SHUT IT!

SHUT IT!

A Fan's Guide to 70s Cops
on the Box

Martin Day & Keith Topping

First published in Great Britain in 1999 by
Virgin Publishing Ltd
Thames Wharf Studios
Rainville Road
London W6 9HT

Copyright © Martin Day and Keith Topping 1999

The right of Martin Day and Keith Topping to
be identified as the Authors of this Work has been
asserted by them in accordance with the Copyright,
Designs and Patents Act 1988.

ISBN 0 7535 0355 7

Typeset by Galleon Typesetting, Ipswich
Printed and bound in Great Britain by
Mackays of Chatham PLC

Acknowledgements

We would like to thank the following for their help and contribution to this book: Ian Abrahams, Daniel Ben-Zvi, Stephen Cole, Paul Cornell, Chris Cornwell, Mark Cullen, Helen Fayle, Liz Halliday, Paul Matthews, Audra McHugh, John McLaughlin, Amanda Murray, Felicia O'Sullivan, Paul Rhodes, Gary Russell, Felicity Shea, Ed Stradling, Rob Stradling, Dave Stone, Kathy Sullivan, Gareth Thomas, Susannah Tiller, Colin Topping, Graeme Topping, Peter Ware, Julie Wilson, Simon Winstone, Nicole Yates, and to everybody on our favourite usenet newsgroup, alt.fan.*t*n*c*t*e*s.

And, especially, Dave Matthews and Martin Wiggins.

For those who are interested, Andrew Pixley's excellent article 'Compulsive Viewing' in *Prime Time*, issue 13, paints in much of the background to *The Sweeney*; Dave Matthews's official web pages (www.carnfort.u-net.com/~/Professionals/) do much the same (and more besides) for *The Professionals*.

Dedicated to . . .

Sarah and Paul (MD)

Ian Atkins, for a decade of encouragement,
and Steve 'The Guvnor' Purcell (KT)

Contents

Introduction

It is a strange irony (which is not lost on the authors) that one of the main catalysts for this book's existence is a pair of car adverts. The fact that *Shut It!* is here, in your hands, is clear evidence of the cyclical nature of television: what goes around comes around.

The televisual wheel of fortune was certainly on the move in the mid-1970s. The very nature of TV crime drama was changing. It is easy to forget that the first season of *The Sweeney* (1975) coincided with the penultimate season of *Dixon of Dock Green*. If *Dixon*, with its Olde Worlde values, had been something of an anachronism in the 1960s, it was absolutely out of its depth in the Glam-Rock final years of the Wilson administration. Despite the best intentions of all involved, it wasn't so much TV for another era as for another planet.

Z Cars, which had started in 1962, proved the point. With its very human police officers, and stories rooted in contemporary, working-class reality, it dared to show the fine line between police officer and villain. The best stories were extraordinary, and it is fair to point out that *The Sweeney* outlived *Z Cars* by only three months. But times were changing, and the audience (whether they realised it or not) wanted something different.

That something was, of course, Jack Regan and George Carter of *The Sweeney*. If it can be stated that *The Avengers was* the 1960s, then in many ways there is no better summation of 1970s Britain than *The Sweeney*. In essence, it paints a picture of how men and women tended to view themselves back then. The 1970s were the awkward adolescent stage between the joyful youth and vigour of the 1960s and the hard-headed, supposedly sophisticated 1980s. In temperament, Jack Regan was the man who had never truly grown up (he could never get a grip on marriage, authority or any form of progress); in word and deed, he was brash and instinctive; in outlook, he was sexist, racist, homophobic, you name it. He wasn't evil (in fact, given this frame of reference, he's absolutely moral, without necessarily being honest) so much as unchannelled – but, as a copper, he got results.

Any discussion of 1970s cops, then, begins with Jack Regan. But there is a flip side to this coin, and it takes the form of the escapist exploits of *The Professionals*. Bodie and Doyle of CI5 might seem to have little in common with Regan and Carter of the Flying Squad, but it was their well-tailored shoulders that carried the genre into the 1980s. When the Sweeney were nicking villains, the Sex Pistols dominated the charts; by the time CI5 were in full tilt, so were Culture Club.

But even *The Professionals* had tricks up its sleeves – it could hardly have been so popular otherwise. Yes, many episodes put explosions and car chases in the foreground at the expense of even a sniff of characterisation. Yes, 'surface' was everything – but beneath that surface, in the better episodes, lurks a wryly reflective heart. If *The Sweeney* wonders aloud whether policemen hanging around with villains the whole time can be an entirely good idea, *The Professionals* begins to probe the nature of killing, and what it does to the hearts and minds of those sanctioned to murder by the State. What *Callan* did week by week, *The Professionals* did during those episodes where it allowed itself a breather. And if, like 'Dirty Harry' Callahan, it's very easy to see Bodie and Doyle as the ultimate right-wing role model, there's just enough discussion about freedom, liberty and justice to give one pause. In turn, Regan wasn't above 'fitting up' his suspects: maybe he gets the right man, but is he right to behave in this way? Neither *The Sweeney* nor *The Professionals* is able to give easy answers: the former, because the writers understood that life is rarely monochrome; the latter because the production team were usually too busy devising the next shoot-out or tyre-shredding handbrake turn.

This book

Shut It! examines the 1970s cop show by detailing these two programmes. *The Sweeney* and *The Professionals* were either violent, sexist, clichéd rubbish from an age of crushed-velvet flares and bad haircuts, or they were two seminal social documents of their era. We write, as our comments and these linking essays make clear, in part from an unashamedly 1990s perspective. No matter how justified or realistic racism and sexism were in terms of the individual characterisation, we cannot pretend not to see them when they are there (and, let's face it, *The Sweeney* loved to titillate its – largely male? – audience). But neither are we ignorant of the context of these programmes, of the very many steps forward they make in all sorts of areas. We list birds, booze and shooters with a kind of reluctant enthusiasm: it's all there; it's central to the (ongoing?) appeal with these programmes, so we may as well accept that and move on. In much the same way as both 'Lad' and 'New Man' have given way to 'New Lad', and with politics becoming obsessed with the middle ground, we too try to strike a balance. George Carter and Ray Doyle, at least, would probably approve.

Shut It! is, hopefully, also a fun reminder of what those days were all about. 'In the seventies, there was long hair,' Denim once said, and indeed there was. There was also a plethora of other kitsch, throwaway garbage cluttering up the shops, the TV screens, and the charts. But 70s icons, once reviled, are now in fashion again as a Day-Glo pop-art nostalgia trip. Lava lamps, Star Jumpers and Hai Karate! aftershave, Chopper bikes and Spacehoppers. If we spend as much time mulling over such things as we do the deep significance of a certain episode's post-Freudian view of the Neo-Platonic family, we make no apologies. Our emphasis is very much what appears on the screen: there *is* some background information in this book, but it's not our primary concern. Even the occasional reference to an actual location, for instance, is usually prompted by something that you can see in the episode itself.

The headings

At the start of each season, we list the technical details and regular and returning cast. We've deliberately avoided telling you the plot of each episode since we intend *Shut It!* to be a companion to watching episodes, not a replacement for it. If you want to know the plot of 'Selected Targets' or 'Discovered in a Graveyard' – go and get that video, and watch it . . . with *Shut It!* in one hand, and your VCR remote control in the other. At various points you might want to look up one of our headings. These are:

Keep Your Mincers Peeled For . . .: All sorts of people who were either quite well known before they did *The Sweeney* and *The Professionals*, or subsequently became famous, have a tiny part of their past captured on the celluloid of these series. You'll also find in these episodes a bunch of jobbing character actors whom you may recognise from that episode of something-or-other you were watching the other week. 'Where've I seen his/her boat race before?' you may well ask yourself. We will tell you. We also list various 'of-their-era' objects – so that you can say, 'You don't see many of *them* these days . . .' – and anything else that takes our fancy.

Birds: As the comedian Sean Hughes has noted, after a while *The Sweeney* just became an excuse for 'boobies alert', a sexual awakening for twelve-year-old boys everywhere. *The Professionals* has a bit of this, too, though it's less obvious. We note the girls at whose bums our heroes stare, and into whose knickers they want to get.

Booze: How did TV cops of the 1970s manage to arrest *anybody* considering the amount of alcohol they put away? We give you the full breathalyser details.

Shooters: In those days, every slag worth his salt went on a blag with a tasty piece of steel. They'd normally find the law ready to give them both barrels back. If you're interested in the body count, this is the category for you.

Each episode gets a 'star rating' for birds, booze and shooters, just as a bit of fun. That's not to say that, if you boil *The Sweeney* and *The Professionals* down to their base ingredients, this is all you're left with. In fact, you might be surprised how many cracking episodes don't score too well on the bums 'n' beer 'n' bangs stakes. (Incidentally, the rankings for **Shooters** are relative: owing to the high-octane nature of *The Professionals*, five *Sweeney* stars is likely to equate to about three in the later programme!)

Motors: Ah, the 1970s – the halcyon days of the British motoring industry. Not. We don't quite list every car we see but, frankly, what can be more evocative of the era than Jack Regan's big Granada screaming after villains in an old Jag? Or, for that matter, Allegros and Maxis in every stomach-churning shade of the rainbow. We tend to concentrate on Brit motors, for obvious reasons, but we've done our best to identify every *major* car in the various stories. But forgive us sometimes if we can't help but laugh at the dreadful, soggy handling of some of the cars, or the amount of rubber the CI5 boys burn.

Threads: Those were the days when villains wore flared strides and shirts with very big collars. And then there's Martin Shaw's haircut. Never have so many people laughed at something so curly. As the critic Phil Purser noted, 'The curly-headed one reminds me fatally of Harpo Marx!' Compared with this, Lewis Collins's bonehead look was almost restrained. With Jack and George, it is more the case that their wardrobe has aged so badly. We check the quality, *and* the width.

Jazz Funk?/*Shaft* Guitar?: Harry South's classic theme tune for *The Sweeney* was bold, brassy and brash – an instant funk classic for thousands of school-age boys to bellow along with tunelessly (as Sean Hughes notes, there are few series in which the title fits so seamlessly into the theme – try it: 'The Sweee-nee, The Sweee-nee!'). Squeeze and later Renegade Soundwave brilliantly used images of the Flying Squad in 'Cool for Cats' and 'Probably a Robbery' respectively. At the

time of writing, a dance-ish, terrace-rousing single – 'We're
the Sweeney and You're Nicked' – is heading towards the
charts.

Laurie Johnson's theme for *The Professionals* took up
where his previous *The New Avengers* tune left off: a brassy,
up-tempo tune with a disco-funk bass line, masses of
teeth-shattering hi-hat, *shakkashakka* rhythm guitar, and a
solo straight out of the Alvin Lee book of rock-and-roll
histrionics. Ironically, both series also used the device of
having a slower, jazzy secondary theme. *The Sweeney* used
theirs (a beautifully haunting effort) over the end credits, and
it remains one of the most memorable aspects of the show.
The equivalent in *The Professionals* was less successful,
normally being used in the scene immediately following the
titles, often to accompany a sweeping shot of whoever was
coming to Cowley's office walking through Whitehall.
Anyway, the rest of the music is discussed in this section.

Bill the Driver: An occasional category for *The Sweeney*
(and a few *Professionals* episodes!) where we watch out for
our favourite bit-part character, Bill the Flying Squad driver.
He's in loads of episodes, often with dialogue or action, but
he never once got a credit. We presume he was played by one
of the stunt team, but we really don't know. So, if you're out
there, Bill, drop us a line, c/o Virgin . . .

Doyle Cooks a Bit of Pasta: In some ways, Ray Doyle can
be seen as one of television's first New Men (with more than
a few laddish aspects). It was quite revolutionary to have a
hard-man character in the late 70s who was a wine drinker,
did some cooking, was reasonably politically literate (and
liberal), and well read and educated. Most of the series'
attempts at showing the softer side of Doyle's character
were heavy-handed, and obvious, and so we've created this
category to have a good laugh at them. We also use it, very
literally, to keep a track on the lad's culinary escapades.

Slash Fiction Moment: This one might require a bit of
explanation. Some years ago, a trend in fan fiction began of
writing erotic stories about same-sex characters in popular

TV (the first series to garner such attention, amazingly, was *Star Trek*!). *The Professionals*, however, could almost have been designed with this in mind (pretty boys in leather jackets and cowboy boots playing with lethal toys). Fanzines (and now the Internet) are full of such fiction (most of it pretty good, and a lot of it written by women, interestingly). In these stories, Bodie and Doyle, erm, discover their attraction for each other. The strange thing is, if you watch the series with this in mind, you find a lot of subtle (and probably completely unintentional) homoeroticism, the sort of thing that *The Comic Strip* lampooned so vigorously. On the one hand, it's almost a shame it's impossible to present a same-gender relationship without someone thinking that sex must play a part somewhere. On the other . . . Oh, watch a few, and you'll see what we mean.

Non-PC Moment: It's somewhat inevitable that two series that were made in another era, when attitudes (both in television and in real life) were different, will produce moments that make today's viewer think, Ouch! A lot of this can be forgiven, and some of the stories tried hard to grapple with a few very important and contentious issues, but, where something particularly unfortunate crops up, we note it to keep our consciences clear.

You What?/Jargon: A rough guide to both series' creation of their own vocabulary. The change of heading indicates the passage from out-and-out cop/cockney slang to something a little more influenced by spy dramas and quasi-political buzz words. Many of the more common terms will also be found in the Glossary at the back of this volume.

Larfs/Laughable Dialogue: Bits of dialogue that are worth rewinding the video for. In the past, we've called such categories things like Dialogue Triumphs, whereas 95 per cent of these examples are chosen because they're very funny, and thus survive the translation to the printed page. Here, we acknowledge this fact, although there are occasions when *The Sweeney*'s Larfs are actually very serious bits of dialogue. Similarly, though we're on the lookout for laughably bad lines in *The Professionals*, we should point out that some of them are actually very good!

Notes: Our assessment of the episode's merit (or lack of it), plus sundry notes on continuity, topical references which may require a bit of explanation, mentions of other texts and so on.

The Glory Days of the Glam-Rock Cops

The Sweeney was a series in which every rule of formula television was broken joyously.

For a start, the battle between good and evil is not fought by distinctly separate groups, but by individuals who often find themselves on one side or other through no more than good or bad luck. When Jack Regan goes drinking with villains, it's in part because he's just the same as they are. And George Carter's upbringing, and interest in boxing, would have placed him firmly on the side of the crooks had fate not conspired to propel him into the Met.

Still, this gives them a good sense of what makes other people's minds tick: George and Jack often simply *know* who's to blame for any given incident. This isn't Miss-Marple-like detection, but pure, animal instinct. Thus often deprived of this progression and unravelling, the viewer can instead concentrate on characters and motivations, in much the same way as more modern crime novels are less whodunnits than whydunnits. One of the great joys in *The Sweeney* is the time taken over creating and breathing life into its supporting characters: sometimes the people we see veer a little too close to working-class caricature, but usually there's just that touch of eccentricity to ring true to life. The end result is that, while obviously poles apart from 'kitchen-sink drama', there's just a hint of reality about the London of *The Sweeney*. Which means that, when Jack and George wander those Soho streets, you can almost smell the cheap cigarettes and stale perfume.

In turn, this means that, although the leads are likable, they're not likable in the same glorified way that George Dixon was. But we're given more of an opportunity to understand their frustrations, too – to come so close to nailing a villain, and then to have the case thrown out because a

form has been incorrectly filled in. This too smacks of real
life more than dramatic norms. The bottom line is, in *The
Sweeney* the villains aren't always captured or, sometimes, a
mere patsy carries the can. (The Professionals, on the other
hand, get their man or woman without fail, which makes the
programme more satisfying but in many ways more bland.)

If this reflects real life – and the 1970s probably saw the
first large-scale worries about the British legal and judicial
system being raised – then it's difficult to say for sure how
'realistic' other elements of the show are. At the very time
that, in real life, Robert Mark was leading his anticorruption
drive through the Met, and a lot of former members of the
notorious Obscene Publications Squad were getting arrested
for corruption, Ernest Bond, the Metropolitan Police's Chief
of Operations, called *The Sweeney* 'a load of old rubbish'
after watching one episode. But the genuine Flying Squad
officers who drank with the cast and crew on a regular basis
said differently. And so did the public.

This is important: it's not that *The Sweeney* is more realistic than, say, *The Bill* or *The Cops* (it certainly isn't), but it
feels right. We do get a hint of procedure, of the mundane – of
the hours spent staking out a building or tailing a suspect –
but not so much that bores us. And if we get a really good
scrap most weeks – well, no matter, we're just seeing the
edited highlights of the life of the Flying Squad.

One thing that *The Sweeney* does reflect very well is the
battle within the police force for its very identity. As the pilot
episode, 'Regan', makes clear, Jack is, in his own way, as
old-fashioned a copper as George Dixon. Jack's bottom line is
results – getting villains banged up. More and more of his
superiors, though, realise that, not only do they need to do
things by the book, but they need to be *seen* to be doing
things by the book. Ian Kennedy Martin had realised that this
sort of conflict was opening up in the police force; that use of
'interrogation' and informants was becoming increasingly
regulated. He approached Thames Television with a format
for a show originally called *The Outcasts*, based around the
exploits of the Flying Squad, that most notoriously macho of
all police divisions.

Ted Childs – then producing *Special Branch*, which was very much a proto-*Sweeney* with its use of grainy film stock and plenty of action sequences – was assigned to a pilot film (now called *Regan*), which would form one of six dramas to be transmitted under the banner *Armchair Cinema*. *Regan* went into production in early 1974. The series that ensued wasn't quite what Ian Kennedy Martin had planned, and so he left the programme entirely. But Ted Childs and the rest of the staff had a strong sense of what they wanted to achieve, and they set about bringing their vision to fruition with a vigour that would have impressed Jack Regan himself.

The Sweeney

1: 'Regan'
4 June 1974

An 80-minute film[1] in the *Armchair Cinema* series
Euston Films/Thames Television
Created by Ian Kennedy Martin

Associate Producer: Mary Morgan
Producer: Ted Childs
Executive Producers: Lloyd Shirley, George Taylor

Title music by Harry South

Regular Cast: John Thaw (Detective Inspector Jack Regan),
Dennis Waterman (Detective Sergeant George Carter),
Garfield Morgan (Detective Chief Inspector Frank Haskins),
Janet Key (Kate Regan),
Morris Perry (Detective Chief Superintendent Maynon),
Carl Rigg (Detective Sergeant Kent)

Writer: Ian Kennedy Martin
Director: Tom Clegg

Cast: Lee Montague (Dale), David Daker (Tusser),
Maureen Lipman (Annie),
Stephen Yardley (Detective Inspector Laker),
Barry Jackson (Morton), Miquel Brown (Miriam),
Peter Blythe (Peter), Michael Da Costa (South),
Ronald Pember (Landlord), Jonathan Elsom (Interviewer),

---

[1] Timings given for television episodes include advertisements, i.e. a standard sixty-minute episode is likely to be actually about fifty minutes in length. Actual running time is given for the two *Sweeney* films.

Betty Woolfe (Mrs Berry), Seymour Matthews (Doctor),
Don Henderson (Strip-Club Heavy),
Nancy Gabrielle (Johno's Wife),
Del Baker (Detective Sergeant Cowley)

Sergeant Alan Cowley is killed in a vicious gangland attack.
His boss, Jack Regan of the Flying Squad, is determined to
avenge his death, even if the case has been assigned to the
rival Serious Crime Squad.

Keep Your Mincers Peeled For . . .: A fine cast is headed by
David Daker (Harry Crawford in *Boon*, and a *Z Cars* veteran),
Stephen Yardley (Spider Scott in *The XYY Man*, Max in
Secret Army, and later Ken Masters in *Howards' Way*), Ron
Pember (Alain in *Secret Army*), Maureen Lipman (you must
know who she is – she's on telly more often than the news),
and Lee Montague (whose numerous TV and film credits
include *Yesterday's Enemy* and *How I Won the War*). But
probably the most recognisable face in the episode is only in
one brief scene. Don Henderson has a CV as long as the arm
of the law, but he's best known for his portrayal of George
Bulman in *The XYY Man*, *Strangers* and *Bulman*.

Birds: ** The film begins with a big cleavage on display in
the pub. There's a girl in bed during the initial arrest. At the
hospital, Regan and Kent cast admiring glances at one of the
nurses as she passes them. Later Regan and Carter sit in their
car assessing the talent ('Cor dear, look at the state of
'er!'). There's also Miriam Lesley, a black jazz singer who
is Mallory's girlfriend, and 'Uncle' Ernie South's (unseen)
'naughty photos'. But what's the fascination with the girl
figure skater, whom we get three or four shots of for no
apparent reason?

Booze: *** 'Funny fellah, my guvnor. He hates publicans!'
Two large whiskies for Jack and George cost (get this) 76p!
Regan drinks Scotch while confronting his wife's new Ger-
man boyfriend (he says he doesn't like 'Krauts'). Miriam:
'You don't drink on duty . . .?' 'Only Scotch!'

Shooters: *** Regan and his boys are tooled up when they go to arrest their suspect. Later both he and Carter spend time on the firing range in preparation for their showdown with Arthur Dale (whose mob is also heavily armed).

Motors: Dale has a white Mercedes. Our first sight of the Sweeney is in a red Rover, an orange Escort and a blue Ford Zodiac. Regan's own car is a blue Granada Ghia.

Threads: Several sheepskin coats are on display (it's April so it must have been a cold spring that year!). Kent's ginger shirt is quite nasty while George's black boxing shorts are rather tight. We've also got to mention Regan's paisley neckerchief. Best of all, the TV interviewer's horribly oversized spotty bow tie.

Jazz Funk?: 'Don't Dilly-Dally on the Way' is sung in traditional cockney knees-up style in the opening pub sequence. The incidental music seems to have been influenced by *Get Carter* (as was much of the series' aesthetics): bongo rolls and throbbing bass lines over which there's the odd stab of jazzy piano or smooth organ. The title music is very different from that of the series that followed, sounding quite like the famous theme of *Callan*.

Non-PC Moment: In keeping with 1970s norms, Miriam is called a 'coloured bird'.

You What?: Regan: 'We've had one of our young skippers smashed up in Tusser country.'

Carter on Regan's driving: 'I never had you for a wheels man, guv.'

Dale: 'I've got three boys with three shooters . . . My boys will zero you.'

The Sweeney refer to the Serious Crime Squad as 'The Gangbusters'.

Larfs: Regan's first line on screen, arresting a man in his bed, is the immortal: 'Get yer trousers on, you're nicked!'

Regan gets Carter back into the Squad: 'I'm not trying to start an affair with you. Don't lift a bloody finger for me – I'm not asking for that. But you can help me put these bastards away. They've done one of ours.'

Regan, after he's just thrashed a confession from Dale for Cowley's murder, looks at the villain's car: 'This stinking heap is licensed till March. It's April twentieth. I'll have you for that an' all!'

Notes: 'Odd sod, Regan. Twenty years ago, he'd have been the perfect cop in the days of individualists. Now he's out on a limb.' Wonderfully sleazy and violent (the scene with the ice skate is terrific). It's easy to see what got everybody so excited in 1974. Here is a police 'hero' who is not a nice man at all – who lies to his superiors, gets confessions at any cost, beats up suspects, and drinks like a fish. The opening is stunningly filmed in the crumbling docklands around Butler's Wharf and Tower Bridge.

Regan is divorced from his wife, Kate. The couple have a daughter called Susie. He is 35 (Kate thinks he looks more like 45), and he pays £200 a year towards the house. Regan's current girlfriend, Annie, is a make-up artist at a (rather dubious-looking) film company. She gets the costume department to iron his shirts for him. She loves Jack, but leaves him for her husband Eddie, who has come back from the navy. Jack says he once worked in 'swinging Ruislip'.

George Carter was a boxer in his youth. He had eighteen months with Regan at the Flying Squad before leaving to work in CID, where he is doing well and up for promotion. He says he didn't like Regan's methods and there are implications that he left the Sweeney because of the hours and pressure from his new wife. He grew up in South London, and his father was a docker. Carter speaks a tiny bit of Italian, though he mixes it up with Spanish quite easily (see 'Hard Men').

Haskins has an ulcer and takes medication for it. He drinks milk to ease his suffering.

First Season

Thirteen 60-minute episodes
Euston Films/Thames Television
Created by Ian Kennedy Martin

Associate Producer: Mary Morgan
Producer: Ted Childs
Executive Producers: Lloyd Shirley, George Taylor

Title music by Harry South

Regular Cast: John Thaw (Detective Inspector Jack Regan),
Dennis Waterman (Detective Sergeant George Carter),
Garfield Morgan (Detective Chief Inspector Frank Haskins,
2, 4–6, 8–9, 11–14), Colin Douglas (Commander, 2, 13),
Jack McKenzie (Len, 2, 3),
John Flanagan (Detective Sergeant 'Matt' Mathews, 3–5),
Morris Perry (Detective Chief Superintendent Maynon, 3–5),
Martin Read (Detective Constable Jimmy Thorpe, 3–5, 10),
Dennis de Marne (Fred, 6, 10),
Stephanie Turner (Alison Carter, 6, 14),
Nick Brimble (Detective Constable Gerry Burtonshaw, 7),
Carl Rigg (Detective Sergeant Kent, 8),
Janet Key (Kate Regan, 14),
Jenny Thanisch (Susie Regan, 14)

2: 'Ringer'
2 January 1975

Writer: Trevor Preston
Director: Terry Green

Cast: Ian Hendry (Brooker), Brian Blessed (Kemble),
Jill Townsend (Jenny), Alan Lake (Merrick),
June Brown (Mrs Martin), Toni Palmer (Edi),
Ray Mort (Driscoll), Angus MacKay (Prosser),

Leslie Sarony (Soldier), Steve Gardner (Billy Martin),
Colin Prockter ('Stupid Hawes')

Regan's surveillance of the notorious gangster Frankie Kemble
comes unstuck when his girlfriend's car, containing much of the
evidence, is stolen.

Keep Your Mincers Peeled For . . .: In an episode chock-
full of recognisable faces (Ian Hendry, Brian Blessed and
Alan Lake need few introductions to TV fans of the 1960s
and 1970s), Ray Mort (from *It's a Lovely Day Tomorrow*)
provides a welcome bit of comedy. And it's nice to see that in
the 1970s June Brown (Dot Cotton in *EastEnders*) was
already playing the mother of a dangerous tearaway.

Birds: ** Regan's girlfriend (she insists he's just an 'acquaintance') is Jenny, a pretty air hostess who starts the episode in
bed and gets menaced by Brooker and Merrick. She gets a
great scene at the end asking (as many girlfriends will subsequently ask) why Jack doesn't change jobs. There's a girlie
calendar on display in Brooker's office.

Booze: ** Pubs are mentioned several times, but all of
Regan's drinking is done at home with Jenny (there's an
empty vodka bottle on the table at the start, and in the final
scene Regan's got the inevitable Scotch in his hand). Kemble
and Brooker share a red wine.

Shooters: *** There's a nasty assortment of weaponry in the
pre-titles, and Brooker later carries a gas-launcher and a
particularly vicious-looking double-barrelled shotgun.

Motors: Brooker drives a yellow Capri I. Jenny's white
Mini is the episode's linchpin. Prosser's Rolls-Royce Silver
Shadow gets only one scene but steals the show. Kemble
drives a white Daimler Sovereign.

The standard *Sweeney* cars early on are as follows: Regan
is in a golden-brown Ford Granada Consul GT V6 3.0
(NHK 295M), as seen in the title sequence. Backup comes in
the form of a blue Cortina Ghia (DLO 97M). The opening
credits feature an S-type Jag (DWD 606C).

Threads: Jack is wearing Jenny's dressing gown at the start. It's significant that our first sight of Regan is with his trousers off! He wears a brown sheepskin and a horrible green tie throughout the episode. Carter responds with a green velvet jacket for the fight at the end. Most of the rest is standard for the era, but a special mention for Merrick's general Jackson the Tailor look, large earring and Jason-King-style facial hair. And 'Stupid Hawes' lives up to his name by wearing some of the most moronic clothes you'll see this side of a Gerry Anderson series – multicoloured tank top, half-Nelson jeans, with bright-red socks and baseball boots.

Jazz Funk?: The pre-titles music is great – heavy bass and flutes. 'Stupid' is listening to some horrible rock on the radio when Regan and Carter turn up at the lockup.

You What?: Carter: 'They'll have that motor stripped down to its knickers by now and going out in boxes.'

Billy: 'You pigs would fit anybody up.'

Carter on Kemble: 'Underneath, he's as smooth as a coal bunker.'

Regan: 'By the time Kemble's brief has had his say I'll be back wearing a tall hat.'

Larfs: Carter on the theft of the car Regan was using: 'This should raise a smile on *Junior Police Five*.'

Regan's reaction to Soldier's opinion that he 'looks a bit evil': 'My mother was frightened by a one-eyed taxi driver.'

A 24-carat moment of TV history as Regan tells Billy: 'We're the Sweeney, son, and we haven't had any dinner!'

Notes: 'Aw, the bloody Sweeney, that's all we need, isn't it?' An absolute classic, Trevor Preston setting the tone for the series immediately with loads of action (the climactic punch-up, especially). Excellent use of locations (Peckham Rye station for a chase sequence, and the Valley, Charlton Athletic's football ground), and a brilliant, understated performance from Brian Blessed. The real world gets a look-in with oblique references to widespread corruption in the Met ('This is the Sweeney, Mr Prosser – you don't buy them!'), and to 'the twins' (who never bothered Kemble).

George eats up to three cartons of yoghurt a day after being told it was an aphrodisiac. Regan had a goldfish but says next door's cat got it. He tells Jenny he's resigned from the job four times. Both Regan and Carter claim to have been Boy Scouts.

Haskins makes a reference to Samuel Beckett's *Waiting for Godot*. George thinks he's talking about a QPR fullback.

3: 'Jackpot'
9 January 1975

Writer: Tony Marsh
Director: Tom Clegg

Cast: Ed Devereaux (Biggleswade), Richard Davies (Doctor), Morgan Sheppard (Morrison), Bernard Gallagher (Desk Sergeant), Carolyn Jones (Irene), Murray Brown (Simmonds), Sally Faulkner (WPC Bond), Natalie Kent (Doris), Bart Allison (Wilf)

The blag is busted, the villains arrested, the poppy recovered . . . Except for 35 grand, which seems to have gone walkabout.

Keep Your Mincers Peeled For . . . : Bernard Gallagher was one of the stars of the first season of *Casualty*, playing the hospital manager, Ewart Plimmer. Richard Davies was TV's stock Welshman for many years. Older viewers will remember him as Mr Price in *Please, Sir!*

The sports page of the *Daily Chronicle* features a headline concerning the Derby County and (briefly) England centre forward, Kevin Hector.

Birds: * WPC Pat Bond is tasty, in a uniformed-crumpet sort of way ('Nice one if you like it a bit on the heavy side,' notes Mathews).

Booze: *** 'Give 'em a drink, and take 'em down the station!' An unseen trip to the pub (''Ere, guv, do you fancy a drink?' 'Yeah, the pubs are open, aren't they?') is followed by another, involving pints of what looks like brown ale, and a spirit that costs 'a hundred and four' (probably the vodka and tonic the newspaper man is drinking). Later, it looks like brandy back at the office.

Shooters: None, but plenty of hand-to-hand violence.

Motors: The arrest of the criminals at the beginning involves a blue police Rover and a green Granada (NHK 292M) plus Jack's usual bronze Granada.

Threads: When Jack is listening to the taped report from Bond, one of the other officers is wearing an especially horrid pink-shirt-and-sideburns combo. One of the robbers wears a pair of hugely flared denims.

Jazz Funk?: Mathews whistles the Laurel and Hardy theme.

Non-PC Moment: Harry on his ex-wife: 'She ran off with a poof!'

You What?: Regan: 'Oi! Pick up those oners, will you? And turn that hooter off.'

Maynon (quoting from a report about Regan): 'You said "Don't worry, old cock, you'll have half the heavy mob sitting on your tail." '

Mathews: 'He's clean, guv, and so's his oppo.'

Larfs: George, waxing lyrical about the missing bag full of money: 'It described an arc, a parabola, into a crowd of disinterested spectators, before it disappeared.'

Carter: ' "Tel," I said, "you were arrested carrying a four-foot length of heavy-duty chain. Now, do you still insist you were taking your dog for a walk?" "Yes," he says. "He's a very big dog." '

And, later, after Carter has informed Tel that the dog was found locked in the kitchen: ' "He used to be a circus dog, he knows quite a lot of tricks!" '

Regan on the 'Peter principle' and the dangers of being promoted 'upstairs': 'You stay at what you're good at . . . There's nothing up there but ulcers and disappointment.'

Doctor (to Regan): 'Once again I break my Hippocratic

oath signing you up as serviceable . . . Putting my signature to this document is fraudulent, as well, no doubt, as contravening the Trade Descriptions Act.'

Notes: 'Someone's run off with thirty grand.' A wonderfully well-structured episode, full of real-life ambiguities, with a smashing conclusion. It's more of an ensemble piece than most (and, as such, provides an interesting template for what *The Sweeney* might have been like had it not concentrated primarily on Regan and Carter). The sequence where they all watch (and comment on) the film of the arrest is sensational ('Self-defence, that,' as a bar is used against a prone man).

Carter seems especially violent in this (his idea of a sensitive interrogation is smashing a slag's face against a fence while shouting, 'Where's the money?'), and he breaks in without a warrant. Seems like the moral high ground adopted in the pilot episode didn't last long. George says Charlie Quigley and his father ran a bookie's together, but they quickly went bankrupt (it was the first year in decades when the favourites of the Grand National and the Derby both won!). 'I was brought up with nappies made out of newspapers,' he says.

It seems that 'Oscar 2-4'[1] is the call sign for the usual brown Sweeney car, and 'Oscar 3' is Regan himself. Regan busted Biggleswade's gang a year ago during a similar blag, but the DPP fouled up the charges and they were prosecuted for only minor weapons offences; Regan swore revenge.

Regan refers to 'an old Tory saying, "Switch Off Something Now" ', one of the slogans of the 1973 power crisis and the three-day week. There are lots of mentions of Arsenal ('Tell him the whole team's been put on the transfer list, shake his confidence!'). When the Sweeney come crashing in on the film, Carter shouts, 'Howay the lads!', the famous chant of Newcastle United's supporters.

---

[1] In common with *The Professionals*, these call signs are usually used over the radio, and thus what might be 'twenty-four' in this case is actually stated as 'two four'. We use the form '2-4' throughout this book.

4: 'Thin Ice'
16 January 1975

Writer: Troy Kennedy Martin
Director: Tom Clegg

Cast: Alfred Marks (Bishop), Peter Jeffrey (Pringle),
Brian Glover (Moose), Bill Dean (Charlie Norton),
Brian Wilde (Stanley), Maurice O'Connell (Morgan),
Margaret Nolan (Betty), Ivan Beavis (Sergeant),
Bridget Brice (Secretary), Robert Gillespie (Steward),
Tony Aitken (Shipping Clerk)

Years of painstaking investigation into Gerry Bishop is blown
away when the man gets wind of the police's interest, and he
flees to France. Still, all is not lost – Bishop's dog remains
behind . . .

Keep Your Mincers Peeled For . . .: An all-star cast headed
by Marks and Jeffrey, two of television's most instantly
recognisable character actors. The late Brian Glover (*Kes*,
An American Werewolf in London, plus numerous TV
credits) provides comic relief, while Brian Wilde, then best
known as Mr Barrowclough in *Porridge*, appears a year
before his debut in *Last of the Summer Wine*. Look out for
the sitcom stalwart Robert Gillespie (*Keep it in the Family*)
in a small role. Bill Dean was previously best known as
Dutchie Holland in *Budgie*, but would become a huge star in
the 80s as the cantankerous Harry Cross in *Brookside*.
Bridget Brice would play a similar secretarial role in many
episodes of *The Professionals*. And watch for a tiny
appearance by Ivan Beavis, one of the original stars of
Coronation Street.

Birds: ** Betty Bishop is a buxom creature in a variety of
disgustingly coloured swimsuits and dresses. Regan asks his
current secretary if she goes out with married men? 'Only for
money,' she replies without a pause. Jack later leaves a
message for an unseen woman called Irene (who apparently

has a big chest and ringlets), saying that he won't be able to take her to the pictures.

Booze: * Nothing for Jack and the boys, but Bishop is clearly enjoying himself in France. He prepares a bowl of champers for Archimedes the dog.

Shooters: None.

Motors: The Sweeney/police cars seen include the usual brown Granada, the green Granada seen in the previous episode, plus the usual blue backup Cortina. Moose drives a green Range Rover and a blue 2CV while travelling to meet Bishop.

Threads: Bishop is seen packing a positively lethal Hawaiian shirt.

Jazz Funk?: Pounding Hammond-organ-based funk during the first scene. There's a terrifically groovy flute-heavy theme that sounds not unlike the early 70s work of Eric Burdon's War.

You What?: Mathews: 'It stands to reason, dunnit? It was Charlie who rubbed him; I'd have thought it was case proven, me.'

Regan: 'Get on to Superintendent Pringle. This is his pigeon.'

Larfs: Bishop (on Archimedes): 'As far as I'm concerned, the major source of radiation shines out of that dog's –'

Haskins's surreal sci-fi moment while talking about the 'accountant copper' Pringle: 'You know, somewhere out there, beyond the Post Office Tower, there's a vast committee called Pringle, constantly regenerating itself.'

Carter: 'You see, we live in a world of supply and demand – and you are in demand.' Moose: 'Like a toilet roll.'

Regan, on Carter: 'Loyal, but thick.'

And, later: 'There are some times, George, when I believe you're incapable of looking after a potted plant, let alone personnel.'

Rural Sergeant: 'Detective Sergeant Gallagher is on sick leave.' Thorpe: 'Are there any other human beings in the building?' Sergeant: 'Nope.'

Haskins on the electronic surveillance device that Regan has lost: 'It was working perfectly well on the tea trolley.'

Bishop (on the phone, after the wrong dog has been delivered): 'I'm not upset, Henry. I merely strangled the hound with my bare hands . . . No, it's not a felony here. No . . . No, they eat them here, Henry.'

Notes: 'He who hits and runs away lives to fight another day.' A very funny episode – all the stuff with the dog, and poor Thorpe being left to watch the kennels for three days – but the ending is oddly arbitrary.

Regan can't remember the serial number of his warrant card. He says that both he and Carter were in the Scouts (see 'Ringer'). Bishop says that Regan has 'manufactured' cases before. Regan seemingly isn't keen on nineteenth-century novelists.

This was the only episode of *The Sweeney* not to be repeated during the successful repeat runs on UK Gold and Channel 5 during the early–mid-1990s. No one seems too sure why.

5: 'Queen's Pawn'
23 January 1975

Writer: Ranald Graham
Director: Viktors Ritelis

Cast: Tony Selby (Lyon), Julian Glover (Bernard Stone), Lynn Dearth (Sheila), Tony Caunter (Clarke), Ben Howard (Ronnie), Christopher Ellison (Budd), Malou Cartwright (Angie), Keith Washington (The Reporter), Gertan Klauber (Emilio), Judy Monahan (Mrs Budd), Malcolm Knight (Dodger), Jonathan Blake (The Army Man), Louis Raynes (The Publican)

The acquittal of a team of blaggers persuades Maynon to turn to his 'weapon of last resort', Jack Regan, who is given five days to use any means necessary to incriminate Johnny Lyon.

Keep Your Mincers Peeled For . . .: Tony Selby (*Get Some In!*) and Julian Glover need few introductions, while Tony Caunter is now best known as Roy Evans of *EastEnders*. However, the biggest bonus of this episode is the appearance of a young Christopher Ellison, later the Jack Regan of the 1980s, Frank Burnside, in *The Bill*.

Birds: ***** Boobies alert! A brief shot of Clarke's croupier girlfriend Angie getting out of bed, starkers. Regan notes that she used to be 'on the game'. Sheila Lyon is a brilliant creation – an outrageously dumb gangster's moll whose hair doesn't stay the same colour in two scenes running. Her provocative dancing in the nightclub causes George to note she has 'some lunch on her!' There's a girlie mag in the hit man's briefcase.

Booze: **** Considering that they actually get a result, it's amazing how much time Jack and George spend in various pubs and clubs – and they drink whisky in the office when discussing the case. George drinks a pint of beer at one point, but Regan is a 'large Scotch' man all the way through. There's plenty of 'bubbly' ('fifteen quid a bottle') in evidence at Lyon's acquittal party, and the kidnappers drink cans of Fosters.

Shooters: * The silencer-fitted pistol that Lyon's hit man uses on Budd in a crowded pub.

Motors: Lyon comes away from court in a white Roller; Stone drives a red/purple Beamer. Lyon is later seen in the series' favourite vehicle, a silver S-type.

Threads: A notable turtleneck-sweater fest with George wearing a purple one, and Jack having both a grey one (that actually goes quite well with his tan suede jacket) and a green model. George's pink shirt takes some getting used to, and there's the usual collection of horrible ties (including a dickie bow worn by Lyon). Bonus points go to the shirt Budd wears at one point, which has a collar bigger than the wingspan of Concorde. Virtually every one of the villains has a moustache too, while some of the perms on show would shame Kevin Keegan.

Jazz Funk?: Most of the nightclub music is horrible tinny synthesiser disco. Lyon and Stone play chess to some classical music. There's a nice snatch of heavy-rock guitar in the boozer at the end.

You What?: Regan: 'Go home and get a clean shirt and your wedding whistle, I'm taking you out tonight!'
  Lyon says he has spilt coffee 'right down me strides'.

Larfs: Regan, after Ronnie the saucepan salesman has fouled up in his kidnap plan: 'That nonstick bastard . . .!'

Notes: 'If I can put Lyon away where others have failed, they're finally gonna have to admit that we're what the Squad's all about, and not these new pinstriped pen-pushers with their second-class honours degrees!' They'd never get away with *this* these days. Regan follows the 'end-justifies-the-means' school of policing with that menacing line, 'You can't operate unless you break the rules, everybody knows that!' Some great set pieces, especially the pig-masked kidnappers chasing Clarke in his boxer shorts through the streets.
  Regan appears to play chess, and there are further references to his having been a Boy Scout (see 'Ringer'). Steve Aston, one of the Sweeney's top boys, was maimed by a member of Lyon's gang and ended up at Stoke Mandeville hospital.
  Saucepans are going for a quid at the market.

6: 'Jigsaw'
30 January 1975

Writer: Tudor Gates
Director: Bill Brayne

Cast: Del Henney (Eddie), Sheila Gish (June),
Ken Parry (Fat Eric), Jack Woolgar (Night Watchman),
Richard Hampton (Hilary Elkin), Joan Scott (Headmistress),
Evie Garratt (Night Watchman's Daughter),
Valerie Bell (Barmaid), Alan Collins (Charlie)

A violent wages snatch at a local factory bears all the hallmarks of the work of recently released Eddie Boyse. But Boyse was in a pub with Jack Regan at the time of the robbery. Regan follows his instincts and goes after his man, even if it means facing the attentions of an ambitious MP.

Keep Your Mincers Peeled For . . .: Jack Woolgar made his name playing the cantankerous night porter Carney in *Crossroads*. A bit of typecasting there. Stephanie Turner, making her debut as Carter's wife, had previously appeared in *Z Cars*, but would later become a household name as Jean Darblay in *Juliet Bravo*.

Look out for the series' first use of a Chopper bicycle, one of *the* icons of the 1970s.

Birds: * June, Eddie's girlfriend, wears a black bra under a semitransparent pink blouse. Regan casts an admiring glance at the bottom of a retreating secretary, and, when talking to a pub doorman, a well-built blonde girl in a tight pink top and jeans squeezes past him. Lovely. Judging from his conversation with George concerning the black hospital sister, Regan likes big women!

Booze: ** 'They're closed.' 'Not all of them!' Regan's on the hard stuff in the opening pub scene, but later he and George are seen drinking bottles of bitter and pints. Jack also eats a packet of Golden Wonder crisps! Haskins drinks up to six pints of milk a day because of his ulcer (see 'Regan').

Shooters: None.

Threads: George's green jacket and pink shirt put in another appearance, as does Jack's grey turtleneck. Regan has a horrible big blue tie. Eddie's cream suit, dark-blue shirt and stripy tie at the parent–teacher evening should earn him some sort of reprimand from the fashion police.

Jazz Funk?: Some of the music is ghastly, but there's a great sequence with a jazzy *Shaft*-style organ as Regan and Carter do the rounds of Soho villains. And another pub scene with

hard rock going on in the background. Eddie sings 'I Found
You Just in Time' in the pub.

You What?: Carter: 'Our job is to nick a firm of blaggers, not
crucify an ex-con.'
  Regan: 'There are more fellas doing porridge 'cos a woman
shopped them than any other reason!'

Larfs: Fred, Regan's put-upon driver: 'I should have stayed
in the navy. I was happy there!'

Notes: 'You haven't got a heart in there, it's just a beating
charge book.' A bit of an ordinary episode, though there are
two memorable sequences (Regan and Carter going around
Soho beating up villains, and George and two colleagues
chasing Boyse through a tower block in the shadow of
Battersea power station). The vicar on a motorbike is a nice
touch, too.
  The initial appearance of Carter's occasionally mentioned
wife Alison (a teacher) is well handled. She hates Regan
(calling him an 'anachronistic joke' and 'an animal'), though
this leads to a painful bit of scripting for Dennis Waterman
('He's an animal, but he's an animal in a jungle!'). The scenes
of George in domestic circumstances (doing the washing up
and mowing the lawn, badly) are nice, and we find out he
likes Clint Eastwood films (no surprise there!).
  Regan says his mum considers him 'a genius'! His snout in
this episode is Charlie Harrison, who gives him a 'whisper'
overheard from 'a couple of Irishmen' (Regan suspects that
they're two disgruntled Liverpool fans). Regan's divorce is
mentioned, and his daughter is roughly the same age as June's
daughter Mary.

7: 'Night Out'
6 February 1975

Writer: Troy Kennedy Martin
Director: David Wickes

Cast: Mitzi Rogers (Iris Long), T.P. McKenna (Grant),
David Hargreaves (Jellineck[1]), Peter Childs (Jim),
Christopher Beeny (The Photographer),
Derrick O'Connor (Eagle), Wesley Murphy (Dukes),
John Oxley (Uniformed Policeman),
Tony Sympton (The Old Man),
Brian Coburn (The Scotsman),
Michael Middleton (The Van Driver),
Jeffrey Segal (The Reporter)

Crime Squad are watching a bank robbery, and they need someone to keep the woman in the flat over the pub next door occupied. Thankfully, she's an old flame of Jack Regan's . . .

Keep Your Mincers Peeled For . . .: The Irish actor T.P. McKenna is another of those great character actors who turn up in just about every long-running series. Christopher Beeny (who's in one scene) is best known for his roles in *The Grove Family*, the 1970s revival of *The Rag Trade*, and *Upstairs, Downstairs*. David Hargreaves (one of our favourite actors) played Stephanie Turner's husband, Tom Darblay, in *Juliet Bravo*. For Peter Childs, see *Sweeney!*

Among the posters visible in Iris's flat are one featuring David Essex and a motorbike scene from *Easy Rider*.

Birds: *** Regan's ex-bird, Iris, claims to be a prostitute now, but Jack doesn't believe her. Regan ends up in bed with her. Twice. When she offers to help Regan move a barrel of booze she's wearing only skimpy briefs and a bra under a stripy dressing gown.

Booze: ** Not quite the booze-fest you'd expect from an episode that largely takes place in and above a pub. Regan buys a bottle of Scotch from the pub for £3.31 before visiting Iris. After the massive (alcohol-fuelled?) scrap, Gerry pours himself a half-pint from the (deserted) pub, which Regan drinks.

[1] Not to be confused with James Warrior's character DC Jellyneck in later episodes.

**Shooters: ** The robbers have plenty of shotguns. Regan is given a larger-than-usual revolver by Grant (which Iris later cleans in the dishwasher).

Motors: Regan is taken to see Superintendent Grant in a black Transit.

Threads: Regan's tie is hilarious, while one of the robbers wears the most disgusting pair of purple socks we've ever seen.

Jazz Funk?: An early outing for the frequently used 'suspense theme' (the piano-based music right at the start). There is lots of music heard coming up from the pub. Later, there's another *Sweeney* incidental-music standard, a fastish theme during a high-speed chase.

You What?: Regan: 'There's a bank screwin' going on!'

Larfs: Jellineck, on Grant: 'Sometimes I think he's his own worst enemy.' Regan (aggressively): 'Not while I'm around!'

Regan: 'Look, Iris, the world does not revolve around your body. This bloke Galileo proved it – it goes round the sun.'

Regan: 'Why don't you rest on your reputation as a good lay and leave it at that!'

Notes: 'You've ruined my pistol, do you know that?' Lovely, character-driven stuff – with Iris railing against bald, pot-bellied, double-chinned coppers like Regan – and some marvellous comedy, notably Regan falling into a puddle on the roof, and the big scrap in the pub (complete with stereotypical, tartan-hat-wearing, ginger Scots). Carter's barely in it – apart, that is, from his being beaten black and blue by Crime Squad officers who think he's a villain. The ending is excellent, too.

Regan was about to spend a 'dull' afternoon watching Fulham play (they seem to be his team, see 'In From the Cold'). He was involved with Iris for about eighteen months, some ten years ago. She says that, on a clear day, you can see Centre Point from her window. This is the first time Regan's surname is misheard as 'Regal' (see 'On the Run', *Sweeney!*).

The bank is the National Anglia Bank. This is the same company that's robbed in 'Contact Breaker' (see a variation in 'The Bigger They Are').

8: 'The Placer'
13 February 1975

Writer: Trevor Preston
Director: Ted Childs

Cast: Stanley Meadows (Harry Poole), Susan Tracy (Fran), John Forgeham (Dennis Rawlins), Tony Steedman (Andrew Burkis), Marjie Lawrence (Mrs Harris), Robert Russell (Ari), Jeremy Young (Wren), Terry Cowling (Kesey), William Moore (Detective Sergeant Bowyer), Mollie Maureen (The Old Woman)

After four weeks of undercover working as a long-distance haulage driver, Jack Regan is finally getting to the heart of a group who have pulled off a string of hijacks. But he also becomes the target of a jealous lover.

Keep Your Mincers Peeled For . . .: John Forgeham these days gets plenty of meaty character roles in series like *Prime Suspect* and *Ruth Rendell Mysteries* but at the time was best known as the Brummie garage man Jim Baines in *Crossroads* and for a small role in *The Italian Job*. Tony Steedman was Shirley's dad in the third season of *Citizen Smith* and Socrates in *Bill and Ted's Excellent Adventure*. Carl Rigg subsequently found himself in *Emmerdale*, playing Richard Anstey.

Birds: *** Our initial view of Fran is as a gum-chewing, dumb blonde hitchhiker with a large chest, wearing a daring miniskirt and knee-length brown leather boots. She has a good memory for figures. 'So have I,' notes Jack. Mrs Harris, Regan's randy landlady, manages to get in a couple of filthy bits of innuendo concerning tea (after Regan asks for three sugars, 'That's how my old man used to like it: hot and sweet!').

Booze: ** Jack asks for a large malt while George (tailing him) drinks a light and bitter. Jack sticks to straight Scotch when drinking with Harry Poole, then later meets Fran in a pub called the Winning Post.

Shooters: ** Handguns in the climactic sequence as Harry shoots Denny, and Regan shoots Harry.

Motors: Fran drives a blue Alfa Spider. 'Fast and expensive,' says Carter. His undercover orange Transit is so genuine in its crappiness that it blows a tyre. Rawlins drives a blue S-type, and there's also a left-hand-drive, blue Ford Mustang on display.

Threads: Undercover he might be, but Jack's fashion sense seems to be hidden, too. He spends the episode sporting a horrible moustache (which makes him look like Bernard Cribbins), a red and blue cravat and, in one scene, a disgraceful geometrically patterned shirt. Denny's stripy shirt with white collar and cuffs isn't much better, and his driving gloves stand out a mile. Carter's purple turtleneck puts in another appearance. Big Arnie's cream flares deserve a mention as the camera lingers on them for several seconds. Haskins's golf wear (a mauve sweater and sporty cap) is hilarious.

Jazz Funk?: Mainly bass and piano. There's some strange, whistling keyboard music to accompany the sequences at the petrochemical plant, which rather resembles the language of the Clangers.

Strangely PC Moment: Fran says she got suspicious of Regan because he didn't touch her while riding in the lorry.

You What?: Carter: 'Your young lady is no roadrunner. She had wheels at the pub.'
    Fran is asked, 'Is he cushty?'
    Regan, undercover: 'They bloody nigh finished me – you're trying to make me the onion. Leave it out!'
    'If he is the filth . . . I didn't know.'

Larfs: Fran: 'Married?' Regan: 'Nah, I've always walked with a limp.'

Regan: 'Haskins is doing for the Sweeney what the Boston
Strangler did for door-to-door salesmen!'

Regan to Haskins: 'How else am I expected to get close?
Put a small ad in *Villains News*?'

Notes: 'Jack Regan, this is your life!' *Z Cars*' creator, Troy
Kennedy Martin, once described Trevor Preston as 'the best
TV writer in the world', and with episodes like this it's hard
to argue. Less overtly dependent on locale than previous
episodes (lots of it takes place in warehouses and industrial
settings), but shockingly violent.

Regan's cover story concerns his wife running off with the
insurance man and selling pot plants and budgies in Penge.
He is staying in Willesden. His cover name is Thomas
Brackwell. Sergeant Kent contemptuously refers to Regan
and Carter as 'Ratman and Bobbin'.

9: 'Cover Story'
20 February 1975

Writer: Ranald Graham
Director: Douglas Camfield

Cast: Prunella Gee (Sandy Williams),
Bernadette Milnes (Maureen Whittle),
Michael McStay (The Nightclub Manager),
Timothy Carlton (Justin), Mike Savage (Ward),
James Marcus (Myles), Thalia Kouri (The Maid),
Los Gitanos (Flamenco Artistes)

Attempts to recover the stolen money from a bank robbery bring Regan into the sophisticated world of Sandy
Williams, a photojournalist on *Nuance* magazine. But can she
be trusted, or is she part of the gang?

Keep Your Mincers Peeled For . . .: Prunella Gee was the
memorably abrasive (and possibly alien) Miss Griffin in
Nigel Kneale's SF sitcom *Kinvig*.

Some nice 70s elements (the setting is during a dustman's

strike): Sandy's pad is gloriously of the era, down to the scatter cushions and Scandinavian pine, and the then state-of-the-art cassette player with BASF C-60 tape. Only the lava lamps are missing!

Birds: ** Sandy Williams – upper-crust totty, for whom Jack Regan may be a bit of rough, or a genuine interest. Initially seen in a silk dressing gown. Her flamenco dance in white boots is rather nice. 'She's my kind of girl, son,' Jack tells George. They seem to have taken a bath together.

Booze: **** Jack drinks Scotch on the rocks with Sandy, who describes herself as 'a Bloody Mary girl normally' (with lime, not lemon). So he makes one for her, which she considers 'excellent', and later she downs a pint in five seconds. There's lots of champagne at the restaurant. In his local, Jack gets slammed on whisky (when George turns up he asks for a half of bitter).

Shooters: None, although Carter gets beaten up towards the end.

Motors: Sandy drives a red Reliant Scimitar. Carter turns up at Nick's Café in a bright-green Austin Allegro. Later, there's a chase scene involving the Allegro and a police Rover, which is about as exciting as watching paint dry. Both cars handle like beached whales and have the ride of a packet of marshmallows.

Threads: Standard stuff mostly, although the ties are particularly horrible in this episode (Myles's especially). Justin's silk scarf and Sandy's peach headscarf show that even the rich succumbed to ugly 1970s fashions.

Jazz Funk?: Music ranges from some groovy guitar rock in Sandy's pad to sinister spacy background stuff to accompany Jack mixing the Bloody Mary.

Non-PC Moment: Regan: 'Something tells me that prison would not appeal to you, Miss Williams. Your poofter friend might have the time of his life flitting from cell to cell, but not you.'

You What?: Carter: 'Don't half pen and ink down here.'

Larfs: Carter: 'We're not asking him to shop his mates, we're asking you to do it for him!'

Regan (before he realises Sandy is a woman): 'Who the bleedin' hell's this Sandy Williams think he is? Scotch-Welsh git!'

Sandy: 'Limes – little green things, eaten at half-time on the equator.'

Notes: 'Cop meets journalist. The End!' A dull episode, enlivened by some interesting directorial touches and a lot of good dialogue, but not much else. The story limps through about half an hour and then gives up completely, with the rest of the episode being padded out by the sad scene of Jack alone in the pub, with only his black-and-white flashback sequences for company. There's a cool fist fight for George to get beaten up in, but the ending is obvious.

Carter mentions the French oceanographer Jacques Cousteau.

There is plenty of location filming around the South Bank. And the Flamenco troupe are rubbish: Gitanos by name and Gitanos by nature. As often happens in TV, one of the worst episodes of the season was also the one with the highest viewing figures (8.75 million and number two in the audience charts for that week).

10: 'Golden Boy'
27 February 1975

Writer: Martin Hall
Director: Tom Clegg

Cast: Dudley Sutton (Max Dellar), John Nolan (Conway), Anthony Morton (Fuller), Colin Campbell (Potter), Tony Jay (Lambourne), Anne Zelda (Joanne), Peter Miles (Bradshaw), Tim Wylton (Customs Man), Michael Segal (Reporter), Fran Fullenwider (Girl in Pub), Helli Louise (2nd Girl in Pub)

There's a big blag in the offing, and the Sweeney's only lead is a suddenly rich drunk. Still, anything to get the organisation-and-efficiency officer off their backs.

Keep Your Mincers Peeled For . . .: Dudley Sutton will be familiar (if almost unrecognisable) to viewers of *Lovejoy*. Peter Miles is probably best known to telefantasy fans for his chilling performance as Nyder, Davros's Nazi sidekick in *Doctor Who*.

Cool 70s bits: George and Jimmy Thorpe play an electronic Ping-Pong-type tennis game (pre-Space Invaders!) in the pub. George is losing 4–1. The robbers use a state-of-the-art U-Matic VCR (with spools of tape!) that looks as if it came out of the Ark.

Birds: * Harry Fuller has picked up a pair of well-endowed slappers.

Joanna Drummond, the spoilt, Twiggyesque daughter of an industrialist, seems to take quite a fancy to the 'nice, quiet' George Carter!

Booze: **** Harry Fuller drinks double brandies with his lady friends. In a lengthy pub scene, George, Jimmy Thorpe and the other Squad lads drink pints of bitter while Jack inevitably goes for a large whisky. He manages to get Bradshaw, the officious time-and-motion man, drunk by slipping vodka into his lemonade. Jack has a can of bitter in the office.

Shooters: None.

Motors: Conway drives a white Triumph 2000 after using his company car, a blue Rover, to dispose of Fuller's body. He's later driven away in a horrible Morris panda car.

Threads: One of Max's suits has enormous lapels while his green-velvet abomination was the worst bit of tailoring on British TV in 1975. His fuzzy ginger perm is quite startling, too. Regan's blue-, green- and white-striped shirt just falls shy of interfering with TV signals.

Jazz Funk?: There's a funky little theme to accompany the arrival of the Kleen Floor blaggers at the bank.

Non-PC Moment: Joanne on her intended: 'Course he's a Mick, Inspector.'

You What?: Max: 'Remember the time you smashed that screw over the back of the swede with a shovel?'

'That's right, it's a blag. And a bloody big one!'

Max: 'They wanted to know where you had your jam jar pinched. You told 'em, right? Now stop flapping.'

Larfs: Regan tells a joke with the punch line 'How low can you go?' to which the reply is 'A little Jack Russell like that!' (It was a Yorkshire Terrier when we both fell out of the cradle laughing at it . . .)

Regan: 'Now look, Harry, if I was in a bad mood, I could nick you for being drunk and incapable.' Carter: 'Or unlawful possession of money.' Regan: 'Being a public nuisance.' Carter: 'Insulting behaviour.' Regan: 'Disturbing the peace.' Carter: 'Ruining my jacket.' Regan: 'Ruining his jacket . . .'

Notes: 'Forget about your own problems, put the nation first: have a bath!' This is a great episode – another attempt to get overt comedy aspects into *The Sweeney* (although it's still early days and the episode is, in places, very nasty). Great performances from Dudley Sutton and Anthony Morton, who get most of the best lines between them. There are some terrific moments (like the bored girl with the tennis racket waiting for George to get off the phone).

George has a ticket to that evening's football international that he got from the father of one of the Squad boys. The next day, he says he enjoyed the game (but confesses to Regan that the second half was rubbish). Regan's father came from Liverpool and not County Clare in Ireland, as he claims to Conway (although his family *are* Irish – see 'Nightmare'). Joanne refers to Regan and Carter as 'Batman and Robin' (cf. 'The Placer'). Jimmy Thorpe has just had his beard 'chopped off'.

The pre-titles sequence was filmed in the Long Room in the pavilion at Lord's cricket ground.

11: 'Stoppo Driver'
6 March 1975

Writer: Allan Prior
Director: Terry Green

Cast: Nicola Pagett (Sara), Billy Murray (Cooney),
Wolfe Morris (Greg),
Aubrey Morris (The Card Player),
Paul Angelis (Barney), Paul Henry (Morris),
Carrie Lee-Baker (Marie), Hugh Futcher (The Porter)

After their driver is killed, a criminal gang urgently need to recruit a new 'chauffeur'. Who better than the new wheels man at the Flying Squad?

Keep Your Mincers Peeled For . . .: Nicola Pagett starred as Elizabeth Bellamy in LWT's *Upstairs, Downstairs*. Paul Henry was, at the time this episode was made, probably the most famous man on television with his performance as Benny Hawkins in *Crossroads*. Billy Murray is now best known as Don Beach in *The Bill*.

Birds: ** Sara Prince, divorced from her boxer husband. According to Carter, she 'puts it about a bit, apparently!' Marie, Cooney's new missus, is as wet as a slap in the face with a haddock. Mind you, being kidnapped while getting your kit off on your honeymoon would do that to anyone.

Booze: *** There's a lot of champagne at the wedding. Haskins (who makes another reference to his ulcer: see 'Regan') drinks brandy, but Jack's still on the Scotch. Later, a delighted George finds a bottle of whisky and two glasses in the office.

Shooters: * Barney and Morris carry lethal-looking sawn-off shotguns during the hotel heist.

Motors: During the initial chase, Barney and Morris are in a silver S-type (the boot pops open at one point, and then magically shuts itself). It comes to a sticky end, but they replace it with another (and newer!) one. Cooney drives a BMW during the heist ('One of those fast, foreign jobs').

Threads: George's purple turtleneck is on show again. The Swiss card player's white suit is more camp than Butlins, while his minder has one of the widest ties in TV history. Cooney's checky trousers make him look like a stunt double for Rupert the Bear. Morris's red bowling vest is just as horrible.

You What?: Morris: 'Crap! The Old Bill. Where'd they come from?!'

Carter: 'Careful, Cooney, you got a lot of mouth for a strapper on Ap-Pro.'

Sara: 'Oh, Mr Cooney, no cavalry, or we'll stripe her.'

Carter: 'We could spread a few bob around, see if any grass comes up with the latest SP.'

Cooney: 'Oh, shut up. This is my manor, remember?'

Larfs: Carter: 'Who taught you to drive, Evel Knievel?'

One of *the* great *Sweeney* moments: Regan: 'You fancy a drink?' Carter: 'Nah, I told the wife . . . Yeah, all right, come on!'

Haskins: 'Go back in there, get Carter, go home and settle for *Match of the Day*!'

Notes: 'If you can't take a joke, you shouldn't have joined.' Another episode full of cool car chases – one aspect of *The Sweeney* that they usually did well. The opening sequence includes the (now clichéd) slow-motion slide into a handily placed stack of cardboard boxes, but back then it seemed fresh and exciting, like a low-budget *Bullitt*.

Carter refers twice to *Hawaii 5-0*. Cooney's wage is £35 a week – a poor wage even by 1975 standards. There's a mention of the 'Clunk Click' seat-belt campaign (Regan and the others never strap themselves in, so Jimmy Saville was having little effect on *them*).

The credits are unusual for this episode: Thaw, Waterman and Morgan, plus guest stars Pagett, Murray and Morris, are all credited at the end of the episode as well as at the beginning. The stunt arranger, Peter Brayham, also gets a credit among the cast.

12: 'Big Spender'
13 March 1975

Writer: Allan Prior
Director: Viktors Ritelis

Cast: Warren Mitchell (Wardle), Catherine Schell (Stella),
Godfrey James (Charley Smith),
Julian Holloway (John Smith),
Billy Hamon (Barry Smith), Maureen Pryor (Enid Wardle),
Peter Armitage (Jacko),
Peter Glaze (Joe Spratt), Sally Knyvette (Angela)

How can Wardle, a mild-mannered accountant at a multi-storey car park, afford to lose thousands of pounds at the races, and keep an expensive mistress like the glamorous Stella? And what is his connection to the villainous Smith family, whom Haskins wants incarcerated once and for all?

Keep Your Mincers Peeled For . . .: An incredible cast is led by the great Warren Mitchell, whose performance as Alf Garnett in Johnny Speight's *Till Death Us Do Part* (and several sequels) makes him one of TV's most recognisable faces. Catherine Schell will be well known to Gerry Anderson fans as Maya in *Space: 1999*. Peter Glaze was a children's TV legend, spending almost twenty years as one of the *Crackerjack* team. A young Sally Knyvette appears in a small (but perfectly formed) role – she later went on to break millions of teenage boys' hearts as Jenna in *Blake's 7*, and millions of women's hearts as Joe Sugden's wife, Kate, in *Emmerdale*. It's also nice to see Julian Holloway (whose face you'll recognise from just about every sitcom of the 1970s, usually playing bank managers or policemen) getting a meatier and more villainous role.

Birds: *** Our first sight of Angela is a close-up of her low-cut neckline and heaving bosom. Our second is a retreating shot of her in leather boots and a short brown miniskirt. Hubba hubba. Plus, Stella – Wardle's 'high-class scrubber' –

is seen in a bikini and in bed. Charley bids her a fond farewell by kissing her chest and stomach.

**Booze: ** Carter and Regan drink cans of light ale in the office. Barry Smith seems also to drink this curiously 70s abomination. Stella and Wardle quaff much champagne. Later Wardle has a whisky and asks Regan and Carter to join him – despite being on duty, they do.

Shooters: * There are lots of pistols in the climactic shoot-out at the Smith's scrap yard ('We're armed as well, you know!').

Motors: There's a gorgeous E-type convertible at the beginning. However, as if any further evidence were needed that the 70s were the decade that taste forgot, Barry drives a purple and silver Jag. Wardle hasn't blown the gaff by driving a flash motor: he's still going around in a terrible yellowy-green Allegro.

Threads: Barry's *Italian Job*-style look is *great* (dark glasses, leather gloves). This episode sees a fine collection of horrible kipper ties (Regan wears at least three different ones). Charley's stripy swimming trunks don't leave a lot to the imagination. During the second race-meeting scene, keep your eye on Carter – at one point a blink-and-you'll-miss-him extra walks past wearing a checky jacket and one of the loudest lemon-yellow shirt-and-tie combos you'll ever see. Then there's the fur coat and white platforms Wardle wears ('Hello, Mr Wardle, you *do* look nice!').

Jazz Funk?: Some powerful and funky piano and percussion-based music to accompany the motorway chase sequence.

You What?: Charley: 'A little graft and a lot of bread.'
    John Smith: 'This mug's a very important mug . . .'
    And: 'That Jacko's bottling out . . . He's always on the sauce and he's stopped pulling birds. That's a sure sign!'

Larfs: Charley on Stella's dodgy past: 'In those days you did a hell of a lot for ten quid!'

Notes: 'This is not a college debating society, it's a police force.' A camp classic; an episode made by the scenes of Warren Mitchell in women's clothing ('Oh 'eck!'). Full of tasty little moments, with just about everybody getting some good lines.

Regan's call sign in this episode is 'Oscar 7'. Regan isn't interested in the chances of promotion to Chief Inspector ('finding stolen bikes in Pinner'). Carter's mum used to work in a pie factory – he gets halfway through an anecdote about 'the stories she used to tell' (concerning a 'poor little cat') when Regan, thankfully, stops him!

Regan misquotes Robbie Burns's 'To a Mouse'. Wardle earns about £3000 a year (legitimately, at least!).

13: 'Contact Breaker'
20 March 1975

Writer: Robert Banks Stewart[1]
Director: Bill Brayne

Cast: Warren Clarke (Danny Keever), Coral Atkins (Brenda),
Tony Anholt (Mark), John Collin (Parish),
Jim Norton (Harrister), Kenneth Gardiner (Arthur),
Cheryl Hall (Jenny), Jill Balcon (Miss Hepple),
Sydney Arnold (Tilley), Ivor Roberts (Sale),
David Jackson (Eddy Cory), Frank Jarvis (Prison Officer),
Patrick Durkin (Foreman Decorator)

A blag goes off, right under Haskins's nose. There's no lead – except a name overheard by a crooked antique dealer.

Keep Your Mincers Peeled For . . . : Warren Clarke is now best known for his role as Andy Dalziel in the BBC's *Dalziel and Pascoe*. Previous high-profile performances include *Nice Work*, *The Manageress*, *Shelley* and the film *A Clockwork*

---

[1] On-screen credit is 'Banks-Stewart', but the author's name is usually written thus.

Orange. Cheryl Hall played Wolfie's girlfriend Shirley in *Citizen Smith*. Handsome Tony Anholt was Paul Buchet in Gerry Anderson's *The Protectors*, Tony Verdeschi in another Anderson series, *Space: 1999*, and Charles Frere in *Howards' Way*. John Collin played Sergeant Hagger in *Z Cars*. David Jackson was one of the original crew on *Blake's 7*, as Gan.

The *Daily Chronicle* headline, concerning the bank robbery is 'SNATCH OF THE DAY!' There's a sign for Wall's Ice Cream that the camera lingers on for several seconds, bringing back lots of memories of Mivvis and Fabs and the like! One for all the technoheads out there: the VCR Regan uses is a Phillips 1501 (a top-loader, which cost a fortune in 1975, and took chunky sixty-minute tapes that went for nearly twenty quid a throw!).

Birds: * Jenny in the hairdresser's is more than happy for George to take her to lunch (she thinks he's 'fresh').

Booze: * Haskins and Regan have champagne during an interminable Scotland Yard retirement function for Ben Sheppitt (who has six months to live according to Haskins).

Shooters: None.

Motors: There's much banger racing at the beginning, and the villains make off from the bank in an ambulance. Phil Harrister drives a grey S-type; Parish a white Range Rover. The backup Sweeney Cortina (blue) is in evidence (this time with the number plate NHK 296M, so it could be a different car), as is a little Morris panda car (twice). Mark Colebrook drives a brown Capri.

Threads: Brenda's flares and the bright-yellow trouser suit of Jenny vie for attention, while both Regan and Carter wear a series of mile-wide ties. The worst threads in the episode, however, are Mark's general 'Total Look of Debenhams' *Persuaders*-type suit. He looks like a walking advert for That Shirt. Now there's a man with Hai Karate! in his bathroom cabinet if ever we saw one.

Jazz Funk?: There's a piano-based cheesy sitcom-esque theme for Harrister's Jag, a loud rock song playing in Brenda's flat, and a strident organ theme at the end.

You What?: When talking to the bank manager, Haskins uses the term 'wire man', meaning the individual responsible for fixing the alarms. Regan says, 'It's a tough drum to blag without an assist', which Haskins translates as the robbery would be difficult without inside knowledge.

Carter: 'You are nicked, sonny Jim!'

Regan: 'Come on, Brenda, if your family had a coat of arms, it'd have crossed jemmies on it!'

Larfs: Regan notes Haskins got news of the bank job 'during the middle of his bacon and mushrooms!'

Danny Keever: 'The only bank I ever did was a piggy bank.'

Notes: 'It's a sloppy mistake to make for a bunch of pros.' A nice little episode, with Haskins for once the man with the grudge, and Regan wanting to do things properly.

Carter plays darts (seemingly pretty well), and displays a dodgy Jamaican accent (see 'The Bigger They Are'). Danny Keever broke Haskins's jaw when he was arrested three years ago. Keever says it was an accident!

14: 'Abduction'
27 March 1975

Writer: Trevor Preston
Director: Tom Clegg

Cast: Stuart Wilson (Inspector Knowles),
Wanda Ventham (Brenda),
Patricia Maynard (Miss Alexander),
Joe Gladwin (Stan Preston), Reginald Marsh (Foss),
Arnold Diamond (Dr Cohen),
Naomi Chance (Miss Mayhew), Eric Mason (Kenny Jarvis),
Jonathan Dennis (Alan Foss), Michael McVey (Paul)

When Regan's daughter is kidnapped, Jack must balance interdivisional rivalry, his wife's bitterness towards him, and his own feelings as he and George seek the abductors and the reasons behind the crime.

Keep Your Mincers Peeled For . . .: Wanda Ventham is one of the most popular actresses in Britain with roles in series as diverse as *The Lotus Eaters*, *UFO*, and *Only Fools and Horses*. The lovely Joe Gladwin was for several years the best reason for watching *Last of the Summer Wine* for his performance as the dour Wally Batty. Reginald Marsh made a long career out of playing pompous bank-manager types (exactly the sort of role he plays here) in sitcoms like *The Good Life* and *Terry and June*, but older readers may remember him in the 1960s as *Coronation Street*'s proto-Mike Baldwin, Dave Smith.

This episode sees the first appearance of one of *the* icons of the 1970s, a green fur-trimmed Parka with orange lining! All of the kids in the opening scene are wearing them, and we get a close-up on the one worn by the little boy who saw Susie abducted. Takes you back to Hereford beating Newcastle on *Match of the Day*, doesn't it?

Birds: ** Anything with Wanda Ventham can't be all bad, but there's little in the way of comedy crumpet here. Except . . . the early scene in which Regan and Stan stare admiringly at the knickers of one of two girls in tennis gear when she bends over to tie her laces. ('I could be arrested for what you're thinking,' notes Stan. Jack agrees, he could!)

Booze: ** Jack spends most of the episode drinking whisky: several times on his own, and twice with Kate. 'This isn't gonna help, you know,' he says, hypocritically. 'Hasn't helped you for years,' replies Kate.

Shooters: * Fay, Brenda's 'friend' (that's a 70s euphemism for 'lesbian lover' if ever we heard one), holds a .45-calibre handgun on Jack and George but is too scared to use it. Regan wields a pretty fearsome truncheon during the episode's conclusion!

Motors: A gold Capri with a vinyl roof is said to be the kidnap car, but we don't see it. Jack drives a green one.

Threads: Jack's really-rather-OK tan jacket and grey polo-neck put in another appearance alongside some less successful efforts – like Kate's suede jacket and orange loon pants.

Alison Carter wears a blouse with a collar big enough to cover Western Europe. Divorce her *now*, George. (Mind you, he can't complain: his blue tracksuit is horribly 70s.)

Jazz Funk?: The edgy, aggressive strings as Jack and George discover old Stan's body are good, but the best music here is the recurring rock theme as Carter trails Brenda up the Northern Line.

You What?: Regan: 'The ladies are gonna love her in Holloway.' Carter: 'Not many! Nice blonde barnet . . .!'

Carter's memorably incompetent attempt to get Regan to stop beating up one of the blaggers in a lift: 'Guv! Guv! Leave it out!'

Larfs: Kate: 'A lot of kids her age go to school on their own.' Regan: 'Well, a lot of mothers need a kick up the arse, then!'

Haskins: 'How you feeling?' Carter: 'I could do fifteen rounds.' Haskins: 'With the tea lady, I suppose?!' Carter: 'I'd still lose . . .'

Regan: 'We're the two biggest male chauvinist pigs in the Sweeney, and if you don't start telling the truth we're gonna throw the lot at you and your friend.'

And, in one of the finest moments of the series, Trevor Preston gives Regan a speech of Raymond-Chandler-like streetwise poetry: 'I sometimes hate this bastard place. It's a bloody holiday camp for thieves and weirdos. All the rubbish. You age prematurely trying to sort some of them out. Try to protect the public and all they do is call you "fascist". You nail a villain and some ponced-up, pinstriped Hampstead barrister screws it up like an old fag packet on a point of procedure, then pops off for a game of squash and a glass of Madeira. He's taking home thirty grand a year and we can just about afford ten days in Eastbourne and a second-hand car. Nah, it's all bloody wrong, my son.' Jack Regan, philosopher and renaissance man!

Notes: 'Some screwed-up bitch has got my kid somewhere, and I'm going to find out where!' They saved the best till last – as epic and towering now as it was twenty-odd years ago, with an anger that is timeless. John Thaw delivers the full range of emotions (his scene in Haskins's office with Wilson is almost too painful to watch). Don't miss this one.

Regan's pad is a bit cluttered and small (not that we'd expect anything else) and he spends the episode chain-smoking (which is understandable). He seems to have the *Daily Telegraph* delivered. He never had a dog. The episode is set in October, and Haskins wants Regan to book next year's holiday. Regan says he has nine days annual leave 'owed' from last year (so he really is married to the job), and calls Haskins 'Frank' for about the first time (there seems to be a softening in the relationship between the characters – certainly Haskins shields Regan from Wilson's vendetta despite Jack's awful description of him as the 'oily rag'). One of Regan's teachers at school was the sixty-year-old Miss Beeston, who had a fifty-inch bust, halitosis, and knuckles like a navvy. Jack says she needed to shave twice a day, and it seems she gave the young Regan bottom many a beating.

George is on sick leave (and is taking pills for whatever it is that's made him ill). He seems to have studied security systems while out of the Flying Squad.

Kate has split up with the German man seen in 'Regan' (variously described by Jack as her 'Aryan language-laboratory boyfriend' and a 'Kraut divorcee'). Susie is eight years old: Jack has seen her twice in six months.

Second Season

Thirteen 60-minute episodes
Euston Films/Thames Television
Created by Ian Kennedy Martin

Associate Producer: Mary Morgan
Producer: Ted Childs
Executive Producers: Lloyd Shirley, George Taylor

Title music by Harry South

Regular Cast: John Thaw (Detective Inspector Jack Regan),
Dennis Waterman (Detective Sergeant George Carter),
Garfield Morgan (Detective Chief Inspector Frank Haskins,
16, 18–19, 21, 23–27),
Martin Read (Detective Constable Jimmy Thorpe, 16),
Stephanie Turner (Alison Carter, 19),
George Layton (Ray Stackpole, 21, 24),
Patrick Mower (Colin Magruder, 21, 24),
Anne Stallybrass (Doreen Haskins, 21[1]),
Jennifer Thanisch (Susie Regan, 21),
John Alkin (Detective Sergeant Tom Daniels, 22, 25),
Nick Brimble (Detective Constable Gerry Burtonshaw, 27)

15 'Chalk and Cheese'

1 September 1975

Writer: Trevor Preston
Director: Terry Green

Cast: Shane Briant (Giles Nunn),
Lesley Anne Down (Caroline Sewell),
Paul Jones (Tommy Garret), David Lodge (Pop Garret),
Peter Howell (Alan Sevier), Ken Wynne (Albie Fenner),
Jeremy Child (Gil Elphick),
Raymond Adamson (Mr Tolman), Terence Seward (Prees),
Eric Dodson (Mr de Courey), Stephen Bent (Scouler),
Ivor Salter (Ibbitt), Betty England (Mrs Tolman),
Maggy Maxwell (Mrs de Courey)

Rich people are being robbed by a pair of masked 'high-waymen'. A gold lighter leads Regan to a well-to-do establishment in Kensington, while Carter investigates his old boxing club.

Keep Your Mincers Peeled For . . .: Lesley Anne Down made a career playing upper-class totty, notably as Georgina

---

[1] Character played by Sheila Reid in the fourth season.

Bellamy in *Upstairs, Downstairs*. Shane Briant was one of Hammer's young stars during the early 70s, appearing opposite Peter Cushing in *Frankenstein and the Monster from Hell*. Paul Jones was a huge pop star in the 1960s, the lead singer with Manfred Mann ('Do Wah Diddy Diddy' and 'Pretty Flamingo' among others). He also starred in the highly acclaimed film *Privilege*. David Lodge was a long-time friend and collaborator with both Spike Milligan (in the *Q* series) and Peter Sellers. He was also the star of the BBC's 1960s football soap *United!*. Jeremy Child is one of those great character actors who seem to be in everything. His credits include *Bird of Prey* and *First Among Equals*.

An eight-track cassette is seen in one of the cars, and a THINK METRIC poster is visible at the boxing club (where there's also a poster for a fight between Joe Frasier and Joe Bugner).

Birds: ** It's got Lesley Anne Down in (and getting out of) a rather nice dress.

Booze: ** Not much consumed, although while at work Regan is passed a suspiciously wrapped bottle which he puts straight into his cabinet. He later refuses a double whisky during his meeting with Sevier (though George has one). George claims at one point that both he and Regan are teetotal!

Shooters: *** Garret tells Nunn that the shooters 'are just for show', but Giles seems rather turned on by the possibility of violence. Tommy Garret resorts to his boxing when one robbery threatens to go wrong, but the next attack concludes with a fatal shooting. Nunn shoots at Regan with a pistol towards the end.

Motors: The episode begins with a Rolls-Royce Silver Shadow. Nunn and Garret steal a yellow Porsche 911 and a white left-hand-drive MGB to rob their victims. Tommy Garret has saved enough money to buy a blue Ford Mustang.

Threads: The garish ski masks. Tommy's ill-gotten gains don't seem to have bought him any taste in clothes if his white strides and horrible pair of shirts (one red, one multi-coloured) are anything to go by.

Jazz Funk?: Giles Nunn prefers listening to ethereal electronic music (man).

Non-PC Moment: There's a 'coloured boy' at the boxing club . . . Called 'Chalky'.

You What?: Tommy tells Nunn to get Mrs de Courey's fur coat: 'Grab the pussy.' (At least, that's what we think he's talking about.)
    Regan to suspect: 'If you don't come across you're going to end up wearing the paper hat, son!'
    George on Tommy's motor: 'Tasty bit of steel.'
    Regan: 'You're a thief. You've been laying your thieving Germans on everything that wasn't nailed down ever since your voice broke.'

Larfs: Regan gets philosophical: 'Son, at the moment I'm treating you as a sad casualty of our corrupt and degenerate society. Don't make me think otherwise.'
    Elphick says Giles is 'good-looking, in an androgynous sort of way'.
    Regan: 'Plenty of money?' Elphick: 'I don't know. One can never tell nowadays. We live in an age of endless credit!'
    Regan says, 'Get yer trousers on', although this time it's because Giles Nunn has injured his leg.

Notes: 'You wouldn't credit what goes on down at their polished country seats at weekends. It's a hedonist utopia.' The pre-title sequence – as Nunn and Garret stage a robbery in the countryside – is staggeringly surreal, with ambient music and no sound effects until the sudden blast of a horn brings us back to reality. This episode's treatment of the various classes is hysterical: the upper class are utterly decadent and, as one of Regan's contacts indicates, just as prone to crime as the working classes, albeit with (allegedly) a greater sophistication. Caroline Sewell is a well-bred, spliff-smoking young thing who considers marriage a 'suburban' institution, and is prone to spout lines like 'I am not one of your mindless little East End scrubbers talking about television and worrying about split ends.'

Carter and Tommy Garret grew up together and were like brothers, 'Pop' Garret seeing potential in both of them as professional boxers. Nunn makes an oblique reference to *The Merchant of Venice*.

16: 'Faces'
8 September 1975

Writer: Murray Smith
Director: William Brayne

Cast: Colin Welland (Tober), Barry Stanton (The German), Jeffry Wickham (Major Carver), Keith Buckley (Jake Jenkins), John Cording (Evil Willie Sanders), Grahame Mallard (Ingram), John Vyvyan (Albert Milligan), John Bardon (Doc Boyd)

Three blags in two days, and the Sweeney suspect the driver to be thug-for-hire Tober. However, he seems to be working for a right-wing terrorist, and Regan is warned off by the intelligence services.

Keep Your Mincers Peeled For ...: The Yorkshire-born writer/actor Colin Welland will be familiar to anyone who's seen *Z Cars*, *Kes*, or *Chariots of Fire* (for which his script won an Oscar). Diminutive Johnny Vyvyan was a long-time collaborator with Tony Hancock in *Hancock's Half Hour*.

Birds: * This episode is almost entirely female-free, barring a Whitehall secretary called Samantha and the nurse who treats Carter's injuries.

Booze: No booze, either. According to Regan, George's coffee tastes like 'liquid concrete'.

Shooters: *** The masked men have shotguns, and they're not afraid to use them. Evil Willie talks of his desire to have an Israeli Uzi sub-machine-gun, and the Sweeney prepare for their confrontation with 'shooters, iron bars, the lot'. Plenty of fisticuffs and hand-to-hand combat, too: Tober wields a commando knife, and beats up the other hired thugs. Carter takes him on, unarmed, only for Regan to intervene ('Come on, George, stop messing about!').

Motors: Tober's white Austin van almost collides with a Rover 3500 and is then pursued by a blue police Cortina with lights (NHK 296M – seen as a Sweeney car in other episodes) and Regan's Granada. The 'sheriff' turns up in a blue Austin Allegro (poor soul). Ingram gets to drive the blue Cortina, and Tober steals an S-type. Towards the end, Haskins arrives in a lurid yellow Rover.

Threads: Regan's still got his gross brown flares on. All of Tober's gang wear large 'Dan Dares' (Jake's are probably the most outrageous; he's got to be the most conspicuous under-cover agent in history, what with that sheepskin coat and droopy moustache!).

Bill the Driver: In a classic moment, Bill the driver injures himself playing football with Regan.

You What?: Carter's snout, Albert, knows all about the recent blags and says things like 'The word's out . . .'

Regan: 'Do you want to go through the comic book?'

Regan tells General Carver to 'Cut the bunny and come clean.'

Larfs: Carter: 'Football?' Regan: 'Yeah. You know, football? Little round thing. People kick it. It's all the rage.'

Carver, after George has asked to go into an office because it's more private: 'This is Whitehall, Sergeant, not the Kremlin.'

Tober, after Evil Willie has suggested that he might have fought him in Northern Ireland: 'No, sonny. If you had we'd have been doing business by the spiritualist.'

Haskins: 'I've just been with the assistant commissioner.' Regan: 'Not, I trust, in the biblical sense of the word.'

Tober, to the German: 'Then that's your Wagnerian funeral, Heinrich. Don't expect me to sit in the bunker till we're down to the last cartridge.'

Haskins, of all people, gets to say, 'Drop it, you're nicked!'

And, the final moment: Major Carver: 'Must go. Toodle-pip.' Regan: 'Bastard!'

Notes: 'Have you ever fought the Sweeney? They're the real heavy mob.' A lovely script from Murray Smith, with the Sweeney coming up against the delicate machinations of the intelligence community. In its ambiguity it prefigures the much later *Between the Lines* and Smith's own involvement in *Strangers*. However, Colin Welland puts in a convincing but occasionally stilted performance, and the plot does rather leap about all over the place.

George places a £1 bet in the bookie's. He's been working with Regan for about eighteen months (see 'Regan'). When they go undercover as repairmen, the call signs used are 'Whisky' (appropriate in any other story!) and 'Zulu'. Hysterically, Regan's operation at the end is called 'Penguin': his own call sign is 'Lollipop'!

17: 'Supersnout'
15 September 1975

Writer: Ranald Graham
Director: Tom Clegg

Cast: Bill Maynard (Quirk), John Tordoff (Stickley),
Vernon Dobtcheff (Kretchmar), Carl Duering (Dantziz),
Rosemarie Dunham (The Dowager),
Christopher Coll (The Shop Owner), George Silver (Yannos),
Vincent Wong (Japanese Tourist), Frank Coda (Quirk's Snout),
Geoffrey Drew (Stooge), Brandy di Frank (The Stripper)

Regan's snout, Joey Stickley, claims to know nothing about the forthcoming jewellery heist. Regan is forced to rely on information that has somehow filtered through to his ambitious, temporary boss, Quirk.

Keep Your Mincers Peeled For . . .: Bill Maynard was the star of *Oh No! It's Selwyn Froggitt* ('Magic!') and *The Gaffer*, and continues in regular TV employment in *Heartbeat*.

There are a number of *very* 1970s items easily visible, including a vintage British Gas van, a miniature reel-to-reel tape recorder and the interior lighting at Regan's flat.

Birds: **** Regan, his shirt open to at least the navel, is about to get it on with a luscious brunette (cue soft jazz and cocktails) when Stickley phones. Later, he and Stickley meet in a seedy club, and watch a stripper.

Booze: ***** An absolute booze-fest: Regan is plying his lady friend with drinks when we first see him, and he knocks back a whisky while cooking a couple of enormous steaks for himself and Carter. He asks George to stick a bottle of red wine under the hot tap (other disgusting culinary habits include flinging spaghetti at the wall to see if it's cooked: this would be fine if he cleared up after himself!). They then have a drunken conversation about Moby Dick and good marriages (both being impossible dreams: lovely to see that, twenty years before *The X Files* did it, *The Sweeney* was using Ahab as a metaphor for one of its central characters!). Regan downs a beer in the pub before meeting Stickley (next to an outside toilet!), and later buys George a treble whisky.

Shooters: ** Regan warns Stickley that even blanks can be 'bloody lethal' at close range, but all the fights we see (including a massive scrap between the Flying Squad and the Serious Crime Squad) involve fists and batons. George is carrying a revolver when driving the taxi undercover.

Motors: The cigarette-lorry robbery utilises a Jag and a Bedford van. George gets to be a cabbie (there's a great scene with a Japanese tourist wanting to go to 'Piccalilly Circus'). The dowager tries to tempt Regan into being her new chauffeur (it's the 'only powder-blue Camargue in Europe').

Threads: Let's start with the lorry driver's neckerchief, George's tie, and, while undercover as a taxi driver, his horrible moustache and red T-shirt. Stickley's skinny tie and thin-lapel jacket was ten years out of date in 1975 (though a couple of years later, thanks largely to punk, the mod revival and the advent of Eddie Shoestring, they would be fashionable again!). Watch out, also, for the first scene of Regan arriving at the snooker club to rough up Stickley – the man who meets him as he gets out of his car has a terrible pair of tan-brown flares. Also, on the subject of 'Dan Dares', exactly 41 minutes into the episode, just as Carter and Quick's snout arrive outside the bank, there's a quick shot of a woman with an enormous pair of electric-blue Oxford bags. And there's a blink-and-you-miss-it sight of a young boy in one of *the* 70s fashion excesses, a Star Jumper, during one of the taxi scenes. (One of this book's authors is *still* upset about his magnificent black and red Star Jumper being stolen, along with a pair of clackers, from Walker Swimming Baths in 1975. If *you* know who was responsible for this crime, please contact the police *immediately*.)

Jazz Funk?: Some *Shaft* guitar during the fight scene at the beginning. There's some funky woodwind when George is cabbying. The strip-joint music is soulful, while the song playing in the pub where Regan meets Stickley features some country-and-western steel guitar.

You What?: Joey Stickley wants a 'oner' plus ten per cent of the insurance for his information.

Quirk: 'You've got no style, Jack, but you're a great scorer of goals. I'm glad you're on my team.'

Carter on Quirk: 'I think he's a diddlo.'

Regan: 'You're *my* snout, sweetheart. I'm very possessive!'

Larfs: George, throwing the Japanese tourist out of his cab: 'Sorry, pal. Look now we're not all like this, and it's nothing to do with the war!'

Technician to Quirk, after the shambles at the jewellery store: 'Shall I accidentally erase the tape, sir?'

Notes: 'Some things about this job are great, and some things *stink*!' Some memorable moments, and a terrific central idea, though the story is hampered by a destabilising comic tone and Bill Maynard's *Caine Mutiny*-style perform-ance. There's a great scene with Quirk explaining his plan with the aid of cardboard cutouts and model cars, but in the presence of the German police observers he comes across as a buffoon. Regan's anger at Stickley's stitching up of Quirk (a 'good copper') is well judged, however, and the last scene is excellent. There are some nice directorial touches too, such as the cat mewing on top of the pub's outside lavatory, and the sleazy strip-joint scenes (which are *very* influenced by *Get Carter*; ironically there's a long-overdue punning reference to the Michael Caine film during Quirk's planning meeting). Good location filming around Gloucester Road tube station.

Regan was commended for bravery for getting beaten up by Stickley during the cigarette-lorry snatch. His flat is directly below one shared by 'two birds'. Carter can speak a little bit of French (to go with the smattering of Italian and Spanish he has) and at least one word of Japanese! Haskins is in Toronto.

During the raid, Carter is Charlie 1, Regan is Charlie 2, and the backup team are Charlie 3. Quirk is Oscar 1.

This was the episode that the BBC chose to represent *The Sweeney* during their 1995 'Cops on the Box' theme night (albeit edited with a hacksaw). The 1977 repeat of this episode (on 5 December) gained viewing figures of 16.2 million, and was number two in the weekly charts.

18: 'Big Brother'
22 September 1975

Writer: Trevor Preston
Director: Tom Clegg

Cast: Michael Robbins (Lee), Gwen Taylor (Anne Knightly), Maurice Roëves (Phil Deacon), David Dixon (Andy Deacon), John Clive (Frewin), Roy Boyd (Traynor), John Halstead (Betty), Keith Bell (Swan), Merdelle Jordine (Angela), Doyle Richmond (Rea)

A suspect collapses in a cell during questioning by Regan, and is rushed to hospital for renal surgery consistent with a severe beating. Even Regan's colleagues are not convinced by his protestations of innocence . . .

Keep Your Mincers Peeled For . . .: Michael Robbins played Arthur, Olive's husband in *On the Buses*. Maurice Roëves's career included roles in *Danger UXB*, and the film *Escape to Victory*, but he's probably best known for his performance as a pyrophobic guitarist in *Tutti Frutti*, while David Dixon had a cult following as Ford Prefect in *The Hitch-Hiker's Guide to the Galaxy*. Gwen Taylor was one of the *Rutland Weekend Television* team, and had the memorable role of Golden Gordon's long-suffering wife in *Ripping Yarns* before parts in *Duty Free, A Bit of a Do* and *The Sharp End*. John Clive was the manic Professor Summersby in *Robert's Robots*; he also appeared in *The Italian Job* and *Carry on Abroad*, and that's his voice you'll hear as John Lennon in *Yellow Submarine*. John Halstead was the comedy porter, Arnold Capper, in *General Hospital*.

Among the words Regan comes up with during his two games of scrabble with Anne are 'kill' and 'zombie' (one-track mind!). But he doesn't know what a 'duiker' is (and neither did one of the authors of this book, worryingly!). The graffiti seen in the episode includes 'Help' twice inside the derelict flat Rea hides in (desperate cry from the alienated urban scum, or a couple of references to the 1965 Beatles film? Your choice . . .) and one celebrating the Canterbury hippie ensemble Caravan. There's also a reference to 'Prince Gypsy Lee', but we haven't a clue what that's all about.

Birds: * Regan spends much of the episode in the company of the brunette Anne Knightley. George seems very keen on a new wine bar: 'Thirty bob a bottle and all the arthritis you can take,' he says, miming women's breasts.

Booze: * George is part-way through a pint of stout in the boozer. Regan drinks red wine with Anne.

Shooters: * Eddie the psycho carries a tasty bit of kit in a foam-filled suitcase, but he never gets to use it. The initial robbery involves ammonia and coshes. Carter carries a small truncheon with him when apprehending Rea.

Motors: Phil Deacon drives a Merc. Watch out, also, for a long shot of a street on which a light-brown Hillman Imp and a very battered-looking white Mini are clearly visible.

Threads: Anne's white collars are so wide they flop down over her shoulders, though Stan's shirt just about takes the honours in this regard (nice sideburns too, by the way!). Regan's grey kipper must be a foot wide. Andy Deacon's perm and general threads are relics from an average 1975 disco (he looks like the kind of geezer who'd smooth up to a girl shaking her stuff to Bachman Turner Overdrive and ask if she wanted to come back and see his etchings). His brother's threads are much more tasteful, though even this is spoilt by his tie. Best of all, though, is Rea's massive maroon flares – dig that, honky.

Jazz Funk?: No (though Rea himself wouldn't be out of place in *Shaft*). The 'suspense theme' returns as Eddie tries out his weapon. There's a rather funky little tune during the pursuit of Rea.

You What?: Carter: 'That Hammersmith wages snatch. We've had a reliable snout on. He's put two names in the frame.'
　　Regan: 'You're done, Deacon. Stone cold. You can drop the Old Vic.'
　　Carter: 'You did have him on his toes earlier.'
　　Stan: 'You kill a kozzer, you take the lot on.'
　　Rea, on Angela: 'She's got a thing about honkys.'
　　Regan: 'She still a tom?' Carter: '. . . Nah, if she tapped him, he wouldn't spend the whole night with her, would he? . . . Is she just earning a bit on the side, or is she under a wing?'

Larfs: Haskins: 'You're building an image, Jack. A broken marriage, drinking, deliberate flouting of authority. The whole damn thing is symptomatic.' Regan: 'Of what?' Haskins: 'A man who's heading for a fall.'
　　Frewin: 'Today's headline, tomorrow's chip wrapper.'

Notes: 'You're too quick with your hands, sometimes, guv, and you know it.' Rather run-of-the-mill and predictable, with workmanlike characterisation and a pay-off (Eddie's hit on Regan) that is promised but never materialises.

A10 is the internal-investigations department (see 'Golden Fleece', *Sweeney!*). 'Matt' (presumably Mathews) is mentioned, but not seen. Regan has nicked Stan Traynor twice. Angela has been busted five times since she was fourteen, including a period of four months in an approved school and two spells inside.

19: 'Hit and Run'
29 September 1975

Writer: Roger Marshall
Director: Mike Vardy

Cast: Gary Waldhorn (Fowler), Sheila Ruskin (Judy),
Patrick Troughton (Crofts), Margaret Whiting (Fladga),
Michael Sheard (Mr Penketh), James Snell (Johnny Moxom),
Liz Smith (Landlady), Terry Hale (Minicab Operator),
Katherine Parr (Mrs Carter)

George's wife is killed by a hit-and-run driver. But did they mean to get her, or were the murderers after someone else?

Keep Your Mincers Peeled For . . .: Gary Waldhorn will be familiar to fans of *The Vicar of Dibley* as David Horton. Liz Smith was the mum in *I Didn't Know You Cared*, while Patrick Troughton was a TV legend as the second Doctor in *Doctor Who*. Speaking of *Doctor Who*, Michael Sheard was one of the most regular guest actors on the BBC show, appearing with five of the eight Doctors over the years; he's probably best known to readers as Mr Bronson in *Grange Hill*.

A good game when watching this episode is to see how many 'You don't see *them* very often these days' items you can spot in the supermarket scene, green-label Heinz Baked Beans and that particular packaging of Bacofoil being two obvious examples.

Birds: ** A knackered George Carter watches his wife getting dressed. 'Give us a flash, darlin'.' 'Fat chance.' Regan glances admiringly at a couple of nurses. Regan seems to be bombing out his latest flame, but it turns out that it's his *daughter* that he isn't taking to the zoo because of nasty 'Uncle Frank'.

Booze: ** Jack brings George a bottle after Alison's death – for therapeutic reasons – and offers to help him drink it 'down to the label'.

Shooters: None.

Motors: The Sweeney car is 'undertaken' by a yellow Datsun, much to Jack's annoyance. 'Get over, ya bastard! ... Drive a Jap car, and they think they're kamikaze pilots!' The vehicle that kills Alison is a stolen blue Allegro. We also see a yellow MG Mk III Midget.

Threads: George's grey flared strides, Fowler's black polo-neck and Judy's enormous blouse collar.

Jazz Funk?: Some choppy Isaac Hayes wah-wah guitar as Fowler visits Judy. The episode also features (at regular intervals) a syrupy pop song the lyrics of which concern a dead love. Much use of discordant piano, bass and percussion mood music. Also, in the scene where Alan visits Judy, there's a little bass-and-trumpet theme – it goes 'dum-dum-dumdum-dum (parp, parp!)', and turns up quite a few times in other *Sweeney* episodes. Other stock music includes a rather comic 'boinging-bass' piece, much used during this season.

You What?: Regan: 'Lawyers. I could have chinned him!'
   Crofts: 'What's the SP on that Richard of yours?'
   And: 'I've tumbled you, Alan, you're all bunny!'
   Regan: 'Another couple of tips like that and I'll be back wearing a tall hat . . .' Fladga: 'Next one'll be a stone ginger.'
   Croft offers to pay Johnny a 'oner' now, with another after the job is complete ('Two hundred sobs').

Larfs: Haskins: 'Your snout either needs elocution lessons, or his ears syringing.' Regan: 'With sulphuric acid!'

George Carter's moment of Marshall poetry: 'Body on the slab, that's all. Nothing. You can't relate to them all, can you? Only this time it isn't *just* a body, [it's] my wife's body. Sudden death. My wife's sudden death. Form 44. How many of those have we had to fill in, eh, guv?'

And: '[If] this world runs another million years . . . she'll still be twenty-nine.'

Regan gets philosophical: 'Church has me foxed. Always rooking you for not going, and then when you do go all they do is tell you how corrupt, how sinful, how unworthy you are.'

Regan: 'People like you make me puke!'

Notes: 'We've got problems enough without some rotten little slag running out on us.' A cracking episode (the two scenes Regan has with Fladga, his snout – and implied girlfriend – are among the best in the series). There are loads of great moments, like Regan finding a vandalised telephone box ('Wouldn't you bloody *know* it?!'), and his joke with Haskins that Wyatt Earp was in 'F division'.

The first murder case Regan worked on seemed to have involved a card game. His dad worked on the Manchester Ship Canal. Fladga says, 'I like it when you've got your Irish up', another nod to his Irish ancestry (see 'Nightmare'). George knows the plot of *Othello* (sort of!), and is aware of the works of Frankie Howerd (telling Alison to 'Titter not, madam'). He is 26. Alison (whose middle name was Mary and whose younger sister is called Betty) was 29. She worked at St Bartholomew's Comprehensive School. George Carter (then a PC) was married the day after a policeman was shot in Mayfair, and was back on duty by 11.15.

Haskins refers to Regan and Carter as 'Batman and Robin' (cf. 'The Placer').

20: 'Trap'
6 October 1975

Writer: Ray Jenkins
Director: Jim Goddard

Cast: Sydney Tafler (Manny Bellow),
Elizabeth Begley (Mrs Riley), Kenneth Colley (Noah Riley),
Bernard Kay (Thomas), Geoffrey Whitehead (Mills),
Brian Hall (Davies), Harry Jones (Hooter),
James Valentine (Woods), Sean Clarke (Danny),
Polly Perkins (The Singer)

One of Regan's snouts has gone to the papers, claiming that Regan is corrupt. Jack has less than 24 hours to clear his name . . .

Keep Your Mincers Peeled For . . .: This episode is full of excellent character actors who've been in *everything* (Bernard Kay and Sydney Tafler, especially). Viewers will recognise Brian Hall as Terry the chef from *Fawlty Towers*.

Watch out for a 1975 anti-Common Market referendum poster (JOBS FOR THE BOYS) and a DIAL BEFORE YOU DIG sign in the call box Regan uses.

Birds: * There are one or two nice bits of crumpet in the pub scene (in particular, keep your eyes on the girl in the low-cut red and white dress).

Booze: * Noah drinks plenty of vodka in the hotel room. Regan invites Carter to a 'Knees-up Mother Brown' at 'Fred's Pub' to celebrate the release of the villains. 'There's nothing stopping us having a drink, is there?' asks Regan. 'Well, it never has before, has it?' complains George bitterly. Tragically, they get a good kicking almost as soon as they arrive: the only alcohol we see is smashed during the fight.

Shooters: None. When Regan calls for the 'cavalry', Haskins asks him if they need 'firearms'. Regan says the backup team merely need 'plenty of muscle', and a big scrap ensues.

Motors: At the beginning, Regan and Carter eschew the usual brown Granada for a blue one (XAN 921N). Jack spends much of the episode driving a brand-new, vomit-yellow Mini, and is tailed by Woods and Davies in a pale Morris 1800. The criminals try (and fail) to escape in a white Transit.

Threads: The singer at the knees-up wears a horrid silver cap. Cor blimey! Regan's tie is pretty vile. The general Bowie (circa *Man Who Sold the World*) 'tranny' look of the girl in the pub wearing the fedora hat and wide tie is also worth noting ('It *is* a madam, isn't it?'). Watch out for Danny's Bay City Rollers tartan-edged jeans, and the garish shirts worn by several Squad members (notable mentions for the scarlet one, and the nasty orange one).

Jazz Funk?: Some gentle, funky guitar-and-bass licks as Regan and Carter leave the newspaper offices in Fleet Street. The pub singer does 'On Mother Kelly's Doorstep', à la Danny La Rue.

Non-PC Moment: Two uses of the word 'ducky' (one by Regan, one by the pub singer).

You What?: Carter: 'Guvnor, we're being smudged!'

Regan: 'They want to see me put myself about a bit; they want the joy of jumping up and down on me when I'm under the pancake.'

Carter: 'I mean, Noah's got form, right? He'd never hold water in the box.'

Regan: 'Well, it's a long, complicated story for a trumpet call, so I'll explain later.'

Larfs: Regan to Noah: 'Hold you lot up to the light, and not a brain in sight.'

Mills on Regan's desperate attempts to extricate himself from trouble: 'These are the nails we need for running through his hands and feet.'

Danny: 'Leave me dad alone . . . You pulled 'is hair off!'

Notes: 'I dunnit. I was with 'em. I was the third man, the one that got away.' Well directed, if a little dull. As with a number of *Sweeney* episodes, the climax comes a tad too early, and the rest of the episode collapses rather than concludes.

Five years previously (in 1969), Regan was a second-class DS working in the Robberies Squad of Divisional CID, Cholmondeley. His eventual promotion was in part helped by the arrest of two out of three of the men who executed the

Golden Maid dairy robbery on Panda Street. It is stated that rules governing informants have been tightened to make corruption less likely. Regan contemptuously refers to Woods and Davies as 'Ratman and Dobbin' (cf. 'The Placer'). Regan first nicked Davies when the latter was eighteen.

George makes a passing reference to the 1920s music-hall song 'Red Sails in the Sunset'.

21: 'Golden Fleece'
13 October 1975

Writer: Roger Marshall
Director: David Wickes

Cast: Cheryl Kennedy (Judy Collier),
Philip Madoc (Pettiford), Madhav Sharma (Earle),
Peter Godfrey (Wally Vince), Michael Latimer (Jackman),
Nicholas Smith (Simpkins), Martin Wyldeck (Cowley),
Damaris Hayman (Mrs Cowley), Allyson Rees (The Au Pair)

A pair of flash Aussie criminals, Colin and Ray, are blagging their way right across Regan's manor, but, just as the Sweeney seem to be getting a lead on the bad lads, Haskins is fitted-up with the naughties . . .

Keep Your Mincers Peeled For . . .: Patrick Mower was one of *the* faces of British TV in the 1970s. A star since his noted performance in the Hammer film *The Devil Rides Out*, Mower really made his mark playing a proto-George Carter, Haggerty, to George Sewell's proto-Jack Regan in *Special Branch*, and the smooth secret agent Cross in *Callan*. Subsequently, he was picked up by the BBC to front their own *Sweeney* clone *Target*, as the maverick Inspector Hackett. George Layton's many sitcom roles include Paul Collier in *Doctor in the House* (and several of its sequels), and a lengthy run in *It Ain't Half Hot, Mum*. Also a noted comedy writer, Layton contributed scripts to many series (including *On the Buses*) and created *Don't Wait Up* in the 1980s. Nicholas

Smith's name may not be too familiar to viewers, but his face (and his ears) will be instantly recognisable as those of Mr Rumbold in *Are You Being Served?*. Anne Stallybrass is well remembered for her roles as Jane Seymour in *The Six Wives of Henry VIII* and as Peter Gilmore's first wife in *The Onedin Line*. Philip Madoc would later join Patrick Mower in *Target*, though he is chiefly remembered as a sadistic SS officer in *Manhunt* and for his award-winning role in *The Life and Times of Lloyd George*. Damaris Hayman still gets invitations to *Doctor Who* conventions the world over after her memorable performance opposite Jon Pertwee as the white witch Mrs Hawthorne. *Young Ones* fans will remember her as the woman who asks Neil if he 'digs graves'!

Birds: **** As much of this episode takes place in the swimming pool of the Trans-World Oil sports centre, this is, therefore, brimming with large-chested, scantily clad young lovelies (the woman in the black swimsuit that Colin is chatting up at the start is the best example!). The blonde 'Sheila' au pair at the house Colin and Ray are casing wears jeans so tight they look as though she'd been poured into them ('Let her force my rhubarb any day!'). Judy Collier in her swimsuit looks gorgeous – the briefs are rather skimpy (we subsequently find out she swam for New Zealand in the Commonwealth Games, so she's obviously a fit girl).

Booze: *** Colin, Ray and 'Woeful' Wally (inevitably) drink cans of Fosters (Colin has another can in his hand during their final meeting with Judy). In the pub, George has a pint of light and bitter and Haskins an orange juice, while Jack sticks to whisky. He also has a shot in the office, explaining that it 'relaxes the throat'. So, *that's* his excuse! Regan also accepts Mrs Haskins's offer of a can of lager from the fridge.

Shooters: * Colin and Ray use a sawn-off in the opening blag; Regan discovers it in the boot of the Jag at the end.

Motors: Wally drives a white Mini Cooper; Colin and Ray a grey S-type. Pettiford has a black Austin 1800. Regan turns up to see the suspended Haskins in a white Morris Marina van (pretending to deliver a television). Colin and Ray sell their ill-gotten goods to a man in a blue Volvo estate. Judy drives a bright-yellow MG Midget.

Threads: *The* episode if you're looking for Fashion Victims. The only question is where to start . . .? Colin's tennis-wear, his Rubettes cap (!) and stars-and-stripes baseball boots, Ray's rainbow shirt (people have been shot for lesser crimes), Haskins's appalling red tie.

Jazz Funk?: Music in this episode includes 'The Entertainer' by Scott Joplin, and Brian Bennett's 'Holy Mackerel!' (the theme tune to BBC's *Rugby Special*). Colin and Ray sing insulting versions of 'Puff the Magic Dragon' and 'Get Along Little Doggie' to Mr Simpkins, and we also hear snatches of the Beatles' 'Something' (sung by Colin) and, what is obviously their theme song, Sinatra's 'Nice 'n' Easy'. There's a snatch of the 'boinging-bass' stock music during the Cowley robbery.

You What?: Carter: 'Straight up, guv, she hasn't even got the bread to go and visit her old man.'
    Regan: 'Ten jobs and not one ricket.'
    Colin on a girl who fancies Wally: 'Word is, she singed her tights last time she saw you down the Kangaroo Club.'
    Regan: 'Shut your rabbit, George.'
    Judy: 'It's time to blow.' Colin: 'Who says so?' Judy: 'The big, bad fuzz!'

Larfs: Colin: 'Stand and deliver, your money or your wife!' (Loud scream.) 'On second thoughts, we'll just settle for the money.'
    Colin: 'Eight o'clock, at Mel's place.' Ray: 'Party?' Colin: 'Yeah. You gotta bring a bottle, a bird and an alarm clock.' Ray: 'Ah, *beaut*!'

Notes: 'I'm on about a pair of flash boys from down under.' Utterly magnificent, Marshall doing the kind of thing he used to do so effortlessly on *The Avengers*, creating hilarious comedy out of very serious situations. Colin and Ray are a pair of inspired characters and their getting away with their crimes at the end perfectly encapsulates the strange nature of

The Sweeney for viewers – sometimes you *want* the villains to escape.

George has been reading a lot since the death of Alison (see 'Hit and Run'), as the evenings seem very long. (The inference is that he's been reading about Charles Darwin.) Regan tells him that his new girlfriend is an air hostess, and that she may have a friend, but Carter isn't interested.

Haskins is married with two school-age children who are privately educated, one of whom is a girl called Lucy (she is also alluded to in 'Down to You, Brother'). The family are regular churchgoers (though Mrs Haskins says 'Christ' as a swear word at one point). We are also told that the family lives near the football ground 'at London Road' (the actual ground used on the location is Griffin Park, Brentford). Also on a football theme, Wally Vince's criminal brother-in-law whom Haskins allegedly threatened to have fitted-up is called Barry Butlin, and he shares his name with a legendary Luton Town and Sheffield United player of the era.

A return fare from London to Durham is £11.24. A dock strike is mentioned (again, *very* 70s!). A10 (the Met's internal-investigation department) are known as 'The Gestapo' by other policemen. The Lone Ranger and the Israeli politician Moshe Dayan are mentioned, and there is a direct reference to the BBC's then main competition to *The Sweeney*, *Kojak* (Regan giving Carter a lollipop and saying, 'Who loves ya, baby?').

This was the first episode of *The Sweeney* to make number one in the TV viewing charts with 8.8 million viewers.

22: 'Poppy'
20 October 1975

Writer: Trevor Preston
Director: Tom Clegg

Cast: James Booth (Labbett), John Rhys-Davies (Brett),
Veronica Lang (Mrs Labbett), Helen Gill (Kay Nolan),
Frank Middlemass (Sterndale), John D. Collins (Vane),
Patsy Smart (Alice), Virginia Moore (Veronica)

Vic Labbett, a robber, returns to the UK for the money he left behind – intending to exchange it for diamonds, with the help of the very bank he originally robbed . . .

Keep Your Mincers Peeled For . . .: Before his star-making role in *Raiders of the Lost Ark*, John Rhys-Davies was mainly known for his stage work in Britain. These days, he's one of Hollywood's most in-demand actors, probably most recognisable as Professor Arturo in *Sliders*. Fans of *Auf Wiedersehen, Pet* will remember James Booth as the exiled criminal Kenny Ames (another slab of typecasting!). Frank Middlemass is another much-loved actor whose chief claim to fame was a notable performance in *Poldark*. John D. Collins's TV credits stretch back to Spike Milligan's *Q* series and *A Family at War*, but he is doubtless best known as one of *'Allo 'Allo*'s stranded English airmen.

Birds: ** Sterndale's secretary wears a rather tight grey jumper and black miniskirt. 'My wife thinks Veronica is too thin,' notes the bank manager. 'I could give her some exercises,' observes Regan. Labbett's mistress, Kay Nolan, has a nice line in 'Come on, upstairs'-type lead-ons, and later enjoys an obviously post-coital fag. Regan notes that one of Labbett's known associates has been shacked up with 'some hippie slag in Leicester'. 'Lucky toerag,' notes George.

Booze: * The opening scene takes place beside a pub called the Crown. At Sterndale's office, Regan turns down the offer of a sherry ('No, thank you, sir, I'm on duty'), but accepts a whisky ('A little water, no ice') without complaint a moment later. He says it's the best malt he's ever tasted!

Shooters: ** Labbett shoots Vane, killing him. There are plenty of handguns in the scrap at the end.

Motors: Vane owns a rather lurid blue-and-white Corvette, and the Sweeney are seen using a Triumph 2000. Mrs Labbett favours the rather more sophisticated Stag, in white. Brett drives a blue S-class, while Labbett has got hold of a white Mini. The final chase, involving various of these vehicles, is across waterlogged fields, where the terrain is as soggy as the handling.

Threads: Ron Brett's stripy shirt and big red tie. Stan the driver's nasty burnt-orange tie.

Jazz Funk?: There's a funky little brass-and-bass theme that's used at various points throughout the episode.

You What?: Regan to Carter (on Mrs Labbett): 'You just wanted to squeeze her toothpaste.'

Mrs Labbett: 'You're clean, Ron. He'll put the hand on all Vic's associates with form first.'

Regan: '. . . Sterndale would be under orders – blind, dumb and daft – or he'll never see a dirty Deutschmark of that poppy.'

Daniels, on Vane: 'Last time I saw him he was barking at the porcelain in some Richmond pub.'

Larfs: Vane: 'You try to out-think Vic Labbett and you're going to end up with a chalk line around you.'

Sterndale: 'It is still inspector?' Regan: 'I don't play golf!'

Regan (to parcel-carrying Daniels): 'Oi, what've you got under yer arm?' Daniels: 'Hairs, guvnor. What have you got under yours?'

Notes: 'When Vic was on remand in Brixton, I remember him telling me he'd been nicked by the sharpest bastard in the job.' A bit of a standard runaround, with the wit of the script not quite disguising the linearity of the plot. And using three different angles of the same car crash at the climax seems a little bit like overkill.

Haskins is mentioned ('It's like talking to a half-hundred-weight of condemned veal') but not seen. Regan calls Carter and Stan the driver 'Handsome and Gristle'. Regan's snout is 'Alice the Malice', owner of a fruit-and-veg stall. Carter seems not to be very good at crosswords.

There's plenty of location filming around Farringdon tube station and Tower Bridge. Watch out for the hair caught in the camera during the pursuit of Mrs Labbett. We have a point-of-view shot of Labbett looking through his binoculars – the image 'zooms in', just as a TV camera would, but quite unlike any binoculars we've ever seen. Labbett pays 'ten pence' for two apples. A bit steep? Inflation, probably – *very* 1970s.

23: 'Stay Lucky, Eh?'
27 October 1975

Writer: Trevor Preston
Director: Douglas Camfield

Cast: Peter Vaughan (Kirby), Ken Hutchison (Vaughan),
Alun Armstrong (Jenner), Paul Moriarty (Tyson),
Sandy Ratcliff (Liz), Brian McDermott (Algar),
Michael Ripper (Herbie Mew), John Woodnutt (Dr Clare),
John Challis (Skef), Donald Webster (Llewellyn),
Ray Barron (Bobby Haigh), Gloria Walker (Kirby's Girl)

Tony Kirby, a gangster, has financed a big blag, and is less than happy when the ill-gotten proceeds are themselves stolen . . .

Keep Your Mincers Peeled For . . .: Peter Vaughan and Alun Armstrong were both regulars in *Porridge*, playing Harry Grout and Spraggon respectively. Vaughan went on to star in another Euston production, *Fox*, played the role of Shirley's dad in *Citizen Smith* and, more recently, an award-winning part in *Our Friends in the North*. Armstrong, who first came to prominence with a small but crucial part in *Get Carter*, continues his association with John Thaw via a semiregular role in *Inspector Morse*. Michael Ripper appeared in numerous Hammer films (often playing the innkeeper who says that they don't get many strangers round these parts), as well as Leonard's chauffeur in *Butterflies*. John Challis, once a *Z Cars* regular, later achieved comic immortality as Boycie in *Only Fools and Horses*, while Sandy Ratcliff found fame as troubled Sue Osman in *East-Enders*. Ken Hutchison will be remembered by millions of football-obsessed youngsters as Matt Murphy in ITV's long-running *Murphy's Mob*.

Watch out for Herbie's ugly chrome-covered radio, which Vincent uses for target practice (and a prominent poster for *La Folies Bergère* in his flat).

Birds: * We hear about Deirdre, Carter's companion from the night before ('If Freud had met her, he'd have thrown away his couch and become a tattooist'). Liz Jenner wears a short blue skirt, and Kirby has his shoulders massaged by his 'girl', Jenny.

Booze: ** Jack and Algar share wine over an Italian meal. Herbie and Regan knock off a couple of bottles of brown ale (Regan gets his in a glass, the sophisticate). Haskins, Regan and Carter drink whisky to celebrate the arrest of Kirby, which Haskins says is a long-held ambition of his. Tyson gets offered a brandy before being roughed up by Kirby and Skef. Dr Clare also drinks brandy from a hip flask.

Shooters: *** Jenner is shot in the leg at the episode's introduction; Herbie later finds himself looking down the wrong end of Vincent Vaughan's silencer-clad gun. During the episode's conclusion, both Kirby and Skef use handguns (the former not very accurately!), while the Sweeney – including Haskins – use slightly more discreet revolvers.

Motors: Kirby has a Mercedes 200.

Threads: Vaughan's wig (and hair clips!) are pretty hysterical. Skef's rainbow shirt and green strides and Kirby's very wide red tie are also worth a mention.

Jazz Funk?: There's some more 'boinging bass', plus bongos, as Regan and Carter pursue Tyson. Plus some plinky-plonky background music as Carter interrogates Llewellyn.

You What?: Regan to Herbie: 'You're still the number-one earwig in the business.'

Herbie: 'It was this big feller ... Made me this offer. He said if I told him all I knew about the job, he'd give me a monkey in straight money.'

Herbie: 'There's this geezer I know. He's got a safe full of snide money. If he gets turned over, he isn't going to dial three nines, is he?'

Regan: 'He wants that info and he's got your old bottle quacking!'

Kirby: 'You've got a terminal mouth, friend.'

Larfs: Dr Clare (after Jenner has been shot in the leg): 'He's a lucky man. Any higher and . . .'

Regan: 'Someone put something in my drink last night.' Carter: 'What?' Regan: 'Alcohol.'

Regan on Jenner: 'He's got a face the colour of a cheap envelope.'

Ken, suggesting that Regan should leave the force: 'Get out, Jack. Get out while you've still got your own teeth.'

Regan (with radio in hands): 'It's not working, Herbie. You think these bullet holes could have anything to do with it?'

Haskins: 'Whatever happened to the honest villain, Jack?' Regan: 'He just about disappeared – like the white whale, and cheap housing.'

Notes: 'Drop it! We're the Sweeney!' Another top-notch Trevor Preston script, with a great cast and some lovely directorial flourishes.

Algar says he's sorry to hear about Jack and Kate ('I thought you two had all the answers'). Haskins thinks he could have gone a long way in the force. There is another reference to Haskins's wife ('Well, if she rings again, tell her I'm out on a case'). Carter says he works sixty hours a week, and gets paid a brickie's wage. Regan lives in 'two rooms in Hammersmith'.

24: 'Trojan Bus'
3 November 1975

Writer: Roger Marshall
Director: Ted Childs

Cast: Lynda Bellingham (Nancy King),
Robert Dorning (Leonard Geisler), Frederick Jaeger (Goldman),

Leslie Dwyer (Ted Greenhead), Carol Macready (Kath),
Roger Sloman (Cosby), Frederick Schiller (Austrian Tourist),
Gillian Duxbury (Goldman's Girlfriend)

Those Australian villains Colin and Ray return to the UK,
hoping to steal a Goya worth £250,000 with the help of
Nancy King, an art dealer's glamorous assistant.

Keep Your Mincers Peeled For . . .: A very young Lynda
Bellingham was a big star in the hospital drama-soap *General
Hospital*, before becoming the most famous mum on telly in a
two-decade-long series of adverts for Oxo. The late Leslie
Dwyer had a film and TV career stretching back to the 1930s,
but is probably best remembered as the permanently drunk
Punch-and-Judy man in *Hi-De-Hi!*. Roger Sloman's face will
be familiar to fans of 1980s comedy – he was one of the *Kick
Up the Eighties* team, and was the TV Detector Man in *The
Young Ones*.

There's a great big advert for Green Shield Stamps at one
point.

Birds: ** Colin is clearly impressed with the 'very trim'
bikini-clad girlfriend of the corrupt art dealer Goldman ('All
shipshape and Bristol fashion,' he remarks), although he fails
in his attempts to glimpse her prize assets. (Colin and Ray are
nothing if not one-track minds, joking about 'bristols' and
'melons' while running sightseeing trips on the Thames.)

Booze: *** Regan walks into an Aussie bar, but declines a
drink. Instead, he seems more concerned by who's been at his
'sauce' (the secret whisky drinker proves to be Haskins – so,
if George's detective skills are all they're cracked up to be,
Haskins is left-handed).

Shooters: **** The supermarket stakeout ends with a virtually gun-free fist fight, during which Carter gets his lights
punched out. ('Why's it always me hooter?' he moans; later
there are the inevitable – and brilliantly played – jokes about
Cyrano de Bergerac and Jimmy Durante). The gun battle at
the end is magnificent, with Colin and Ray, armed with a rifle,

a pump-action shotgun and grenades, taking on the pistol-armed Flying Squad.

Motors: Regan drives a black Morris 18-22 (the precursor to the British Leyland Princess) during the undercover job. The blue Sweeney Cortina (NHK 296M) reappears. Colin and Ray are variously seen in a flash Pontiac and a red double-decker bus!

Threads: Regan wears a hideous pair of brown flares and stacked shoes during the supermarket stakeout. Colin's open-necked shirt reveals an ankh medallion. His white flares are way cool, but not in the same league of horridness as the red, white and blue elasticated belt (with twin-star buckle!) that keeps them up! Oh, and there's an Austrian tourist in full national dress (including lederhosen) . . .

Jazz Funk?: Another collection of great music with the recurring themes of 'Golden Fleece' repeated ('The Entertainer', 'Holy Mackerel!', Colin and Ray singing 'Nice 'n' Easy'). We also get George Carter whistling 'An Ordinary Copper' (the theme tune to *Dixon of Dock Green*), and Colin and Ray doing a virtual stand-up routine with the bus conductor around 'Let's Call the Whole Thing Off'. Best of all, though, is the jazzy, summery theme used early on as Regan and Carter drive around London. *Very* Average White Band. *Niiiice!*

You What?: Haskins: 'Remember, it's top-weight info.'

Regan smacks an unconscious villain around the head, shouting, 'Come on, you slag, wake up!'

Colin: 'As they say in England, looks like it's Shanks's Pony again . . .'

Is this the only *Sweeney* episode to feature 'Cover me!'?

Larfs: Haskins to a returning Regan: 'Busy day at the store, dear?'

Regan (on Haskins's 'snout'): 'The sharpest ears in West One. Mr Spock, they call 'im.'

Nancy (looking at the safe): 'It's a Goya.' Ray: 'Can it breathe all right in there?'

Colin to Nancy: 'We're wasting our time... You need Raffles, and who have you got...?' Ray: 'Ned Kelly!'

Cosby (asked if he has ties with Australia): 'Guv, I've never even been to Manchester!'

There's the brilliant policing aphorism: 'A vindictive copper... is no good to his old mum'!

Regan: 'There should be a couple of inches left.' Carter: 'As the bishop said to the actress!'

Notes: 'Flash monkeys! It's happening again, isn't it?' Colin and Ray's return owes much to *Butch Cassidy and the Sundance Kid* ('This never happened to Paul Newman,' says Ray) and *The Sting* (the returning musical nods to 'The Entertainer'). The episode contains some brilliant cameos, including Mr Greenhead, the boat owner, talking about the changing face of the Thames (while quoting *Hamlet* and John Masefield's 'Sea Fever'), and a puzzled man trying to restart his car as the villains and the Sweeney run past. Only the supermarket-blag subplot seems superfluous.

As before, Mower and Layton turn in assured comic performances. Their discussion about Ray learning Portuguese in Rio (so he can order a Fosters), and where flies go in winter, are obvious highlights. We learn that a young Colin Magruder sold a sundial outside the Sydney Botanical Gardens seventeen times in one weekend.

There is a darker undercurrent to these jokers, though, as Regan is quick to point out. The shoot-out at the end, with Tower Bridge in the background, underlines that Colin and Ray are dangerous men. This sequence's final moment is glorious, like something out of a Tarantino movie.

There are many references to Australian cricketers – Colin and Ray being compared to the contemporary fearsome pace duo Dennis Lillie and Jeff Thomson. Don Bradman is also mentioned (it's probably no coincidence that Ray shares his surname with another 1970s Aussie cricketing hero, Keith Stackpole). There are loads of continuity references to 'Golden Fleece', Colin and Ray having returned from their sojourn in Rio with Judy for more action. They plan to go to Leningrad next, where they say there are 322 art galleries. They ask for two five-pence bus fares!

The filming on the Thames, around the Tower (Colin laughs as they pass Traitor's Gate) and at St Katherine's Dock is gorgeous.

25: 'I Want the Man'
10 November 1975

Writer: Ray Jenkins
Director: Tom Clegg

Cast: Roy Kinnear (Frankie Little),
Michael Coles (Maynard), Russell Hunter (Popeye),
Elizabeth Cassidy (Sandy Little),
Peter Halliday (Chief Inspector Gordon),
Patsy Dermott (Christine),
Henry Woolf (Jimmy Dancer),
Walter McMonagle (Bell),
John Gleeson (Flying Squad Officer)

Regan gets a tasty whisper of an impending blag from one of his snouts. But when the Sweeney move in to arrest Frankie Little, they find his female contact escaped, and the snout, Popeye, has gone missing.

Keep Your Mincers Peeled For ...: The late and much-lamented Roy Kinnear needs few introductions to TV fans of any age. The versatile Scottish actor Russell Hunter will mainly be remembered for a very similar role to this, as Lonely, the scared, smelly sidekick of Edward Woodward in *Callan* (he also played another variation on the same character in an episode of *Minder*). Henry Woolf's most memorable appearances in a long TV career remain those alongside Eric Idle in *Rutland Weekend Television*.

Towards the end, watch out for the man in the white coat behind Bill and Carter. He's so excited he runs into a lamppost, nearly knocking himself over in the process.

Birds: * Little on offer here, as Christine's appearances are too fleeting to get excited over. George glances admiringly at a passing secretary ('I wish I wasn't so tired . . .').

Booze: * Or here, though Maynard is a heavy whisky drinker. The opening restaurant scene, at least, features whisky, sherry and a carafe of white wine along with the king prawns and steak. Jack buys Haskins a bottle to sweeten his disposition after he has upset a uniformed chief inspector (Haskins declines the 'bribe'!). Significantly Regan, anticipating a brainstorming session with Haskins, Carter and the boys, calls for coffee and sandwiches.

Shooters: During the climactic fight sequences, the Sweeney seem to carry only truncheons and wooden staves.

Motors: Maynard uses a white Mercedes 600 limousine to whisk Popeye away, and a blue Ford Zephyr to watch Frankie Little. Both vehicles, and a blue van, are used during the attempted robbery of the Bedford truck carrying used bank notes bound for the incinerator. The Sweeney's usual brown and blue Fords are supplemented by Carter in a dark blue Rover.

Threads: Christine's kooky sixties-style cap. Regan's corduroy jacket is plain vulgar.

Jazz Funk?: In keeping with a slightly substandard episode, the music is very plinky-plonky and unmemorable, apart from a bizarre and discordant theme as the green truck is observed.

You What?: Regan: 'Knock on every door in the manor.'

Carter: 'They reckon she might be the bird on that sparklers blag in Hatton Garden . . .'

Regan: 'The word is, there's a big tickle.'

Maynard: 'I can't tolerate a grass, know what I mean?'

Plus Carter's magnificent reaction to being up all night: 'Haven't got a couple of matchsticks I could borrow, have you, [to] keep me mincers open . . .?'

Larfs: There's one so-bad-it's-funny exchange between Haskins and Regan: 'Hijack . . .?' 'Hello, guv.'

Notes: 'You're lucky I'm a thief and not a gangster, son.' It's
a shame that such a good cast didn't have more to get their
teeth into. There's precious little in this episode to excite
(although, by the same token, there's not much wrong with it,
either). Regan's completely illegal threats to arrest Frankie's
daughter to make him talk are a highlight.

The car tailing the truck has the call sign 'Pathfinder',
while the squad cars are all called 'Hawk' (Carter is 'Hawk
2', Daniels 'Hawk 3' and presumably Regan is 'Hawk 1'').
Maynard is a former middleweight boxer, and plays back-
gammon in one scene. Bobby Moore (West Ham United,
Fulham and England captain) and Harold Wilson (the Prime
Minister) are mentioned in the same line of dialogue (!). The
James Bond actress Ursula Andress and the film *On the
Waterfront* are also referenced. Some of the filming took
place at Stamford Bridge, Chelsea's football ground.

The big brawl at the climax at what seems to be a disused
railway siding is very impressive. In fact, Tom Clegg's direction is one of the best things about the episode – little touches
like filming the loading of the van during a flurry of snow
give the episode a realistic quality.

26: 'Country Boy'
17 November 1975

Writer: Andrew Wilson
Director: Jim Goddard

Cast: Robert Swan (David Keel), Myra Frances (Liz Keel),
Christine Shaw (Kathy Peters),
Andronia Katsaros (Annie Clark), Leslie Schofield (Ian Ross),
David Belcher (Police Inspector), Shaun Curry (Peters),
Malcolm Kaye (Brian Slater), Alan Brown (The Consultant),
Roy Sampson (Uniformed Constable),
Bobby Collins (Young Boy)

A firm seem to be playing games with the local constabulary:
setting off all of the alarms on their manor, then taking pot

shots at passers-by. The guvnor calls in Regan and the boys for help, but Jack has problems enough with a know-all wetback from the sticks.

Keep Your Mincers Peeled For . . .: Leslie Schofield is an instantly recognisable face from many series of the 1970s (including *The Fall and Rise of Reginald Perrin*). He's now Jeff Healy in *EastEnders*.

Birds: ** Is that a girlie mag Inspector Burrows is reading in the opening scene? Looks suspiciously like it. Jack's 'sort-of' female friend, is Annie Clark, a big-breasted 'tart with a heart'-type with a bad back. Wonder how she got that?

Booze: *** Mrs Peters seems very partial to vodka on the rocks (Smirnoff red label). Jack, David and Annie have Scotch in the local, while Liz goes for a brandy.

Shooters: **** 'Get the shooters together, George.' Slater has a tasty high-velocity rifle, but the most extraordinary scenes are the rescue of Peters and the climactic gun battle.

Motors: Keel drives a mustard-yellow Morris Marina, poor sod. If the number plate is any guide, the Sweeney Granada seen in 'Trap' (XAN 921N) has changed from blue to silver!

Threads: 'Get my anorak, George,' says Regan! His dark suit (seen a couple of times previously) is in evidence again, but it's only when it's sideways on that you realise just how big those flared strides actually are. Liz's medallion must weigh a ton. Slater wears a denim jacket with sheepskin collar. David sports a bow tie (he's been to a concert: 'Hope we didn't spoil your final movement,' notes Regan with a smirk) and, later, a shirt with an *enormous* collar.

Jazz Funk?: Lots of really throbbing bass in this, plus the usual stock music.

You What?: Regan: 'Would you Adam-an'-Eve it?'

Larfs: Regan: 'From Bristol?' Haskins: 'They've got a good team down there.' Carter: 'City or Rovers?'

Notes: 'Come off it, Frank. I need a boffin from Bristol like I need a hole in the head!' A terrific episode in which Regan comes face to face with the future of the force, takes the piss but ends up rating Keel highly ('He'll do,' he tells Haskins, which, you suspect, is as close as Jack Regan will ever get to genuine praise). The scene where Jack withholds a man's pills to enforce his cooperation is excellent. Some fine location work around Westminster Bridge, and a great climax. Strange coda, though.

The Squad are all listening to a boxing match at the beginning. Haskins reckons Regan couldn't mend a fuse without 'blacking out half of London'. Keel's call sign is 'Oscar 1-4-2'; Regan is 'Oscar 7' in this episode.

Minor note of interest to TV historians. David Keel was the name of the character played by Ian Hendry in the first season of *The Avengers*. The line 'Keep 'em peeled' is presumably a nod to *Police Five*. And, when Keel says, 'I'm fond of theatre, music, literature, art – but I'm a copper . . .', you can't help but think of Morse.

27: 'Thou Shalt Not Kill!'
24 November 1975

Writer: Ranald Graham
Director: Douglas Camfield

Cast: Ronald Lacey (Barry Monk),
Dean Harris (Jimmy Wands), Harriet Philpin (Julia Coulson),
Barrie Cookson (Assistant Commissioner),
Olive McFarland (Mrs Dowland),
Nicholas McArdle (Inspector Wilson),
Iris Russell (Miss Lewis), Hubert Rees (Reginald Dowland),
Christopher Crooks (Frank Gough), Mike Lewin (Johnson),
Stuart McGugan (Hicks), Sally Lahee (Bank Clerk),
David Masterman (Greg)

An armed blag at the National Mercian Bank on the campus of Faraday University turns into a fiasco when a siege ensues and the decision on how to deal with the situation is taken out of Regan's hands.

Keep Your Mincers Peeled For . . . : Ronald Lacey's range runs from a semiregular role in *Whatever Happened to the Likely Lads?* (as Terry Collier's brother-in-law), to much more villainous, slimy parts like Harris in *Porridge* and a horrible Nazi in *Raiders of the Lost Ark*. Iris Russell will be remembered by telefantasy fans as the mother in *Timeslip*. Ironically, the best-known face in the episode has a tiny part: Stuart McGugan, who plays one of the police marksmen, was a regular *Play School* presenter, served ten years on *It Ain't Half Hot, Mum*, and was also in both *Tutti Frutti* and *Hamish Macbeth*.

Birds: * There are a few lovelies in jeans hanging around the crime scene at the beginning, but, once the siege takes over, unless seeing Harriet Philpin in terror is your bag, there's not much to get excited about here.

Booze: * Regan and Carter spend the episode dry. Luckily for the series' reputation, two bottles of champagne *do* put in an appearance.

Shooters: ***** *Everybody*'s tooled-up in this episode, with a positively lethal array of arms: the villains favour automatic pistols and sawn-offs, the Sweeney their usual revolvers.

Motors: One of the villains tries to escape in a crappy blue Vauxhall Velox. Haskins turns up in a brown Rover. The initial getaway car is a blue Morris 1800, but they swap this for a blue Hillman Minx hijacked from two policemen. The second getaway car is a blue Jaguar ('Freedom is a warm Jag,' says Woods).

Threads: George and Jack both wear crushed-velvet jackets (green and royal blue respectively) that, after five minutes of running around a dusty campus, throwing themselves behind concrete slabs to avoid getting shot, are *filthy*. George's grey strides are bad, but nowhere near as bad as the pair worn by the reporter, Gough, with a dodgy bum-fluff beard. As for the rest of the Squad, Gerry Burtonshaw's suede boots are pretty nasty, Greg wears a pair of cheap shades throughout, and one of the Flying Squad boys has a frizzy perm that wouldn't have looked out of place on a mid-70s second-division footballer (and a horrible orange tie, too). But *everything* pales into insignificance beside Wands's cream flares – some of the widest known to humankind. Even after he's changed clothes, he's *still* the centre of attention with a checky jacket. Julia's lime-green T-shirt is horrible too, and this is also the episode in which we see the colour of George Carter's boxer shorts. Light blue.

Jazz Funk?: A very definite Isaac Hayes influence on a lot of the music, with really choppy guitar and the rolling percussion of a very powerful rhythm track.

Hardly a Barrel of Larfs: One of Regan's finest 50 minutes, beginning with the quintessential: 'This is gonna be a right *bastard*!'

Regan goes all Bodie and Doyle on us: 'Cover 'em, George! With me, Gerry!'

'This guy Wands was always gonna take a piece of the world with him.'

And his angry rant at Haskins at the end: 'If you'd have ordered us to fire when you had the chance, Dowland would still be alive, that girl's face wouldn't be scarred for life, a policeman wouldn't have been smashed up, and, more importantly, the chances of a villain ever taking hostages again would be a lot less than they're gonna be now!'

Notes: 'If we give in now, we give in all down the line . . .' Utterly brilliant, probably the best ever episode of *The Sweeney*, though certainly one to avoid if you're looking for quick laughs. The episode was due to be shown a month earlier, but was swapped with 'Trojan Bus' shortly before transmission, because a real-life armed robbery had taken place on the day it was scheduled. Ironically, this works much better at the end of the season. Haskins bottling it, and *not* ordering his men to shoot, remains one of the most powerful and memorable moments in *The Sweeney*.

Regan is 'Oscar 2-3' in this episode. Carter is 'Oscar 3-7'.

One tiny point of interest: the cast list at the beginning of the episode gives Dean Harris's character as Jimmy Wands, but he is called Terry throughout the episode.

Third Season

Thirteen 60-minute episodes
Euston Films/Thames Television
Created by Ian Kennedy Martin

Associate Producer: Mary Morgan
Producer: Ted Childs
Executive Producers: Lloyd Shirley, George Taylor

Title music by Harry South

Regular Cast: John Thaw (Detective Inspector Jack Regan),
Dennis Waterman (Detective Sergeant George Carter),
Garfield Morgan (Detective Chief Inspector Frank Haskins,
29, 31–33, 35–40),
John Alkin (Detective Sergeant Tom Daniels, 29, 31–33, 37),
Jennifer Thanisch[1] (Susie[2] Regan, 36),
James Warrior (Detective Constable Jellyneck, 37[3]),
Morris Perry (Detective Superintendent Maynon, 30),
George Sweeney (Tim Cook, 32, 40)

---

[1] Incorrectly credited as Thanish on screen.
[2] Credited as 'Susan Regan' here.
[3] Here credited as 'Taffy'. It is difficult to be certain if the characters are the same – certainly 'Taffy' is a lot less scruffy than Jellyneck, and sports only a moustache, and no beard . . . But then, in two years a lot can happen to a geezer. Perhaps it was marital problems . . .

28: 'Selected Target'
6 September 1976

Writer: Troy Kennedy Martin
Director: Tom Clegg

Cast: Lee Montague (Kibber), Ronald Fraser (Oates),
James Aubrey (Reynes), Peter Schofield (Boothroyd),
Maureen Lipman (Mrs Smedley),
Jonathan Elsom (Mr Bradshaw), Basil Dignam (Moberly),
Deirdre Costello (Gwen Kibber), Roger Hammond (Finch),
Judy Matheson (Kibber's Girlfriend), Bill Treacher (Tom),
Hugh Martin (Murray), Annie Lambert (Air Hostess),
Frederick Marks (Detective), Roger Putt (Prison Officer),
James Fagan (Hotel Receptionist), Mike Elles (Porter),
David Barham (Toby Bradshaw),
Tracy Strand (Annie Kibber)

The Sweeney tail a recently released thief, Kibber, convinced
that he is planning a bank job. Trouble is, the notes he made
in jail are rather ambiguous . . .

Keep Your Mincers Peeled For . . .: Bill Treacher (*East-Enders*' Arthur Fowler) gets about two lines! Both Maureen
Lipman and Lee Montague appear again (see 'Regan').
    It seems that Jack is reading Ken Kesey's *One Flew Over
the Cuckoo's Nest* (the Picador edition to tie in with the film).
There's a Paddington Bear toy in Mrs Smedley's bedroom.
Oates reads a kung-fu magazine.

Birds: *** A casual glance at a passing American air hostess
leads Regan to her room ('I want you to get into bed with
me'). Jack checks his watch and asks her to give him five
minutes. As a result, he 'loses' Oates (he resents George's
suggestion that she's a plant, but, let's face it, the rest of the
plan seems immaculately set up). Kibber's girls strip for the
cameras (frequently, it seems – the Squad are getting through
a vast amount of film).
    There's a very prim-looking woman in glasses and a red

sweater in the Squad office, seen on a couple of occasions. Whose secretary is she?

Booze: * There are bottles of stout in Oates's room. Regan refuses champagne there, *and* a whisky at the bank. Is he feeling all right? Haskins seems to keep a bottle of Scotch in the safe in his office. Maybe the ulcer's cleared up.

Shooters: One enormous fist fight only. The stunt co-ordinator, Peter Brayham, is the Squad officer in dark glasses during this sequence.

Motors: Kibber's usual transport is a silver Roller. The yellow MGB we see is, apparently, 'harvest gold'. Thanks, George. A yellow Opel Kadett, containing Oates's shoe, is dredged from the quarry lake. A 'maroon' BMW plays rather an important role in the conclusion . . . by sitting in a driveway doing nothing. There's also a horrible yellow 2CV parked next to Kibber's car at one point. One of the Squad cars is a dirty white Cortina.

Threads: Some glorious kipper ties: Regan goes for some sort of square patterning, while George's seems to be knitted. And as for the Squad officer who loses Kibber and Finch . . . Just how many years away is Eddie Shoestring? Reynes's pinstripe suit wouldn't have looked out of place on a Chicago mobster. One of Kibber's girlfriends wears (briefly, before taking them off) a pair of skin-tight yellow pants and a leopardskin top.

Jazz Funk?: Some rather whistly Van-McCoy-style elevator music in the hotel.

You What?: Carter: 'You're not turning over your own guvnor, are you, guvnor?'

Larfs: Regan: 'Every spring, five thousand officers break into their guvnor's office and raid the contents of his desk trying to find out what he's written about them.'

    Kibber: 'What are you going to be when you grow up?'
Daughter: 'A social worker.'

    Carter: 'There's blood and teeth all over the floor. Poor old

Toby's weeping – they smashed all his lenses. Dave's in hospital, and Mike's downstairs with concussion.'

And (on police jargon): 'It's like joining the masons all over again.'

Notes: 'A massive defeat for the forces of law and order, wouldn't you say, guv?' Not quite as extraordinary as you expect from the pen of Troy Kennedy Martin, but there is still some good material here. Proceedings are enlivened by George's very procedural narration and some fantastic fight scenes (the way the big scrap towards the end smashes into other flats is hysterical). Lovely location filming around Waterloo ('You wouldn't recognise it now,' Tom tells Kibber. 'All plate-glass and one-way').

Colly Kibber shares his name with the English actor, dramatist and poet laureate (from 1730) Colley Cibber (1671–1757), author of *Love's Last Shift* and *Raving Madness* (and immortalised in the Julian Cope song 'Kolly Kibber's Birthday'). The original Titus Oates (1649–1705) was a seventeenth-century conspirator and perjurer, expelled from various religious orders for 'infamous practices' and the instigator of the Popish Plot in 1678. Regan says Oates is 'A much underrated fellow', echoing Judge Jeffreys's view of his namesake. There's an oblique reference to Cinderella.

29: 'In From the Cold'
13 September 1976

Writer: Tony Hoare
Director: Terry Green

Cast: Anthony Heaton (Billy Medhurst),
Maureen Sweeney (Pauline Medhurst),
Lewis Fiander (Ashby-Jones), Martin Fisk (Jackson),
Johnny Shannon (Mason), James Beckett (Stan),
Paul Kember (Mickey), James Taylor (Gregory),
Peter Clapham (Local Inspector),
Miranda Bell (Mrs Jackson)

Regan and Carter arrest Billy Medhurst, a man involved in the shooting of a policeman, Eddie Jackson. Regan is out for revenge, but Medhurst's flash lawyer is quickly on the scene.

Keep Your Mincers Peeled For . . .: Anthony Heaton is one of those 'third villain from the left' character actors, whose face everybody will recognise (older viewers may remember him as Snowey in Southern TV's *Dick Barton – Special Agent*).

Birds: ** There's a girlie poster on display at the factory Billy and his mates are blagging, and a naughty mag on the floor of the trailer park. Pauline (her back to the camera) flashes her knockers at Regan and Carter ('Have a bloody good look').

Shooters: ** In the flashback to Eddie's shooting, Regan and Medhurst are armed. Billy's escape is engineered by a gang arriving mob-handed, and tooled up with sledgehammers, baseball bats and at least one sawn-off shotgun.

Motors: Eddie is driven away from the identity parade in a blue Marina. His (adulterous) wife gets into a blue right-hand-drive Alfa Spider. Medhurst's prison van is blocked by a white Princess and what seems to be a red Cadillac, converted into a truck, complete with winch! That should be pretty inconspicuous on the streets of Old London Town . . .

Threads: Beware! You are about to enter *The Flare Zone* . . . *Everybody* packs a really naughty pair of 'Dan Dares' in this episode, but a special mention for Mrs Medhurst's electric-blue pants: never mind the quality, feel the width . . . Ashby-Jones's apple-green-tinted glasses and gold briefcase are obviously necessary accoutrements for a man with a pink handkerchief in his top pocket. Mickey's green parka with fur collar and Stan's red tank top deserve mention. And Regan wears a hugely impressive open-necked shirt. He also has two disgusting kipper ties: one looks as if it's made from grey, slanted camouflage, and another is covered with a dark diamond pattern.

You What?: Billy: 'I wanna ring my brief.'

Pauline: 'They're gonna see you go down, and they're talking telephone numbers.'

Stan on how cold the back of the lorry is: 'It's a bit bloody taters in there.'

Billy on the same subject: 'I've got two of the chaps in the back of the wagon. They're gonna think a brass monkey had a result if they have to stay in there much longer.'

Billy: 'Things have gone a bit reels-of-cotton.'

Regan to Mrs Medhurst: 'You've been telling Uncle Jack pork pies.'

Carter: 'Oh, come on, you knew he was a bit ginger.'

Larfs: Haskins, after Regan has suggested he welsh on a deal with Medhurst: 'You know, Jack, there's something deeply immoral about you!'

Regan on the body: 'I'll tell you this: having his head cut off hasn't helped identification.'

Notes: 'I'd know that bastard anywhere.' The director Terry Green obviously took his Douglas Camfield pills that morning: the flashback and slow-motion sequences are glorious. There's a great scene where we hear the carefree whistles of the mortuary attendant while watching the (mute) reaction of Pauline Medhurst to the corpse. Some lovely location footage, too – particularly in the scene on a rooftop overlooking London Bridge with Mason – and 'Hyphen-Jones' is hilarious.

George suggests he and Jack go to see Fulham on their Saturday afternoon off. They're paged during the game, but don't seem too bothered as the Cottagers are getting beaten 1–0 at the time. George says he's thinking of 'scrubbing round' a holiday in the Seychelles this year and staying in London.

30: 'Visiting Fireman'
20 September 1976

Writer: Troy Kennedy Martin
Director: Tom Clegg

Cast: Nadim Sawalha (Shebbeq),
Valentine Palmer (Carew), Jim McManus (Ollie Parsons),
Frederick Treves (Beemax),
Michael Cronin (Sergeant Chivers),
Ian Thompson (Thompson), Ronnie Brody (Mechanic),
Anthony Langdon (Shand), Katya Wyeth (Helga),
Laurence Harrington (Lawyer),
Richard Felgate (McFarland), Joe Griffiths (Pianist),
Pauline Cunningham (Typist), Durra (Belly Dancer)

When Carew is arrested for a bank job, his alibi is simple: he was drinking with Jack Regan . . .

Keep Your Mincers Peeled For . . .: Just as Ed Bishop was British TV's stock American for most of the 1970s, so Nadim Sawalha has spent most of the last twenty years as British TV's stock Arab, as his several appearances in this book will make clear! His daughters, Julia and Nadia, have also enjoyed very successful TV careers. Michael Cronin is best remembered as Mr Baxter in many early seasons of *Grange Hill* (he also played an Irish builder in an episode of *Fawlty Towers* – here, he's Welsh!). Incidentally, that's the legendary stuntman and bit-part actor Nosher Powell (*The Comic Strip Presents . . .*) playing the motorist who confronts Jack Regan as he tries to chase the man who's been spying on him. The diminutive Ronnie Brody is one of those faces that seem to crop up in all sorts of places on TV, in his case usually playing small put-upon men in sitcoms.

The prominent book in Regan's flat is *The Comeback* by Barnaby Williams. Watch out, too, for a game of bar football in the Turkish bar. Regan has a bullworker in his flat.

Birds: *** The young woman jogging in denim shorts and matching coloured boots has a very big bum. Regan's current secretary wears a fetching blue cardigan (partly unbuttoned). He fails in his attempt to peer down her cleavage. Helga – the blonde Teuton in the Turkish club – wears a couple of fetching blouses, tied just above her navel. The Turkish belly dancer is well endowed (in the tummy area, at least).

Booze: *** 'Get these boys a tonic water!' Shebbeq brings a Turkish liquor back for Regan. They drink something alcoholic and milky-looking in the bar. There are more drinks later with Chivers. At the end, Regan makes a (vast amount of) vodka-based cocktail.

Shooters: * Shebbeq carries a pistol – Regan asks if he bought it in the Portobello Road.

Motors: The arresting officer at the beginning is driving a disgusting brown Rover 3500. Carew has told Regan that the getaway car will be a white Jag (that'll be difficult to spot, then). Regan drives a faded green Cortina II (in reverse) at a burgundy Mk I Cortina, containing the man who's spying on him. This in turn crashes into a grey S-type. We also see the Sweeney's blue Mark III Cortina. Regan's car later proves reluctant to start – this is probably something to do with the fact that there is a bomb wired to the ignition.

Threads: Regan's disgusting, purply jacket and his equally upsetting brown-orange dressing gown. Thompson's ginger shirt and brown three-piece suit are similarly nasty. Joe the pianist's sickly yellow flares almost qualify as the worst thing in the episode, but are beaten by the vile pair of blue-check strides worn by the man standing behind Regan and Carter when they're doing their song-and-dance routine.

Jazz Funk?: Joe the pianist is playing a jazzy tune as Regan comes into the club to meet Shebbeq. Regan and Carter do an excellent version of Jimmy Durante's 'As Long As It Comes From the Heart', with Joe on piano. There's much throbbing bass in the episode.

Bill the Driver: Bill finds himself caught up in the fire seen at the end of the episode.

You What?: Regan to Thompson: 'Furthermore, it's not the first time you've stolen my gravy.'
Shebbeq: 'Jack, are you carrying?'

Larfs: Carter: 'Guvnor, "God" wants to see you.' Regan: 'What, "God", or *God*-God?' Carter: 'If it was *God*-God, there would have been a flash of lightning and the summons would have been delivered by an angel with wings.'

Shebbeq translates George's Turkish greeting: 'Happy birthday. May the horse dung you are about to eat on this trip taste sweet.' (No surprise, as this was given to him by the local *Greek* restaurant.)

Regan: 'I feel like the prophet Isaiah, come out of the wilderness.'

Notes: 'Jack, there are enough people in this building trying to bury you – don't do it yourself!' An excellent central performance from Sawalha, and stuffed to the gills with great moments, including Regan incompetently trying to catch a fag in his mouth, and the bomb that destroys £1,000 worth of cucumbers (or is it rhubarb?).

Regan can do a reasonable Humphrey Bogart impression. Shebbeq last came over to England during the 1966 World Cup finals: he mentions Bobby Charlton, and he and Jack discuss the special qualities of Nobby Styles ('Where are you now, Nobby, when we most need you?'). The Squad station house is near Tower Bridge.

There's a reference to the opera soprano Maria Callas.

31: 'Tomorrow Man'
27 September 1976

Writer: Andrew Wilson
Director: David Wickes

Cast: John Hurt (Grey), George Cole (Longfield),
Peter Bayliss (Burnham), Ann Curthoys (Dr Jenny Smart),
Nina Thomas (Caroline),
Lawrence James (Desk Sergeant), Keith Ashton (Massey),
Jason James (Police Sergeant),
Dennis Blanche (CID Detective)

Tony Grey, recently released from stir for dangerous driving, hatches a scheme to exact revenge on his former business partner. Regan and Carter are dragged into the world of high technology and computers.

Keep Your Mincers Peeled For . . . : Any episode featuring John Hurt and George Cole doesn't really need you to look much further, but the vigilant will be rewarded, with Dennis Blanch (Derek Willis in *The XYY Man* and *Strangers*) appearing in a small role.

In the garage there's a big sticker proclaiming, THE NEW FIAT 131 MIRAFIORI. A briefly glimpsed *Evening Standard* headline concerns a 'bomb threat' – a bit of horrid 70s realism creeping in.

Birds: *** Angela, Longfield's secretary: George says he 'would', to Regan's amusement. Both men are after Jenny Smart, whom Jack 'found hanging around the national police computer'. They both attempt to drive her home, and Regan pulls rank in a desperate attempt to get intimate with her at the hotel. But she knocks the pair of them back and ends up going out to dinner with Haskins! (Thought he was supposed to be happily married . . .) When Regan discovers a rather hot-and-bothered-looking Grey under the quilt at Caroline's hotel room, Grey remarks, 'We don't all go to bed just to sleep.'

Booze: ** Regan has a whisky at Longfield's office. Grey smashes a bottle during his initial visit. Philistine. Regan and Carter drink at the Heathrow Hotel.

Shooters: * There's a shotgun evident during the fight with the hockey-mask-wearing goons. George proves pretty tasty with a baseball bat in the same scene.

Motors: The villains use a dark-blue Triumph 1500TC and an old, light-blue Vauxhall Velox when attempting to rob the van.

Threads: Tony Grey has just spent two years in prison, which may explain his 'fashion-victim' status in this episode: dreadful, checky, knee-length greatcoat and almost-matching cap, green velvet jacket, cream flares and brown rollneck sweater. And he has the audacity to criticise Longfield's 'appalling' taste! Give him life, judge. (Still, this all seems to be part of his plan, as the suits he later wears are a vast improvement.) Caroline's enormous flares are matched only by those of the policeman climbing up the ladder at Data Task. Carter looks a right pudding in his ill-fitting security uniform.

Jazz Funk?: There are a lot of nice bass riffs throughout the episode. And there is yet another use of the piano-based piece of music *The Sweeney* often trots out in moments of suspense.

You What?: Regan: 'Smudge him when he comes out.'
    Carter's version of a popular term for nothing: 'Sweet Felicity Arkwright!'

Larfs: Regan on computers: 'What's a cursor?' Carter: 'Someone we nick for obscene language?'

Notes: 'He was using a double. We've blown it.' A cracking revenge saga, very well written and with an excellent ensemble cast performance (John Hurt is especially impressive). If *Bugs* had been around in 1976, it would have looked a bit like this. The night filming next to Tower Bridge is especially evocative, although the view from Longfield's office looks suspiciously like that seen in 'Golden Fleece' (were both scenes filmed at LWT's head office?).

Regan goes under the alias of 'Casey' at the hotel. He says he doesn't know what a doppelgänger is, but threatens to look the word up in a dictionary. Certainly, by the end of the story, he's happy to drop it into everyday conversation. The wage Grey's firm are offering for computer programmers (£5,000 per annum) seems a bit on the low side even for 1976 (it's only a ton a week).

32: 'Taste of Fear'
4 October 1976

Writer: Roger Marshall
Director: David Wickes

Cast: Norman Eshley (Robert Hargreaves),
Arthur English (Tug Wilson), Bernard Spear (Benny),
Lesley Dunlop (Eileen Shaw), Ralph Arliss (Ames),
Norma Streader (Helen Hargreaves),
Anne-Louise Wakefield (Susie Farmer),
Shay Gorman (Shaw)

A pair of army deserters kneecap an Irish bookie during
a robbery at his home. Regan's team investigate, with an
ambitious new colleague. But Jack harbours doubts about the
newcomer.

Keep Your Mincers Peeled For . . .: Norman Eshley was the
Roper's put-upon neighbour in *George and Mildred*. Arthur
English's career in light comedy took in roles in series like
Are You Being Served?, *Follyfoot*, *The Ghosts of Motley Hall*
and *In Sickness and In Health*. George Sweeney was hilarious
as the thuggish Speed in *Citizen Smith*. Lesley Dunlop made
her name in *Angels* before becoming the star of *May to
December*. Bernard Spear spent most of his career playing
Jewish tailors (just as he does here!), most notably in *Albion
Market*.

Carter uses a Pentax camera. There's a big advert for the
German airline Lufthansa in the window of Tramper's Travel.

Birds: ** Regan glances admiringly at the bottom of Bianca,
Haskins's new secretary. George seems very interested in a
schoolgirl on a bicycle and, after noting how much he likes
white socks and short skirts, asks Hargreaves about what
fetish he's into.

Booze: *** George takes Eileen to the pub and has a whisky
while buying her a snowball (which he seems not to have
encountered before). Regan jokes that Hargreaves drinks only
cider (in halves). At the caravan stakeout, Regan passes his
hip flask around. He also gets out a bottle in the office;
George isn't supposed to have any after his trip to the
hospital. Unfortunately, he forgets ('You don't think me leg'll
fall off, do you?').

Shooters: *** Cook has a pump-action shotgun. All the Squad are tooled up at the caravan site (where the only injury is to George, who stands on a pitchfork and requires stitches and a tetanus jab), and also when Cook and Ames are finally arrested.

Threads: Look out for George's suede boots. There are some good laughs at the expense of Regan's suit (a theme continued into the next story). When Benny inspects the garment, he says, 'Your tailor. He was annoyed with you, was he? . . . I know the cutter. He used to work at the delicatessen. He couldn't cut salt beef, either.' Later, Carter asks Regan, 'How much did you pay for that whistle?' Regan: 'Forty quid.' Carter: 'Could have got a new one for that!' George offers to buy it off him: 'My mum's dog needs something to sleep on, see.'

Jazz Funk?: There's a poppy little theme to accompany Regan going to the launderette. We're treated to what sounds like a violin-led jig as the Sweeney take up their positions, and blaring trumpets during the siege proper. There are some funky guitar licks during the observation of Susie Farmer's house, and the 'suspense' music makes its second appearance in two stories.

You What?: Tug: 'You start cracking skulls, you get Old Bill out in strength. A straightforward blag, nobody bothers.'

Cook: 'There's two things I like. Really like. One's kicking Micks, and the other's thumping birds.'

Haskins: 'You're trying to snow me.'

Regan: 'Give his drum a spin . . . Put the breeze up his kilt!'

Cook: 'I'm warning you, ya poxy filth!'

Larfs: Carter, on Hargreaves: 'Tall for his height, isn't he?'

Regan, on the same: 'Pound to a penny he's a God-botherer!' (He could be right: one of the books Hargreaves is reading at home seems to be a bible, complete with indented tabs.)

Regan: 'The first hairy one I was on – you know, shooters, et cetera – there was a real old sweat. "Weren't you nervous?"

somebody asked him afterwards. "Nah," he says. "Not even a little bit?" "Nah. Funny thing is, though, somebody peed my pants!"'

Regan and Carter eat the same brand of cereal, and get their jokes from the packet: 'How do you tell the sex of a chromosome?' 'Look up its genes!' (Both have made the joke wheel from the back of the packet, though Regan claims this is for his daughter. Of course it is, Jack.)

Notes: 'It's a hard world, guv.' 'Yeah, but keep it to your-self, George. No one else wants to know.' As with Roger Marshall's previous pair of scripts, 'Taste of Fear' is the first part of a dramatic two-parter (see 'On the Run').

The Sweeney are also known as C8 (and 'the Heavy Mob' according to Haskins, reflecting a phrase from such episodes as 'Jackpot' and 'Faces'). Carter makes a reference to the (then current) England football manager Don Revie. Regan joins in with an oblique nod to the (real-life) 1975 London Spaghetti House siege. He also alludes to Uri Geller's alleged spoon-bending abilities. Regan knows, off the top of his head, that 45 per cent of the population have the blood group O ('Why couldn't it be AB rhesus negative for a change?' moans George).

It costs Cook £6.50 to get his leather coat repaired and dry-cleaned.

33: 'Bad Apple'
11 October 1976

Writer: Roger Marshall
Director: Douglas Camfield

Cast: Norman Jones (Perrant), John Lyons (Huke),
Sheila Brennan (Marge Proctor), Brian Poyser (Ash),
Rod Culbertson (Grigg), Colin Rix (Letts),
David Miller (Hudson),
Kenneth Gilbert (Superintendent Reynolds),
Patricia Franklin (Mrs Perrant),
Ellis Dale (Bank Manager),

**Maggie McCarthy (WPC Collins),
Billy James (Drag Stripper),
Steven Hatton (Johnny Peters)**

Haskins's investigations into a corruption case lead him to suspect widespread immorality in a provincial police force.

Keep Your Mincers Peeled For . . .: There are two Led Zeppelin posters on the wall of Johnny Peters's bedroom.

Birds: **** WPC Collins gets up to some rough stuff at the beginning ('You don't know your own strength, girl!'). In a subversion of the norm, we watch a male stripper in drag. When Johnny Peters is taken away by the bent coppers, his girlfriend's knockers are on display ('Cover 'em up, love. Put me off my breakfast'). Jack seems rather taken by the redhead Marge.

Booze: * Jack gets a job behind the bar of Marge's club, but he spends more time smashing bottles than drinking from them. He knows what's in a Bloody Mary (see 'Cover Story') and a Screwdriver. Perrant and Huke drink cans of light ale.

Shooters: None. Perrant has a big stick. Regan breaks his knuckle (a seemingly common occurrence); Carter says at least it's not his drinking hand.

Motors: Perrant seems to prefer boats. There's a disgusting green Allegro taxi at the beginning.

Threads: Letts: 'Tell me, does the Met dress like that these days?' Regan: 'Yeah, most of 'em.' Letts: 'Thank God I wore [a] uniform.' A very hurt Regan says he pays his tailor £10 a month! Watch out for George's tie, Huke's checky flares, Perrant's lime-green socks, and Jack's purple shirt, open to his navel.

Jazz Funk?: Sleazy stripper music. Regan sings the first line of 'Stranger in Paradise'. There's a great jazzy organ-and-brass theme when Jack's working in the Blue Parrot.

You What?: Perrant: 'What do you reckon you'll draw?'

Grigg: 'About two penn'orth.' Perrant: 'Double it.'

Grigg: 'Look, I'll give you a long 'un for an acquittal.'

Regan: 'Don't play barrack-room lawyer with me, Uncle!'

And: 'I know if I was you, I'd sing like a hot canary.'

'Whilst in his cups' is Haskins's euphemism for being under the influence.

Regan: 'He must be off his chump.'

Huke: 'Listen, pillock, I'm the fuzz. You raise one finger at me and your feet won't touch, savvy?'

Larfs: Regan: 'You've been on the wrong end of one of these inquiries, Frank . . . Sifting through your private life, pricing your home – everything from the sideboard to your wife's second best bra.'

Haskins: 'He's either got a bee in his bonnet, or an ounce or two of high-octane honey.'

Regan (on an incorruptible police force): 'There's only one force got that.' (He points heavenwards.) 'St Peter's AC Crime.'

Notes: 'Not a bent copper?' A lovely episode, with John Thaw, as always, seeming to revel in Regan's undercover operations. Smashing script and visuals from our favourite writer/director team (put Marshall and Camfield together and you *always* got something that's watchable).

Carter tries to interest Regan in the porn films being shown by the 'dirty squad' (taken from a raid in Greek Street). However, Regan's is the least busy of Haskins's teams, and so they're called into this case. Haskins is old enough to remember V-J Night. He has been investigated for corruption himself (see 'Golden Fleece').

Shaw Taylor is mentioned, as is 'the Police Act of 1964', and there are countless anti-government jokes. Regan refers to Leeds United's midfield duo of the era, Johnny Giles and Billy Bremner (as 'a pair of villains'!), and there are boxing references to the then British and world light-heavyweight champion John Conteh, and Muhammed Ali's trainer Angelo Dundee. George seems something of a film fan, referring to both Sydney Greenstreet in *Casablanca* and *Butch Cassidy and the Sundance Kid*.

34: 'May'
25 October 1976

Writer: Trevor Preston
Director: Tom Clegg

Cast: Marjorie Yates (May), Karl Howman (Davey Holmes),
Geraldine Moffatt (Sheila Martin), Brian Gwaspari (Cree),
Frank Mills (Len), Tim Hardy (Francis),
Jeremy Sinden (Feast), Roger Booth (Ashcroft),
Tim Meats (Jessop), Cyril Shaps (Turner),
Adrian Shergold (Don Edwards),
Kathleen St John (Miss Finch)

A 'thieving old Shylock' gets a kicking and the local plod
finger Davey Holmes. His mum, May, is an old flame of
Jack's, but what has the boy got to hide?

Keep Your Mincers Peeled For . . . : Long before he was
Jacko in *Brush Strokes*, Karl Howman was the man who took
over from Robert Lindsay as Jakey Smith in *Get Some In!*
Jeremy Sinden, Donald's son, was a regular in *Crossroads*,
playing one of Jill Richardson's numerous boyfriends.

Birds: * Sheila Martin, whose husband is a gangster serving
a three-stretch (but it should have been life according to
Regan). Her clandestine affair with young Davey may have
dire consequences for them both.

Booze: ** Jack and George's 'breakfast' is a bottle of vodka.
Later, Regan, Carter and May have (respectively) glasses of
whisky, beer and vodka. Davey seems to only drink 7 Up.

Shooters: None.

Motors: Another appearance by the villain's friend, the
silver-grey S-type, only this time it's a police car (*very*
undercover!). It still does its usual trick of flipping open the
boot in the middle of a chase sequence. There's a very
prominent Norton Commando 850cc motorbike, and Sheila
drives around in a left-hand-drive American Motors AMX

('Car wouldn't start . . . I don't use it much'). Francis has a grey Bentley.

Threads: Don Edwards's flared jeans.

Jazz Funk?: Discordant and sinister music during the beating up on the old man gives way later to a horrible honkytonk piano theme more in keeping with a best-forgotten sitcom than the sharpest cop show on TV. There is, however, a nice, summery guitar tune to accompany Sheila driving to meet Davey.

You What?: Regan: 'Five weeks to sort this job out, and some daisy from Division screws it up in five minutes.'

And: 'Look son, I've been on me pins for twenty-nine hours. Up the reports!'

Don: 'I know Davey, that's not his bag . . . Our Davey's so straight he wouldn't put a washer in a parking meter.'

Regan: 'Look, Len, I didn't come here to have a bull and a cow with you.'

Len on Regan's patch: 'I thought your manor was the slag and dipper mile!'

Larfs: May (as Davey is arrested): 'You lay one finger on him . . .' Cree: 'It isn't like that now, missus, haven't you heard? It's all psychology.'

Regan: 'If you weren't who you are, I'd kick your arse up to your shoulder blades.'

Sheila: 'I was taking the dog for a run.' Francis: 'You'll have to watch it round here. He might get eaten by the squirrels.'

Notes: 'Young Davey's been practising his postural variations with someone.' It takes three-quarters of the episode to work out what crime is being committed here (it eventually turns out to be blackmail). A change of pace from the usual *Sweeney* knockabout, with some reflective moments, although the scene with Sheila's dog is amusing.

Regan reckons he's getting too old for 'all-night obos'. His gaff is 'a bit of a tip' with dirty plates and coffee cups, and empty booze and milk bottles much in evidence. He has a painted mural in his bathroom (it had been previously seen in 'Visiting Fireman' but we get a better look at it here), and there's a *Peanuts* cartoon book visible in his kitchen. He thinks he doesn't have a beer gut but is carrying 'relaxed muscle'. George thinks he should 'cut out the spuds'.

Regan and Bobby Holmes were once close friends (May tells George a story about their dressing up in drag to go to a party) before Holmes turned to crime and died in prison. Jack always fancied May Holmes, and she helped him through his divorce from Kate. Davey calls Regan (sarcastically) 'Uncle Jack'.

Haskins is mentioned (twice) but not seen.

Warren Beatty, Frosties cereal, and the Beatles' *Magical Mystery Tour* are all mentioned, and there's a possible oblique reference to *The Likely Lads*. Most of the locations are in the Chelsea area.

35: 'Sweet Smell of Succession'
8 November 1976

Writer: Peter Hill
Director: William Brayne

Cast: Hywel Bennett (Steven Castle),
Peter Dyneley (Tarley), Sue Lloyd (Arleen Baker),
Willoughby Goddard (Kitter),
Maxwell Shaw (Colin Raleigh), Alan Tilvern (Walters),
David Sterne (Parkin), Gail Grainger (Jill),
Geoffrey Todd (Nairn), Jack Allen (The Vicar),
Peter Brayham (Johnno)

They're burying Joe Castle, 'one of the biggest villains in West London'. The Sweeney gear up for a right royal battle for Castle's turf, but, when the old man's son turns up, complications ensue.

Keep Your Mincers Peeled For . . . : Hywel Bennett will be most familiar to viewers as the eponymous hero of *Shelley*.

Sue Lloyd was a regular face in various ITC film series of the 1960s (including a semiregular role in *The Baron*), *and* was later David Hunter's wife, Barbara, in *Crossroads*. Peter Dyneley's voice was that of Jeff Tracy in *Thunderbirds*.

When Regan removes the tape recorder from Kitter's desk, the lid falls off. Watch out for the very prominent bottle of pickled onions in the cheap café, and for the horrible orange lamp shade on display in Castle's office.

Birds: *** Arleen Baker, Castle's 'personal assistant'. 'How personal?' asks George. 'Enough to make your eyes water, sunshine,' is Regan's reply. She keeps the stolen jewels in her stocking tops, and we see her in bed with Steven Castle.

Regan and Carter ogle a girl in a very tight sweater and gypsy skirt in the café. 'If this keeps up we're gonna have to take you down to the vet's,' notes Regan. Carter briefly goes out with Haskins's secretary, Jill.

Booze: ***** Carter shares a bottle of wine over a meal in an Indian restaurant with Jill. He asks if she'd like to go with him to 'a little club' he knows. Later, they have another (candlelit) meal, with more wine at his gaff (with whisky to follow after she goes off in a huff). Steven spends most of the episode drinking with Kitter, Walters and Arleen (sherry, whisky and champagne, respectively). Arleen seems to prefer vodka. Regan and Haskins drink whisky with Walters and Parkin. Given the amount of alcohol on display here, it's a miracle that Carter turns down a drink with Regan in the office (Haskins, though, is quick to accept a little later).

Shooters: ** There are loads of shooters visible in the climactic sequence at the disused market, including the rather nasty shotgun that polishes off Tarley.

Motors: Tarley drives a white Merc saloon, and Arleen a red MGB Mk II. A grey S-type comes a cropper at the end.

Threads: The usual: Jack's corduroy jacket, Carter's grey polo-neck. Look out for Castle's black-and-white spotted shirt, and Jill's fluffy white jacket thing.

Jazz Funk?: Carter and Regan meet in a café with some groovy rock guitar as background music. When George and Jill have a meal at his place, there's some smoochy jazz on the record player. There's also some bassy electronic music to accompany the car chase. Steve Castle's preferred choice is classical. There's a wicked bass riff during the pursuit of Raleigh, and a choppy guitar-and-organ rock theme during his abduction. And we mustn't forget Carter's a cappella version of 'The Red Flag'.

Non-PC Moment: Carter mentions other candidates' attitudes to 'coloured police officers' in a fairly derogatory way. If George had got his promotion, he'd be (according to Regan) 'Nicking the local poof in the recreation-ground toilets!'

You What?: Carter: 'Who's the kiss of death in the fifty-bob overcoat?'

Regan: 'That's the kosher SP, Patsy. You ask Kitter.'

Tarley: 'Get stuffed, Regan. The day ain't come when the Sweeney can snow me.'

Regan: 'There's been a right bull and cow in there.'

Haskins: 'Is he on the turn?' Regan: 'Nah, he's in a bit of a two-and-eight about this selection business.'

Carter: 'I dipped the board. Well, I had to, really, didn't I? Lost the gaff, bird pulled up the ladder. It's not my bleedin' day, is it?'

Larfs: Tarley: 'Drop dead, Kojak!'

Regan: 'How'd you get on last night?' Carter: 'All right.' Regan: 'No naughties?' Carter: 'Nah, it was back home to mum, wannit?' Regan: 'Cocoa and the family album . . .'

Carter: 'He's a commander. That's only two down from God!'

Notes: 'On the chandelier again, George?' A terrific episode about lack of honour among thieves, with a smooth and cynical performance by Hywel Bennett. The violent black-and-white sequences at the start are an added bonus, and Thaw pulls off a more convincing Yorkshire accent when joking with Carter than he often does in *Kavanagh, QC*!

Regan is placing a bet the first time we see him (£2 'on the nose'). His tax disc's expiry date is 'Nov 1975' (a year out of date by the time of the episode's transmission). Jack and George discuss whether they're 'going down QPR tonight'. They eventually decide not to. George is 28 (presumably he's just turned 28 as he was 26 in 'Hit and Run' just over a year ago) and has been in the Sweeney for two years (probably since his return from CID – see 'Regan').

Location work includes scenes near the Westway flyover and in West London (Brentford).

36: 'Down to You, Brother'
22 November 1976

Writer: Richard Harris
Director: Chris Menaul

Cast: Derek Francis (Meadows), Terence Budd (Owen),
Tina Heath (Deborah), Kenny Lynch (Holder),
Malcolm Tierney (Miller), Ron Pember (Apps),
John Barrard (Chauffeur),
Simon Callow (Detective Sergeant),
Michael Logan (Joke Teller), Jenny Cryst (Girl at Hotel)

Raymond Meadows, a retired villain, gets drunk and admits to Jack that he was responsible for a blag some years ago. Regan wants to reopen the case, but does Meadows have an ulterior motive?

Keep Your Mincers Peeled For . . .: Tina Heath, the first of two *Blue Peter* presenters to play foxy chicks in *The Sweeney*. Previously she'd been the teenage star of *Lizzie Dripping*. Kenny Lynch and Simon Callow (in a blink-and-you'll-miss-him role, complete with cropped hair and wicked 'tache) surely need no introduction. That's Nosher Powell again, playing the 'other gorilla'! For Ron Pember, see 'Regan'.

Watch out for the *Valley of the Dolls* novel and *A Fistful of Dollars* and *Hang 'Em High* posters in Owen's room, plus a poster for the *QE2* at the hotel. Regan and Carter play the

Mastermind game in the back of the van (see *The Professionals* – 'Hijack').

Birds: ** While at the dinner-jacket do, Regan asks the brunette behind the bar if she's looking for love (she says she isn't). Carter 'wouldn't say no' to the lovely Deborah, Meadows's blonde-ish daughter. She has two scenes swimming in the pool (wearing dark and pink bikinis respectively).

Booze: * Regan's piling away the Scotch (without ice) at the drinks party-cum-boxing match. They've got Double Diamond and Skol on draught. Meadows has a whisky while Owen and his gang are attempting the diamond job.

Shooters: None.

Motors: Meadows's thugs turn up at Owen's place in a red Jaguar XJ-S. Owen himself is seen in a black and a yellow Capri. Meadows has a Roller (Carter never fancied one himself), while his daughter drives a blue Spitfire (much more up George's street).

Threads: The Detective Sergeant sports an offensive yellow kipper. There are some very tasty checked jackets on display.

Jazz Funk?: Vivaldi! (An extract from the first movement of his Concerto No. 1 in E major ('Spring') as we see Meadows's Rolls-Royce, and from the first movement of Concerto No. 4 in F minor ('Winter') during Owen's attack on Meadows.) And there's some baffling country-and-western, complete with slide guitar and mandolin, at various points, most noticeably when Owen arrives in the yellow Capri.

Non-PC Moment: 'You don't half rabbit, you blackies,' says Owen while talking to Holder, shortly before lapsing into an appalling West Indian accent.

You What?: Meadows: 'Six years ago I did my last little tickle.'
   Cameraman: 'Wanna smudge?' Carter: 'Yeah, let's immortalise him.'

Larfs: Regan: 'Meadows? He's about as kosher as butter on a ham sandwich.'

Notes: 'When I was a kid no one used to lock their door. What sort of world we living in?' There's just enough plot and depth of characterisation to keep this simple tale ticking over quite nicely.

Haskins has a ticket for a boxing match between 'whatsisname' (Sutherland) and 'the American fellow' (Vicenzo). George is keen to go, but is not senior enough. Regan speaks to Kate on the phone twice, and meets Susie. He lives in flat 7, and his call sign in this story is Oscar 2-4. Carter says he comes from a family of healthy eaters, and is thinking of taking up golf. He is impatient for the job to be over so that he can go home and watch West Ham on the TV. Haskins has a daughter (who currently has a cold). It may be Lucy mentioned in 'Golden Fleece', but see also 'Victims'. There is a reference to Cinderella.

37: 'Pay Off'
29 November 1976

Writer: Peter J. Hammond
Director: Douglas Camfield

Cast: Dave King (Drake), Geraldine James (Shirley Glass),
Ken Kitson (Killick), George Harris (Franklyn),
William Armour (Murdock), Anthony Douse (Millan),
David Ellison (Vaughton)

Carter's current girlfriend, Shirley, wants to establish if her former partner really is dead. George should know better than to try to mix business with pleasure . . .

Keep Your Mincers Peeled For . . .: Geraldine James is well remembered for her roles in *The Jewel in the Crown*, *Blott on the Landscape* and *Band of Gold*.

Items in Shirley's flat include a very 70s orange mushroom lamp, a trill phone and a psychedelic mural. There's also a possible sighting of a lava lamp near the wrought-iron spiral staircase, but it's a fleeting glimpse and it's difficult to be certain. The staircase, incidentally, is a dead ringer for the one in Ray Doyle's flat in *The Professionals* episode 'Involvement'!

Birds: *** There are plenty of blonde bimbos at the Drake's Drum casino, one of whom (Shirley) George chats up. (Regan: 'You dirty bastard.' Carter: 'Have you met my father?' Regan: 'Jammy sod.') It seems that Carter suffers from brewer's droop during their first attempt at lovemaking (but he later does much better!). Not surprisingly, he describes his relationship with her to Haskins as 'purely heterosexual'. Also, you've got to love the sequence with Jack and the surly, smoking, blonde schoolgirl. She's not much older than your daughter, Jack . . .!

Booze: * Haskins, Regan, Carter, Daniels, Bill and some other boys from the Squad are drinking in Drake's club (Regan orders the 'same again, no sherry this time').

Shooters: *** The animal-mask-wearing thugs in the pre-titles flashback are suitably tooled up with pistols and shotguns (and explosives!). The final shoot-out sees Drake armed with a wicked silencer-fitted rifle, Zac carrying a pistol and Killick with a revolver. They are no match, though, for the trained police marksmen!

Motors: In the pre-titles sequence, the villains use a blue Mark I Cortina, a yellow and white VW Caravette and a black Austin Cambridge. Haskins turns up in a dark greenish-brownish Rover 3500, with Daniels in a white Cortina (DLO 97M, which used to be *blue*!). Carter drives a yellow-green Mini to the quarry; Killick arrives in a blue Land Rover. There then follows a virtual cavalcade of police and Sweeney vehicles, including Haskins's Rover, a brown police Maxi, a green VW van, a panda car, a Transit and the usual silver Granada/white Cortina Sweeney combo.

Threads: Haskins wears some tasty shades during the initial shoot-out. And what about Shirley's baseball boots?

Jazz Funk?: There's an excellent little bass-guitar riff in the quarry.

You What?: Regan: 'George, the local factory dropped it like a hot potato. Get smart, son. Do the same. This Glass obviously did someone's petty cash and had it away on his toes. The bird's either diddlo or she's the victim of a hoax. It's all very sad, but it's a cruel world!'

Haskins: 'Did Millan put Glass in the frame – if you'll forgive the pun?'

Carter: 'Item: a year ago one Edward Fitzpatrick Glass was hired as a stoppo driver to take part in a security blag, right?'

Shirley: 'Could I have an interpreter, please?'

Zac: 'That's all I did, man, I wanted the chick to know where she was at!'

Carter: 'You gotta be out of your tiny Chinese.'

And what's probably Regan's first use of 'On yer bike!'

Larfs: Carter: 'What if I found Eddie Glass? And he's alive and well and living in Stoke Newington?'

Haskins: 'Come on, you've been the Lone Ranger in your time.' Regan: 'But I don't intend to end up as bloody Tonto.'

Haskins (looking at an X-ray): 'Well, at least Eddie's teeth lasted longer than he did.'

Regan: 'Eddie's turned up ... Dead, but he wouldn't lie down. Yeah, up he popped, out of the quarry, as large as ... well, you know what I mean.'

Regan, on what sentence Jamie Murdock can expect: 'Twenty-five, maybe thirty if the judge's arthritis is playing him up on the day. What's inflation gonna do to your cut by 2001?'

Regan: 'Now, shut it!'

Notes: 'Here he is: the Valentino of the Victoria line.' An excellent story, with a nice climax in a *Doctor Who*-like quarry. Hammond's script cleverly pitches Carter and Regan against each other, though we're not convinced that he's got their dialogue quite right. There are some great lines about a villainous, misunderstood midget!

Carter makes a Charles Laughton/*Hunchback of Notre Dame* reference ('The bells!'). Carter takes one sugar in his coffee. Regan is Oscar 2-3, Haskins is Oscar 7, and Carter is Oscar 4-3.

There are references to the explorer Marco Polo and the

then current kung-fu craze. Carter's line about marks for 'content, presentation and star quality' is a reference to the categories used on the ITV talent show *New Faces*.

38: 'Loving Arms'
6 December 1976

Writer: Robert Wales
Director: Tom Clegg

Cast: Roy Sone (Arthur Ward),
Clifford Kershaw (Fred Booth), Anne Dyson (Lilly Booth),
Alan David (Blakeney), Mona Hammond (Ann Robson),
George Tovey (Len Walters), Julian Littman (Jeremy Clarke),
Steven Pacey (PC McKenna), Max Mason (PC Adler),
Douglas Anderson (Faith Healer), Perry Balfour (1st Youth),
Angela Phillips (1st Girl Robber),
Raymond Winstone (2nd Youth)

Some right dodgy geezer has flooded the streets with replica shooters. Regan and Carter are on the case, hoping to track him down before anyone gets hurt.

Keep Your Mincers Peeled For . . .: Mona Hammond played Blossom Jackson in *EastEnders*. Steven Pacey was the heartthrob Del Tarrant in *Blake's 7*. Alan David began his TV career as a presenter of the BBC's 'with-it' 60s pop show *Gadzooks! It's All Happening*, before becoming one of the stars of Eric Chappell's office sitcom, *The Squirrels*. Long before he shortened his name, starred in *Robin of Sherwood*, *Get Back* and the film *Nil By Mouth*, and finally received acknowledgement as one of the finest actors of his generation, Ray Winstone was a teenage protégé, with meaty (often thuggish) roles in *Fox*, *Scum*, and *Auf Wiedersehen, Pet*.

The *Evening News*'s second story (beneath 'HOME MADE GUN KILLS PC & YOUTH') is 'HOLIDAYS ABROAD BOOM DESPITE THE INFLATION' (sic). Things worth trying to spot in this episode: a box containing Sanyo stereo speakers; some Chelsea graffiti; an advert for Tizer; and a wad of mid-1970s £20 notes (purple-backers, featuring William Shakespeare's boat race).

Birds: * There are some girlie mags in the newsagent's at the beginning (one of the magazines seems to be called *Vibrators*!), and some 'interesting' posters on Arty Ward's walls. Blakeney's thugs drag a startled prostitute from Ward's bed.

Booze: None, though Carter suggests some as a viable alternative to their investigations. Carter gives two bottles of Black Label to somebody in the crime labs to get a look at the gun (Regan queries why it cost two bottles: 'Inflation,' he is told).

Shooters: ** The whole story is based around the lethal Colt replicas. 'You're in the wrong place, son,' says Len the newsagent when confronted with one of them. 'You want the OK Corral.' Jack and George tread carefully when arresting Ward. Similarly, Regan takes no chances as he bursts in on Mrs Booth, gun in hand – to find the room full of praying Christian Scientists.

Motors: There's a lovely orange Ferrari and a load of Rollers outside Blakeney's garage. The thugs pick up Arthur Ward in a convertible left-hand-drive Pontiac.

Threads: Bill's disgusting blue parka, complete with fur-lined hood, makes another appearance. The flares worn by the (innocent) young man chased by Regan and Carter must surely have gone out of fashion with the Bay City Rollers. McKenna wears an especially toffish pin-stripe suit. Ward's nasty yellow shirt and sheepskin coat are especially noteworthy.

Jazz Funk?: The Sweeney lads sing 'Where Have All the Bog Rolls Gone?' Haskins, on the other hand, is seen humming 'Ode to Joy' (Beethoven's Ninth Symphony). There's some terrible jukebox rock in the boozer, but a poppy little theme is used during the rainy-night-in-Soho montage. Arty sings a couple of lines of 'If I Was a Rich Man' from *Fiddler on the Roof*.

Bill the Driver: The best scene in the episode is George, Jack and Bill chomping away on some cream slices.

You What?: Len: 'Young, cocky bloke. Very tricky. Well, you know, it's all lardy with the dialogue.'

Regan: 'Yeah, well he did Old Len right up. Gave the press boys a dialogue about it only being a toy gun, and Old Len here being diddlo.'

Carter: 'Aw, leave it out, guvnor. It was all Gunga Din, wasn't it? It was just bad luck.'

Arty: 'I thought everything was all straight and legal, all six and eight and lovely, you see.'

Larfs: Carter: 'Guvnor, that's fifteen we've been through – and all of them couldn't have been more surprised if we'd stuffed their shirts with ice cubes.'

Notes: 'I knew there was a bit of skulduggery . . .' Some nice contrasts are established between the adult world and the 'kids' with 'toy' guns, and between the evil 'villains' (see how quickly Art tries pinning the blame on Booth and Blakeney) and the selfless love of Fred and Lilly. The (very grainy) Soho-esque sequences do drag on a bit, though, but Alan David puts in a suitably nasty, understated performance.

Regan begins the episode trying to find the rightful owners of a consignment of stolen toilet products. Matt is mentioned, but not seen. A uniformed copper gives chase to the two girls – there must have been a lot of bobbies on the beat back then. There's also a (seemingly obligatory) reference to *Butch Cassidy and the Sundance Kid*.

39: ' "Lady Luck" '[1]
13 December 1976

Writer: Ranald Graham
Director: Mike Vardy

---

[1] The title appears on screen within quotation marks.

Cast: Moira Redmond (Marcia),
Norman Rodway (Edmunds),
James Cossins (Colonel Rosier),
Daphne Oxenford (Mrs Rosier),
Peggy Bullock (The Old Lady),
Carolyn Hudson (Marcia's Friend)

A woman comes to Regan with some information about a recent blag at a bookie's. Trouble is, it seems she wants to incriminate her own husband . . .

Keep Your Mincers Peeled For . . .: James Cossins seemed to make a career out of playing military types and bank managers, normally in sitcoms. Norman Rodway played the spy Cummings in *Reilly – Ace of Spies*.

Birds: * Regan and Marcia Edmunds seemed to have a one-night fling, though it didn't last beyond the revelation that she was trying to shop her husband ('You lost interest in me overnight').

Booze: * In the pub, Regan buys 'Carole' a large vodka and tonic, and a (very) large Scotch for himself. The total cost: £1.14. A 1945 Château d'Yquem has a pivotal role in the plot.

Shooters: ** Pistols and a double-barrelled shotgun (held in one hand and, we are later informed, used for hunting duck!) are used during the initial robbery. 'Get the team tooled up, George,' says Regan as they prepare to arrest Edmunds.

Motors: There is a blue Vauxhall Viva and a nice silver XJ6 on display at the beginning. Haskins is again seen in a Rover 3500, this one being a horrible sort of brown. Regan describes the orange Granada as a 'high-performance squad car'.

Threads: Edmunds's shirt collar is simply *vast*, but it would need to be to contain that gold-coloured tie! George's white crash helmet is *so* uncool.

Jazz Funk?: Actually, some *Shaft* guitar, when Regan and Carter have a look at the park. Before then, however, we've been subjected to some dreadful Muzak in the boozer, and a much nicer bass-driven theme as Regan and Carter time the route to the bookie's. The motorbike sequence is accompanied by a choppy guitar riff that's a dead ringer for the Jam's 'Precious' (the bass line is quite similar, too).

You What?: Carter: 'There you go, guvnor, full house, aces on the roof. Don't look so surprised, they're all contenders.'

Carter: 'Guvnor! Dog and bone – urgent.'

Larfs: Regan: 'You spend months slouching around, drinking with social vermin, mortgaging your liver for a pension. But every now and then I feel I really deserve it when something nice, clean and unexpected lands in me lap, like a ripe apple.'

Haskins: 'You mean we're going to have a Grand Marnier soufflé, mixed up and baked in court?'

Notes: 'Detective Inspector Regan, Flying Squad. You're nicked!' A well-written story, with very few characters, that tries to make the most of its few locations and basic plot.

The lead story in the *Evening Standard* seen in the pre-titles sequence is 'RUSSIAN SHIP SEIZED BY NAVY'. The events in this story form 'Operation Ladybird'. Haskins mentions Regan's snout Stickley (see 'Supersnout'), so presumably their relationship did continue after that story. Regan says that Marcia saw his name in an old newspaper (the 'London Airport job'). He's not above asking Marcia to lie under oath. During the motorcycle sequence there's a lovely homage to *Butch Cassidy and the Sundance Kid*.

The Flying Squad has groupies according to Regan ('less than our fair share!').

40: 'On the Run'
20 December 1976

Writer: Roger Marshall
Director: David Wickes

Cast: Brendan Price (Pinder), John Sharp (Uncle), Jan Harvey (Pat), Dave Hill (Shayler),

Alan Mitchell (Stackman), Keith James (Lakin),
Anna Wing (Mrs Haldane),
Roger Brierley (Psychiatrist), Malya Woolf (Nurse)

Tim Cook – dubbed 'The Leopard' by the papers – is sprung
from jail, and sets out to have his vengeance on the man who
put him behind bars: Jack Regan.

Keep Your Mincers Peeled For . . . : Jan Harvey, later star of
Howards' Way (as Jan Howard) and *Bugs*, puts in a great little
cameo as Regan's latest pissed-off girlfriend. *EastEnders* fans
will spot Anna Wing (Lou Beale) in a small role.
     The boys who discover the Jeep are riding Chopper bikes.

Birds: ** Regan takes a fishing holiday in Suffolk with his
girlfriend Pat Nightly (George says he knew her sister –
'Twice!'). She says Jack left a cigarette burn on her duvet,
which seems to be a euphemism for *something*, but we
hesitate to speculate . . .

Booze: * Jack and George order whiskies at the pub in
Suffolk, but Pat drinks George's before he can. Carter orders
three large ones at the end. (Look out for the big advert for
Skol on one of the pub tables.)

Shooters: ** Cook steals a twelve-bore from a local manor
house. When the Squad track him through the forest, several
– including Jack and George – are tooled up. They've also
got dogs with them.

Motors: Pinder borrows a blue left-hand-drive Jeep Renegade
from the garage where he works.

Threads: Watch out for the outrageous red, white and blue
kipper worn by the Squad switchboard operator about ten
minutes into the episode. (Almost as bad is the pattern on
Haskins's smartish tie. It looks like alligator skin!) Also look
out for Cook's bobble hat and donkey jacket. Regan and
Carter both discard their ties before chasing Cook through the
woods.

Jazz Funk?: There's some sinister flute-and-piano music, plus a loud guitar rock theme heard on Pinhead's radio in the garage.

Bill the Driver: He gets a tiny piece of the action – smacked in the face by a gun stock.

You What?: Carter: 'A little bird tells me that you had a bunny with Cook.'

And: 'He wouldn't have the nous to pull a stroke like that.'

Larfs: Carter: 'What name could I mention that'd bring you back?' Regan: 'There isn't one.' Carter: 'Raquel Welch?' Regan (after a long pause): 'Never heard of him!'

Pat, after George has told her that the newspaper report talks about a Detective Inspector Jack Regal: 'Imagine you as a cinema! Or have they turned you into a bingo parlour?'

Notes: 'Cook's mad – stark, raving mad.' Another astonishingly violent season closer (for the third year running). A direct sequel to 'Taste of Fear' with many references to the events of that story. It takes a while to get going, though, and the ending isn't quite as tense as it probably should have been.

Regan quotes loads of dialogue and character names from *Jaws*, which seems to be a particular favourite film of his. He plays bar billiards (presumably, like everybody else in the country, he picked it up watching *The Indoor League*). On the stakeout Carter has corned-beef sandwiches: Regan thinks this is cheapskate, telling George, proudly, that his are ham and tomato! Haskins asks Regan if he reads his Bible, but Jack notes he is 'more a Harold Robbins man!' Carter's first pinch was a Peeping Tom.

There are references to the real-life spy George Blake (who spectacularly escaped from Wormwood Scrubs in the 1960s) and *The Birdman of Alcatraz*, along with nods at *Dr Jekyll and Mr Hyde*, Dusty Springfield's 'I Close My Eyes and Count to Ten' and Laurel and Hardy.

Sweeney!
Theatrical Release: January 1977

An 89-minute feature film
Euston Films/Thames Television
Based on *The Sweeney*, created by Ian Kennedy Martin

Producer: Ted Childs
Executive Producers: Lloyd Shirley, George Taylor

Music composed by Denis King

Regular Cast: John Thaw (Detective Inspector Jack Regan),
Dennis Waterman (Detective Sergeant George Carter),
John Alkin (Detective Sergeant Tom Daniels),
Nick Brimble (Detective Constable Gerry Burtonshaw),
Morris Perry (Detective Superintendent Maynon[1])

Writer: Ranald Graham
Director: David Wickes

Cast: Barry Foster (McQueen), Ian Bannen (Baker),
Colin Welland (Chadwick), Diane Keen (Bianca),
Michael Coles (Johnson), Joe Melia (Brent),
Brian Glover (Mac), Lynda Bellingham (Janice),
Paul Angelis (Secret Serviceman), Bernard Kay (Matthews),
Anthony Scott (Johnson's Henchman),
Anthony Brown (Murder Inquiry Superintendent),
John Oxley (Chadwick's Deputy Editor),
Peggy Aitchison (Carter's Neighbour),
Hal Jeayes (Manservant), Sally Osborn[2] (Sally),
John Kaye (Special Branch Sergeant),
Chris Dillinger (Johnson's Henchman),
Peter Childs (Murder Inquiry Inspector),
Alan Mitchell (Detective Inspector),
Leonard Kavanagh (Pathologist),

---

[1] Credited on screen as 'Flying Squad Cmdr.'
[2] Incorrectly credited on screen as 'Osborne'.

Anthony Woodruff (Coronor), Michael Latimer (PPS),
Matthew Long (Traffic Police Sergeant),
Joyce Grant (McQueen's Secretary),
Johnny Shannon (Scotland Yard Duty Sergeant),
David Corti (Young Boy),
Susan Skipper (Chadwick's Secretary),
Nadim Sawalha (Chairman of the Oil Producer's Conference)

One of Regan's snouts complains that his girlfriend's recent suicide was really murder. When Jack begins to investigate, he finds himself fitted up and under Special Branch's scrutiny.

Keep Your Mincers Peeled For . . .: Welland, Kay, Bellingham, Glover, Coles and Sawalha had all previously appeared on *The Sweeney* (see 'Faces', 'Trap', 'Trojan Bus', 'Thin Ice', 'I Want the Man' and 'Visiting Fireman' respectively). Barry Foster made his name playing the tiepin psycho in Alfred Hitchcock's *Frenzy*, before becoming TV's best-loved Dutch detective in *Van Der Valk*. Ian Bannen's film roles included another not-quite-as-good-as-the-TV-series movie *Doomwatch* and the excellent *Fright* (opposite a young Dennis Waterman). His TV appearances include *Tinker Tailor Soldier Spy* and the 90s remake of *Dr Finlay's Casebook* (as Dr Cameron). Diane Keen, before the lure of coffee adverts, was then best known for the sitcom *The Cuckoo Waltz* (with the future *Professionals* star Lewis Collins), though *The Sandbaggers* was just around the corner. Telefantasy fans will know Joe Melia from his brilliant comic turn in *The Hitch-Hiker's Guide to the Galaxy*. Peter Childs would soon work with Waterman again in *Minder* (as Sergeant Rycott).

Items visible in George Carter's bathroom include a bottle of Hai Karate! talc (just above the sink), a bottle of TCP, which must come in very handy given the number of beltings he gets from villains (on top of the medicine cabinet), and a copy of *Private Eye* (next to the lav). He's also got a bar-football game in his front room.

There's some Queens Park Rangers graffiti visible in the vandalised telephone box Regan tries to use. They were a good team back then . . .

Birds: ***** Boobies alert! Janice is stripped three minutes into the film. Later, Bianca's dressing gown falls from her shoulders, and then she sits up a bit too sharpish in bed, and, wey-hey, cop an eyeful of *them*. George and Jack still have a thing about air hostesses. And Jack has a go at Doreen the big-chested (and probably married) barmaid, but fails miserably.

Booze: **** Jack gets a bottle out in the office after the arrest of the wages blaggers. There's booze all over the place, including a pub scene (with George and Jack knocking back the whisky), Baker and Chadwick sharing a drop of the hard stuff, and two party sequences with wine and champagne. Plus, Regan is force-fed whisky, which makes a change from his force-feeding whisky to others! Jack and Bianca later drink some in bed. Obviously the experience hasn't been too harmful to him.

Shooters: *** All the lads are tooled up for the wages snatch at the beginning, but it ends without a shot fired ('Remember, no guns unless they use them'). Johnson's crew use a pair of positively lethal Ingram sub-machine-guns when doing McQueen's dirty work – all in extreme, and very bloody, close-up.

Motors: The (attempted) wages snatch involves a red Jag XJ6 and a white Lancia Flavia. Unique to this film is another silver Granada (registration LYN 266S – a registration used for a BMW in the second film!) for Bill to drive Regan around in. Ronnie Brent uses a yellowish Mercedes. The false cops turn up for Brent in a blue Princess, complete with lights. They also have access to a white Rover. Jack trashes his red Cortina, very much under the influence. He and Bianca are later pursued by a Volvo estate. We see that George's own car is a light-blue Vauxhall Viva. Seriously.

Threads: Can we start with the gold lamé bedspread in the hotel room? One of the Squad has purple- and pink-striped Y-fronts. 'Big Tiny' is wearing a black-and-white scarf (indicating possible support of Notts County, Newcastle United, or, more likely, Fulham!). McQueen's lime-green shirt and stripy tie, Ronnie's gigantic flares and George's suede boots are also yucky.

Jazz Funk?: As befitting a big-screen crime movie, there's plenty of strident snare-drum and timpani percussion. Deprived of the use of Harry South's theme tune, what we get instead is an awful, squeaky synthesizer-based thing that is so instantly forgettable, we've already forgotten it. Later, there's some driving rock guitar at the pub, and the main instrumental passages seem very influenced by *Starsky and Hutch*, with lots of *Shaft* guitar and drop-dead-cool saxophone.

Non-PC Moments: Brent talks about 'wogs in the oil game'. McQueen tells a very off-colour joke about Arabs having lots of food at their weddings 'to keep the flies off the bride'.

You What?: George: 'Guvnor, I think you've gone diddlo!'

Larfs: Regan's response to the sarcastic calls of 'Afternoon, guvnor': 'Shut it!'

Daniels, on 'Big Tiny': 'When they had him down Wood Green nick, he wouldn't come out of his cell, so they sent this big Alsatian in. Do you know, he bust its jaw and threw the bastard out!' George: 'Yeah, I saw the film. *Dog Day Afternoon*!'

Regan, inevitably: 'All right, Tinkerbell, you're nicked!'

Murder inquiry superintendent: 'Now, will you and your sergeant go back to your strip club, or wherever it is you masquerade as police officers.'

Notes: 'Yeah, and we're the Sweeney, and this man is under arrest.' Much more violent than the TV series was ever allowed to be (that amazing sequence of the bullet through the head of the uniform PC, for instance) and, because of that (and because it tries a little too hard to be different), the film doesn't quite pull off its aim of being bigger *and* better than the TV series that spawned it.

Carter is now living in a flat (number 3), with a bathroom that includes a shower but no bath. He gets the *Daily Express* delivered, and picks up a copy of the *Evening Standard* on his way home from work. He quotes from *On the Waterfront* ('I could have been a contender') and makes references to *Dog Day Afternoon* and James Bond. He seems to have been quite good at physics at school. For the second story running, Regan is called 'Regal'. Mention is made of A10, Watergate and the famous Yellow Pages ad ('Let your fingers do the walking'). There's a reference to Regan, like Don Quixote, 'still tilting at windmills'. Burtonshaw is left-handed.

Locations include Baron's Court and Rayner's Park tube stations, Whitehall, Lambeth Bridge and Westminster. The UK television première of this film was on ITV on 22 December 1980 at 9 p.m. It was watched by 14.8 million viewers.

Sweeney 2
Theatrical Release: April 1978

An 108-minute feature film
Euston Films
Based on *The Sweeney*, created by Ian Kennedy Martin

Producer: Ted Childs
Executive Producers: Lloyd Shirley, George Taylor

Music composed by Tony Hatch

Regular Cast: John Thaw (Detective Inspector Jack Regan),
Dennis Waterman (Detective Sergeant George Carter),
John Alkin (Detective Sergeant Tom Daniels),
James Warrior (Detective Constable Jellyneck)

Writer: Troy Kennedy Martin
Director: Tom Clegg

Cast: Denholm Elliott (Jupp), Ken Hutchison (Hill),
Anna Gael (Mrs Hill), Barry Stanton (Big John),
John Flanagan (Willard)[1], David Casey (Goodyear),

---

[1] 'Willie' Willard seems to be a different character from Mathews, whom John Flanagan played in the first season. He's got a cockney accent for a kick-off (Matt was a Scouser).

Derrick O'Connor (Llewellyn), Guy Standeven (Logan),
Brian Gwaspari (White), Frederick Treves (McKyle),
Johnny Shannon (Harry), Clifford Kershaw (Gloria's Father),
Toby Salman (Doctor), Nigel Hawthorne (Dilke),
Lewis Fiander (Gorran), Anna Nygh (Shirley Hicks),
Michael J. Jackson (Soames), Lynn Dearth (Mrs White),
Fiona Mollison (Mrs Haughton),
Sarah Atkinson (Mrs Mead), John Lyons (Mead),
Brian Hall (Haughton), Matthew Scurfield (Jefferson),
Gareth Milne (Bank Teller),
Sebastian Witkin (Skateboarder),
Hubert Rees (Bank Manager), George Innes (Pete Beale),
Roddy McMillan (Collie), Michael O'Hagan (Doyle),
Arthur Cox (Detective), Georgina Hale (Switchboard Girl),
Patrick Malahide (Conway), Max Mason (SPG Constable),
Frank Coda (Commissionaire), Yvon Doval (Mr Mahmoun),
James McManus (Barman), John Vine (PC),
David Gillies (PC), Seretta Wilson (Girl),
Diana Weston (Air Hostess),
George Mikell (Superintendent), Marc Zuber (Anoy),
Joe Zammit-Cardona (Customs Official),
Leon Lissek (Alexandros), Marilyn Finlay (School Teacher),
Seymour Matthews (Harry), Stefan Gryff (Nino),
Michael Scholes (Boy in Bed), Danny Rae (Taxi Driver),
Rosario Serrano (Mrs Konstantikis),
Eamonn Jones (Barman), Alan Ross (Fiddler)

When Superintendent Jupp is sent to trial at the Old Bailey,
his last assignment for Regan is to track down a brutal gang
who specialise in bank jobs and steal precise amounts of
money. One blag goes horribly wrong, but the robberies
continue ...

Keep Your Mincers Peeled For ...: Denholm Elliott and
Nigel Hawthorne surely need no introduction to anyone with
the vaguest knowledge of British TV or film over the last
30 years. Patrick Malahide would later work with Dennis
Waterman again, in *Minder*, as Sergeant Chisholm. Georgina
Hale was Budgie Bird's wife, Jean, in *Budgie*. Stefan Gryff

appeared in Michael J. Bird's beautiful pair of Mediterranean dramas *The Lotus Eaters* and *Who Pays the Ferryman?*. Fiona Mollison played the dangerous Vanessa Bennett in *Strangers*.

Many of the faces here had previously appeared on the TV series, including Barry Stanton ('Faces'), John Lyons ('Bad Apple'), Seymour Matthews ('Regan'), Clifford Kershaw ('Loving Arms'), Johnny Shannon ('In From the Cold' and *Sweeney!*), Lewis Fiander ('In From the Cold'), Frederick Treves ('Visiting Fireman'), Brian Gwaspari ('May'), Lynn Dearth ('Queen's Pawn'), James McManus ('Visiting Fireman'), Brian Hall ('Trap'), and Max Mason ('Loving Arms'), not to mention Ken Hutchison.

George Innes's character, some years before *EastEnders*, is 'Pete Beale'. The kid with the skateboard, rather than being a piece of contemporary background, is actually crucial to the plot. Check out the advert for the Pifco Teamaker. Hands up who bought one of them for their mum, Christmas 1978? There's some Tottenham Hotspur graffiti visible.

Birds: ***** Shirley Hicks is the flat-chested 'lovely lady' with a Nazi fetish. Regan thinks her friend Gorran 'gives her one dressed up as Adolf Hitler'. He has a film of her (he says it's part of his 'private collection') doing a very saucy strip while draped over a Panther Deville. (The piece ends with the rather stern narration, 'Remember, rubber is a natural resource. Recycle rubber!' Maybe that's what public-information films have always been lacking . . .)

Regan fails in his attempt to pull the blonde switchboard operator (he's asleep), but Carter has better luck, phoning his guvnor while in bed with a woman. A sozzled Regan gets to put his face in the bosom of the blonde air stewardess (see *Sweeney!*) before saying how terrible it must be dealing with all the 'drunks, sex fiends [and] villains' on such flights. (Oh, the irony!) Carter has been busy chatting up another stewardess, and mimes the size of her chest with gusto (and, he says with delight, she's a Chelsea supporter!). When Regan and Carter arrive at the Malta 'HQ' of the villains, each of them seems to have a very tasty-looking bikini-wearing wife (several have children, but not a stretch mark in sight!). Mrs Hill later strips for the camera.

On their return, Carter starts seeing a schoolteacher who doesn't like policemen. Llewellyn ogles two extremely well-endowed girls from the car while bragging about his 'hard-on like a milk bottle'. And this was when Viagra wasn't available on the National Health? Yeah, right . . . When Carter and the others break into the hotel room, the young man is in bed with two women (double boobies alert!). At the end, Jack's little black book seems to have drawn a blank: Carter, on the other hand, is considering dumping the schoolteacher for the well-endowed barmaid.

Booze: ***** Carter and some of the others, having investigated a brewery threatened with arsenic poisoning, return to the station somewhat the worse for wear (Carter notes it would have been cheaper to pay the ransom). Regan offers to buy George a drink after telling him that the woman hostage has died in hospital. During the porn film, somebody makes a reference to the famous adverts for Strongbow cider. Regan discusses a bomb in a hotel 'over a large Jack Daniel's' ('You could call it a briefing. On the other hand, you could say it was a piss-up for ten public servants'), and Carter has a vodka and tonic. At the end, the whole Squad get slaughtered in a pub called the George (Regan and Carter are on pints of Young's bitter), and (attempt to) dance a jig or two. Daniels slips something that looks suspiciously like vodka into Robert's orange juice. Bill the driver has got his trousers off, but seems in little danger of being nicked . . .

Shooters: ***** The carnage! This couldn't have had a bigger body count if Sam Peckinpah and Quentin Tarantino had been directing it. At the beginning, Frank Hill goes all Harry Callahan on us: 'You're privileged to be looking down the barrels of a gold-plated, sawn-off Purdey shotgun. Now, as a bank manager, you'll appreciate that any man capable of cutting a gun like that in half wouldn't think twice about cutting you in half.' We see the (messy) result of the blag that went wrong. 'Then the shooters were out. It was like D-Day.' 'What was the score?' 'We got two of 'em.' As Regan

complains bitterly, 'I've never seen so many dead people.'
There's a lot of discussion about what shooters to take on the
final raid (it will have to be the second Purdey, which Hill
saws in half, having lost the other in London), which proves
to be less than a complete success (Hill uses one barrel
to shoot one of his fellow villains and the other on the
car's petrol tank). The conclusion is sickeningly bloody, and
includes a spectacular shotgun suicide.

Motors: The opening shot may be the only appearance in *The
Sweeney* of a (pink) Reliant Robin (for people who can't
afford a proper bike . . .). The first car the Sweeney are
interested in is a 'big Merc, lime-green' (it's probably a
W116-type S-class). Carter is initially seen in a yellow Vauxhall Chevette. If that's bad, poor old Regan is seen driving
himself about in a blue Maxi. In among a *vast* number of
Granadas and Cortinas, watch out for Carter's black Rover P6
(Mk II), a blue police Triumph that crashes through a shop
window, the BMW police and getaway cars, and the lovely
Jag XJ6, used as a getaway car towards the end. We mustn't,
of course, forget Regan's film of the Panther Deville and a
half-naked woman. ('Do you realise every single part on that
has been machined by hand?' enthuses Jellyneck. We presume he's talking about the car . . .) Daniels thinks it's a
Datsun.

Robert – the well-spoken, vegetarian replacement driver –
turns up in a brand-new silver Granada 2.8S (VHK 491S). It
appears a lot in the fourth season as a backup car.

Threads: It's all a question of smalls: watch out for Frank's
rather tight red-and-white trunks, and Bill's disgusting Y-
fronts. We'll also point you in the direction of Shirley's
fluffy bra for extra laughs. Jellyneck, the scruffy little Welsh
Flying Squad constable, appears for the first time (but see
'Pay Off') in his nasty tank top, shirt permanently sticking
out of his pants and leather jacket that has, most definitely,
seen better days . . .

Jazz Funk?: No: the incidental and theme music comes cour-
tesy of Tony (*Crossroads/Neighbours*) Hatch. Say no more

(though, to be fair, the sinister cello opening is quite effective). The little wind-up toy that plays the German national anthem is a triumph of nasty kitsch. Is it just us, or does the choral music on Regan's naughty movie sound like the (modern) theme to the UEFA Champions League? Incidentally, a reference is made to the composer Henry Mancini, and you can see bill posters for the Jam, Split Enz and X-Ray Spex (the villains' car crashes into the latter two!).

Bill the Driver: His finest moment! See **Booze** and **Threads**.

You What?: 'Two-tones' are police sirens.

Corruption is known in the Met as 'the big C'.

This is the only *Sweeney* product to feature the 'f' word (many, many times!).

Larfs: Regan: 'Your client is so bent that it's been impossible to hang his picture straight on the office wall for the past twelve months.' (And, in flashback, we see that he's right!)

Regan: 'Loyalty is like a girdle – it should stretch two ways.'

And (on the gleaming new Sweeney car): 'Bash it up, smash it up, cover it with stickers – Vote Tory, that sort of thing . . . I want the glove compartment filled with Mars bars, wine gums and jelly babies. And ham sandwiches. The sort that come in cellophane packets. And sausage rolls. But no potato crisps. They interfere with transmission.'

Carter, to the schoolteacher: 'What's a virgin, miss?'

Regan: 'No dogs. The last time we had dogs they bit every bleedin' man present but the villains.'

Notes: 'Well, well, if it isn't Jack the lad.' As with the previous film, this is much more violent – and brash in all directions – than the TV show, but the end result has much in its favour. As a showcase for Troy Kennedy Martin's brilliant dialogue and attention to detail (the procedural aspects, as one should expect of the creator of *Z Cars*, are very well handled), it can't be bettered. There's a great contrast, for instance, between the awful aftermath of the robbery that went wrong, and the earlier scenes of the relaxed Sweeney officers and drivers tucking into bacon butties. Loath though we are to agree with Leslie Halliwell, the conclusion is, however, a bit of a disappointment (the villains are dealt with in scenes of precious little tension). Mind you, Regan's reaction to Hill's death – first shambling incomprehension, then a desperate attempt to wash his face clean – is memorable, as are the closing moments in the pub.

Carter's call sign is Oscar Charlie 2-5; Regan's is Oscar Charlie 1-1; Daniels is Oscar Charlie 1-3. Superintendent Jupp (the film indicates that he is Regan's most recent boss) is likely to be imprisoned for seven years on corruption charges. It's stated that Regan has worked for him for the past three years (we wonder, was the role originally written for Frank Haskins?). Regan borrowed a German 1945-issue helmet from Gorran (who wants it back): see the fourth season's 'Hard Men' for the next instalment concerning this item! It is implied that Big John is Regan's usual driver (and not Bill, even though we see the latter driving him at the start of the film: just to confuse matters, the implication from Regan's conversation with the doctor is that Bill the driver is actually called Jim the driver in this film!). Big John loses a foot in the abortive attempt to stop the robbery of the National Metropolitan Bank (Daniels holds a collection for him into which Regan puts what looks like two tenners). In Malta Regan says he is aware of the UK law that concerns a solicitor being present during the questioning of suspects (too bad he rarely remembers this fact back on his home turf!).

There is a mention of Sexton Blake's detective novels. Jupp quotes the first Baron Acton (1834–1902): 'Absolute power corrupts absolutely.' Jellyneck's 'Evenin' all' was George Dixon's opening line for 24 years on *Dixon of Dock Green*.

Some of the filming took place at Hanger Lane tube station on the Central Line. *Sweeney 2*'s UK television première was on ITV on 21 December 1981 at 9.15 p.m., and it got 16.1 million viewers.

Fourth Season

Fourteen 60-minute episodes
Euston Films/Thames Television
Created by Ian Kennedy Martin

Associate Producer: Mary Morgan
Producer: Ted Childs
Executive Producers: Lloyd Shirley, George Taylor

Title music by Harry South

Regular Cast: John Thaw (Detective Inspector Jack Regan),
Dennis Waterman (Detective Sergeant George Carter),
Garfield Morgan (Detective Chief Inspector Frank Haskins,
44–46, 50–51, 53–54),
James Warrior (Detective Constable Jellyneck, 42–43, 52),
Benjamin Whitrow (Detective Chief Inspector Braithwaite,
42–43, 50, 51,[1] 52),
Roger Davidson (Major Chapman, 42, 52),
John Alkin (Detective Sergeant Tom Daniels, 43–45, 50, 53),
Nick Brimble (Detective Constable Gerry Burtonshaw, 48),
Sheila Reid[2] (Doreen Haskins, 53)

41: 'Messenger of the Gods'
7 September 1978

Writer: Trevor Preston
Director: Terry Green

Cast: Diana Dors (Mrs Rix), Malcolm McFee (Lukey),
Dawn Perllman (Linda Rix), James Ottaway (Uncle Billy),
Richard Adams (Ray), Andrew Mussell (Rick),
Rosemary Martin (Mrs Lipman),
Fanny Carby (Dot Plummer), Michael Melia (Rudd),

[1] Uncredited.
[2] Character played by Anne Stallybrass in the second season.

Derek Martin (Spooner), John Judd (Sergeant),
Rosie Collins (Gloria), Michael Tarn (Charlie Pearce),
Timothy Kightly (Vicar Dennison),
Bernard Stone (Mr Lipman), Helen Keating (Cathy),
Patrick Hannaway (Bernie), Cliff Diggins (Olly),
Del Baker (Sid), Chris Webb (Arthur)

Carter's snout has a whisper about the theft of 200 flasks of mercury. A name is in the frame: Lukey Sparrow, the 'Clapham Casanova'. But Lukey is about to get married, and his arrest brings Regan and Carter into conflict with something much worse than hard-nosed criminals – a fire-breathing mother-in-law.

Keep Your Mincers Peeled For . . .: Diana Dors, once 'Britain's answer to Marilyn Monroe' but, by the 70s, the star of *Queenie's Castle* and other second-division sitcoms. Michael Melia would later play Eddie Royle in *EastEnders*, while Derek Martin's most memorable role was as Detective Pyall in the BBC's incredibly violent *Law and Order*.

Some of the graffiti on the wall as Carter chases Spooner says CHELSEA and HUDSON IS GOD (a reference to Alan Hudson, the Chelsea and England midfield star of the early 1970s – he'd been playing for Stoke City since 1974, however, so it must have been there for a while!).

Birds: *** It's inevitable that somebody who 'carries his brains in his trousers' like Lukey will be surrounded by big-chested beauties. He chats up two little punkettes in his first scene, and gets more than a chip pan as a wedding present from his future wife's friend Gloria. And then there's the leggy blonde he hitches a lift with at the end. Cath Clayton hurriedly repositions her negligée when Regan and Carter burst in. The man who spots Lukey watches a rather chunky girl playing tennis, and in the next scene Gloria finds it rather hard to keep her skirt from blowing up in the wind.

Booze: *** Jack spends the opening scene preparing for a Social and Athletics Club speech with a whisky bottle in his hand (he thinks he sounds 'like a sauced-up old pudding').

Shooters: No guns, but there are some great fight sequences – including Carter and Spooner going for it with a rubber hose and a spade respectively (during which George gets kneed in the balls). The fight in the park is similarly well-staged (albeit with some well-OTT sound effects).

Motors: This story sees the introduction of a new brown Granada Ghia for the Flying Squad (registration number: RHJ 997R). The bronzed blonde who picks up Jakey drives an open-top Mercedes.

Threads: Jack's blue dressing gown (he looks good in a dinner suit, though). His taste in 'work clothes' – a light-blue suit – seems to have improved somewhat. Lukey's brown velvet suit and wide-collared shirt (not to mention his general Stan Bowles look). Lily Rix's fake-leopardskin coat.

Jazz Funk?: There's some really funky bass-and-drums stuff as George investigates various condemned buildings. And, the comedy snare-drum ending with Regan and Carter running away from Lily Rix.

Non-PC Moment: Mrs Rix: 'I hope he's had his hair cut . . . I don't want him looking like a poof in the photographs.'

You What?: Lukey: 'I'm getting hitched tomorrow . . . Straight. Clean fingernails, best whistle . . . To Linda Rix, daughter of Stanley, unfortunately deceased, and Lily, just unfortunate! . . . I've got me orders, Mr Regan. Get the barnet notched, pick up the whistle. . .'

'Go and give his drum a spin, George.'

Regan: 'Look, slag, I don't give a toss who you have in your bed. But don't you try and run your numbers on me. Now, you know something about that blag. You've got a simple choice. You tell me what you know, or you get your arms broken when the old man comes out.'

Regan: 'I know for a fact those two Herberts did time in the same college.'

Rudd: 'If that little snot's grassed us, I am gonna personally put his lights out.'

Rudd: 'There's a century in it for the face that spots him.'

Uncle Billy on his aching feet: 'Me dogs are barking, Lil.'

Spooner, on Lukey: 'That horny little bastard who grassed me. He's earnt himself a spankin'!'

Carter: 'Nearly had me bleedin' swede off.'

Larfs: 'Well laugh, y'bastards, that one cost me a fiver.' Regan, practising for his stand-up routine for the Flying Squad Social and Athletics Club dinner, tells a couple of halfway decent jokes, particularly the one about the recently promoted Alsatian. And he impersonates Tommy Cooper.

Lukey gives Mrs Plummer a rather phallic cactus. Mrs P: 'I'll put it in the lav. It'll be nice and moist in there.'

Regan: 'If we find out you're fibbing, Lukey, I'm gonna come down so hard on you, you'll have to reach up to tie your shoelaces . . .'

Carter (after the fight): 'Your nose is bleeding.' Regan: 'Must be the altitude.'

Uncle Billy on his recently arrested nephews: 'What a pair of tearaways, eh?' To which Regan responds: 'Nick him an' all!'

Notes: 'Who the hell are you?' 'The Sweeney, watch your mouth!' The closest *The Sweeney* ever got to pure sitcom. A brilliantly funny episode – the scene of Regan and Carter turning up at the Rix household and arresting nearly everybody is priceless. And a quick word about Uncle Billy – he's in only three scenes but he's the best thing in the episode.

There are references to Oddjob from *Goldfinger*, *Jaws* and the Ali Shuffle (Muhammed Ali's famed boxing-dance). From Dot Plummer's description of the horror film she was watching (Christopher Lee's in it, along with a severed hand), she could be referring to *Dr Terror's House of Horrors* (Amicus, 1964).

This is the first appearance of the series' new title sequence: Regan and Carter (to the sound of a ringing bell) chase a criminal (played by the stunt coordinator, Peter Brayham, in a pair of villainous dark glasses) prior to beating the crap out of him. The episode title appears after Regan's fist smacks straight into the camera. Shot through a triangular prism, the effect is spoilt as Thaw and Waterman pause (*not* in freeze-frame!) as they emerge from their car so that their name captions can appear – watch out for Waterman's tie wobbling slightly! (In the episodes in which Haskins appears the sequence is slightly different, and Garfield Morgan at least *does* get a freeze-frame as he gets out of a different car).

The closing credits, which also feature the kaleidoscopic look, are much better – Regan and Carter wander (rather sadly) around Soho to the accompaniment of the melancholic, slower version of the theme music. The suggestion is of two lonely men in search of something to do. It ends with Regan throwing down his cigarette packet and grinding it with his foot on the pavement. Impressively downbeat.

42: 'Hard Men'
14 September 1978

Writer: Troy Kennedy Martin
Director: Graham Baker

Cast: James Cosmo (Detective Sergeant Davy Freeth),
Ronnie Stewart Preston (Ross), Jonathan Carr (Stronnach),
Brian Hoskin (Bramley), Ronnie Letham (Hodgy Laing),
Alan Norton (Gibson), Michael Beint (Dubbin),
Julian Gough (Guards Officer), Janet Ellis (Marge's Friend),
Miranda Forbes (Maggie's Mother),
Norman Lumsden (Sir Henry), Ian Ricketts (Boyd),
David Stockton (PC), Natalie Pennington (Maggie),
Sara Simmons (Dinner Party Guest),
David Drummond (Dinner Party Guest),
Vickie Climas (Sir Henry's Wife), Peggy Bullock (Old Lady)

Detective Sergeant Davy Freeth from Clydeside CID has come to London in search of three 'hard men' who, it is whispered, are planning a kidnapping. But the case quickly turns to farce as Jack's overstretched squad become involved.

Keep Your Mincers Peeled For . . .: The memorable scene in which Regan wakes up in bed next to a girl wearing a

German stormtrooper helmet. Yes, that *is* the future *Blue Peter* presenter Janet Ellis!

A visible headline in the *Evening Standard* notes 'BANKS IN INTEREST RATE WAR'.

Birds: *** Regan and Carter, somewhat animatedly, discuss the photo of a 'very tasty' woman, who turns out to be Freeth's wife. Regan's most recent girlfriend was called Marge but she's gone to Africa without telling him. He beds her (very young) friend, Suzie, who's looking after the flat (Jack says he wants to recover a valuable antique which he left behind!). George buys Freeth a porn mag to read on the train back to Glasgow.

Booze: * There's a can of Tartan Export next to the bed when Regan wakes up.

Shooters: ** Carter and Regan, checking their standard handguns, give each other surprised looks as Freeth pulls out a lethal-looking service revolver when they go to make the arrest. 'Get the chaps together, Jelly. We need shooters.' The execution of Ross comes as quite a shock.

Motors: The Flying Squad drive a silver Granada 2.8 S and a blue Cortina. Dubbin has a white BMW.

Threads: Ross's tie and Stronnach's suede jacket (though his sideburns are even more spectacular).

You What?: Regan: 'I'll get you the tin tack for that, mate!'
　　DS Freeth: 'Open up, it's the pollis!'
　　Carter: 'Guvnor, I think we got the wrong gaff.'
　　Freeth: 'That Regan's only interested in booze and hog-magandy.' (Use your imagination!)

Larfs: Carter: 'They left without making the bed. The reason could be there's a dead man in it.'
　　Regan (talking on the phone): 'We've got enough on our hands; we've got a dead man here. Oh sure, natural causes: got a knife stuck in his belly. Course, it could have been hari-kari.'
　　Regan: 'There's only been a break-in at Windsor Castle.'
Carter: 'They haven't nicked the Corgis?!'

Regan: 'Where you come from, they batter everything from fried fish to bleedin' grandmothers.' Freeth: 'Where I come from, we don't batter down doors without a warrant.'

Regan: 'I've just about had enough of this, you Scottish git!' Freeth: 'Isn't that the usual attitude for the Met, patronising in the extreme? All the wogs start south of Calais, and civilisation stops north of Watford!'

Notes: 'These Jocks are cunning bastards, aren't they?' A joyfully amusing episode, with a lot of very serious stuff, but with almost every scene having something uproariously funny about it. It includes the best *Sweeney* comedy sequence as Carter, Regan and Freeth break into the wrong flat, find themselves in the middle of a dinner party, apologise and leave!

George reads the *Daily Mirror*. He makes reference to the traditional song 'D'ye Ken John Peel' and to Lord Rockingham's XI's 'Hoots Mon!' His Italian, at best, is pretty phonetic. One of Ross's killers reads from the Old Testament (1 Chronicles 10:13), predating *Pulp Fiction* by over fifteen years. Locations include Euston station.

43: 'Drag Act'
21 September 1978

Writer: Ted Childs
Director: Tom Clegg

Cast: Katherine Fahy (Julie Kingdom),
Albert Welling (Mike Seton), Patrick Malahide (Mason),
Peter Kerrigan (Bowyer), Roger Hume (Lockhart),
Derek Deadman (Curry), John Rolfe (Brookford),
David Atkins (Marriot), John Hartley (Chief Inspector),
David Foxxe (Cyril), Oliver Smith (Lorry Driver),
Vivienne Johnson (Mavis), Rachel Dix (Marriot's Girlfriend)

Investigating a whisper of a blag, George Carter encounters Julie Kingdom, a saucy young minx of a PC who makes solving his case her top priority. Bad move. If there's one thing Jack Regan and his bosses can't stand, it's the Firm being made a laughing stock . . .

Keep Your Mincers Peeled For . . .: Peter Kerrigan's moment of glory was as George Malone in *The Boys From the Blackstuff*. For Patrick Malahide, see *Sweeney 2*.

Birds: *** Regan is currently seeing a lady called Mavis, who appears to have accompanied him to a force party (judging from the paper hat she's wearing, and Jack's tux). Apparently, she later passed out while doing the conga. Jack and George, emerging from Cyril's sauna club, stare admiringly at a passing girl's bottom. Carter says he's had about six baths before his date with Julie. Marriot's 'niece' wears an outrageously cleavage-revealing dress. Curry, the farmer, tells George and Tom Daniels about a trick he once saw a girl in a club in Amsterdam do with a cigar ('Was it lit?').

Booze: *** Marriot's girlfriend returns to his car with two bottles of vodka. On their date, George buys Julie a white wine, and a bottle of lager for himself, but he doesn't get to drink it. They later have a glass of red wine each. Daniels drinks a can of Skol on the stakeout (during which a milk bottle is passed around the van for the Squad to piss in!).

Shooters: * Curry threatens Seton with a double-barrelled shotgun.

Motors: Marriot's Rolls-Royce Silver Shadow is a suitably gauche bright-gold colour. A Day-Glo-yellow Rover and the usual Sweeney light-brown Granada pursue the Bedford lorry, with, as they might have said in the *TV Times*, devastating results . . . Marriot is taken away in a grey Cortina (it's the same car as seen in 'Messenger of the Gods', but it's no longer blue – one stunt too many, perhaps?).

Threads: Even by his own standards, Regan's tie in this episode is enormous. It hardly goes with his lime-green shirt. Daniels's denim flares are similarly disgusting.

***Shaft* Guitar?:** Mavis sings 'Falling in Love Again' in a thick German accent. There's a romantic piano theme to accompany George and Julie walking through the park, and in the night scene down by the Thames. They are planning to go to a gig, seemingly at Ronnie Scott's Jazz Club (in Soho) – billboards outside the club advertise a forthcoming gig by the jazz giant Dizzy Gillespie.

You What?: Marriot: 'She's a bit mutton. Fell off her bike as a kid . . .'

Regan: 'George, you are not doing naughties on your own doorstep, are you?'

Regan, finding Marriot's fingerprints on the stolen brandy: 'He couldn't keep his thieving Germans off it, could he?'

Larfs: Regan to Cyril: 'You made Uncle Jack and Young Georgie look a right pair of lemons!'

Cyril (looking admiringly at George): 'You're welcome here any time. Looks as if you could do with a bit of quick friction.'

Braithwaite on Carter's impetuousness: 'Hasty? He was bloody supersonic!'

Carter to Curry: 'Listen, you haven't grown anything since the Flood. You're even VAT-exempted in the Domesday Book.'

George tells Daniels a joke about an Irish football manager who had the pitch flooded so he could 'bring his sub on'!

Notes: 'If he hears one more mention of Julie Kingdom, he's gonna have you out at Elstree directing traffic and wearing a tall hat!' If there's one thing guaranteed to exasperate Jack Regan, it's a woman getting in between him and George Carter! This is a cracking episode, full of lovely moments (the outstanding car stunt, for instance), which help you forget that many important strands of the plot develop off screen. Really funny in places, too (Seton's incompetent observation of Marriot, Carter's dreadful Humphrey Bogart impression).

The (fake) headline in the *Evening News* is 'OLD FOLKS TERRORISED BY LONDON FLYING SQUAD'.

44: 'Trust Red'
28 September 1978

Writer: Richard Harris
Director: Douglas Camfield

Cast: John Ronane (Red), John J. Carney (Eric),
Sara Clee (Jo), Gretchen Franklin (Charlady),
Nigel Humphreys (Con), Hilary Crae (Jean),
Anthony O'Donnell (Maurice), Tim Thomas (Billy Boy),
Alec Linstead (Optician)

'Red' Redgrave, a former soldier turned cat burglar, sees one of his young firm killed, falling from a roof after a factory blag. At 45, Red is haunted by the feeling that he's getting too old for the game. But will he find a sympathetic ear in Jack Regan?

Keep Your Mincers Peeled For . . .: John Ronane's next job was to switch sides, playing Sergeant Singer in *Strangers*. Gretchen Franklin was Alf Garnett's original 'silly moo' in the pilot episode of *Till Death Us Do Part*, but most readers will know her better for her performance as Ethel Skinner in *EastEnders*.

Birds: ** George thinks he's managed to pull the 'two riches' at the bar for himself and Jack. Regan isn't interested, leading to his criticism of George's 'overactive finger'!

Booze: * At George's birthday booze-up in the pub, most of the lads are on pints of bitter, but Regan's drinking a whisky as ever. At George's gaff, they share cans of light ale.

Shooters: None, though the main fight involves a broken bottle, which is dangerous enough.

Motors: Eric runs a second-hand-car business, and meets the others in an aquamarine BMW.

Threads: Billy Boy's red balaclava and bright-green trainers. Jo's candy-striped maternity frock. Jack's patterned tie (and his lime-green shirt puts in another appearance). Eric's platform-heeled shoes. Daniels's green turtleneck sweater. And there's a great close-up of Regan's flares.

Jazz Funk?: There's some spacy music on the radio in Regan's flat as Carter cooks breakfast, and some louder, more rocky stuff in the pub (watch out for flyposters in the pub advertising a forthcoming gig by the Lurkers!). There's a funky slap-bass riff to accompany Carter and Regan chasing Burrows.

Non-PC Moment: George tells a joke about an Irishman with a two-piece jigsaw who sent it back because it didn't have a picture on the box!

You What?: Eric: 'What about skirt . . .?' Red: 'There was no one special, no one he was cased up with.'
   George on his picking-up abilities: 'It was all there, I tell ya. Stone ginger!'
   Eric: 'So, you drew a visit? Who hasn't?'

Larfs: Jo on Regan: 'You're like a clockwork ferret.'

Notes: 'It's all a game . . . Cops and robbers . . .' An excellent episode. In Redgrave we have a near mirror-image of Regan, with only a sliver of glass dividing law from lawlessness. Both men seem to have realised that they're getting too old for the game they're playing, with Regan at his most philosophical and world-weary, turning down the possibility of quick and easy sex, and later admitting to Carter that he drinks and smokes too much, that he's out of shape, and that he's starting to think about the consequences of the situations he gets into. Many poignant moments add to the mix, and the ending is a choker, suitably embellished by Douglas Camfield's clever direction.

45: 'Nightmare'
5 October 1978

Writer: Ranald Graham
Director: David Wilkes

Cast: Paul Antrim (Farrell), Tony Rohr (Flynn),
Barry Philips (Keith Wilson),
David Gillies (Norman Charles), Lea Brodie (Jane),
Kenneth Watson (Horrocks), J.G. Devlin (Hay),
Enid Irvin (Mrs Charles), David Ellison (Dutchman),
Alfred Maron (Stirk), Linda Brill (Maire),
Ritchie Stewart (Café Owner)

What are the chances of two different firms going after the
same lorryload of cigars? As likely as winning the pools. But
then, as Carter points out, someone does win the pools, every
week . . .

Keep Your Mincers Peeled For . . . : David Ellison was
Sergeant Joe Beck on *Juliet Bravo*.

The newspaper story below the 'LONDON HOSPITAL DRAMA'
piece is headlined 'INFLATION AT 4-YEAR LOW'. Watch out also
for another example of that most 70s of sporting equipment, a
skateboard.

Birds: *** Jane is Jack's latest, er, partner. As well as having
a precognitive dream, she's a bit of a health freak, and a
nympho to boot. Jack says he should be rewarded for keeping
her away from happily married men. (Whatever it is they
get up to in bed together, Regan considers it 'dangerous'!)
George, on the other hand, gets a bit carried away describing
an advert for cigars involving a bra-less girl in a wet T-shirt.
(His mother is threatening to write to Mary Whitehouse – see
also 'Hearts and Minds'!) He seems to be referring to the
famous series of Castella adverts of the era.

Booze: * 'Let's get down there, I could do with a pint!' The
usual swigs of Scotch from office paper cups. Carter slips
Regan a bottle of whisky while he's in hospital. For most of
the episode, though, Regan is more interested in tea than
booze!

Shooters: **** The Dutch trucker carries a Parabellum
Luger pistol, and there's an almighty kerfuffle in the café.
Only Wilson survives, and Farrell later shoots him with a

small revolver. The two Irishmen aim to swap the cocaine for five high-velocity rifles with laser sights. When Haskins hears of this, his response is unequivocal: 'I want twelve men, fully armed, and five cars outside the front, now. I want tear gas, masks, walkie-talkies, loud hailers, full ambulance facilities, the lot.' Shame they don't turn up in time, and it's left to Carter and Regan to apprehend the would-be terrorists (and Farrell's distraught younger sister): cue big shoot-out.

Motors: Farrell and Flynn trash their (stolen) brownish XJ6 near the beginning. They are later seen in another, newer, Jag.

Threads: Regan's parka and Carter's tight leather jacket are no match for Bill the driver's thoroughly nasty green pullover.

Jazz Funk?: There is some sort of rock music playing on the radio in the background of the motorway caff, which leads into a rather funky theme as the Dutch trucker eats his breakfast. There's some (inevitable) jig-type music in the Irish boozer.

Non-PC Moment: Regan: 'I'm taking a leak, Seamus, and next time I see your face, I'll do it on that!'

You What?: Daniels: 'They're moving the joanna.'
  'Why top a bloke for a few lousy smokes?'

Larfs: Regan (pointing to Haskins's coffee): 'That's the caffeine, you know. Worse than marijuana, that stuff.' Haskins (grumpily): 'And very nearly as expensive.'
  Jane (describing her dream): 'You were trapped in a narrow place, and there was this huge thing, bearing down on you to crush you to death.' Regan: 'Sounds like the barmaid at my local. Did it have a blue hair rinse and look like George III?'

Notes: 'You're in danger, Jack, terrible danger.' Very amusing – particularly the fun and games had with the tracking unit in the commode! – but with a tension underpinning the proceedings. The scenes in the Irish pub in Kilburn are a delight. Come to think of it, we're sure we've both been to that boozer ... There's a lovely moment as Regan and Carter munch their ham sandwiches while watching the makeshift landing strip, and every scene with Jane is a delight. The surreal dream sequence at the start (and the way it crops up throughout the episode) is about as close as *The Sweeney* ever came to telefantasy.

Jane says lemon-grass tea is rejuvenating (well, it seems to work – twice!), and that Jack's planets are in a 'difficult configuration', which sounds about right. Jack hasn't smoked in six days, and has even, it seems, started going to the gym. It's got to be said, he's a lot more pleasant for it! He's stolen a tracking device from C7. Regan's grandmother was Irish (his Irish heritage had been hinted at on occasions but this is the first time it's confirmed).

Jeff is selling five cigars for a pound.

46: 'Money, Money, Money'
12 October 1978

Writer: Trevor Preston
Director: Sid Roberson

Cast: Edward Judd (Eddie Monk),
Vilma Hollingbery (Anne Monk), Tina Martin (Kath),
Glyn[1] Owen (Wally Hough), Michael Culver (Dave Leeford),
John Cater (Slemen), Linal Haft (Fischer),
James Bree (Saxby), William Simons (Pope),
Christine Shaw (Mrs Norris)

A 'retired villain', Eddie Monk, celebrates winning £58,000 on the pools with Jack and George. However, Monk's chequered past makes him a prime target for blackmail ...

Keep Your Mincers Peeled For ...: Edward Judd was Gavin Grant, the star of ABC's *Intrigue*, and had a major role

---
[1] Name misspelt as 'Glynn' on end credits.

in *Flambards*, but most viewers will recognise him from a very famous public-information film about road safety ('Think Once. Think Twice. Think Bike!'). Glyn Owen was a soap-opera veteran, appearing in *Emergency – Ward 10*, *The Brothers* (as Edward Hammond), and, later, *Howards' Way* (as Jack Rolfe). Michael Culver played the real-life spy Donald Maclean in Ian Curteis's *Philby, Burgess and Maclean*. Fans of the excellent *Secret Army* will remember him as the smooth Luftwaffe chief, Brandt. John Cater's supporting roles occurred in a huge number of series, including *Virgin of the Secret Service*, *The Duchess of Duke Street* and *I, Claudius*. William Simons, with a much larger beard than the one he sports here, was Constable Thackery in Granada's handsome Victorian detective series, *Cribb*.

There's some Chelsea graffiti visible in a back alley.

Birds: ** George goes out with Kath Monk, who works as an estate agent's secretary. She's a pretty, chubby blonde who occasionally wears glasses. Frankly, she's much too sweet for a man like George Carter, though at least he doesn't laugh at her when she tells him she's a vegetarian, which surprises her. Jack has known her since she was a little girl and must have mentioned George to her, because she asks if he was the policeman whose wife died (see 'Hit and Run'). Jack says George is 'over it' now.

The (unseen) secretary on the first floor of the police building apparently has a chesty arthritis problem (Regan mimes to show just how big the problem is!). Eileen Norris wears a black bra under a semitransparent blouse.

Booze: ** Regan, Carter and Haskins have a whisky in Haskins's office. 'So what are we going to do now, Frank?' asks Regan, after hearing that a case they've been working on for months has just collapsed. 'Finish the bottle,' says Haskins. 'Yeah, why not? Your bottle.' 'No, as a matter of fact, it's yours. I borrowed it from your desk.' (You'd have thought Haskins would have learnt his lessons after the events of 'Trojan Bus'.) Eddie's local pub seems to be called the Bird in Hand.

When Regan meets Wally in the pub, he's drinking (what

looks like) a half of bitter. Both Anne and Pope drink large amounts of gin in this episode.

Shooters: None. Worth watching, though, for Regan's incompetent attempt to arrest Fischer (and then the way he later kicks the crud out of him for running down his friend Eddie).

Motors: Slemen drives a muddy Renault 16 ('white, foreign,' according to an eyewitness); Fischer has an Austin 1800 (complete with white leather upholstery!). It's 'green' according to Dave Leeford, but it looks black to us.

Threads: Fischer's horrid blue denim flares. Ugh! Both Regan's and Eddie Monk's trousers are of a similarly impressive girth, but they don't catch the attention in quite the same way.

Jazz Funk?: Listen out for a rather nauseating tinkling theme as Carter and Regan search for Eddie. There's a much funkier riff in evidence as they pursue Alec Slemen.

Bill the Driver: A nifty little exchange with Jack on the perils of soft drinks.

You What?: Regan: 'Every time I go into my bank, they look at me like I'm about to blag the place!'

Haskins: 'The legal eagles are worried. They think he's got a shake on.'

Eddie: 'You never did have my funnel. I'd like to kick his lungs in.'

And: 'You bottle on me Alec, and I'll give you real grief.'

Larfs: Regan to Kath concerning George: 'Has he told you he's a practising heterosexual?'

Regan: 'What's up, Frank? You've got a face as long as a baker's round.'

Kath: ' "You can't be optimistic with a misty optic." ... It's an old Balham proverb.'

Notes: 'Eddie used to say you were the only copper he knew who didn't make him feel like a thief.' Another excellent Preston script, but the structure is all over the place. Why the prominence given to the intimidated suspect in an unconnected case? And why draw that strand of the plot to a conclusion with an off-screen reference to goings-on in Bristol? Not that we've got anything against Bristol, you understand.

The National Anglian Bank puts in an appearance (see 'The Bigger They Are'). This may be a completely different company from the National Anglia Bank seen in 'Night Out' and 'Contact Breaker'. Wally 'taught Jack Regan everything he knows'. He says he was 'the best bastard thief-taker there was', but he turned to drink when his wife died of cancer. His scenes are rather moving, and there's a vague implication that this is how Jack Regan might end up in a few years' time. George spends most of the episode looking for a new flat (a really dreadful one, with 'hot and cold running rust', is going for fourteen grand). In the end, Carter decides to stay where he is. The title is, presumably, a reference to the Abba song (Anne Monk mentions singing it, but, conspicuously, she doesn't).

47: 'Bait'
19 October 1978

Writer: Trevor Preston
Director: Sid Roberson

Cast: George Sewell (Vic Tolman), Barbara Ewing (Joan), Di Trevis (Lynn), Edward Peel (Lennie), Arthur Cox (Roan), Eric Dodson (Mr Dodds), Alan Hunter (Stoddard), Steven Barnes (Dr Marland), Judy Buxton (Salesgirl), Frederick Bennett (Gate Keeper), Alan Leith (Sergeant Stern), Diana Rowan (Traffic Warden), Michael Brodie (Guard), Simone Cowdrey (Little Girl)

A woman involved in a car crash is adamant that she does not want to go to hospital, and underlines her intentions with a gun. The Sweeney conclude that Vic Tolman has broken out of prison, and he and his missus are performing jobs just to annoy the police . . .

Keep Your Mincers Peeled For . . .: George Sewell spent much of the early 70s in demand after his star-making performances as Alec Freeman in *UFO* and as the proto-Jack Regan, Alan Craven, in *Special Branch*. These days he tends towards comedy, playing Jasper Carrott and Robert Powell's boss in *The Detectives*. Barbara Ewing is probably best remembered as the impressively cleavaged Agnes Fairchild in *Brass*. Edward Peel had semiregular roles in *Emmerdale Farm* (as Tom Merrick) and *Juliet Bravo*.

Look out for George Carter reading a sex encyclopedia, a Mink de Ville LP cover in Joan's flat, a safety-training poster in the offices where Lynn works, and a chunky 70s reel-to-reel tape recorder.

Birds: * George is clearly taken by the girl in blue in the toy shop. 'I wouldn't mind toying with that,' he says.

Booze: * In the station, Carter makes himself and Regan a coffee (Regan's is 'without' – sugar, presumably). Later on, they drink whisky from cups. Vic sends Lennie out to the offy for whisky, gin and two bottles of champagne.

Shooters: *** Lynn and Vic both have pistols. Even Bill the driver is tooled up ready for some shooting at the end.

Motors: Lynn Tolman is driving a Mini estate at the beginning. Lennie is very disappointed with Vic's latest stolen car, a brown Ford Zodiac. 'I like Jags,' he says. 'They're my favourite.' Tolman says the Zodiac is 'sweet as a nut . . . All the Jags I saw was rubbish.' Tolman and Lennie *cycle* out of the factory they've just robbed and towards the waiting car.

Threads: Lynn's tweed jacket and long woolly scarf make her look a bit like Tom Baker in *Doctor Who*. This is something of a turtleneck-sweater convention: half a dozen are on display and they're all different colours!

Jazz Funk?: There's nasty rock 'n' roll on the radio as Lennie prepares some tea for Lynn. The Group 4 guards arrive at the factory to dramatic trumpet-and-piano music, complete with an OTT sudden ending.

Bill the Driver: Carter, on Regan: 'He's going to drop us right in it one of these days.' Bill: 'Not many.'

Non-PC Moment: Both Regan and Carter are very mean about 'uncle Joan', who they suspect is a 'dyke'. After all, she's been inside, so it stands to reason, right?

You What?: Policeman (on Tolman): 'Yeah, we had him in here once, skip. He's a hard lot. Bet he can lay some down when he's on the malice.'

Carter: 'What do we do, clock her? Put an ear on the telephone?'

Regan: 'You should see your boat . . .'

Vic: 'I've got the Flash Jacks by the short hairs, and I'm gonna give them the treatment!'

Larfs: Lynn, with gun, to ambulanceman: 'Get your mate to stop this bastard!' His response: 'Bloody stroll on . . .'

Regan, after Carter has estimated he will have to do door-to-door on around two hundred flats: 'Hope you've got a sharp pencil, Sherlock!'

Vic's moment of angry poetry about the police: 'I hate 'em, 'cos they're filth. Lying, grafting, thieving lice. They're all so bent they wouldn't know an honest man if he pissed on their boots. I hate 'em 'cos they're stupid and greedy, and bloody vicious with it . . .'

Notes: ' "Maybe" isn't good enough when you're dealing with a vicious slag like Tolman.' A bit of a nothing episode, complete with limp ending of futile bravado. Vic and Lynn are a great pair of characters, however, and some of the dialogue is Preston at his very best.

Regan compares Vic Tolman and Lynn Hurst to Bonnie and Clyde. He put Tolman away three years ago, on a twelve stretch. Tolman recently escaped, seriously injuring a prison officer. Since then, they've done three jobs, netting themselves £42,000 in Sunderland, £38,000 in Doncaster and £60,000 in Cardiff. In the London job we see them pull off, they steal over £82,000.

Haskins is mentioned three times, but not seen.

48: 'The Bigger They Are'
26 October 1978

Writer: Tony Hoare
Director: Mike Vardy

Cast: Colin Jeavons (Gold), Jenny Runacre (Sharon),
Raymond Skipp (Collins), Tony Steedman (Masterson),
Donald Burton (Grey), Colin McCormack (Wade),
Ian Collier (Logan), Trevor Thomas (Leroy),
Richard Wilson (DCI Anderson),
Richard Hampton (Barnes), John Carlin (Pierce)

Brutal events in Malaya in 1953 come back to haunt some of
those involved in a village massacre. Needless to say, the
Sweeney get their snouts in on the action, too.

Keep Your Mincers Peeled For ...: The great Colin
Jeavons has a huge CV that includes work as diverse as
Kinvig, *The Hitch-Hiker's Guide to the Galaxy*, *Sherlock
Holmes* (as Inspector Lestrade), Dennis Potter's *Blue Remembered Hills*, and *Billy Liar*. Richard Wilson spent much of his
career playing dour Scotsmen in sitcoms before *Only When I
Laugh* and (later) *One Foot in the Grave* catapulted him to
superstardom ... playing dour Scotsmen in both. In this
episode he plays, yes, a dour Scotsman. For Tony Steedman,
see 'The Placer'.

Birds: * Sharon, the blonde model girlfriend of Leroy the
photographer. And the tasty monochrome results: 'Artistic
poses for people who've got repressions.'

Booze: * Champagne during the opening scenes at a society
party. Gold spends much of the episode knocking back the
Smirnoff. Jack drinks Scotch in the office from a paper cup.

Shooters: * Masterson takes a sub-machine-gun (an Uzi?)
from the safe prior to the raid on the bank vaults. It and a
handgun are used during the escape from the scene.

Motors: Collins drives a green Cavalier. He is observed by the two mercenaries in a white Commer van and in a green Allegro. At the end, Masterson arrives at Gold's house in a green Princess.

Threads: Sharon's dreadful multicoloured dress, worn with what looks like a public-school tie. The jackets in this episode are particularly bad (see George's leather effort, and Gerry Burtonshaw's suede one). Leroy Gardner's white strides are the business, especially up against Harry Collins's flares.

Jazz Funk?: The opening discordant touches of synthesizer are vaguely disturbing, despite the nice percussion. Contrast this with the awful tinkly piano stuff from the party.

Non-PC Moments: Given the fact that *The Sweeney* is a series about a pair of London-based police officers during the 1970s, one can excuse a few bits of casual racism by Jack and George on the grounds of maintaining realism. However, just occasionally, it all goes a bit too far, and this episode is probably the worst culprit. The tone is set during an early scene when a pretty black woman passes the squad car and Carter makes a tasteless comment ('Look at the state of *that*'). To be fair, he's said this before, about women of various races, as far back as 'Regan'. However, things are compounded when he says, 'Never mind de colour, just feel de width' in the same appalling Jamaican accent he demonstrated in 'Contact Breaker'. There's also a 'humorous' reference to Gold being 'not kosher', and Collins seeing Gold because he is interested in becoming a Rabbi and 'Gold can fix it for him'. But the episode's treatment of Leroy, the jive-talking pseudo-American with the blonde girlfriend, is particularly unfortunate. Some disapproving looks are exchanged when it is revealed that Leroy's girlfriend is white, and Regan later describes the man as 'a pretty shrewd spade'.

You What?: Regan on Collins: 'He got a "not guilty" at the Bailey.' Carter: 'You got the right hump about that, didn't you?'

Collins: 'And there's no way without that lawyer breathing down my Gregory.'

Regan: 'And what would a drummer like Collins be doing socialising with a ponce like Garner?'

Carter: 'Guvnor, I can see you in a tall hat directing traffic . . .'

Leroy Garner's 'jive' moments include: 'I just want to be left alone, man, you dig?', 'Cool it, baby!', 'Hey man, what's going down here?' and 'What are you staring at, you stupid honky bitch?' If they'd wanted Huggy Bear, why didn't they say so?

Collins: 'We end up in one of two places: the river, or the boob.'

Larfs: Gold: 'I grew up amongst scum like that. Pay 'em off and they come back for more.'

Regan: 'Get your coat on.' Leroy: 'What for, man?' Carter: 'Because there's no central heating in the cells, that's what for.' Leroy: 'Hey, man, don't talk that way. I'm clean – ain't that so, baby?' Sharon: 'Yeah, baby. Leroy – he takes a shower at least once a day.'

Masterson: 'I don't even like you, Leonard. A modern-day robber baron, greedy and as crass as they come . . . You were an obnoxious boor when you were a squaddie. Having money has made you even worse.'

Notes: 'That geezer is one tenacious bastard.' Strong stuff indeed, dealing with the nature of authority and responsibility via a well-plotted glimpse at one of the less glorious parts of British military history, namely the Malayan Min Yuen War, which started in 1948 and continued for several years. The various racist elements present in the script, together with a reference to the National Front (by Carter), remind us of a nasty underbelly to the 70s that is often forgotten amid cosy nostalgia.

Haskins is mentioned ('Come back, Frank Haskins, all is forgiven!'). His temporary replacement is DCI Anderson, 'Scotland's answer to Uriah Heep' (the Dickens character from *David Copperfield*, not the contemporary heavy-metal band).

There are references to the bloody end to the Angolan civil war for many of the British mercenaries involved (see *The Professionals* – 'Where The Jungle Ends' for more details), and to Wade having fought in Ethiopia (probably during the civil war that broke out in Eritrea and Tigré after the overthrow of Emperor Haile Selassie, by the army under the command of Colonel Haile Mengistu, in 1974). The bank in which Collins's safety deposit box is held is the National Anglian (see 'Money, Money, Money'). There's a reference to *Andy Pandy*, and to the (vastly different) poets Lord Tennyson and Pam Ayres. Locations include the docklands around Jubilee Wharf.

49: 'Feet of Clay'
2 November 1978

Writer: Roger Marshall
Director: Chris Burt

Cast: Joss Ackland (Alan Ember),
Thelma Whiteley (Margot Ember), Brian Capron (Colin),
David Wilkinson (Paul Ember), Cheryl Campbell (Erica),
Geoffrey Palmer (Commander Watson),
Philippa Gail (DCI Barton), Robert Oates (DI Jim Hinxman),
John Junkin (Taxi Yard Proprietor),
Diana Weston (WPC Janet Reynolds), Stuart Blake (Doctor),
Marc Zuber (Abdul), Carol Drinkwater (Roz),
Richard Mottau (Peck), John G. Heller (Casino Manager),
Lydia Lisle (Mary), Wendy Young (Jo)

Jack Regan, co-opted to the Serious Crime Squad to investigate a spate of muggings, is approached by a reformed grass, Alan Ember. It seems his son has been kidnapped.

Keep Your Mincers Peeled For . . .: Joss Ackland's credits include *Ashenden, Thicker than Water, Z Cars, The Crezz, Enemy at the Door, Shadowlands* and villainous roles in films like *Lethal Weapon 2* and *Bill and Ted's Bogus Journey*.

Geoffrey Palmer is one of Britain's finest actors, his forte
being gentle comedy roles such as those in *Butterflies*, *Hot
Metal*, *Whoops! Apocalypse* and *As Time Goes By*. The
actor-writer John Junkin has a huge list of TV and film
credits, including playing the Beatles' roadie in *A Hard Day's
Night*, and roles in *The Plank*, *Till Death Us Do Part*, *Marty*,
and *Blott on the Landscape*. Brian Capron played Mr Hop-
wood in many seasons of *Grange Hill*. Carol Drinkwater
(in a blink-and-you'll-miss-her role) was the original Helen
Herriot in *All Creatures Great and Small*. Cheryl Campbell
shot to fame opposite Bob Hoskins in *Pennies from Heaven*.

Ember has not one but two trill phones (one a particularly
obnoxious shade of green). Watch out for posters of Charlie
Chaplin (in the kidnappers' flat) and the David Carradine TV
series *Kung Fu* (in Paul's room).

Birds: *** Regan can tell that George is seeing someone
('Aftershave, haircut, bought a new whistle'), though drinking orange juice to lose a little weight is probably the
giveaway. Her name is Jo, and Carter has known her for
'ages'. In the glimpses we get of her, she seems pretty
enough. Regan gets into an open-top Spitfire with an attractive older woman at a set of traffic lights. Without a word
spoken. Blimey! It transpires that she is a prostitute ('I see
business is good.' 'I'm not knocking it.') and that they
already know each other. At the casino, the 'dealer, flashing
her knockers to one and all, is actually Policewoman Janet
Reynolds'. And very impressive they seem, too!

Booze: * Regan apparently had three large ones 'back at the
Crown' before he and George set out in the taxi. Regan and
Carter have some champers at the Embers after Paul's return:
'Never been known to refuse.' 'Not when it's free.'

Shooters: None, though George injures his nose again (see
'Trojan Bus').

Motors: There's the nice yellow Spitfire towards the beginning, plus a shedload of black cabs. (Now, here's a funny
thing. The first attack we see involves one with the number
plate JUL 342K, which is then, apparently, impounded for

fingerprints and forensic analysis. And yet, somehow, the villains get hold of the same taxi again for the second – set-up – job that we see.) An 'old banger' VW Beetle (clock that chrome roof-rack!) is used to pick up the money. Regan and Carter watch it from a blue pickup truck with bottles of gas on the back. Ember drives a white Princess; the second pay-off involves a blue Vauxhall Viva.

Threads: Mrs Ember's rather unflattering, greenish nightwear. George's tartan cap in the taxi, and his black sweatshirt and jacket for the mugging job. Regan's brown delivery coat is hilarious. Jack also has a Cinzano cooking apron in his flat. Special mention for the tight, light-blue (with dark blue stripes) Adidas sports top worn by one of the kidnappers.

Jazz Funk?: Yes, during the blue-van scenes.

Non-PC Moment: Carter: 'You know anything about a new firm, mugging tourists? Schwarzers and A-rabs, mainly.'

Regan's memorable mocking of the casino-visiting Arab gent: 'Oh, who's been a naughty Abdul? You wait till Allah hears about this!'

Regan: 'Delicate bit of machinery.' Carter: 'What is?' Regan: 'The family unit.' Carter (camp voice): 'Makes me glad I'm gay.'

You What?: The taxi company owner indulges in a bit of cockney even George doesn't understand: 'In my office, I've got umberellas [sic] galore, sets of gnashers, twenty pair of Palmer's . . .' 'Palmer's?' 'Palmer's doors. Drawers.'

And: 'You need a bloody degree to drive a flounder these days.'

Colin: 'Hope you haven't done anything silly – like call in the big, bad fuzz.'

Larfs: Regan: 'A couple more and we'll call it a day.' Carter (yawning): 'A couple more and it *will* be day.'

Regan: 'I've just spent two nights in a motor that smells like a wrestler's jockstrap, so either pee or get off the pot!'

Notes: 'You're the only one I can trust.' 'You must be desperate.' In keeping with much of the story, the excellent pre-titles sequence promises a good deal of savagery which never materialises. Instead we're presented with a good, if very predictable, plot, and some excellent moments of humour. The scene where Regan wakes Carter by running his hand across George's cheek, pretending to be his girlfriend, is priceless (George smells 'like a rancid camel'), as is Regan's appearance before Commander Watson with little bits of tissue paper stuck to his face where he's cut himself shaving. The pair later nod off while watching the car containing the ransom money.

Alan Dirkser's confessions (he later changed his name to Ember) helped clear up 100 offences and led to the imprisonment of seventeen villains. The case netted Ember a share of the insurance proceeds, and helped Regan (then working in C Division) win his promotion to detective inspector. Regan talks to Susie on the phone (it's her birthday). Carter now lives in an old terraced house with a lurid pink door (number 5). He has some sort of tabloid delivered (see *Sweeney!*), along with one bottle of milk. Haskins's ulcers have, apparently, perforated.

Mention is made of the music-hall song 'Abdul Abulbul Amir', and the legendary horror-film actor Lon Chaney.

50: 'One of Your Own'
9 November 1978

Writer: Tony Hoare
Director: Chris Menaul

Cast: Michael Elphick (Fleet), Nick Stringer (Kearny), Sion Probert (Phil), Rachel Davies (Tina), Neil Hallett (Morris), Jacky Turner (Taylor), Sheridan Fitzgerald (Jenny), Delena Kidd (Mrs Morris), Iain Black (Prison Officer), Nicholas Owen (Constable), Jonathan Blake (Stephen), David Corti (Richard Morris), Clare McLellan (Sally Morris)

It looks like the tea leaf James Fleet will win his appeal on a technicality. Time for George to go undercover and spend a night in the Scrubs.

Keep Your Mincers Peeled For . . .: Michael Elphick is still, despite many and varied roles, best known as the eponymous *Boon*, playing alongside Rachel Davies in many episodes. Other well-remembered Elphick appearances include *Blue Remembered Hills*, *Private Schultz*, *Three Up Two Down* and *Harry*. Nick Stringer was Ron Smollett in *The Bill*, and also appeared in *Press Gang*. Keen-eyed viewers may be able to spot Nosher Powell again as one of Kearny's thugs (see 'Visiting Fireman').

Birds: **** Jenny, who begins the episode as George Carter's girlfriend, seems to have a uniform fetish. She later sleeps with Regan (and is disappointed when he says he hasn't got a helmet, offering to provide one herself next time) and with Tom (he answers the phone while she's sitting astride him). 'She's too much . . . Do you know what she had me doing?' Fleet offers to take Carter (undercover as 'Charlie Mason', a minor con) to a club full of girls, including a Dutch woman called Wilma.

Booze: ** Jenny works in a pub. Regan pours her what looks like a brandy back at his place. Tina has a bottle of champagne in her hand when Fleet is released after his successful appeal. George drinks a vodka and tonic while undercover.

Shooters: * There's a fist fight with Kearny and his thug, and the very violent interrogation of Fleet and Carter. They have a shooter; Fleet later threatens Kearny with a handgun, thinking he's abducted Tina.

Motors: There's a big Pontiac, and a sunshine-yellow Cortina Mk III driven through a handily placed wooden gate.

Threads: Tom Daniels wears a rather smart black poloneck and grey suit. This is a real big tie gathering!

Jazz Funk?: There is some weird electronic percussive music at the beginning, and much pounding drum and guitar when Regan and Daniels pursue one of the villains. Fleet sings 'Oh I Do Like To Be Beside the Seaside'.

You What?: Carter, to Haskins: 'Look, the thing is, I've gotta meet with this terrific bird, you see. I've give her a tug, and she says I'll be all right if I . . .' He then translates it for us: 'There is this young lady with whom I have developed a wonderful relationship . . .'

Haskins: 'What is important is that he's only served eight months of a ten stretch for a quarter-of-a-million-pound diamond robbery, and the tom wasn't even recovered.'

Regan: 'Geezers in the boob tend to talk about things they wouldn't dream of talking about on the outside.'

Fleet: 'I told ya. They propped me to get you to tell me about all this terrible villainy you been up to.'

And: 'Patsy, you're making a ricky. I never had that tom. They slung me for it, didn't they?'

And: 'Come on, Charlie. You and me, we're just tea leaves. This could get really naughty.'

Larfs: Carter (on seeing Fleet's photo): 'Cor, he looks a bit dodgy, doesn't he?' Haskins: 'The eyewitness at the time thought he looked just like a police officer.' Carter: 'Good-looking geezer, isn't he?'

Fleet: 'He must love you, that . . . wossit? Keegan?' Carter: 'Regan? Oh, that bastard . . .'

Tina: 'He has just got out of jail after eight months, remember? What do you think I did with him? *The Times* crossword?'

Notes: 'You're the Fulham Flasher, intcha?' An excellent and likable performance from Elphick, playing a man who ends up on the verge of prison again while his double-crossing woman and her lover get away scot-free with the money. There's a staggeringly brutal torture scene, and some very naughty humour.

There's a nod to Laurel and Hardy ('That's another fine mess . . .') and another oblique reference to the Krays (the 'Brothers Grimm'). There are jokes that Carter in glasses looks like Clark Kent, and that if he gets hurt they can rebuild him like Steve Austin in *The Six Million Dollar Man*. Tom Daniels is married, but his wife has recently left him.

51: 'Hearts and Minds'
23 November 1978

Writers: Donald Churchill, Ted Childs
Director: Mike Vardy

Cast: Eric Morecambe (Himself), Ernie Wise (Himself),
Edward Hardwicke (Bellcourt), Edward de Souza (Busby),
George Mikell (Danilov), Caroline Blakiston (Hildegarde),
Jenny Quayle (Wendy), Miles Anderson (Hawkins),
Jack Klaff (Al Krim), John Moreno (Doad),
Joseph Charles (Ulysses), Nicholas McArdle (Tridgwell),
Paul Freeman (1st Detective), James Winston (Sid),
Alan Bodenham (Henry), George Irving (2nd Detective),
Jean Boht (Woman Neighbour),
Ronald Forfar (Police Observer),
Gary McDermott (Police Driver),
Martyn Whitby (SPG Inspector),
Anthony Smee (Army Lieutenant), Simon Brown (Gene),
Barbara Grant (Neighbour), John Fielding (Reporter)

What do a break-in at the home of a leading biochemist, a group of Marxist Arabs and a popular comedy double act have in common? Regan and Carter get involved in the shady worlds of international politics and showbusiness.

Keep Your Mincers Peeled For . . .: As a return favour for John Thaw and Dennis Waterman's memorable appearance on their 1976 Christmas Special, Eric Morecambe and Ernie Wise made the trip for the second leg. Edward Hardwicke was Dr Watson in Granada's highly successful *Sherlock Holmes* adaptations in the 1980s. Both Edward de Souza and Caroline Blakiston are easily recognisable TV faces, possibly best remembered for *The Troubleshooters* and *Brass* respectively. Jean Boht, Ma Boswell in *Bread*, has a tiny part as a nosy neighbour who wants to write to Mary Whitehouse. Ironic, really, since Mary and her NVLA pals were never too keen on *The Sweeney*.

The headline of the *Evening Standard* reads '12 HURT IN LONDON TRAIN CRASH'; a smaller and highly plausible story further down is titled 'FARMERS FLEE AS PEASANTS REVOLT'.

Birds: * The chorus girls (including Wendy) all wear rather fetching little pink things. Wendy herself is quite cute.

Booze: ** Regan and Carter drink whisky with Bellcourt and again, later, with Eric and Ernie ('Well, if *he's* having one . . .'). Eric and Ern have given Wendy a bottle of champers, which she gets out for Busby.

Shooters: ** The Arabs use Czech army pistols (with silencers) during the break-in, and carry lethal-looking sub-machine-guns later on. Regan urges Haskins to get as many of the Squad as he can down to the club and to make sure they're all 'tooled up'.

Motors: The Arabs drive a yellow-green Range Rover. Busby's chosen mode of transport is an orange and white VW camper van, until they run him off the road and into the river. At the conclusion, the Transit is pursued by the villains in a yellowish Mercedes, Bellcourt in an enormous black Bentley limousine, Haskins in an eggshell-coloured Rover, a blue Triumph police car, and a couple of Sweeney Fords.

Threads: Mrs Busby's brown frock and matching neck scarf. Busby's light-blue suit and disgusting cravat. Ulysses's yellow dressing gown is almost as nasty as Ernie Wise's purple one. We would mention Eric's oversized flat cap, but it's a TV legend anyway, and part of a stage costume. He also wears an orange-and-white Luton Town scarf (he was, of course, a director of the club). One of the Squad boys wears a pair of light-orange loon pants.

Jazz Funk?: Eric, Ernie and Charlie the Dummy do a version of 'When You're Smiling' on stage. The chase sequence is accompanied by some nice bassy disco music.

You What?: Regan: 'We had a message from MP on the RT there was one going off here.'

Carter: 'I do hope you're not gonna be a completely irresponsible superior officer and creep back to your gaff for a kip?'

And: 'She said that a geezer gave her old man two thousand quid in used oncers and said there was another three thousand when he screwed the gaff.'

And: 'Is that the geezer with the dodgy strawberry?'

Larfs: Eric Morecambe does all of his usual party pieces (the glasses trick, 'What do you think of it so far?' 'Ruggish', etc.). Seeing Eric and Ernie on stage doing their act is a reminder of just how good a double act they were.

Notes: 'He's a big fan of yours ... usually.' Oddly, this isn't anywhere near as funny as it could have been. The pacing is a bit flat and the episode wastes its guest stars, giving them only about half a dozen scenes when they should have had most of the episode. The highlight is Eric Morecambe throwing boxes of frozen fish at the chasing Arab terrorists.

Eric thinks Carter looks like Columbo. Regan watches a fictional episode of Thames's real-life current affairs programme *This Week* ('An Affair of the Heart', about Busby and his work). B12 are responsible for 'dabs'; C7 for the ballistics test on a bullet. Ernie seems to be reading a copy of *Goodbye Emmanuelle*. The name of the company on the side of the van that Eric and Ernie use to escape (Brayham's Fresh Fish) is taken from the stunt arranger Peter Brayham (that's Brayham, incidentally, doubling for Eric as he clambers into the back of the still-moving van).

Viewing figures for this episode were an astonishing 18.25 million (the highest the series ever got). The episode was hampered through an illness to Benjamin Whitrow, who appears, unbilled, in one scene as Braithwaite, with half of the scenes having to be reshot. The day after the episode was broadcast, the club where the cabaret scenes were shot was gutted in an apparent case of arson.

52: 'Latin Lady'
30 November 1978

Writer: Ted Childs
Director: Peter Smith

Cast: Meg Davies (Christobel), Stuart Wilson (Knox),
Donald Morley (Delacroix), Stephen Bent (Eddie Hibbard),
Jack Carr (Pat Tyler), Sandra Payne (Meryl),
Geoffrey Larder (Askew), Elizabeth Bradley (Mrs Hibbard),
Janet Amsden (Betty Edwards), Gladys Powell (Pianist),
Eamonn Jones (O'Connor)

When a gynaecologist is attacked in broad daylight, Regan
and his squad are quick to arrest one of the blaggers, a former
racing driver named Jimmy Knox. But complications arise in
the shape of Jimmy's girlfriend.

Keep Your Mincers Peeled For . . .: Meg Davies would later
play the wife of Van der Valk in the 90s revival of the show of
that name.

The opening scene features a (seemingly French) onion
seller on a bicycle. Minus, sadly, a blue-and-white-hooped
jumper, but *with* a beret! In the TWA offices there are adverts
for flights to New York and San Francisco. Also, there's
another 70s icon, a 'Watch Out! – There's a Thief About'
poster in Camden Hill nick.

Birds: *** Christobel Delgado – Bolivian, of Portuguese
parentage, and the shady Latin Lady of the title – is really an
Australian named Christine Delton. A former nurse, with a
call-girl past, she gets her claws into Regan in a big way
as he sleeps with her, and wakes up knackered, with an
injured shoulder, claiming he's getting too old for this caper.
Later, with a knowing glance at George, he tells Braithwaite,
'Something came up.' Braithwaite innocently remarks, 'I
hope the bird hasn't flown!'

During her initial appearance at the station, George notes,
'It's a bit nice, innit?' and later offers her a 'suggestive

biscuit', to which Regan responds, 'George, on yer bike!'
Carter says he tried to pull the nurse at the clinic, but she
blanked him.

Booze: *** Bill sneaks a bottle of something into Camden
Hill nick for George and Jack while they're interrogating
Knox. Regan drinks many whiskeys at the Irish boozer,
and what looks like three bottles of chilled champers with
Christobel at the hotel before bedding her. George says Regan
uses a boozer in Charlotte Street called the Black Bull where
he is alleged to be 'giving the barmaid one'. He and Jelly go
for a drink.

Shooters: Tyler has a pistol, to the Flying Squad's surprise.

Motors: Delacroix drives a red BMW. The villains use a
brown Triumph Stag and a Mercedes 200-series.

Threads: Regan's very smart grey suit. Jellyneck's horrible
shirt. Tyler's massive brown flares.

Jazz Funk?: Regan sings 'When Irish Eyes Are Smiling' at
O'Connor's boozer ('It's a grand voice on the man'). There's
some very tinkly music playing in Christobel's hotel room.

You What?: Carter: 'Robbery, possessing an offensive
weapon, driving a stolen car, resisting arrest. Now, that's
got to be a Nevis, hasn't it?'
   And: 'Went all Tom and Dick on me, didn't he?'
   And: 'He's schtum, and crumb, and screaming for his brief.'

Larfs: George Carter with the cliché that launched a thousand
parodies: 'Now, the way I see it, starshine, is we got you
banged to rights anyway!'

Notes: 'Those uniform boys . . . They're the bloody mafia.' A
very funny episode, as camp as Butlins in places. There's a
running gag about George borrowing some traffic lights for a
Squad disco in 1977: now Traffic Division want them back.
   Regan and Carter once won a talent contest at the Irish pub
in Kilburn. The landlord, Sean O'Connor, is a mate of
Regan's, so there is a suggestion that the contest was fixed.
Regan misquotes (drunkenly) from *A Tale of Two Cities*.

George speaks a little Spanish. There's a mention of the bomb squad, and the IRA.

53: 'Victims'
14 December 1978

Writer: Roger Marshall
Director: Ben Bolt

Cast: Lynda Marchal (Eve Fisher),
Peter Wight (Jimmy Park), Elizabeth Burger (Joan),
George Innes (Willoughby), Gillian Rhind (WPC Jackson),
Benny Lee (Tommy Swain), John Biggerstaff (Mr Culley),
Katie Allan (Sharon), Stuart Wilde (Richard Haskins)

A policeman is shot, and Haskins oversees the investigation. Trouble is, it's the least of Haskins's worries: his wife has gone AWOL.

Keep Your Mincers Peeled For . . .: Lynda Marchal was one of the stars on the BBC's first medical soap, *The Doctors*. George Innes (who had previously appeared briefly in *Sweeney 2*) was a veteran of *Upstairs, Downstairs* and *Danger UXB*.

There's a nice bit of Chelsea graffiti behind the uniformed bobby, along with lots of references to somebody called Sid. In Tommy the agent's office, there's a poster for a pantomime starring 70s icon Dick Emery. Eve has a dentist's chair in her flat (kinky!).

Birds: ** Tommy the 'theatrical' agent is watching a beautiful blonde woman dancing provocatively in her white undies. He cuts things short just as she's about to get her bra off, having already decided that she's 'the wrong shape' (picky so-and-so!). Next up is Sharon, a brunette in dark underwear . . . There are, literally, hundreds of photos of seminaked women around the walls. Regan reckons most of them are underage, and points to one who he says looks 'about fifteen'. Tommy tells him she's 21 ('She told me!').

Booze: * George offers to buy WPC Jackson some 'antifreeze'.

Shooters: ** Taylor is shot before the episode begins. 'Has Jimmy got a shooter?' Regan asks Eve. He has, and the episode concludes with a tense stand-off.

Motors: The confrontation at the end involves the usual array of Sweeney Granadas and Cortinas, plus a muddy-brown Rover SD1 (Haskins), a blue Transit and an ambulance. Watch out, also, for a BP oil tanker, and a bright red taxi.

Threads: Willoughby's avocado-green jimjams, Eve's mustard-yellow top, Jimmy Park's parka and George's flat cap and donkey jacket are all hysterical.

Jazz Funk?: A snatch of loud rock during the 'strip'. There's a touch of the 'suspense theme' as Park watches Daniels and Barry.

You What?: Haskins: 'I want you to find anybody that Sergeant Taylor knew who lives around here – anybody that any of us know that live around here. Villains, snouts, grasses. I want the bastard that fired that.'

Regan: 'I'll bell Catford, find out the strength of this Malone knock-off.'

Daniels: 'You know a brief named Grow?' Regan: 'David Grow? . . . Bent as a banana.' Daniels: 'He's pulled a bloody habeas corpus on me.' Regan: 'Well, that's par for the course, innit?' Daniels: '. . . But how did he find out? That's what I can't tumble.' Regan: 'Someone from the nick belled him?'

Regan: 'What about Taylor's drum?' Daniels: 'As clean as a whistle.'

Larfs: Haskins: 'Taylor survived the op.' Regan: 'As a man, or . . .?' Haskins: 'Ask again in forty-eight hours.'

Regan (to Daniels): 'Oh, uncross your legs, son. Don't be such a bloody Boy Scout.'

Carter: 'Bit taters, innit? Who you watching for?' Jackson: 'A flasher.' Carter: 'In this weather? Poor little bastard. He'd get it frostbitten.'

Carter: 'Southend meant fifteen pints to me. Fourteen of bitter, and one of whelks!'

Regan: 'He's got a straight choice. He either listens to you, or he listens to a priest.'

Notes: 'I'm not tired, Frank. I'm just very, very frightened.' Poor old Haskins, the Walter Skinner of the Flying Squad! From the remarkable opening, to that fantastic flashback sequence to a much younger Frank Haskins (complete with hair!), this is just about as good as *The Sweeney* gets. Brilliantly written (what else would you expect from Roger Marshall?), and sensitively acted. As a way of sketching in the themes of the final episode it can't be faulted, either. (Bet Mary Whitehouse loved the conclusion: what's that, three 'bastard's in under ten seconds?!)

Major continuity foul-up (notwithstanding the change in actresses!): Doreen Haskins talks of the 'boys being home from school' (the establishment in question being a boarding school some distance from London), and the implication is that Richard and Brian are the only children the Haskinses have. However, although 'Golden Fleece' mentions two children of school age, it makes it clear that one of them is a girl, Lucy. (A daughter is also mentioned, though not by name, in 'Down to You, Brother'.)

Richard and Brian are both studying for their A levels (and so either they're twins or poor Mrs H was pregnant again mere months after dropping the elder of the two). Richard recognises the (mis)quotation from the Stevie Smith poem 'Not Waving but Drowning' (though he gets the sex of the poem's protagonist wrong), and has recently visited the Tate (there's a reference to Henry Moore). Doreen Haskins hates the police force (Frank is considering his resignation, as he was in 'Golden Fleece'). She was brought up in Southend, and used to work in a bank. Doreen has a sour-faced sister, Joan (who has at least two daughters). Their mother recently died, some time after Frank and Doreen decided that they couldn't look after her (Frank missed the funeral because he was working). Doreen has recently been to the doctor with some sort of phantom or imaginary pregnancy. The Haskinses used to live at number 23 (a terraced house): the whole street is now due for demolition. Haskins takes a size-sixteen collar.

They have a joint bank account at the Nat West. Doreen's maiden name was Masters.

Daniels reads the *Guardian*. The names Geoff Boycott and Freddie Trueman (the Yorkshire and England cricketers) are mentioned as being frequently used aliases for snouts. The bottle of milk that Haskins buys at his local corner shop (which seems to be called Pat and Harry's) costs 12½p. The ha'penny, of course, has long since gone the way of all flesh. There's a reference to the famous Southend funfair ride, the Kursaal Flyer.

54: 'Jack or Knave'
28 December 1978

Writer: Ted Childs
Director: Tom Clegg

Cast: Barrie Ingham (Canning), Richard Griffiths (Harries), Jo Warne (Gloria), Ralph Nossek (Duxbury), David Casey (Jackson)[1], Andrew Downie (Bishop), Jane Cussons (Sonia), Dan Gillan (Desk Sergeant), Anna Nygh (Jean), Matthew Scurfield (Kennedy), Andrew Paul (Teenager), Peggy Ann Jones (Lady), Frank Lee (Driver), Stephen Gordon (Driver's Mate), Linda Hooks (Ivy)

A vicious blag, just outside the Metropolitan area, brings Regan into conflict with a superior officer. Unfortunately, the wind of change is sweeping through the police force, and Regan finds himself on the receiving end of some serious allegations.

[1] The character is called Colin Anderson by other characters (see **You What?**). David Casey had previously appeared in *Sweeney 2* playing Goodyear. Although the characters are clearly different (Anderson is a photographer with C10), both wear identical Liverpool scarves (see the final scene of *Sweeney 2*).

Keep Your Mincers Peeled For . . .: Richard Griffiths's
TV credits include *The Cleopatras*, *Bird of Prey*, *Whoops!*
Apocalypse, and, latterly, *Pie in the Sky*. Anna Nygh played
Desirée in *Citizen Smith* (she'd previously had a small role in
Sweeney 2, as had both David Casey and Matthew Scurfield).
The Bill's Dave Quinnan (Andrew Paul) here appears as the
'teenager'! Barrie Ingham was the eponymous star of *Hine*.

Watch that scene of Regan and Carter meeting in a crowded
market for the brilliant sight of dozens of passers-by trying
desperately (i.e. not very hard) *not* to look at the camera, or
the actors. One woman even starts laughing, and points at
John Thaw and Denis Waterman. To think, she was probably
completely unaware that twenty years later her inability to
remain calm when spotting two television celebrities in the
street would become a source of great amusement to two
authors writing a book about *The Sweeney*!

The fake headline in the *Sun* is 'SECURITY MAN KILLER
KENNEDY GETS 30 YEARS', with the secondary headline 'JUDGE
PRAISES FLYING SQUAD'.

Birds: ** 'Do you reckon she's had an accident?' asks
George Carter, watching Ronald 'Tottenham' Harries's latest
girlfriend. On the cleavage of another he states, 'Don't get
many of those to the pound, do you?' We see one of Harries's
birds in more detail later, and, yes, she is rather big up top.
'They're all like that,' says Colin.

'Ahoy there!' says Carter from a boat to two passing Abba
lookalikes ('Didn't like yours much anyway,' he says, noting
Regan's disgusted look). Jean Jackson is resigned to having
her room searched by Carter and says, 'Oh, I suppose I'll
have to strip next', but Carter looks less than impressed. 'No
thanks,' he says.

Further to Regan's seeming fascination with air hostesses,
we find out a possible reason – that his wife was one.

Booze: * Carter has a bottle of whisky in his pocket when he
goes to visit Gloria. Later, he tries to calm Regan down by
taking him for a drink 'before they open', but Regan refuses.

Shooters: ** The gang at the start use a sawn-off and a pistol plus some big batons. The arrest of Kennedy at the marina involves two marksmen and some tooled-up Sweeney boys, led by Carter (who falls in the water) and Regan. Kennedy has a shotgun, but is hit in the leg by one of the marksmen.

Motors: Harries drives a yellow Merc. We glimpse Carter on a motorbike (again – see ' "Lady Luck" '). Canning has a nice yellow Rover. At the end, Regan disappears into the distance in a black taxi cab.

Threads: Sonia the reporter's white poloneck. And the usual array of flares, kipper ties, horrible polyester shirts and bad haircuts, one last time . . .

Jazz Funk?: The overdramatic disco piano theme at the start, and much 'boinging bass' later on. Regan whistles 'An Ordinary Copper' (see 'Trojan Bus'). In Jean Jackson's flat there's a stack of LPs visible while she talks to Carter. It's difficult to make out many of the titles on freeze-frame, but among those we can see are *Led Zeppelin 2*, *Deep Purple in Rock* and the Jam's *This is The Modern World*. The one on top of the pile looks very like Bob Dylan's *Bringing it All Back Home*. Colin hums 'You'll Never Walk Alone.', somewhat inevitably.

Bill the Driver: Bill has won just over £200 on a yankee (a racing bet).

Non-PC Moment: Gloria: 'There's me laid out in Paddington General; Jack the lad's in Jamaica nicking spades.'

You What?: Stuttering security man: 'Going for a slash, Dick.'

Colin: 'Lovely bristols . . .' Carter: 'Who?' Colin: '[Your] skin and blister . . .'

Carter: 'Colin Anderson, C11 smudger, reckons Tubby here has been showing out.'

And: 'You won't believe this. He only had an old brass with him.'

Larfs: Regan: 'Cyril Edward Rayner, clearly identified in the Letchmore branch of the National Mercia Bank, with a shotgun in one hand, and five grand's worth of used fivers in the other, is now walking tall and free.'

Regan: 'You don't have to take that from a polisher like that, Frank.' Haskins: 'What do you suggest I do, Jack? Punch him in the head, or will it be all right if I just tell him to get knotted?'

Carter: 'Get yer vest on, Sid. You're nicked.'

Gloria (to crying child): 'Shut it!'

Carter (on the caged birds that fill Gloria's flat): 'What happens if they all talk at the same time?' Gloria: 'Why do you think Stan works at nights?'

And Jack's memorable, vitriolic parting words to Haskins: 'I am utterly and abjectly pissed off with this little lot. I've given the best years of my life to the job, I've got eighteen bloody commendations if you include the one I *didn't* get yesterday, and how does this wonderful police force show its gratitude for all my years of unstinting effort? It bangs me up in a crabby little cell like some cheap little villain. All because a toerag called Hutchinson's got a few bottles twitching on the fifth floor. Now, because that poor little bastard [Carter] had the guts to get off his arse, I'm going to have to be reinstated – and what do you bunch of bleedin' double-dyed hypocrites want now? You want me to crawl back to work and be terribly *grateful* that I didn't get nicked for something I didn't do. Well, you can stuff it!'

Notes: 'He was a right sod, our Jack.' Absolutely fantastic, and a fitting end to this great series. Having diced with some sort of official sanction before, it's only fitting that the nuclear option was finally pressed in the last episode. Seeing Regan cooped up in the cell is something to behold. The scenes of Regan wandering around Soho are some of the best in the series.

Bribery allegations have emerged concerning the West London subdivision between May and August 1968. At this time, Canning was Regan's skipper in O Division (Regan himself was a detective sergeant, second-class). 'He was a pain in the arse then as well.' Canning (now a regional detective chief superintendent) hasn't gone to the Met for help, even though the blag was only half a mile inside his territory. Gloria Barclay is an old flame of Regan's, dating back to 1968 when she was a police typist. He got her pregnant, but 'nearly ruined my life . . . He didn't do the right thing by me.' He transferred from O Division to the Murder Squad soon after (see **Non-PC Moment**). Regan's full name is John Albert Regan. He is very dismissive of 'left-wing intellectuals', and considers Carter a 'prince'.

In 1968, Haskins was at Hendon (preparing for his next step up the ladder). CIB are mentioned for the first time (a decade and a half later *Between the Lines* would dramatise their work in much greater detail).

The Liverpool footballers Steve Heighway and Tommy Smith are both mentioned (as are their moustaches!). Regan says 'the world doesn't end at Stamford Bridge, you know, George', indicating Carter's love of Chelsea (see *Sweeney 2*). George tells Colin that his mother hates Everton (as a way of getting more information out of him). There is a poster of Kevin Keegan on the wall of Colin's darkroom, along with an action shot of what looks like the 1972 England v. Wales game (England won 3–0 with goals by Emlyn Hughes, Colin Bell and Rodney Marsh). Colin reckons a recent world championship boxing match was fixed ('He couldn't have gone five rounds with a geriatric gerbil').

'He'll be back. He needs the job like an alcoholic needs booze.' 'Yeah . . .?'

'Call Yourselves Professionals . . .?'

It was going to be *so* different.

If there was one single, overriding influence on the creation and direction of *The Professionals*, it was the astonishing success in Britain of the American series *Starsky and Hutch*, which began in 1976. The concept of the 'buddy series' replaced the previous Hollywood penchant for loner, maverick cops who bucked the system. In *Starsky and Hutch* two men of vastly different backgrounds and attitudes work as a team, and have a friendship to boot. Television executives are keen to exploit new trends and, when Brian Clemens approached Brian Tesler at London Weekend Television with a couple of series formats, one, *The A-Squad*, about a pair of specialist antiterrorist agents, raised a few eyebrows.

'Britain's answer to *Starsky and Hutch*' was used more than once in pre-publicity about *The Professionals* during the autumn of 1977, and it's not hard to see the connection. You could never really describe *The Sweeney* in these terms: true, Regan and Carter were friends, but they rarely lowered their defences for anyone, still less each other. Bodie and Doyle, on the other hand, seemed to have more fulfilled lives (at least, if you count an almost endless stream of girlfriends and one-off encounters as 'fulfilled'), but were actually more intimate, more able to live out of each other's pockets, intellectually if not literally. Indeed, it's the interplay between the two CI5 agents that gives many of the early episodes in particular a real dramatic bite: in the absence of any great characterisation elsewhere, at least the two leads (three, if you include Cowley) are engaging. The sheer presence of Martin Shaw and Lewis Collins saves more than one dull episode, and with the late Gordon Jackson on the sidelines, lobbing in pithy aphorisms and a hint of world-weary *realpolitik*, you can almost excuse the more mindless excesses of some of their exploits.

For this element really to have worked well – and, in effect, to carry the series – character development should have been central. Attempts *were* made ('Klansmen' is a good early example), but Shaw and Collins became increasingly frustrated that the writers seemed as keen to split them up and place them with other CI5 operatives as to let the banter and the slow revealing of character take place. Things were not helped by the *shambles* that is the original transmission of *The Professionals* (see below). It would perhaps take a book as big as this to really dig down and find the truth, but the upshot was that episodes were shown wildly out of order. Any hope of a continuing narrative was lost.

There are still points of light, however: episodes that show a quirky edge that might be expected as the follow-up series to *The New Avengers*. Episodes like 'Mixed Doubles' and 'Discovered in a Graveyard' show a metaphysical bent, with surrealism and a very real reflection on the ease and difficulty of killing. Most weeks, *The Professionals* was content to just blow away its extras (how many enemies are shot while resisting arrest: did they *ever* take anyone alive?). There is a casualness about the deaths in *The Professionals* that is more sickening than, say, the violence of the two *Sweeney* films – but at other moments one is brought up short. In trying to bring some British quirkiness to a fairly Americanised format, *The Professionals* does occasionally nod towards that most underrated show of the era, *Strangers*.

Even its defenders and strongest fans would probably admit that *The Professionals* rarely scales the heights of great drama. But few would deny that there's usually something – even if only another excellent stunt or tense stand-off – to keep even the worst episode afloat. If *The Sweeney* appealed to the unregenerate 'bloke' in its male viewers, *The Professionals* took us all back a few years to children playing with toy cars and cowboy guns. And that's easy to excuse, given the odd moment of self-doubt displayed by Doyle, Cowley or even – heaven help us – Bodie himself.

A Note on recording blocks

As mentioned above and in the following episode guide, *The Professionals'* recording and transmission order differs wildly. Here is a list of the probable production order:

> *First filming block* (started June 1977)
> 'Old Dog with New Tricks'
> 'The Female Factor'
> 'Long Shot'
> 'Private Madness, Public Danger'
> 'Killer with a Long Arm'
> 'Heroes'
> 'Where the Jungle Ends'
> 'Close Quarters'
> 'Stakeout'
> 'Everest was Also Conquered'
> 'When the Heat Cools Off'
> 'Look After Annie'
> 'Klansmen'
>
> *Second filming block* (started June 1978)
> 'Rogue'
> 'Hunter/Hunted'
> 'First Night'
> 'The Rack'
> 'Man Without a Past'
> 'In the Public Interest'
> 'Not a Very Civil Civil Servant'
> 'A Stirring of Dust'
> 'Blind Run'
> 'Fall Girl'
> 'Backtrack'
> 'Servant of Two Masters'
> 'The Madness of Mickey Hamilton'
>
> *Third filming block* (started April 1979)
> 'Stopover'
> 'Runner'

'A Hiding to Nothing'
'Dead Reckoning'
'Mixed Doubles'
'Need to Know'
'The Purging of CI5'
'Fugitive'
'The Acorn Syndrome'
'Slush Fund'
'Weekend in the Country'
'Take Away'
'Involvement'

Fourth filming block (started June 1980)
'The Gun'
'Wild Justice'
'Blackout'
'It's Only a Beautiful Picture . . .'
'Blood Sports'
'Hijack'
'You'll Be All Right'
'Kickback'
'Foxhole on the Roof'
'Discovered in a Graveyard'
'Operation Susie'
'The Ojuka Situation'
'The Untouchables'

Fifth filming block (started March 1981)
'Cry Wolf'
'A Man Called Quinn'
'Lawson's Last Stand'
'No Stone'
'Spy Probe'

The Professionals

First Season

Thirteen 60-minute episodes (including one untransmitted)
An Avengers Mark 1 Production/London Weekend Television
Created by Brian Clemens

Associate Producer: Ron Fry
Producer: Sidney Hayers
Executive Producers: Albert Fennell, Brian Clemens

Title music by Laurie Johnson

Regular Cast: Gordon Jackson (George Cowley),
Martin Shaw (Ray Doyle), Lewis Collins (William Bodie),
Bridget Brice (Betty, 1–4, 6–9),
Trevor Adams (Benny, 1, 11),
Howard Bell (CID Sergeant[1], 3, 4),
Joseph Charles (Jax, 7, 13)

1: 'Private Madness, Public Danger'
30 December 1977

Writer: Anthony Read
Director: Douglas Camfield

Cast: Keith Barron (Nesbitt), Donald Douglas (Sutton),
Di Trevis (Susan Fenton), Angus Mackay (Gerald Harvey),
Christopher Ellison (Biggs), Peter Penry-Jones (Cummings),

---

[1] Since Bell's two appearances are under exactly the same character description, we assume he was playing the same CID sergeant in both episodes.

Penny Irving (Pam), Gloria Walker (Pretty Nurse),
Donald Maciver (Hoskins), Melanie Peck (Barmaid),
Ian Fairbairn (Miller), Malou Cartwright (Miller's Secretary)

CI5 investigate a number of mysterious deaths at a chemical company, and uncover an ambitious attempt to hold the country to ransom by threatening to contaminate water supplies with a hallucinogenic drug.

Keep Your Mincers Peeled For ...: Keith Barron surely needs little introduction: he had been a TV star since his groundbreaking work with Dennis Potter in the two *Nigel Barton* plays in 1965, and his subsequent career has ranged from hard-hitting drama (*The Odd Man*, *It's Dark Outside*, *The Further Adventures of Lucky Jim*) to sitcom (*Duty Free*, *Haggard*, *Room at the Bottom*). The CI5 agent Biggs marks Christopher Ellison's next major stepping stone on his way to *The Bill* (see *The Sweeney*'s 'Queen's Pawn'). Penny Irving was Grace Bros' lift girl in *Are You Being Served?* (it's her voice you hear on the sitcom's opening credits), and starred in the infamous mid-70s British horror movie *The House of Whipcord*.

Bodie and Doyle are seen shooting at cans of Coke, Heineken and Newcastle Brown Ale. One of the posters in Nesbitt's lab reads NUCLEAR BASES MUST GO. Right on!

Birds: ** Betty, Cowley's secretary, is prim and efficient in a sexy sort of way (Bridget Brice had, of course, previously played Jack Regan's secretary: see *The Sweeney* – 'Thin Ice').

In the pre-titles there's a well-built girl in figure-hugging black shorts, water-skiing. Bodie patronises the company secretary ('sweetheart'), and clearly fancies Susan and the blonde nurse, too ('Plenty of girls think I should be put down'). Benny meets Doyle at a strip club and says 'After curtain-down, the dressing room will be crawling with birds ... Birds in a very singular state of disarray. Birds with very few feathers indeed.' When we get inside, there's little to get excited about, however: a few women stand around in their underwear. This isn't *The Sweeney*, after all.

Booze: * Nesbitt orders a half of bitter and a beef sandwich in the pub as a ruse to infect one of the barrels. Cowley offers Bodie and Doyle a 'wee nip' of 'medicinal' Scotch after their dip in the reservoir. There's a huge advert for Smirnoff in the pub.

Shooters: ** We first see Nesbitt practising with his rifle. Bodie and Doyle have constructed a makeshift shooting range for themselves. There is a gun battle at Nesbitt's house, and again at the reservoir.

Motors: In the first two stories, Doyle's preferred vehicle is a blue Triumph TR7 (OOM 734R), with Bodie driving a white Triumph Dolomite (POK 79R). In this episode, Cowley has a red Princess. Nesbitt owns a bronze Mk III Cortina; Sue Fenton a red Mini. The patrons of the Black Bull smash up a variety of cars, including a Mk II Jag, a dark-blue Ford Zephyr and an Allegro. The last of these crashes into a police car.

Threads: Watch out for Bodie's pink shirt and black-and-white spotted jacket (was the costume designer colour blind or something?) and Doyle's lumberjack-y jacket. They're so bad, they return at regular intervals. Nesbitt has a pretty extreme pair of faded denim flares on at the beginning. Keep a lookout also for Benny's 'windmill' T-shirt.

***Shaft* Guitar?:** We must start with the title sequence itself, featuring Laurie Johnson's legendary theme music, which will be familiar to every reader. (We *love* the middle-eight section where the guitar player just freaks out and goes for a Ritchie Blackmore moment ... Didn't these people know punk had happened?)

There's a lovely big Wurlitzer pushing out Hendrixy riffs in the pub – but Doyle pulls out the plug after only a few seconds. Nesbitt's transistor radio seems only to pick up news bulletins and *dreadful* rock.

Slash Fiction Moment: They bravely face death together, in the water.

Jargon: Bodie: 'It'd be easy to boss that lock.'

Benny: 'Sutton's in there, dropping off a little packet of big H to a good customer.'

Laughable Dialogue: Cowley: 'World Chemical Products. Man just fell out of a seventh-storey window.' Doyle: 'That's police business.' Cowley: 'He jumped.' Bodie: 'Then that's his business.' Cowley: 'Someone had slipped him a drug . . .' Bodie and Doyle: 'Well, that's drug squad business . . .'

Cowley: 'Will she live?' Bodie: 'God knows.' Cowley: 'Yes, but, unfortunately, I haven't been in touch with him for some time.'

Cowley: 'God save us from all idealists.' Bodie: 'I thought you and he weren't talking.' Cowley: 'Oh, he does me the occasional favour . . .'

Notes: 'The sky is very big.' Definitely *not* the episode they meant to start with (see 'Old Dog with New Tricks'), as it gives the viewer no clues as to the format – apart from the fact that it involves cars and guns and flip humour and threats to national security. The contrast with a programme like *The Sweeney* is still pretty obvious, though: here, Nesbitt is presented to us as a nutter (albeit with – these days – quite understandable desires, namely the reduction in the UK's stocks of chemical weapons). No more, no less. He uses evil means, and has designs upon the authority structures of the country, and thus must be stopped. We don't know what drove him to these lengths, or whether he feels any guilt about the depths he is stooping to: in fact, his characterisation is next to nonexistent (just how many lines does Keith Barron get in the *whole* episode?). Brian Clemens's influence comes through loud and clear: don't worry about characters, just make sure the end result is thrilling and exciting. So, whereas *The Sweeney* began with something of a character study, *The Professionals* starts with a brash and thoroughly linear template. That it entertains the viewer (and it *does*) is perhaps due to Douglas Camfield's careful direction (even if the drug trips are another excuse for him to dig into his bag of special camera lenses). There is one genuinely great moment, though: Cowley's words to Doyle while they consider the interrogation of Sutton. 'Did you ever know a pusher who was a user . . .? Get me a hypodermic and some heroin.'

Cowley has fought in 'several' wars. CI5 seem able to interrogate their prisoners in any way that they see fit.

The news headlines are suitably bizarre: all the political parties have agreed to defence cuts (thus placing *The Professionals* firmly in the realm of telefantasy!), a woman has been acquitted on pornography charges, and the US president hopes to visit the UK to discuss 'the African problem'.

The scene of the man crashing into the police car has been edited during most recent reruns.

During the initial first-season run, a less familiar title sequence was used. In it, Cowley, Bodie and Doyle scream up in a Rolls-Royce. Bodie and Doyle then do an assault course with two other men, abseil from a great height, dive through a plate-glass window (in slow motion), then get back in the car and drive off at speed. The logo used before and after advert breaks is also slightly different from subsequent seasons (no silhouettes). The more familiar, 'car-crashing-through-a-plate-glass-window' title sequence was devised for the second season and featured on all subsequent episodes, including repeats of the first season, having been dubbed on by LWT (but see 'When the Heat Cools Off'). In an attempt to let the viewers know who these people are, over the opening credits Cowley gets a short voice-over ('Anarchy. Acts of Terror. Crimes against the public. To combat it I've got special men . . .'), which also appears in 'The Female Factor', but was dropped thereafter.

2: 'The Female Factor'

6 January 1978

Writer: Brian Clemens
Director: David Wickes

Cast: Anthony Steel (Sir Charles), Walter Gotell (Baker),
Felicity Dean (Sara), Pamela Salem (Ann),
Barry Justice (Simon Cilver), Maggie Wright (Paula),

Patrick Durkin (Terkoff), Fredric Abbott (Big Man), Stefan Kalipha (Wences), Michael Burrell (Reeve), Sally Harrison (Jo), Kenneth Watson (Tilson)

The apparent suicide of a high-class prostitute of Doyle's acquaintance leads CI5 into a complex plot to incriminate an opposition minister.

Keep Your Mincers Peeled For . . . : Pamela Salem was a telefantasy icon of the 70s and 80s, starring in *Tripods* and *Into the Labyrinth*. Walter Gotell appeared in six James Bond films in the role of the Soviet spymaster, General Gogol. Patrick Durkin was a reliable character actor who seemed to specialise in two sorts of role: Eastern Bloc spies (as here) and Scouse labourers (as in *The Sweeney*'s 'Contact Breaker').

Items worth spotting in Doyle's flat: a fourteen-inch TV set (couldn't he afford anything bigger?), a backgammon game and a trumpet. You'll also be able to spot a number of record covers on the wall of the disco. These include the Doobie Brothers' *Stampede* LP, ELO's *A New World Record* and a Donna Summer cover (possibly a twelve-inch single).

Birds: **** An absolute babe-fest, this one. Ann strips down to her briefs and bra as she climbs the stairs (and escapes from the house wearing nothing but her knickers and a big fur coat). Sara spends much of the episode in a bikini. She and Sir Charles are, of course, photographed while writhing on the shagpile. Bodie and Doyle escape from a wedding reception with (respectively) a brunette (called Sue) and a blonde. Doyle even gets to visit Joanna, the blonde hooker (he tells her to 'Get 'em off!'), with lousy alcohol, which leads us to . . .

Booze: *** Bodie, Doyle and Cowley tuck into Cowley's whisky in the office. Baker and Terkoff share an inevitable Smirnoff, and, when the latter dies in the car park, there's a large cardboard box that once contained Cinzano behind him. There's Möet in the club, though Bodie prefers a pint . . .

Shooters: ** . . . And with said pint in one hand, he has a really cool (one-handed!) fist fight. As for shooters, Terkoff and 'Uncle Sam' Baker have guns; the CI5 chaps return fire. Doyle is shot in the leg. 'At least I haven't got your problem. It's gone right through,' he says to Cowley, before collapsing. (See 'Old Dog with New Tricks' for the (delayed) explanation of Cowley's limp.)

Motors: Sir Charles drives a dark XJ-S. Ann has a nice yellow Spitfire. Wences the pimp drives a 'big American car' (it's a Mustang). Apparently, it's 'gold'-coloured, but in most conditions it seems to look grey. Simon Culver drives a grey Granada Ghia (when Sara tries to get away in it, dramatic convention dictates that it doesn't start first time – either that, or mid-70s middle-of-the-road cars really were as unreliable as we have been led to believe). We reckon we never saw the TR7 again because Doyle destroyed too many tyres screeching to a halt.

Threads: Bodie and Doyle look pretty cool in their dark suits, though Ray Doyle's collars do look somewhat like the wings of Concorde. Bodie's brown, leatherish jacket makes its first appearance. If we had to walk on crutches for any length of time, we wouldn't wear flares as wide as Doyle's. And a special word about Simon's dirty-yellow check jacket. Vile. Yes, that'll do.

***Shaft* Guitar?:** Lots of sinister cello. The disco scene has two main bits of music; one a dreadfully plinky-plonky xylophone-led bit of background Muzak, the second a more strident rock-guitar theme.

Doyle Cooks a Bit of Pasta: He knows the rules of backgammon, and says 'Ciao' on the phone, which must mark him out as some kind of pre-New Man New Man.

Non-PC Moment: Actually, Bodie, Doyle and Reeve all very carefully use the word 'black' to describe Wences, but does 'a big flash car driven by a black guy' (automatically) mean he's a pimp, as Doyle suggests?

Laughable Dialogue: Cowley (to Doyle): 'I can sell your

body to science if I want while it's still alive!'

Sir Charles: 'What the devil do you mean?' Cowley: 'Ah, the devil. Yes, I think the devil had something to do with it.'

Notes: 'You're not coppers.' 'No, we're worse. Much worse.' Oh dear, oh dear. Only the second episode, and we already have a plot repetition (drug-dependent women used for nefarious ends). Still, the rest of this episode is fine eye-candy, and there is at least a hint that Cowley doesn't always approve of the people he's charged to 'protect'. Sir Charles gets his comeuppance in a very smart conclusion.

Doyle's first name is revealed as Ray. When he worked in the drug squad he used to live in a flat north of the river; now he lives in Chelsea. He doesn't smoke. It is stated for the first time (in this transmission order!) that Bodie has an army background. Cowley says nothing is outside of CI5's jurisdiction. Certainly, we see that they can take over any investigation from any branch of the police force (and have their own forensic teams); that they can imprison without charge; and that (as in the previous episode) interrogation is very much in their purview. The shadow minister expects his party to be back in power within the year (so, presumably, he's a Tory: he certainly has the morals of one!).

Jo the prostitute charges £50 a half-hour (blimey, that's a bit steep *now*, let alone in 1978 – she *must* have been good!). There are references to Sherlock Holmes and Batman. Some of the location filming took place close to the Royal Albert Hall.

3: 'Old Dog with New Tricks'
13 January 1978

Writer: Brian Clemens
Director: Sidney Hayers

Cast: Johnny Shannon (Charley Turkel),
Stephen Chase (Dapper), Philip Davis (Billy),
Richard Hampton (Morgan),
Pamela Stephenson (Nurse Bolding),

Anthony Morton (Henry Turkel),
John Judd (Police Inspector), Basil Hoskin (Dr Brook),
Edward Dentith (High-Ranking Police Officer),
Sammie Winmill (Young Lady)

Gangland boss Charley Turkel's plans to kidnap a 'top cop' to use as a hostage to gain the release of his brother come to the attention of George Cowley at CI5. His brief is to 'use any means necessary' to foil Turkel's scheme.

Keep Your Mincers Peeled For ...: Pamela Stephenson (these days Mrs Billy Connolly), fresh from Australia and a year before her star-making role as a member of the *Not the Nine O'Clock News* team, has a small (but beautifully formed) role here. Some of the faces in this episode will be familiar from *The Sweeney* – Johnny Shannon and Anthony Morton for instance (see 'In From the Cold' and 'Golden Boy' respectively). Older telefantasy fans will remember a teenage Sammie Winmill as Carol, one of the originals from *The Tomorrow People*.

There's a BEAT THE BURGLAR poster in the police station. Two Silver Jubilee posters are visible in shops near the station, which gives a rough indication of the likely month in which the location filming was done. There's a (seemingly genuine) copy of the *Evening Standard* (the date looks like 24 September 1977) but with a mock headline MILITARY HOSTAGE.

Birds: ** The two nurses at Dartingford hospital in flowery dresses (see **Non-PC Moment**). Bodie's current sleeping partner Clare (and *not* Cowley's secretary Betty, as Doyle says), walks around his flat wearing nothing but a blouse.

Booze: ** Cowley's a whisky drinker (chiefly to mask the pain from the bullet in his leg). He invites both Bodie and Doyle to share a glass with him in his office. Most of the Turkel gang are on the hard stuff, too.

Shooters: ** The episode begins with an 'Irish gang' raiding an armoury, involves a hand grenade, and ends with Doyle sticking a lethal-looking shotgun against Henry Turkel's head.

Motors: Poor old Bodie and Doyle drive around in a dark-brown Rover 3500 (EMK 760J – it's not even new!). Just look at how (badly) the suspension fares when it comes round the corner and then brakes to a halt. (Incidentally, the same car can be glimpsed in *Sweeney 2*.) We've seen better road-holding in a blancmange. (The Capris must have been a comparative relief after this!) Cowley's got a pale-brownish-yellow Rover SD1. There are vast amounts of police Triumph 2000-type cars, a big army truck – and a copper-coloured Princess.

Threads: Let's start with Bodie's sheepskin bedspread, and continue with his flared strides. There's the first appearance of two of the series' most memorable images, Doyle's checky blue and white shirt, and Bodie's white poloneck (with his gun holster worn, rather obviously, on the outside). Big leather-jacket era, too!

***Shaft* Guitar?:** The pre-titles have a heavy bass theme, laced with trumpets. There's a snazzy little piece as Bodie and Doyle enter the hospital. The slower, more jazzy secondary version of the main score accompanies one of the final scenes.

Slash Fiction Moment: At the end, Bodie and Doyle walk down the corridor together. Almost holding hands, but not quite.

Non-PC Moment: The famous sequence where Bodie rips open Nurse Bolding's blouse to get out the hand grenade, and we get a close-up of Pamela Stephenson's breasts ('Your lucky day, Nurse Bolding!'). He ends up on top of her, of course. The scene is, however, preceded by one of Bodie's finest moments: 'He's holding a Webley .44 . . . along with a 38B cup!'

Jargon: Doyle: 'He coughed.' Cowley: 'If you mean he talked, then say so.'

Laughable Dialogue: First Irishman: 'Roight [sic], let's be havin' yer.' Second Irishman: 'We did it. By God, we pulled it off!'

Billy: 'I want a lawyer.' Bodie: 'Why, son? Do you want to make a will?'

Cowley to a bunch of CI5 recruits: 'You'll be paired off and from then on you're the Bisto Kids. The slightest whiff of anything and you move in, shake him down, crush him before they even start to grow, like an alley fight. And that's what it is, an alley fight. So kick him in the goolies first. Do unto others now what they're still thinking about. Oh, there'll be squeals. And once in a while you'll turn a law-abiding citizen into an authority-hating anarchist. There'll be squeals and letters to MPs, but that's the price they have and we have to pay to keep this island clean and smelling, even if ever so faintly, of roses and lavender!' Even Bodie notes the Fascist overtones!

Notes: 'You CI5 boys think you're the cat's whiskers, don't you?' This was the first episode filmed, and certainly *should* have been the first shown. In places, it's actually pretty well characterised: Cowley gives a speech of fire-breathing right-wing menace (see **Laughable Dialogue**), then we find out he got his limp taking a bullet in the Spanish Civil War fighting the Fascists. Bodie served in Belfast, 'keeping the peace', to which Doyle asks 'Whose peace?'

Bodie knows the work of Samuel Beckett. Doyle was a former policeman – though, perhaps surprisingly, he never rose above the rank of detective constable. Cowley could have the bullet removed from his leg, but is fearful that it might lead to amputation.

CI5 have no ranks, but their authority places them above the police chain of command. There's an oblique reference to the St Valentine's Day massacre. CI5's nicknames, according to Cowley, include 'the Action Squad', 'the Big A' and '*the* Squad'! They 'work for' the Home Secretary. In keeping with the 'pilot episode' feel of this episode, the radios are rather different from the norm, too (these are small 'boxes' with aerials; the usual ones look more like slimline shavers).

Is the mention of Wood Lane police station a subtle dig at the Beeb?

4: 'Killer with a Long Arm'
20 January 1978

Writer: Brian Clemens
Director: David Wickes

Cast: Michael Latimer (Georgi), Diane Keen (Hilda),
Milos Kirek (Costa), Alan Tilvern (Tarkos),
Jonathan Hyde (Tommy), Anthony Carrick (Mervin),
Mitzi Rogers (Barbara), James Leith (Carter),
Hal Jeayes (Poacher), Suzanne Danielle (Pretty Girl)

A top Greek assassin has entered the country and killed a policeman. Of slightly more interest to CI5 is the lethal weapon he is carrying. And finding out who his intended target is.

Keep Your Mincers Peeled For . . . : Suzanne Danielle, one of *the* sex symbols of the 1970s. She's not in the episode for long, but, since she wears virtually no clothes whatsoever, that's quite all right with us. For both Michael Latimer and Diane Keen, see *Sweeney!*.

The high-rise apartment that Costa and Georgi break into is a hideous example of 1970s design. See how many ugly specimens of modernist architecture, dated furniture, electrical items and ornaments of the era *you* can spot!

In Tommy's flat, there are a couple of posters worth looking out for: Che Guevara (an obvious choice for a poster, since he's a terrorist . . .), and, of course, one celebrating the beauty of his homeland (with GREECE written in English on it!).

Birds: *** Hilda, a gypsy-dress-wearing member of the Greek terrorist group, although she isn't Greek herself ('I believe in the cause'). This was the era of attractive Bad-Girl Terrorists (Leila Khaled, Marion and Dolours Price) so she's not as ridiculous as she sounds. Her *other* look (stretch pants, black leather gloves) is much more in keeping with her role as a cold-eyed bomber.

Investigating the apartment block where the Greeks are hiding, Bodie meets a pretty young woman wearing only a blue towel and a smile. They make a date for tomorrow, but he later has to burst into her apartment and climb on to her sunroof, by which time she's changed into a kimono-style dressing gown. At the end, Doyle and Bodie use the long-distance gun to check out the bedroom of a girl wearing a white bra and knickers and black suspenders and stockings. She's a natural blonde, notes Cowley with some interest!

Booze: * Ouzo is mentioned in the Greek restaurant. Bodie drinks a can of Heineken. Several bottles of Möet champagne are seen in ice buckets at Wimbledon.

Shooters: *** A policeman is killed with a shotgun in the pre-titles. The whole plot concerns a very special (and extremely tasty) piece of weaponry ('Good tool, this,' notes Doyle). Georgi also toys with a lethal-looking sub-machine-gun. There are various shotguns and handguns on display.

Motors: There's a nice grey Jag XJ6 and a white Range Rover. Bodie drives a white Triumph Dolomite (POK 79R) for the first time. Cowley's yellow Rover 3500 SD1 automatic has the (hysterical) registration number MOO 229R! The Greek royals are whisked to Wimbeldon in a Roller, of course.

Threads: Bodie's *Saturday Night Fever*-style double-breasted brown jacket and cream strides. His salmon-pink shirt, seen later, is a crime against humanity. Georgi's general *Jason King* look in the opening scene.

***Shaft* Guitar?:** Some wildly choppy *shakkashakka* guitars to accompany Costa and Georgi driving up the motorway, and the inevitable sinister keyboard music when the golfer gets shot. There's a nice cello variation on the title music.

Slash Fiction Moment: A beauty. Doyle does the paperwork in the Squad rest room, while Bodie, having had a shower, wanders around in his dressing gown drying his hair.

Non-PC Moment: Doyle: 'Irish Greek?' Bodie: 'Well, perhaps his granny had a bicycle!' And various other tasteless, racist observations about the Greek community.

Laughable Dialogue: Cowley: 'I'm a man with a tidy mind, you see: I enjoy stamping "Case Closed"!'

Cowley: 'There's one thing you and I share, Bodie . . . We share an animal instinct and a nose for trouble. You too, Doyle. You can't teach it, you can't learn it. You've either got it or you haven't got it.'

Notes: 'Two dead, neither of them us. We did OK.' A horrible episode – outrageously racist and sadistically violent. For long stretches it's not even particularly funny either. Nice location work in South London, and some of the images (the scarecrow in the cornfield, the golfer carrying on putting, unconcerned, as shots are flying around him) are suitably bizarre. (A shame that the rifle seems to fire the world's slowest bullets.) Bodie and Doyle's argument over the risks taken in their simultaneous entry into the flat ('Next time, you can be the monkey on the string') is also worthy of a second look. Much of the acting, though, is one-dimensional.

Bodie and Doyle refer to Cowley as 'the Cow'. The Wimbledon stock footage features Bjorn Borg.

5: 'Heroes'
27 January 1978

Writer: James McAteer
Director: William Brayne

Cast: John Castle (Tommy), Rufus Collins (Tin Can),
Ralph Michael (Estate Car Driver),
Dorothy White (Mrs Lewis), Thomas Baptiste (Huntley),
Damien Thomas (Raider), Robert McBain (Mr Lewis),
Jim McManus (Lorry Driver's Mate),
David Baron (Mr Sumner), Chris Dillinger (Raider),
Neil Kennedy (Raider), Luan Peters (Lady in Sports Car),
Gay Close (Bride), Christopher Neil (Bridegroom),
Jonathan David (Raider), Peter Davidson (Lorry Driver),
Peter Craze (Security Man),
Valentine Palmer (News Reporter)

An American bigot called John Gerry Patterson is murdered, despite the protection of CI5. The killing is witnessed, and filmed, by a number of people, whose lives are put at risk by a newspaper printing their names and addresses . . .

Keep Your Mincers Peeled For . . .: Bruce Boa plays Patterson (uncredited); he's probably most famous for his roles in *Fawlty Towers* (playing Mr Hamilton in 'Waldorf Salad') and *The Empire Strikes Back*. The *Fawlty Towers* connection continues with Luan Peters, who played Raylene Miles in 'The Psychiatrist' (notably getting Basil's soot-covered hand on her bosom). John Castle crops up in all sorts of stuff, from *I, Claudius* to *The Vanishing Man*.

Watch out for two quite lengthy sequences featuring Cowley's primitive Sony VCR. One of the posters in Huntley's club refers to MILITARY GENOCIDE IN ETHIOPIA (see *The Sweeney* – 'The Bigger They Are').

Birds: * The two truckers look down on the blonde in the sports car. 'Shall we let her in?' 'I wish she'd do the same for me.'

Booze: ** Bodie offers to buy Cowley a pure malt. Later, while watching one of the witnesses, he complains that Doyle should have brought some drink for them. 'I'm like a fine piece of machinery: I need lubrication,' he says. 'Yeah, well, too much lubrication and that fine piece of machinery might finish up with a bullet up its crank case,' retorts Doyle. Cowley in turn offers to buy Bodie a malt whisky, but instead proceeds to Latymer's club, where (after all this talk!) they finally consume some champagne. The hit men all drink cans of Skol.

Shooters: ***** Plenty of guns for the failed hit outside the hotel, and the successful killing on the road. Some CI5 chaps turn up to protect one of the witnesses with just about the biggest rifles you ever did see. There is a confrontation between the villains, armed with handguns and a sawn-off, and Bodie, Doyle and Tommy. Tommy has a pump-action shotgun with a folding stock. Most of the killers escape, then proceed to take pot shots at people from a variety of cars (and a speedboat). Tommy responds with (get this) a grenade launcher!

Motors: There's a whole load of vehicles caught up in the roadworks, including Minis, Cortinas, Transits, Volvo trucks and a gold MGB. The assassins escape in a yellow Mercedes. Mr May's disgusting yellow Marina gets what's coming to it when the villains shoot at it from a passing Mk II Jaguar. Tommy drives a black Capri II Ghia. The killers observe the newly-weds from a black Triumph 2000; some CI5 chaps turn up in a black Maxi, of all things. A black Dolomite is used during the attempt on Mr Sumner's life.

Threads: Bodie's pink shirt (a different one), Doyle's check shirt, both worn with holsters over the top. Tommy's light-blue flares and Guinness T-shirt. Tin Can's red San Francisco T-shirt isn't exactly rasta-natty-dread either.

***Shaft* Guitar?:** There's some supposedly tense music during the confrontation in the abandoned warehouse: full of violins, tingly keyboards, even that thing that sounds like a rapidly played comb.

Non-PC Moment: Another black man, another junky . . . Still, there is quite a nice bit where Doyle appeals to Huntley's sense of ethnic betrayal as a way of getting information.

Laughable Dialogue: Cowley: '. . . tighter than a Scotsman on Burns Night . . .'

Notes: 'Because our killers are British – British northerners – and they've got nowhere else to run to.' The plot is wafer-thin and something of an excuse for some nice gun battles, but at least Bodie's crass humour in the face of the deaths of innocent people is jumped on by Doyle and Cowley. The stupidity of some aspects of the script is staggering, however – a team of hit men from the north (where? Liverpool? Newcastle? Leeds? – they've all got RSC accents anyway, so it seems not to matter) who get their info on their targets from the press (as if any British newspaper, no matter how sensationalist, would print the names *and addresses* of witnesses in a murder case!).

There is another reference to CI5 also being known as 'the Big A'. Doyle loses 50p on the horses. Bodie tells a story from his days in Africa (a nurse tried to commit suicide and blamed him for it). Cowley quotes Harry Truman: 'The buck stops here.' References are made to the Lone Ranger and Tonto, and *Nineteen Eighty-Four*.

6: 'Where the Jungle Ends'
3 February 1978

Writer: Brian Clemens
Director: Raymond Menmuir

Cast: David Suchet (Krivas), Del Henney (Benny),
Geoffrey Palmer (Simon Sinclair),
Christopher Reich (Franky), Paul Humpoletz (Tub),
Leon Lissek (Pole), Jeremy Bulloch (Denver),
Robert James (Cusak), Georgina Kean (Cynthia),
Arthur Blake (Butler), Desmond Jones (Bank Manager)

A bank raid is carried out in military style. Bodie knows the group responsible. He was once a friend of several of them. And a sworn enemy of the leader, Krivas.

Keep Your Mincers Peeled For ...: David Suchet subsequently won popular acclaim for his definitive portrayal of Hercules Poirot in the handsome Carnival Films series of the early 90s. For Geoffrey Palmer, see *The Sweeney* – 'Feet of Clay'. Jeremy Bulloch was a teenage star in the 1960s in the BBC's soap opera *The Newcomers*. Fans of *Robin of Sherwood* will remember his semiregular performance as Edward, although he's probably most famous as the man behind the mask of Boba Fett in the *Star Wars* trilogy.

Watch out for a horrible pair of orange-patterned curtains – the sort that everybody thought were as cool as a polar bear's naughties in 1976, but five years later had found their way either into a jumble sale or on to a bonfire. One of the best bits of the episode is when Bodie and Doyle visit the block of flats in which Benny's girlfriend lives. Keep your finger on the freeze-frame for some excellent 70s graffiti, including FONZIE FOR KING! (well, *Happy Days* was *very* big back then!), THE FUZZ ARE PIGS, THE HAMMERS (West Ham United) and QPR. (We'd love to know where it was filmed as those two teams are from opposite ends of London and don't have many areas of crossover support!)

A copy of the *Daily Express* for 22 November 1977 is visible. The headline DARING ARMED BANK RAID! seems to have been especially for the episode, however.

The aerial sequences – presumably a montage of RAF stock footage and specially shot scenes of the light aircraft – are hysterical. The Harriers that we watch take off (and see in formation and manoeuvring) keep changing into Jaguars, and the landscape beneath the light aeroplane – gently rolling farmland – clashes with the military aircraft banking over windswept Scottish moorland!

Birds: * When Bodie and Doyle pretend to kidnap Sinclair's daughter, little Miss Cynthia proves to be a right saucy minx, hitching up her skirt and wondering why Doyle doesn't try to 'ravish' her ('Aren't I pretty enough?'). Doyle feigns an illness, and they share some chocolate. Now, if it had been Bodie in the car, we dread to *think* what might have gone on.

Booze: * Sinclair and Krivas share a whisky.

Shooters: *** Vast amounts of sub-machine-gun fire during the bank raid, and during the escape. More weapons (including knives) in the conclusion.

Motors: A 'grey Air Force truck'. Various police Triumphs, a couple of panda cars (Allegros), a grey Rolls-Royce, and a police Range Rover. A yellow and grey Ford three-ton truck, and some scrambling bikes. Cowley's usual yellow Rover, plus Bodie's Dolomite.

Threads: Bodie's checked jacket and his dark suit with turned-up cuffs. His salmon shirt puts in another appearance, while later he wears a garish scarlet one with a collar so wide it's a surprise he doesn't need a police escort. Thankfully it gets ripped to shreds during his fight with Krivas, so hopefully that's the last we'll see of it. One of the customers in the bank wears a disgusting open-necked brown shirt with an equally massive collar: sadly, nobody thought to shoot him. Benny's red tie. Doyle's awful ginger checked jacket.

Shaft **Guitar?:** Throbbing disco music, with plucking basslines for the bank raid, and, indeed, much of the episode. The kind of 'porno funk music' that *The New Avengers* specialised in. In places it sounds not unlike Atomic Rooster. There's a cool jazz theme to accompany Bodie and Doyle's visit to Cusak, and the slow cello variation on the title music reappears.

Slash Fiction Moment: The charged tension when Bodie stops Doyle from beating up Cusak. Handbags at ten paces.

Jargon: Bodie: 'You could be giving me a bum steer. Convince me.'

Laughable Dialogue: Bodie: 'Drink?' Doyle: 'You buying?' Bodie: 'I'm buying.' Doyle: 'I'm drinking!'
  Sinclair: 'I've told you what I want done. How you do it is up to you. When you have done it, I think your Swiss bank manager will nod his gnomish little head with delight!'
  Bodie gets philosophical: 'Britain's become a funny bloody place.' Doyle: 'Social revolution?'
  Bodie: 'Screech owl.' Doyle: 'Screech owl? What are you, Bodie, a bird-watching freak?'

Notes: 'I'm not breaking the law, just bending it.' A completely moronic episode, but ultimately great fun. The dialogue is so overblown that after half a dozen scenes it becomes hilarious. The episode is packed with really good actors giving it their resigned best (notably Geoffrey Palmer and David Suchet, who are always worth watching, and a lovely little cameo from the actress playing Cynthia). And there's the mother of all gunfights at the end. A good one to watch with your mates, with a chicken-and-prawn curry, after a few bevvies.
  There are several references to the (real-life) civil war in

Angola. During the mid-1970s many British mercenaries were involved in this (particularly bloody) conflict, which reached a climax in 1976 with the Marxist-Leninist MPLA emerging victorious (hands up everybody who finally understands the last verse of 'Anarchy in the UK'!) over the government forces of UNITA.

Bodie seems to be very good at darts (three double tops, one when he wasn't even trying). A couple of years ago (presumably just before he joined CI5 and teamed up with Doyle – see 'Close Quarters'), Bodie was in Holland. There were rumours that he was dead, and Franky says the last he heard Bodie was rotting in a Congo jail (this must have been some time ago, as Congo was called Zaïre at the time). The bank robbed is a branch of the London & National.

Stock footage of Heathrow airport, and of various RAF fighter planes, forms up to five minutes of the episode. Other directorial failings (see **Keep Your Mincers Peeled For . . .**) include less-than-successful, speeded-up sequences (for instance, as the police car crashes) and some very poor editing during the Bodie–Krivas fight sequence. When Bodie mentions the '.44 Magnum. At close range . . .', is he alluding to Dirty Harry in *Magnum Force*?

7: 'Close Quarters'
10 February 1978

Writer: Brian Clemens
Director: William Brayne

Cast: Hildegard Neil (Sara), Gabrielle Drake (Julia), Clive Arrindell (Myer), Madlena Nedeva (Inge), Allan Surtees (Vicar), David Bradley (Kristo), Barney James (Hans), Rowland Davies (Doctor)

Given time off because of a hand injury, Bodie takes his girl-friend for a relaxing day on the Thames near Marlow. And runs into a group of fanatic German anarchist terrorists. As you do.

Keep Your Mincers Peeled For ...: Gabrielle Drake's legion of fans followed her career through *UFO*, *The Brothers* and (even) *Crossroads*. She's the main villain in the best ever episode of *The Avengers* ('The Hidden Tiger'). (One of the authors of this book also possesses a copy of her 1972 film *Au Pair Girls* – though the least said about that the better.) Fans of *Ace of Wands* will remember Hildegard Neil's performance as Madame Midnight.

Two amusing gaffes are worth looking out for. Doyle insists on calling Julia 'Julie', while the female HQ radio voice tells Cowley that 'Brodie's car' has been found. Also watch out for the dramatic pratfall by the stuntman whose car Bodie has just stolen as the terrorists drive past.

Once again, the *Daily Express* (at the time the most reactionary and right-wing of all the British press) seems to be the production team's choice of newspaper. The headline says 'VIP KILLED IN AIRPORT LOUNGE!'

Birds: * Bodie's current girlfriend is the lovely Julia, a sensible redhead with a tasteful choice in clothes. Come *on*, what's a goddess like her doing with a prat like Bodie?!

Booze: * The terrorists seems to be planning a nice night in with a meal and white wine when Bodie arrives! Bodie is about to drink what looks like a brandy at the vicarage, but is distracted. Cowley tells Bodie and Doyle to be in the Red Lion at 8.30 – he wants the cost of his car window back in single-malt Scotch.

Shooters: *** The Myer-Helmut group are all tooled up with sub-machine-guns. Bodie and Julia take them on with one semiautomatic pistol.

Motors: A pivotal moment: the first CI5 Capri! Bodie drives a bronze Mk II 3.0 Ghia (top speed: 120 m.p.h.). It's from CI5's car pool, which is specifically mentioned for the first time. Bodie steals a brown Cortina estate (check out that wood-veneer trim!), and is chased by a red Audi 80. Cowley's changed to a yellowish Granada.

Threads: Bodie's horrible brown jumper, and a white one

with what looks like a club motif on it. Doyle's taste in chunky jackets gets worse and worse.

Shaft Guitar?: Snare drum and violins in the opening. The cello version of the theme makes a reappearance. There is a funky, up-tempo wah-wah-guitar sequence as the terrorists drive through the front door of the vicarage, and some nice stabs of brass at various points during the siege.

Laughable Dialogue: Bodie: 'Take your choice: you can walk, or I'll pistol-whip you and carry you.'

Inge: 'You English, you know nothing about politics!'

Notes: 'You fight fire with fire in this job.' Again, this one is so stupid, it's brilliant. A mini *Die Hard* in which an injured Bodie single-handedly takes out a crack team of international terrorists while protecting 'two hysterical women'. What a guy! Actually, some of the dialogue strives for philosophical impact: there's an interesting discussion between Bodie and Myer about how alike they are. Let's ignore, however, such contrivances as Bodie encountering the terrorists in the first place. And leaving his walkie-talkie switched on, and in plain view, on the seat of his car. And that wildly improbable shot of his to attract Cowley and Doyle's attention. The vicarage he discovers must be about the most opulent in the entire C of E. Complete with perhaps the most cowardly vicar!

Bodie says he never gave much thought to where he would die – it could be down a dark alley, in the African jungle, or running for the last bus! He misquotes James Cagney's dialogue from the end of *White Heat* ('Look, see, Ma – made it! Top of the world!': 'He died' notes Julia). Cowley put Bodie and Doyle together two years and three months ago. They were chalk and cheese, he says, but have worked well together (though they both infuriate him).

The piece of stock Heathrow footage that begins this story is very similar to the clip used at the beginning of the previous episode. The pre-titles murder of the businessman with a lethal injection in broad daylight was probably inspired by the (real-life) murder of the Bulgarian dissident broadcaster Georgi Markos at Waterloo Bridge in 1977 by a member of the Bulgarian secret police, the Darjavna Sugur-nost, using a poison-tipped umbrella as the murder weapon. The Myer-Helmut group, seem to have been directly inspired by the activities of the West German anarchist group the Red Army Faction led by Andreas Baader and Ulrike Meinhof. (Their motto was 'Don't argue, destroy.')

This was the highest-rated episode of the first season (and the second-highest of all time), getting 17.4 million viewers and fifth place in the weekly viewing charts.

8: 'Everest was Also Conquered'
17 February 1978

Writer: Brian Clemens
Director: Francis Megahy

Cast: Michael Denison (Lord Derrington),
Richard Greene (Neil Turvey), Ann Lynn (Ann),
Kathleen Byron (Mrs Turner), Charles Keating (Sammy),
Gary Waldhorn (Turner), Helen Cotterill (Sally),
Roy Boyd (Hamer), Llewellyn Rees (Sir Arden French),
Jeremy Hawk (Sir Frederick Tallen),
Andrew Downie (McKay), Graham Padden (Angus),
Caroline Argyle (Julia Turvey), Peter Blake (Tony Miller),
Robert Booth (Bremner), Mark Colleano (Mark),
Dick Sullivan (Priest)

The deathbed confession of a man opens up all of the gory details of a 25-year-old crime. But people in high places want to stop George Cowley uncovering the truth.

Keep Your Mincers Peeled For ...: Richard Greene was one of television's biggest stars of the 1950s, as the eponymous hero of *The Adventures of Robin Hood*. Michael Denison was another star of the era, in *Boyd QC*. Peter Blake's most memorable roles were in two sitcoms, *Agony* and *Dear John*. For Gary Waldhorn, see *The Sweeney* – 'Hit and Run'.

Prominent in several scenes is the *Daily Express* from 2 June 1953, celebrating the Queen's Coronation and the first conquest of Mount Everest. It seems that fans of half the football teams in the country have been in the Star Hotel, Bayswater judging by the graffiti on the walls (Fulham, Spurs, Manchester United (MUFC), Everton and QPR all being represented).

Birds: * Bodie and Doyle use a photograph of a topless woman to make an unflattering montage of Cowley in the locker room. There are also several girlie posters in the Squad rest room. Bodie tells a girl on the phone that he loves lasagna.

Booze: ** Turvey hurls a glass of 'particularly good' Scotch in Bodie's face, a compliment Bodie later repays. With Cowley, at least he and Doyle have the decency to drink the stuff.

Shooters: * The hit man's high velocity sub-machine-gun. Hamer is armed only with a 'camera gun'.

Motors: Turner's possession of a Rolls-Royce is taken as being proof that he's corrupt. The introduction of Bodie's Capri in the previous episode is followed by a short sequence involving Doyle's silver Capri 3.0 'S' (check out those body skirts!). Bodie's Capri (we see its number plate clearly for the first time: PNO 580R) has its windscreen and tyres shot at by Frank Goodman, the hit man (who drives a dark-brown Mark I Capri). The deer hunters – Hamer, McKay and Angus – have breakfast in the back of their white Range Rover. Bodie and Doyle pick up Goodman in a blue Cortina, but switch back to a Capri before gate-crashing Turvey's grand-daughter's party.

Threads: Doyle's patchwork-quilt jacket makes another appearance. Julia Turvey wears a reasonably OK white blouse.

***Shaft* Guitar?:** The party disco sequence. Shake yer booty.

Non-PC Moment: The Irish Catholic priest in the opening

scene is a bit stereotypical. Begorrah. There are also several very unflattering references to lesbianism from Bodie, but then we think he's just jealous that anyone's getting more women than he is.

Laughable Dialogue: Cowley's frequent aphorism: 'Never send a boy on a man's errand. They'll only pinch his bike.'

And: 'Are you deaf or something, or are you just plain pig-ignorant?'

Notes: 'I killed Susie Carter.' A very obvious (and long-winded) conspiracy episode that takes far longer to reach its conclusion than it needs to (though the scene in the CI5 locker room is rather good). Satisfying last few scenes, however.

Cowley took karate. Tongue-in-cheek, Bodie and Doyle suggest that the new recruit, Tony Miller, should not call Cowley 'the Cow' until he's completed a year's service (and then not in the building). Bodie refers to the Icarus legend, and seems to be a fan of Gary Cooper movies. Doyle makes reference to Orwell's *Nineteen Eighty-Four* (specifically Room 101). Cowley's allusion to 'The Third Man' is more likely to be about Burgess, Maclean and Philby than the Joseph Cotton/Orson Welles film (but see *A Stirring of Dust*).

Bodie's memory plays tricks on him in this episode: he says that Cowley warned them off Turvey before the murder of Tony Miller and Ann Berry. In fact, the meeting to which he refers took place *after* the murder of Miller (and Turner).

9: 'When the Heat Cools Off'
24 February 1978

Writer: Brian Clemens
Director: Ray Austin

Cast: Peter Hughes (Bill Haydon), Lalla Ward (Jill),
Bernard Kay (Harry Scott), Gerald Sim (Minister),
Graham Weston (Syd Parker), Shelagh Fraser (Mrs Wilson),
Arthur White (Freddy), Alistair Cameron (Car Salesman),

Michael Sheard (Merton), Geoffrey Hinsliff (Sergeant),
Robert Mill (Fitch)

Seven years ago, Constable Ray Doyle's partner was gunned down in the line of duty. The man convicted of the dirty deed has been banged up in stir ever since, but now his daughter is making waves and trying to get the case reopened.

Keep Your Mincers Peeled For . . .: Lalla Ward, daughter of Lord Bangor, first came to prominence as the teenage vampire in Hammer's *Vampire Circus*. Her other credits include a memorable appearance as Mary Godwin in John Elliot's 1972 biography of Shelley, a regular part in *The Duchess of Duke Street*, and the second Romana opposite her future husband Tom Baker in *Doctor Who*. Geoffrey Hinsliff was Don Brennan in *Coronation Street*. For Michael Sheard, see *The Sweeney* – 'Hit and Run'. For Bernard Kay, see *The Sweeney* – 'Trap'.

The 1977 sequence begins with a shot of the *Daily Mail* with the headline 'QUEEN'S JUBILEE CELEBRATIONS START WITH A BANG' (which dates it somewhere around 6 June). Doyle's apartment features lots of Scandinavian pine.

The 1971 sequence has a cricket match on television. It's on screen for only a few seconds, but it *looks* like a clip from the 1975 ashes series between England and Australia with Dennis Lillie bowling to Tony Greig.

Birds: ** Bodie has arranged a double date for himself and Doyle. Bodie's bird (name unknown) is a tasty blonde thing, while Doyle's is called Eva (she's 'tall, nubile, accommodating,' says Bodie). They're in a restaurant, with plans to go on to a disco, and are getting on terrifically well when Jill's appearance puts a mocker on things.

Jill herself is a well-spoken strawberry-blonde whom Doyle eventually falls for. Bodie once set Doyle up with a date with a 'big' gymnast. Doyle doesn't seem keen on a repeat. Cowley's secretary (presumably Betty) has 'awfully nice legs' according to the minister.

Booze: ** Doyle and Bodie share a whisky after the

disastrous night out. Cowley and the minister indulge in Cowley's 'awfully good' single-malt Scotch.

Shooters: * The search for the .38 Police Special that killed Fitch and Syd Parker is the focus of the episode.

Motors: We see Syd and Doyle in an Austin 1300-type panda car. Haydon drives off in a grey Jag XJ6; this is later 'rediscovered' by Bodie and Doyle in a Datsun dealership. It, and the panda car, both have K (August 1971 to July 1972) registrations, so the 1971 sequences must take place in August.

We get our first good look at Doyle's Capri (SOO 635R); Bodie is still in the bronze Ghia.

Threads: Doyle's tight black T-shirt and flying jacket (*very* Julian Cope). His scarlet overalls. The 1971 material features some contemporary fashions including a girl in a black miniskirt, and another in blue hot pants and knee-length, white, leather boots.

***Shaft* Guitar?:** Lots of hi-hat and percussion, and a really heavy disco theme as Doyle chases Haydon in his car.

Doyle Cooks a Bit of Pasta: He spends a lot of time working on his vintage Harley-Davidson. He seems to drink cocoa in bed.

Slash Fiction Moment: It occurs late in the episode, Doyle giving Bodie a crushed look after he discovers his betrayal by Jill. Poor lamb.

Jargon: Doyle: 'You're busted.'

Laughable Dialogue: Doyle: 'What kind of gun?' Scott: 'How would I know? . . . The kind that kills you!'

Scott: 'You were always close to death, then, but at least you knew you were alive.'

Notes: 'It's always a set-up with me as the pigeon.' A right load of old cobblers, though the twist in the tale five minutes from the end of the episode is clever. A lot of the story's execution is nonsensical, however (the second Jill starts telling Doyle where the gun might be – alarm bells should start ringing in his mind).

As an additional stick to beat the episode with, the time scale is up the spout. The murders took place in 'the long hot summer' of 1971 (probably August – see **Motors**), while the present-day sequences are set in 1977 (probably June, maybe a bit later). But Haydon has been in jail for seven years and five months according to his daughter, which would place events in about January 1979 (or the flashback in January 1970). And, just as a matter of pure disinterest, the summer of 1971 was one of the coldest of the decade!

When shown in the 1997 repeat season on Granada Plus, this episode featured the original season-one title sequence (aside from the original video release of 'Klansmen', it's just about the only place you'll see it these days).

Bodie can't ride a motorbike according to Doyle (he's joking, of course – see 'Wild Justice'). Cowley used to be a very good tennis player. In 1971 Ray Doyle was a uniform constable (and presumably became a detective constable later, as mentioned in 'Old Dog with New Tricks'). His partner (and friend) was Syd Parker. CI5 was just being formed at this time and Doyle thought it sounded 'exciting, different'.

Six days sounds like a very short trial (especially for a double murder). Cowley believes British justice is near perfect ('God and prevailing winds permitting'). So did most people in 1978 . . .

10: 'Long Shot'
3 March 1978

Writer: Anthony Read
Director: Ernest Day

Cast: Roger Lloyd Pack (Ramos), Martin Benson (Villa),
Robert Gillespie (Sammy), Peter Cellier (Walton),
Nadim Sawalha (Sheikh Achmeia), Ed Bishop (Dr Harbinger),
John Horsley (Mitchell), Shaun Curry (SAS Sergeant),
Tony Caunter (Detective Sergeant), Brian Haines (Agent),
Judy Matheson (Mandy), Max Mason (Corporal),
George Mallaby (Driver), Archie Tew (1st Security Guard),

John Hamill (2nd Security Guard),
Gillian Duxbury (Girl in Gym)

Ramos, a world-class assassin, is in England. His target may be an American diplomat attending a peace conference. Or it may be someone considerably closer to home.

Keep Your Mincers Peeled For ...: Roger Lloyd Pack, complete with a Beatle haircut and shades that make him look like Joey Ramone, is almost unrecognisable to fans of *Only Fools and Horses*, who know him as Trigger. Ed Bishop was, for years, Britain's favourite American actor. Most viewers will know him as the tough Commander Straker in *UFO*. John Horsley was the porn-obsessed Doc Morrissey in *The Fall and Rise of Reginald Perrin*. For Tony Caunter, see *The Sweeney* – 'Queen's Pawn'; for Nadim Sawalha, see *The Sweeney* – 'Visiting Fireman'; for Robert Gillespie, see *The Sweeney* – 'Thin Ice'.

Watch out for Doyle's Adidas sports bag (both of the authors used to have one, as did most of the teenage boys in the country). Is this the first episode to feature a London *A–Z*?

Birds: ** Susie, the karate girl, impresses both Doyle and Bodie. And bombs them both out at one time or another, before going out on a date with Doyle at the climax. Mandy Mitchell is rather pretty, but she falls for the chloroform-over-the-mouth trick almost straight away, and spends most of the episode with a gag in her mouth.

Booze: * The state of Morani seems not to be strictly Islamic, as the Sheikh shares a drink of whisky with Cowley and Harbinger.

Shooters: * Ramos has a lethal array of weaponry.

Motors: Mitchell's daughter is first seen driving a brown Triumph Stag. Ramos has a nice black Jensen Interceptor. Sammy and his pal case the Mitchell place from their yellow Cortina. Mitchell himself has a blue Jag.

There is a continuity error in this episode: Bodie and Doyle race off to the airport in a brown Rover but arrive back at HQ in a white Dolomite.

Threads: The horrible matching jogging suits worn by Harbinger, Bodie and Doyle (see 'Mixed Doubles'). And yet another appalling jacket for Doyle.

***Shaft* Guitar?:** There's some great sinister cello music as Bodie breaks into Mitchell's house.

Non-PC Moment: Bodie on the girl in the gym: 'Women's libber. The way to her heart, and all places south, is to let her beat you!'

Laughable Dialogue: Sheikh Achmeia: 'You people in the West are too damn soft . . .'
    Bodie: 'You heard the man. If you want to catch a tiger . . .'
Doyle: '. . . or lose a good goat?'

Notes: 'Know thine enemy.' This episode has aged so utterly badly that it now looks like brilliant satire of an entire era (complete with an offensive Arab stereotype who goes on all the time about executing people). Watch out for Bodie's reaction to Doyle getting the crap kicked out of him by Susie – it's worth the price of the video on its own!
    Bodie says he has a better head for heights than Doyle (see 'Foxhole on the Roof' for an example). Cowley hates rats. His office has an *en-suite* shower.
    There are references to *Bridge over the River Kwai*, while Cowley's line 'shades of Dallas' may be a nod towards the Kennedy Assassination (although, since he's talking about oilmen hiring assassins, we could assume he's talking about *Dallas*, which had started transmission in the US a few months earlier).
    That bit of stock footage with a Jumbo at Heathrow turns up again!

11: 'Stakeout'
10 March 1978

Writer: Dennis Spooner
Director: Benjamin Wickers

Cast: David Collings (Frank), Barry Jackson (Bob),
Pamela Stephenson (Attractive Blonde), Jack Lynn (Fat Man),
Peter Armitage (Peanut Eater),
Tony Osoba (Handsome Negro),
Ronald Leigh-Hunt (Doctor), Gerald James (Hunter),
Brian Hawksley (Man in Raincoat), Malcom Hayes (Jack),
Barry Stokes (Major), Andrew Bradford (Fraser),
Sarah Grazebrook (Sarah), Fiona Reid (Young Girl),
Brigette Fry (Young Girl)[1]

A CI5 agent stumbles by chance upon a deadly plot, but is
killed soon after phoning Cowley. Bodie and Doyle are
assigned to stake out . . . a bowling club.

Keep Your Mincers Peeled For . . .: David Collings played
Silver in *Sapphire and Steel*, and was later Mr Winter in *Press
Gang*. Tony Osoba is best known for his roles in *Porridge* (as
McLaren), *Coronation Street* (as Peter Ingram) and *Dempsey
and Makepeace* (as Chas Jarvis). Pamela Stephenson appears
for the second time this season (see 'Old Dog with New
Tricks'). Ronald Leigh-Hunt has a career stretching back to
the 1950s when he played King Arthur in *The Adventures of
Sir Lancelot*. A decade later, he played the lead role of
Colonel Buchan in *Freewheelers*, and he was Dr Thorne in
General Hospital.

Cowley has that most 70s of communications devices, a
trill phone!

Birds: ** At the bowling club, Bodie takes a special interest in
two lovelies wearing white T-shirts, slips and knee-high socks.
'How do you score?' asks Doyle, struggling with the com-
plexities of ten-pin bowling. 'I just get lucky, I guess,' says
Bodie modestly, eyeing the gorgeous blonde who's hanging
around the place. She proves to be a junky. Funny how the only
addicts we see in *The Professionals* are either black or good-
looking young women in the thrall of the bad guys.

[1] Sometimes *The Professionals* would jointly credit actors (in this
instance, Reid and Fry are credited as 'Young Girls').

Booze: None, since most of the episode takes place in a bowling alley.

Shooters: * The army soldiers carry rifles; Kerrigan and the others watching the fat white supremacist have pistols.

Motors: John Fraser drives a white Cortina into a handily placed pile of cardboard boxes. Benny, Bodie and Doyle are seen in a Granada; the fat man drives a yellow Merc. Doyle drives his silver Capri again. Police Rovers take Cowley and the army chaps to the bowling alley.

Threads: Doyle's Dennis the Menace top. The black guy's fawn poloneck and enormous flared strides.

Shaft **Guitar?:** The dramatic single chord to accompany the murder of Fraser is nice. Lots of wah-wah guitar in the Fat Man's theme.

Slash Fiction Moment: Bodie gives Doyle a manly thump on the back a couple of times.

Non-PC Moment: Tony Osoba playing a 'handsome negro' (see cast list).

Laughable Dialogue: Hunter: 'What about the little people?' Cowley: 'Like you and me, you mean?'

Notes: 'Swallows!' The scenes during the stakeout are a welcome change of pace, with a few red herrings that would be quite fun if we didn't already know who the terrorists are. You've got to hand it to Shaw and Collins: they really do try their best despite the awful lines they're given. We see another example of the standard *Professionals* episode structure where Bodie and Doyle, and Cowley, arrive at the same conclusions (or location) via separate strands of the investigation.

Doyle has size-nine feet, and plays pool quite well. Neither he nor Bodie seems entirely familiar with bowling (which costs 40p a game). Bodie says he hasn't been to a dentist in years. Benny's shaved off his beard since 'Private Madness, Public Danger'.

Mention is made of the photographer David Bailey, and

there's an oblique reference to *Hawaii 5–0* ('Book him!').
Two Cokes cost 30p.

12: 'Look After Annie'
17 March 1978

Writer: Brian Clemens
Director: Charles Crichton

Cast: Diana Fairfax (Annie), Clifton Jones (Stanley),
Patricia Quinn (Isla), Derek Francis (John Howard),
Keith Buckley (Ben Hymer), Nick Brimble (Big Billy),
Frank Jarvis (Patterson), Michael Walker (Turner),
John Golightly (Police Officer), John Sarbutt (Thug),
David Mallinson (Frank), Jonathan Bergman (Thug)

A radical politician called Annie Irvine, of the Workers'
Christian Alliance, returns to England, with her protection in
the hands of her old flame, George Cowley.

Keep Your Mincers Peeled For . . . : Nick Brimble moves
from Flying Squad Geezer to Butch Biker on Acid! Patricia
Quinn was the villainous Livilla in *I, Claudius*.
  The stock footage of an ecstatic theatre audience used in
the opening scenes seems to have come from the same source
as that used in the legendary video for Sid Vicious's version
of 'My Way'! The headline of this episode's copy of the *Daily
Express* is 'SCANDAL OF POP PUSHERS'. An inside page carries
the headline 'WHY A WOMAN'S LIFE IS ONE BIG HEADACHE'.
Also briefly glimpsed in a broadsheet newspaper carried by
Annie's would-be assassin is an advert for the housing charity
Shelter (which suggests it's a British newspaper, despite the
fact that the assassination attempt was supposed to have taken
place in Chicago). One of the bikers has the legend THE LIVING
DEAD on the back of his jacket.

Birds: * Annie and 'Georgie' Cowley were something of an
item over a number of years after meeting for the first time
when Major Cowley went to university after the war. They

shared a love of opera (one that seems, in Annie's case, not to have survived the relationship). They last met over ten years ago. She has been married (and divorced) twice – odd behaviour for a Christian.

Bodie reads an issue of the soft-core porn mag, *Knave*.

Booze: * Cowley has 'a wee dram of Scotch' with Annie.

Shooters: ** Big Billy Taylor carries a lethal-looking shotgun. The CI5 agents return fire with an array of pistols.

Motors: Cowley and Bodie are seen in the usual yellow Granada and bronze Capri respectively. Bodie uses a blue Transit to take away Annie and the bikers after the shoot-out at the end.

Threads: Bodie's and Doyle's white jackets as they test the security around Annie are rather suave. Doyle's checky shirt and Bodie's sheepskin reappear. There's a nice collection of Y-fronts on display towards the end.

Non-PC Moment: Bodie adopts a really obvious camp accent when asked whether Cowley could be considered attractive.

Laughable Dialogue: Bodie and Doyle on the rather distressing idea of Cowley getting intimate with a woman: 'He'd kick the door down, throw her on the bed . . .' 'And frisk her . . .'

Notes: 'Drop everything! Everything – including your pants!' This episode, directed by the great Charles Crichton, features one of the worst-choreographed fight sequences in TV history, and some appalling editing and acting. Annie, in particular, lacks any hint of the charisma her impact requires.

Cowley never married. It is said he knows which side of whose bed Doyle and Bodie get out of! He was a Major in 16th Special Commando during the war and later served in MI5. He can get tickets for many events, including a forthcoming opera by La Scala. At university, he once got his 'head bust open' at a political meeting, defending freedom of

speech (he implies that he no longer believes as passionately
in this). Bodie makes a reference to Adam and Eve, despite
his agnostic tendencies (see 'Mixed Doubles'). CI5 are not
above planting drugs on people they want to question – or, in
this case, remove from the public eye for a few days.

There are references to Joan of Arc, the Tolpuddle Martyrs,
John F. Kennedy, Eva Perón and Jesus as people whose power
and influence were greater after death than before (the book
The Death of Eva Perón is seen at one point). There is lots of
stock footage of police in riot gear which seems to have been
drawn from news film of football matches and (possibly)
political demonstrations.

13: 'Klansmen'
not broadcast in the UK

Writer: Brian Clemens,
based on a story by Simon Masters
Director: Pat Jackson

Cast: Edward Judd (Hulton), Trevor Thomas (Zadie),
Sheila Ruskin (Helen), Anthony Booth (Dinny),
Lawrie Mark (Tommy), Oscar James (Topaz),
Louis Mahoney (Doctor), George Harris (Arty),
James Coyle (Merv), Madeleine Newbury (Miss Pearce),
Jules Walter (Mr Miller), Trevor Ward (Ben),
Stephen Lawrence (Lenny), Allister Bain (Mr Culver),
Willie Payne (Carter)

A series of racist attacks involves Bodie and Doyle in a
deadly case.

Keep Your Mincers Peeled For . . . : Tony Booth achieved TV
immortality as Mike, the 'randy Scouse git' son-in-law of Alf
Garnett in *Till Death Us Do Part*. These days he's prob-
ably more famous as the father-in-law of the Prime Minister.
Oscar James was Tony Carpenter in *EastEnders*. For Edward
Judd, see *The Sweeney* – 'Money, Money, Money'. Louis

Mahoney played another white-coated doctor in the *Fawlty Towers* episode 'The Germans'.

Birds: * Bodie spends most of the episode deliriously insulting the pretty black nurse, but ends up going out with her.

Booze: ** Cowley and Doyle share a whisky. Tommy gives Doyle some Scotch after he's been beaten up by Dinny.

Shooters: * There are a couple of shotguns visible, along with knives and clubs, but actually much of the violence in this episode is hand-to-hand.

Motors: Zadie has a nice red Merc, as befits a successful lawyer (and much to Bodie's chagrin). Doyle's silver Capri puts in another appearance. Hulton and Dinny are driven around in a blue Cortina.

Threads: Tommy's half-mast denims, red checky shirt and Jackson Five afro. Cowley's enormous black-and-purple kipper tie.

Shaft **Guitar?:** A generally bass-heavy soundtrack. The violin-and-cello music as Arty is killed is excellent.

Slash Fiction Moment: Doyle almost in tears as Bodie lies bleeding on a hospital trolley. 'Bodie, you half-Irish son of a bitch, what do you wanna go and do that for?'

Completely- PC Moment: The entire story. Any episode that displays the sort of anger at racism that this one does can be forgiven a large amount of bad dialogue and plot loopholes (the revelation about Mr Miller, and Doyle's closing comments, threaten to trivialise the polemic, but don't quite).

Laughable Dialogue: Bodie: 'That's overreacting a bit, isn't it? After all, all they did was plant a cross in a spade's garden.'

Doyle (pretending to be racist): 'Who you gonna serve, the real people, or the monkeys?'

Tommy: 'You're going to have an eye blacker than my arse!'

Notes: 'You want to mix it with me, nigger?' An astonishing piece of work, every bit as raw and challenging today as it was in 1978 when nervous ITV bosses pulled it from the schedules (the episode has been transmitted in some overseas markets, and got a belated British debut when it was released on video in the late 1980s). Easily the best episode of the first season: the redemption of Bodie from a racist thug into a human being, despite being something of a contrived revelation, is necessary and laudable all the same.

Doyle refers to the film *In Like Flint*. Bodie watches a game of pitch and toss, and Zadie is interrupted in the middle of a game of bridge (horribly, appropriately enough, bidding four spades). His wife suggests Scrabble after his departure.

Second Season

Ten 60-minute episodes
An Avengers Mark 1 Production/London Weekend Television
Created by Brian Clemens

Associate Producer: Chris Burt
Producer: Raymond Menmuir
Executive Producers: Albert Fennell, Brian Clemens

Title music by Laurie Johnson

Regular Cast: Gordon Jackson (George Cowley),
Martin Shaw (Ray Doyle), Lewis Collins (William Bodie),
Diana Weston (Ruth Pettifer, 14[1], 16, 19[2]),
Trevor Adams (Benny, 15), Allan Surtees (Minister, 15, 18[3])

---

[1] Credited as 'Ruth' in this episode.
[2] Credited as 'CI5 Girl' in both episodes 16 and 19. Cowley refers to her as 'Miss Pettifer'.
[3] Cowley refers to the minister as 'William' in this episode.

14: 'Hunter/Hunted'
7 October 1978

Writer: Anthony Read
Director: Anthony Simmons

Cast: Cheryl Kennedy (Kathie), Bryan Marshall (Preston), John Stratton (Brownie), Tony Caunter (Maurice Richards), Frank Barrie (Martell), Martin Wyldeck (Jack), Malcolm Hayes (Forensic Man), Maria St Clare (Singer), Jeillo Edwards (West Indian Woman), Vicki Michelle (Jo)

Bodie and Doyle are given the job of testing a new American rifle, but, while Doyle is out with an old girlfriend, somebody steals the gun from his airing cupboard.

Keep Your Mincers Peeled For . . .: Cheryl Kennedy was a regular face on TV in the 1970s, though most teenage boys of the era will be more familiar with her bottom and its significance to the plot of Dick Emery's 1971 film *Ooh . . . You Are Awful!*. (Her character in that film has the same surname – Mason – as her role here.) Bryan Marshall appeared in series such as *United!*, *Villains, Warship* and *Out*. He would later star in *Buccaneer*. Vicki Michelle is best known as Yvette in *'Allo 'Allo!*. For Tony Caunter, see *The Sweeney* – 'Queen's Pawn'.

Watch out for more football-related graffiti – CFC (Chelsea, presumably) and the rather bizarre ARSENAL FOR ENGLAND! WOT AGAIN?. There are also two lots of graffiti celebrating THE MEETING, the significance of which escapes us.

Doyle has a new apartment since the previous season – a two-floor, very 70s pad, with a dangerous-looking modernist staircase that we wouldn't set foot on if our lives depended on it. Items to look out for include three postcards on his fridge, a dartboard, a very small portable telly, a Humphrey Bogart poster on his bedroom wall and several shelves of books (so, when does Ray ever get the time to read?).

Birds: ** Kathie Mason, an old not-quite-but-almost girl-

friend of Doyle who turns out to be setting him up with her
ex-husband Preston. Why does poor Ray always go for the
Bad Girls? When she walks with Doyle over the bridge (how
can we put this politely?), she's clearly not wearing a bra and
it's very cold . . .

Bodie and Doyle take Kathie and Bodie's (very sleepy)
friend, Jo, to an East End pub, where Bodie tries to chat up
the singer, while Jo nods off. ('I think she wants to go home
to bed.' 'I should be so lucky.') Doyle notes 'married birds,
not my scene.' Birds in general are, however, 'a natural
obsession'.

Booze: ** In the pub, Kathie drinks white wine and Bodie
red. There's also a bottle of light ale on the table, which
presumably belongs to Doyle. Bodie, Doyle and Brownie
share cans of lager on Brownie's boat. Cowley has a nip of
brandy in his coffee.

Shooters: ** The episode concerns the laser-sighted
American 180 automatic rifle, which can shoot 900 rounds a
minute (or 15 rounds a second) over a range of about 1,000
yards. It is said that it can cut down telegraph poles.

Motors: Doyle's glorious white E-type is destroyed. (We
almost cried.) There's a dark Porsche 911 and an Allegro
panda car. A new season gives Bodie and Doyle some new
toys to play with: Bodie gets a silver Capri S (UOO 303T),
and Bodie a white Escort RS2000 (PNO 641T).

Threads: Bodie's enormous strides. Doyle's shades,
especially when pushed on to the end of his nose.

***Shaft* Guitar?:** 'Following in Father's Footsteps' (a music-
hall song of the 1920s) is sung in the pub, in best cock-er-nee
knees-up fashion. Doyle driving through the Greenwich tun-
nel is accompanied by a really funky theme, with swooping
strings and a choppy guitar, and there is some groovy rock
guitar on the radio as his car goes out of control.

Doyle Cooks a Bit of Pasta: A pasta jar is visible in his new
gaff. He's got nothing in his fridge, though, except for a
rock-hard piece of bread!

Slash Fiction Moment: Bodie telling Kathie Mason that, if anything happens to Ray, he'll find her sadistic husband and kill him (very slowly) and then, to save her from spending the rest of her life in prison, do the same to her, 'with great joy!'

Jargon: Kathie: 'You were a busy young copper. The terror of Stepney Green!'

Notes: 'I want that gun back.' A rather routine episode to begin a season with. The explosion of Doyle's car is a great stunt, and there is a nice procedural feel to much of the action, but the main plot (Doyle set up by a shady lady) is reminiscent of 'When the Heat Cools Off', with a splash of 'Killer with a Long Arm' thrown in. Enigmatic conclusion, though, if a bit contrived.

Bodie carries a Swiss Army penknife (see also 'The Purging of CI5'). Doyle's ex-DS was Maurice Richards, who now runs a pub. Bodie's call sign is 3-7, Doyle's 3-6 (although mention is also made of '4-5's place'), HQ is 2-4. (In subsequent episodes, the call signs – and agent numbers – stabilise as 4-5 for Doyle, 3-7 for Bodie, and Alpha One – or occasionally Charlie – for Cowley.) C11 is part of Criminal Intelligence. It is implied that (in certain circumstances) even CI5 need a search warrant.

15: 'The Rack'
14 October 1978

Writer: Brian Clemens
Director: Peter Medak

Cast: Michael Billington (John Coogan),
Lisa Harrow (Geraldine Mather),
Cyril Luckham (Judge Hall), Robert James (David Merlin),
Ken Campbell (Parker), Peter Marinker (Frank Williams),
Jenny Lee Wright (Lorna), Christopher Ellison (Paul Coogan),
Michael Mundell (Reporter), James Hayes (McKay),
Jonty Miller (Carter), Charles Pemberton (Big Man)

A snout's whisper about ten pounds of uncut heroin sends CI5 to the home of an ex-boxer, Johnny Coogan. Arrests are made, but a death in custody puts Cowley's squad on the rack . . .

Keep Your Mincers Peeled For . . .: Michael Billington was the heart-throb Paul Foster in *UFO*. Lisa Harrow's credits include the sinister *1990* and the leading role in the biographical series, *Nancy Astor*. One of Cyril Luckham's most noted roles was in Rudolph Cartier's classic *Wednesday Play*, *The July Plot*. *Doctor Who* fans will recognise him as the White Guardian. Jenny Lee Wright was the pretty girl on *The Benny Hill Show* who used to chase Benny around at high speed and slap the little bald man on the head. The actor/performer Ken Campbell was a regular contributor to *The Secret Policeman's Ball* concerts, often in a double act with Sylvester McCoy. Peter Marinker's voice may be familiar, as he was one of the actors who dubbed *The Water Margin* into English. For Christopher Ellison, see *The Sweeney* – 'Queen's Pawn' and *The Professionals* – 'Private Madness, Public Danger'.

Some of the graffiti in the interrogation cell is alarming, particularly CI5 – THEY'RE ALL MURDERING BASTARDS! and a reverse swastika. Ellison makes a less than convincing corpse!

Birds: * Bodie says he hasn't met a woman yet he couldn't handle. He's probably lying, but, even if he isn't, he certainly meets one in this episode! Geraldine could 'prosecute me any time'. And she does. There are a couple of dumb(-ish) blondes featured, too – Coogan's bird and Lorna the prostitute.

Booze: * Cowley and the minister have some Scotch the day before the investigation. At the end, Cowley offers to buy beer . . . But the whisky's on Bodie.

Shooters: * There are guns everywhere during the raid. 'All of them were armed,' notes Cowley.

Motors: At the head of a convoy of various CI5 Fords that sweep in to arrest the Coogans is Cowley's new red Granada (YHJ 766T). Paul Coogan tries to escape in a 911. Merlin drives a Triumph 2000-type car. The minister's car is a 3.5 litre Rover ('P5B'). John Coogan drives a Jag XJ6 when looking for Parker. We also see the silver Capri and white Escort.

Threads: Paul Coogan's velvet jacket. Bodie's and Doyle's ties are equally frightening.

***Shaft* Guitar?:** What about that dramatic OTT brass-and-wah-wah-guitar theme to accompany the initial raid on Coogan's gaff?

Doyle Cooks a Bit of Pasta: He's seen reading one of those many books of his (see the previous episode). He eats organic food, according to Bodie.

Slash Fiction Moment: The near lover's tiff, and then the little smirk that passes between them after Bodie has got Doyle to face his self-pity over Paul's death. (You can see the outline of Bodie's, erm, manhood when he comes out of the building where the inquiry is taking place.)

Jargon: Bodie: 'Parker's my pigeon . . .'
   Coogan: 'You grassed on me, Parker!'

Laughable Dialogue: Geraldine: 'It's revolting. Unbelievable. It must be exposed and stopped!'
   Cowley's astonishing defence speech: 'She's used me as a whipping boy because I founded CI5. But I didn't: you did. Society did. *This* society did. If there were no fires, you wouldn't need firemen, and in God's name, and I invoke him sincerely, I wish you would make my job, my organisation, redundant. I wish you would make the streets clean again. I wish you would give every man, whatever his colour or creed, the right to be, to feel, safe again. But that's not going to be. Not yet. And so, you need me. Like it or not, you need CI5. That's why I'm asking you, pleading with you, don't destroy us. Don't cut us down. Not until you've got something better to put in our place. Miss Mather has seized upon the word "jungle". Aye, in the popular vernacular, that's *where it's at*. A jungle with mad beasts crawling through it, and we are the hunters . . . These are the streets we have to walk. Not

the bright streets, the mean ones, devoid of hope and all humanity. We walk them and we brush aside some of the dirt – not much, just some of the dirt – so that there's less to offend when you come along ... The disease hurts, but so does the surgeon's knife. Which would you prefer? It's your choice.' No wonder he gets a round of (muted) applause at the end of all that!

Notes: 'Life's important, any life. I believe that.' This is a really good episode, despite the fascist overtones and the offensively one-dimensional characterisation of Geraldine. When we wrote an essay on *The Professionals* in our book *Classic British TV* and concluded that 'whenever an interfering left-wing reporter-type appeared, they would be either killed, seduced, or converted to the cause', this was the episode we were chiefly thinking about (though there are other examples). There *are* many good things on display here (and some of the acting is top-class), but 'The Rack' does leave a rather bitter taste in the mouth of anyone who believes in civil liberties. Not surprisingly, given its subject matter, this story covers similar ground to *The Sweeney*'s 'Big Brother'. The opening scene in a disused train is wonderfully evocative.

Doyle has a guitar in his flat, which suggests he can play a bit. He was a boxing champion in the police force, and a first-class marksman with both a rifle and a handgun. He is interested in kendo and karate, and started a sports club (mostly to help underprivileged black kids, he says). He also paints (see 'In the Public Interest', 'Rogue').

William Andrew Philip Bodie (his mother was a royalist!) is of Liverpool-Irish descent and left school at fourteen. He joined the merchant navy but jumped ship in Dacca three years later after a fight over a girl. He was a bouncer in an African club, and ran guns for both sides in the Congo Wars (presumably *circa* 1963–5 during the United Nations peace-keeping era). He was a mercenary in Angola and Biafra (both in the early 70s), and was involved in 'dubious activity' in Jordan before returning to the UK to join the army. He became a sergeant in the Paras before being seconded to the SAS and, subsequently, CI5.

Cowley founded CI5. This episode confirms that search without warrant is part of CI5's brief (cf. 'Hunter/Hunted'). He says Bodie and Doyle's appearance with Parker was 'pure Perry Mason'.

Fennell Street seems to have been named after the producer, Albert Fennell.

16: 'First Night'
21 October 1978

Writer: Chris O'Hara
Director: David Wickes

Cast: Tony Vogel (Kidnapper 1 – Frank),
David Howey (Kidnapper 2 – John),
Arnold Diamond (Biebermann), Julian Holloway (Harvey),
John Nettleton (Minister), George Pravda (Hirschfield),
Nadim Sawalha (Arab Diplomat),
John York (Local Police Chief),
Robert Hamilton (Kidnapper 3 – Mac),
Brenda Cavendish (Divorcee),
Pearl Ann Turner (Blonde WPC), Susan Derrick (2nd WPC),
Jean Gilpin (Debra), John Patrick (Soldier),
Jack Elliott (Marksman)

An Israeli diplomat is kidnapped in broad daylight. Cowley's boys are quickly on the case.

Keep Your Mincers Peeled For . . .: Tony Vogel played the eponymous role in *Dick Barton*, Southern TV's version of the famed radio series. Nadim Sawalha (see *The Sweeney* – 'Visiting Fireman') turns up as yet another Arab diplomat (he meets Cowley at the Nadim Investment Group building – see the reverse lettering on the glass behind them). George Pravda played the Soviet Inspector Pushkin in *Strangers*. For Julian Holloway, see *The Sweeney* – 'Big Spender'.

There's a tasty 70s stereo in the neighbours' house as Cowley and Doyle keep tabs on the kidnappers. The child delivering papers rides a wicked Chopper bike.

**Birds: ** Both Bodie and Doyle have to dump dates when the kidnap happens. Bodie is enjoying a day at the tennis club watching his girlfriend Jane Anderson (or, rather, looking at her and her tennis partner's knickers). Doyle and his girlfriend, Debra, are on their way to 'the rock concert' when he gets the call and she pulls a bottom-lip on him. Later, Doyle chats up Ruth Pettifer ('Your clutch is slipping'), and, when she says, 'You're as bad as Bodie', Doyle responds, 'Now, be fair – nobody's as bad as Bodie.'

Booze: None.

**Shooters: ** The kidnapping involves several sub-machine-guns, as does CI5's assault on the siege house.

Motors: The black Mercedes limousine carries the Israeli delegation to the South Bank. We see a number of police Rovers during the abduction, which utilises a hovercraft and a helicopter. The kidnappers also use an orange Rover and a grey Jag. Cowley, Doyle and Bodie are seen in the red Granada, white Escort and silver Capri respectively. Doyle drives Ruth around in a blue Honda Civic.

Threads: Doyle's quilt-like jacket puts in another appearance. Bodie tells Cowley that pink is the 'in shade'. Under normal circumstances we'd think he was taking the piss but this *is* Bodie we're talking about.

***Shaft* Guitar?:** Pretty standard music (including the cello theme), though there are a couple of interesting piano-and-percussion moments.

Doyle Cooks a Bit of Pasta: He chides Bodie on the amount of cholesterol in his body when his partner is eating a bacon sandwich. Bodie is also partial to Swiss chocolate roll, though Doyle won't touch it.

Non-PC Moment: Minister: 'This isn't Italy, or some banana republic.'

And, then there's Bodie (with his 'spotted dick') and Doyle's discussion with two rad-fem WPCs in the canteen about sexual politics. They'd *never* get away with it these days.

Laughable Dialogue: Ruth: 'When I couldn't sleep, I listened to the short-wave. It's better than a king-sized novel. Sex, violence, money, intrigue ...' Cowley: 'You should make a bid for the film rights.'

Notes: 'There are times, Bodie, when I find your ribaldry quite distasteful.' A pretty standard run-around, though the scenes of Bodie and Doyle on the bus (the former looking *very* pissed off) are like a proto-*Pulp Fiction*. (Is everyone on the top deck oblivious to these two guys with gun bulges and hand-held radios talking about kidnappers ...?)

Bodie speaks a bit of Spanish, and isn't interested in the philosophy of Kant ('A load of ...'). Doyle seems to be a Catholic. Cowley calls Doyle 'Goldilocks'! There are references to the Mafia helping Italian terrorists, the IRA running protection rackets and Mossad's spectacular ending of a hijacking at Entebbe airport, Uganda, in 1976.

The villains read the *Daily Express* (was there some sponsorship going on?).

Lots of location filming took place near the Royal Festival Hall and around docklands and Butler's Wharf. There's also a great shot with St Paul's in the distance, and some locations near Willesden Green tube station. Mention is made of Johann Strauss's *Tales from the Vienna Woods*.

17: 'Man Without a Past'
28 October 1978

Writer: Michael Armstrong,
from an original story by Jeremy Burnham
Director: Martin Campbell

Cast: John Carson (Brian Forrest), John Castle (Peter Crabbe),
Rachel Herbert (Madge Forrest), Rod Culbertson (Arthur),
Ed Bishop (Braddock), John Bay (Haskell),
Deirdre Costello (Sally Pendle), Robert Rietty (Gino),

Robert Dorning (Padgett), Hilary Ryan (Carol Forrest),
James Bree (Grant), Alan Leith (MacNeil),
Anthony Bailey (Phipps), Peter Pacey (Attendant),
Neville Barber (Inspector), Ann Michelle (Girl),
Gloria Walker (Nurse), Maya Woolfe (Claire)

A bomb in the restaurant where Bodie and his girlfriend are eating kills two people and injures eleven. But who was the intended target, and why?

Keep Your Mincers Peeled For ...: John Carson's TV credits included *It's Dark Outside* and *The Troubleshooters*. For John Castle, see 'Heroes'. Ed Bishop (see 'Long Shot') plays an American – *big* surprise there!
   Watch out for a blink-and-you'll-miss-it appearance of a boy on a skateboard. There is a Buddha statue in Forrest's drawing room.

Birds: * Bodie takes his girlfriend, Claire, to his favourite trattoria and charms her with his wit. Then she gets blown up. No wonder she's thinking of packing him in. He's interested in the pretty nurse at the end, too, but Doyle says she's his (she comes with the tablets, apparently).

Booze: * Wine, in the restaurant. Bodie refuses an offer of whisky from Forrest (who has one himself).

Shooters: ** Much in evidence during the final, climactic shoot-out.

Motors: Carol Forrest drives a tasty, yellow Jensen-Healey. Bodie's silver Capri is followed by a brown Triumph 2000-series car; Doyle is run down by a big, ugly American motor. Bodie tails and overtakes the green Triumph driven by Braddock.

Threads: Bodie wears an almost tasteful black poloneck. Carol Forrest's sensible jeans and white blouse look pleasant enough. Her taste in clothing is not shared by her mother, who wears a terrible pair of flares to do the gardening. The *Daily Mail* headline after the bombing is 'RESTAURANT HORROR!', which, given the shirt collars on display, is a fair summary.

***Shaft* Guitar?:** There's some unusually raucous rock music on Carol Forrest's car radio. The car-chase sequences are accompanied by pounding music with very prominent scary violins and electric guitars.

Slash Fiction Moment: 'You look terrible', and the hospital visit at the end. We don't believe for one second that those flowers are for Claire . . .!

Jargon: Braddock: 'Twenty years ago, we put the finger on him.'
Doyle: 'You dumb crud. What took you so long?'

Notes: 'The man's a maniac.' A completely over-the-top exercise in violence, explosions and car chases without much common sense, but (thankfully) with an awareness of its own stupidity. Love the bit where Bodie performs a dramatic roll-over-bonnet-into-shooting-position trick, and gets a round of applause from a bus queue! Rod Culbertson hams it up disgracefully.

Bodie speaks a little Italian.

The director, Martin Campbell, graduated (via *Edge of Darkness*) to the James Bond movie *Goldeneye*.

18: 'In the Public Interest'
4 November 1978

Writer: Brian Clemens
Director: Pennant Roberts

Cast: Paul Hardwick (Green), John Judd (Chives),
Stephen Rea (Pellin), Colin McCormack (Edwards),
Tom Georgeson (Reed), Tony Calvin (Terry),
Pamela Manson (Sally), Saba Milton (Female Clerk),
Fredric Abbot (Big Man), Fraser Cains (Cop)

A provincial town has a remarkably low crime rate. But Cowley is suspicious of the local police force's methods.

Keep Your Mincers Peeled For . . . : Stephen Rea was the

Czech dissident in Tom Stoppard's classic *Play of the Week*, *Professional Foul*. Tom Georgeson played Dixie Dean in *Boys From the Blackstuff*. He went on to starring roles in *The Manageress*, *Between the Lines*, and *Liverpool One*.

There are several references to that most 70s of phenomena, football hooliganism.

Birds: * Bodie says he's going out with a redhead. A fifteen-year-old Doyle had an encounter (possibly his first sexual experience) with a blonde girl called Annette close to a dance hall. He also used to borrow his dad's overcoat to get in to see X-rated films. Dirty little boy!

Booze: ** Cowley shares a whisky with Pellin. In the gambling club, Bodie buys a pint (in a Carlsberg glass) and a whisky for Doyle and gives the owner a pound note. 'Keep the change,' he says! Chives drinks whisky in this office (his boss, Green, appears teetotal, offering Cowley a tea and not the expected whisky).

Shooters: * The police are armed with pistols when they go for Bodie and Doyle.

Motors: The cop-thugs turn up at the Gay Youth Organisation in a green Hillman Hunter and a blue Triumph 2000-type; later, they use a black Hillman Minx and another Hunter. Most of the police cars we see are Rover 2000s.

Threads: Pellin's grey strides. Bodie's suede jacket. His blue and white shirts both have enormous collars. Doyle's green T-shirt.

Shaft **Guitar?:** There are some nice blasts of French horn as Cowley is trailed by Pellin.

Bill the Driver: . . . appears as a uniformed copper.

Non-PC Moment: In an episode as potentially liberal as this, it's a pity to have to single out one of the vilest moments of TV history as Pellin, the sympathetic secretary of the Gay Youth Organisation, says, 'I'm not a homosexual myself, but many of my friends are.' He goes on to tell Cowley that he's seen many people suffer through bigotry and ignorance. Lines like the above probably don't help.

Slash Fiction Moment: There's something undeniably kinky about Bodie and Doyle supposedly running a gay centre, sharing a hotel room and cruising around town in their car.

Jargon: Big man: 'The fuzz in this place take a personal interest, don't they?'

Laughable Dialogue: Minister: 'Green runs a very tight ship, George.' Cowley: 'So did Captain Bligh.'

Minister: 'For God's sake, George, to most law-abiding citizens, it sounds like Utopia.' Cowley: 'Aye, that's what they thought about Hitler's Germany.'

Cowley (on Green): 'Suppose he suddenly clamps down on those who don't go along with his politics. Or ethnic groups. Or people who grow their hair below the Plimsoll line. Or anyone who doesn't measure up in his opinion. Unbridled power. That's the thing I've been fighting all my life. It starts wars and it hurts people and it's damn bloody dangerous!'

Notes: 'We don't want your kind in our city.' Despite a few unfortunate sequences (see **Non-PC Moment**), this is a fantastic episode. Contemporary interest in 'zero tolerance' gives it a certain topicality, and overall it has aged better than most. Extremely violent, too, although most of the beatings are administered off screen.

The city isn't named but Doyle went to school there (although he comes from Derby). Bodie mentions that Doyle paints (see 'The Rack'). Cowley lives in a first-floor apartment in King's Court.

19: 'Rogue'
11 November 1978

Writer: Dennis Spooner
Director: Ray Austin

Cast: Glyn Owen (Barry Martin),
Pamela Stephenson (Maggie Briggs),
Tony Steedman (Paul Culbertson),

Neil Hallett (David Hunter),
Robert Gillespie (Steve Ballard),
Teddy Green (Doctor in Mortuary),
Andy Ho (Old Chinaman),
Larrington Walker (Geronimo),
Athar Malik (Doctor in Hospital),
Martyn Whitby (Policeman)

A critical witness in the case against Culbertson, a gangster, is killed arriving at King's Cross station. But only a handful of CI5 agents knew he was coming.

Keep Your Mincers Peeled For . . .: For Pamela Stephenson, see 'Old Dog with New Tricks'. For Tony Steedman, see *The Sweeney* – 'The Placer'. For Robert Gillespie, see *The Sweeney* – 'Thin Ice'. For Glyn Owen, see *The Sweeney* – 'Money, Money, Money'.

The remains of Martin's Chinese takeaway suggest it was a chow mein of some description.

Birds: * Maggie Briggs, Martin's blonde bit of stuff. When Bodie talks of a girl's eyes hinting of eastern promise, Doyle says he thought Bodie more of a 'leg man'.

Booze: *** There's a bottle of red wine in Martin's flat. Maggie drinks vodka and orange. In the pub, Bodie seems to be having a half of lager. Culbertson has a brandy just after his meeting with Barry Martin. Cowley is more than a little miffed at the end when Bodie and Doyle say they haven't brought him any whisky ('hospital rules'). Actually, a bottle is hidden with the grapes, and he smashes it.

Shooters: ** Martin uses a pistol with a silencer to kill Ballard. He keeps a couple of guns and a knife concealed in his flat.

Motors: There's a big yellow VW van at the beginning, delivering papers. Maggie's car appears to be a gold Mercedes convertible. Martin's 'spare car' is a white Mini, although a nice grey Porsche 911 is prominent in the same scene. He escapes from the car park in a dull Cortina II.

Threads: Doyle's white trainers! Martin's red cravat. Culbertson's dressing gown.

***Shaft* Guitar?:** There is some eerie cello music.

Slash Fiction Moment: Bodie and Doyle, in a famous sequence often used in trailers for the series, fling themselves around over boxes and straw bales while 'working out' with Martin.

Jargon: Cowley: 'If you hadn't gone in like gangbusters you might have picked him up alive.'
    Martin: 'When I went on the take with you, I didn't know you were in bed with the reds.'

Laughable Dialogue: Martin: 'We were fighting for the flag while you two were in your prams.'

Notes: 'I'll have to clean my own doorstep.' Not a bad episode, with an excellent cast, although some elements are downright stupid (why don't Bodie and Doyle block the exit of the underground car park when they go in looking for Martin?). There's also that pathetic karate fight between Doyle and Martin.

Barry Martin was Major Cowley's sergeant in the army, and was his first recruit to CI5. Ruth thinks Doyle is very perceptive and Bodie is impenetrable. Doyle's painting is mentioned again (see the previous episode and 'The Rack').

Doyle mentions 'Miss Marples' (*sic*) (seeing as he also talks about 'adenoids' and not androids in a sci-fi movie – Bodie corrects him – perhaps he banged his head training with Martin!).

Much location filming at King's Cross station, and around Rains Street in Westminster (the Chinese-takeaway scene).

20: 'Not a Very Civil Civil Servant'
18 November 1978

Writer: Edmund Ward
Director: Anthony Simmons

Cast: Maurice Denham (Sir James Temple),
Bill Fraser (Colonel Summerville),
Robert Swan (Logan-Blake), Harold Innocent (Repton),
Peter Woodthorpe (Councillor Webb), Tony Church (Minister),
Lyndon Brook (Gillam), Derek Martin (Renshaw),
Anthony Heaton (Singleton), David Hargreaves (Halloran),
Linda Goddard (Jenny Burton)[1],
Andrew McCulloch (Bradford), Frank Jarvis (Musgrave),
Donald Bisset (Judge), Brian Hall (Sam Burton),
Duncan Preston (Karl Drake)

Cowley, Bodie and Doyle are called upon to penetrate the
shady world of . . . building projects and local housing.

Keep Your Mincers Peeled For . . .: The stylish and dig-
nified character actor Maurice Denham will be an instantly
recognisable face from his many roles in series like *Talking to
a Stranger*, *The Lotus Eaters*, *Fall of Eagles* and *The Old
Men at the Zoo*. Bill Fraser is best known as Sergeant Major
Claude Snudge in *The Army Game* and *Bootsie and Snudge*.
Readers will probably best remember Duncan Preston as
Clifford the handyman in the 'Acorn Antiques' segments of
Victoria Wood – As Seen on TV. He was also in *Surgical
Spirits*, *Hunter's Walk* and *Dinner Ladies*. For Derek Martin,
Anthony Heaton, David Hargreaves and Brian Hall, see *The
Sweeney* episodes 'Messenger of the Gods', 'In From the
Cold', 'Night Out' and 'Trap'. Robert Swan also appears in
The Sweeney – 'Country Boy'.

Birds: None, though it's a pity we don't get to see 'Fifi', who
lives next door to the pub and who is available to anybody
knocking three times, apparently.

Booze: * Robert the accountant drinks whisky (MacKenzies)
spiked with weedkiller. Bodie and Doyle meet their contact in
a seedy pub ('I always like a place where I can spit on the
floor,' says Bodie). It has Guinness and Skol on draught. Sir

---

[1] Although credited as Jenny, the character is referred to as 'Linda'
by her husband.

James has a whisky and offers Henry one. Cowley and Webb drink brandy at the golf club.

Shooters: None: there's a great bar-room brawl, though. ('I enjoyed that,' notes Bodie.)

Motors: The accountant has a big Jag (apparently), but is taken home in Sir James's Roller, pursued by Drake in a Mini estate. Doyle observes a house from an orange Escort van. Cowley drives himself about in a red Granada Mk II Ghia.

***Shaft* Guitar?:** There is some cheesy rock to be heard in the pub, and lots of nice bass guitar. Bodie tells Cowley he's 'a disco man' – which we kind of knew anyway.

Doyle Cooks a Bit of Pasta: Alarmingly, Ray accompanies Halloran and Bodie to the local chippie where they tuck into 'plaice and chips twice, and a bag of chips'. Doyle seems to pour the salt on, although at least he doesn't drown it in vinegar as Bodie does.

Jargon: Henry Repton: 'Cowley's taking it very personally. He thinks he was gulled.'

Doyle (looking at some brushes): 'These any good for whitewash? . . . Snow jobs, cover-ups, turning the proverbial blind eye? . . . How much did they pay you, or did they put the frighteners on?'

Laughable Dialogue: Cowley: 'Bodie, there are ways of asking people questions without removing their teeth. For one thing, it makes for clearer diction.'

Repton (on his divorced wife): 'We still talk to each other – by cheque.'

Doyle (on Bodie): 'You'll have to excuse his manners. He hasn't got any.'

Bodie (to Doyle): 'You couldn't stop a fat lady in a thin alley.'

Notes: 'I don't think we can play the usual rules on this one.' One or two directorial flourishes – there's a nice cut between Councillor Webb's patronising talk of housing the citizens, and the crying baby in the squalid Burton house – cannot disguise the fact that this is a tawdry and dull tale, beneath the contempt of Jack Regan, let alone George Cowley. And it's very talky, too. The best thing about it is, in fact, Cowley's obvious distaste for ministerial machinations, and Gordon Jackson's performance.

Cowley is a good sabreur. Bodie and (apparently) Doyle are not. Mention is made of the relief of Mafeking. Doyle has smelly socks according to Bodie.

21: 'A Stirring of Dust'
25 November 1978

Writer: Don Houghton
Director: Martin Campbell

Cast: Robert Urquhart (Darby),
André Morell (Brigadier Stadden),
Alan MacNaughton (Sorenson), Carol Royle (Helen Pierce),
George Murcell (Yashinkov), Billy Boyle (O'Leary),
Robin Parkinson (Taxi Driver), Shelagh Fraser (Elsa),
Myles Hoyle (Lewis), Michael Petrovitch (Callinari),
Chris Dillinger (Russian Aide 1),
Terence Mountain (Russian Aide 2),
Norman Rutherford (Cleric)

A notorious spy, Thomas Darby, is back in England. Everybody and their dog want something from him, whether it's his diaries, his knowledge or his death.

Keep Your Mincers Peeled For ...: Robert Urquhart had been involved in tales of espionage before as *The Aweful Mr Goodall*. He also featured in *The Prime of Miss Jean Brodie* and *The Old Men at the Zoo*. André Morell was a leading figure in two of the most important television events of the 1950s, playing O'Brien in the Nigel Kneale/Rudolph Cartier adaptation of *Nineteen Eighty-Four* and Professor Bernard Quatermass in *Quatermass and the Pit*. Sherlock Holmes fans will remember his excellent Dr Watson opposite

Peter Cushing in Hammer's *The Hound of the Baskervilles*. Alan MacNaughton made something of a speciality playing shadowy figures in the civil service and government in programmes such as *The Sandbaggers* and *A Very British Coup*. Carol Royle was the tortured Jessica in Dennis Potter's *Blackeyes*. Billy Boyle will be most familiar to readers as one of Basil Brush's human sidekicks.

Watch out for a very 70s cassette recorder. There is a lot of West Ham graffiti in the episode. They'd just been relegated, which says a lot.

Birds: * Helen Pierce, Darby's pretty, illegitimate daughter.

Booze: * There is a wagon full of crates of Carlsberg in one scene.

Shooters: ** Sorenson keeps a pistol and ammunition in an empty cigar box inside his bedside cabinet. That's safely hidden away, then. There is much gunfire elsewhere, particularly as Bodie and Doyle rescue Helen Pierce from O'Leary.

Motors: Cowley's red Granada makes yet another appearance, this time driven by Lewis. A blue Hillman Hunter whisks away O'Leary and Helen; Darby is taken away by Sorenson in a black Cortina with Elsa at the wheel. The 'banker' sits in a 'big, expensive car' – actually a white Jag or a Daimler.

Threads: Helen's headscarf.

***Shaft* Guitar?:** The snare-drum-and-kettledrum opening is suitably loud, with sinister piano chords.

Laughable Dialogue: Doyle to Bodie: 'You're a moron!'
Cowley: 'That tired old spy could topple a government, start a fair old massacre and bring a lot of maggots crawling out of the woodwork.'
The Brigadier: 'Sentimentality is a mortal handicap for spies.'
Doyle: 'Execution?' Cowley: 'Well, Sorenson's not going to be playing tiddlywinks with him, is he?'

Doyle: 'You know it's going to be tight in there?' Bodie:
'Like a spinster's girdle, mate!'

Yashinkov, on *Pravda*'s report of Darby's death: 'I think
you will find that he died next Monday.'

Notes: 'You want me to tell you about ghosts?' A really
funny episode, full of the standard staples of fist fights and
gunshots, but with a nicely shadowy feel to it. The opening
car-park scenes are clearly influenced by *Get Carter*, but from
there it's closer to *The Spy Who Came in From the Cold* than
James Bond. The interest of foreign publishers in books about
British espionage never ceases to make stories like this
topical!

Bodie supports his home town team: 'Liverpool for the
cup!' he says to one of the KGB men. Later he changes this to
'Up the Moscow Dynamo!' *The Third Man* was on TV the
week before. Bodie seems not to have seen it, saying 'that
might have been the scene thirty years ago in Berlin'. Thankfully, Doyle knows it was actually set in Vienna. Bodie
suffers from dust allergies and blocked sinuses. Bodie was in
the third year at junior school when Darby defected. Cowley
can order a 'red close' – the equivalent of a D-notice –
stopping the press from publishing particular stories not in
the national interest.

Darby was the top man in Section 9, the SIS. When he
defected, his (ghostwritten) autobiography was published
under the title *Red Spy at Night*. In *The Professionals*'
universe, Burgess, Maclean and Philby were called Furnell,
MacNaught and Darby! The unknown 'fourth man' is
described as having to be rich, influential and a pillar of the
establishment to have escaped detection for so long. This
episode was broadcast over a year before the *real* fourth man
was revealed to be Sir Anthony Blunt, whose career almost
exactly fits in with the above description. Did someone *know*
something?

Tottenham Court Road is mentioned, as are the Spanish
Civil War and Uncle Tom Cobbleigh (by Bodie).

22: 'Blind Run'
2 December 1978

Writer: Ranald Graham
Director: Tom Clegg

Cast: Jasmina Hilton (Leia), Tommy Boyle (Charlie),
Sandra Payne (Phillipa), Tony Jay (Foreign Observer 1),
Kevin Brennan (Minister), Ahmed El-Shenawi (Bodyguard),
Steve Plytas (Foreign Observer 2),
Kevork Malikyan (Hanish (Mr X)),
Rowland Davies (Male Secretary), Tariq Yunas (Georgio),
Yasha Adem (1st Official), Neville Rofaila (2nd Official),
Nayef Rashed (Ambassador 2),
Gabor Vernon (Ambassador 1), Ian Liston (Security Man)

Bodie and Doyle are assigned to escort someone, somewhere.
They quickly work out that they have become expendable,
and that a successful conclusion to their mission may be
impossible.

Keep Your Mincers Peeled For . . . : There's a great shot of
Lewis Collins's belly button at one point, if you're into that
sort of thing.

Birds: ** Bodie is seeing an air hostess (see 'The Ojuka
Situation' for Cowley's thoughts on this tendency of his).
Doyle forms an instant attraction with Leia ('I think I'm in
love'). He even offers to interrogate her thoroughly for information (over dinner). Bodie, meanwhile, is going to ring a
boat girl called Phillipa and give her suitable compensation
for the damage caused. Always assuming he can remember
her telephone number.

Shooters: ***** The episode is full of them: sub-machine-
guns, rifles, shotguns, the lot. There are two ambushes, both
featuring a withering array of arms. The body count (and
ammo expenditure) in this episode is astronomical. One of
the gunmen is able to bring down the radio-transmitter aerial
with a single shot.

Motors: Bodie and Doyle follow the old black limousine in an eggshell-blue Austin 1800. A Porsche 924 gets between the two. The villains use a bewildering array of Cortinas, Granadas and big American sedans. In desperation, Doyle, the bodyguard and Mr X escape from the house in a blue Ford Fiesta van.

Threads: Doyle's grey towelling jogging top.

Non-PC Moment: Doyle's rather uncharacteristically brutal request for subtitles for 'Sinbad'.

Jargon: Cowley auditions for the famous *Beyond the Fringe* 'Initials' sketch: 'You knew about the ISS deal with the CPI . . . I'd rather have been up against BOSS, even the KGB. What the hell do you think my men are, kamikaze pilots?'

This is the first episode in which anyone screams 'Cover me!' Doyle shouts it, amazingly, not to Bodie, but to Leia!

Laughable Dialogue: Doyle: 'I'm a male capitalist pig!'

Bodie on Charlie: 'Case of mistaken identity. The Sheikh of Bethnal Green is now a watering can!'

Notes: 'Don't you know what is your assignment? Or are you just a couple of dumb bodyguards?' A complete run-around; mindless, but well put together.

This episode is the source of a famous *It'll Be All Right on the Night* out-take. As Leia, Mr X and Doyle jump into the back of the yellow van, and it speeds off, Martin Shaw slipped and came crashing back out again. There wasn't time for a retake and so they just had to cut the sequence with the film they had: you can actually see him start to fall backwards before the next shot.

Bodie does a form of Japanese exercise (it looks very like t'ai chi, but that's Chinese). He has a pilot's licence. The last time Cowley shook either Bodie's or Doyle's hand was when they joined the Squad. Cowley refers to Bodie and Doyle as 'my boys'. Cowley's cover name is 'Big Daddy'! Bodie's alias is Dave Bentley. Doyle's is Mark Layton.

There are references to Oddjob (from *Goldfinger*) and Tinkerbell and Wendy (from *Peter Pan*), plus Sinbad. Charlie says 'The Eagle has landed' (Neil Armstrong and Buzz Aldrin's call sign when Apollo XI touched down on the moon), and 'All the way, with LBJ' (Lyndon Johnson's 1964 election slogan). Leia is pronounced 'Leila' throughout the episode.

23: 'Fall Girl'
9 December 1978

Writer: Ranald Graham
Director: William Brayne

Cast: Pamela Salem (Marikka), Frederick Jaeger (Schuman),
Michael Latimer (Willis), Sandor Elès (Kreiber),
Patrick Malahide (1st Security Man),
Phillip Joseph (2nd Security Man),
George Irving (3rd Security Man), Eamonn Jones (Barman),
Christine Shaw (Barmaid), Lydia Lisle (Julia),
Frederick Marks (Knowles),
Gregory Floy (Technician), Michael Redfern (Vic),
Astrid Frank (Anna), John Larsen (4th Security Man),
Lewis Wilson (Old PC), Myrtle Devenish (Old Woman),
Vivien Stokes (WPC)

An old flame of Bodie's arrives in London, and their relationship rekindles. Unfortunately, there is more to Marikka Schuman than meets the eye . . .

Keep Your Mincers Peeled For . . .: Sandor Elès was the slimy restaurant manager Paul Ross in *Crossroads*. You'll probably recognise Michael Redfern as the Oxo dad from that series of adverts with Lynda Bellingham. For Pamela Salem, see 'The Female Factor'. For Patrick Malahide, see *Sweeney 2*.

The front-page story in Bodie's newspaper seems to be 'TED BURNS HIS BOOKS'. The headline about Marikka Schuman reads 'EAST GERMAN STAR VISITS LONDON'.

Birds: *** Pamela Salem puts in another smouldering

performance, this time as the German film star who is Bodie's ex-lover. She has a mole on the back of her neck, which Bodie enjoys kissing, and is drinking champers in a foam-filled bath when they meet (they hope) for a few hours rumpy-pumpy. Bodie does his best to patronise the woman at the pub. ('Cheers, princess.' 'You call me that again, I'll crown you.') Doyle clearly likes the CI5 telephonist, Julia, though she considers him 'all mouth and no trousers'. Bodie uses her to contact a girl called Christine to rearrange a rendezvous. We don't see the events that followed, at Dino's wine bar and beyond, but by all accounts Christine's friend Frankie has an interesting hobby (it could, we later learn, be ballet – which *isn't* very interesting, really).

Booze: *** In the pub's garden area, Doyle has a pint of something in his hand (could be Coke, actually). Bodie has some sort of spirit-with-ice at the swanky hotel. He downs what looks like white wine at the pub the next day. Cowley has a couple of small malts at Doyle's pad. Doyle again meets Bodie in the pub: he asks for a tomato juice (probably feeling a little the worse for wear), and Bodie (already drinking a pint) buys him a vodka and tonic.

Shooters: *** Bodie leaves his pistol and holster in his car before his few moments of passion with Marikka. A sniper's rifle (suitably incriminated) is crucial to the plot. The conclusion sees Bodie, with an FM rifle, taking on the fully armed men of the security forces. Ah, the course of true love . . .

Motors: The German delegation sweep in front of Bodie in a Rolls-Royce Phantom VI. Marikka is taken from Doyle's flat in a brownish Granada. Willis turns up for the final confrontation in a green Princess.

Threads: Doyle's diamond-patterned jumper. Kreiber's black-and-white polka-dot tie is certainly distinctive enough for him to stand out when meeting Bodie for the first time. Bodie's dark shirt and pale jacket are really cool . . . for the 70s. And his ever-present black poloneck puts in a prominent appearance. Doyle's shiny green neo-parka jacket does, too.

Best of all, the second security man with his frizzy perm, light-brown suit, dark-brown shirt and horrible tie – a walking advert for the decade that taste forgot . . .

***Shaft* Guitar?:** The smoochy woodwind music at the start.

Bill the Driver: Watch out for the first bloke the old dear tries to sell the flowers to . . .

Laughable Dialogue: Doyle: 'I'm licensed to thrill.'

Doyle: 'What's this, an up-market Page Three? All the nudes that's fit to print.'

Doyle (on Bodie): 'Well, you've got to hand it to the lad. If he was going to the electric chair he'd have Miss Universe pulling the switch.'

Notes: 'I wanna see the girl.' A bit of a mess. Just what is going on at the conclusion? Who's trying to shoot whom, and why doesn't Bodie take a pop at whoever kills Marikka?

Bodie is an *Express* reader, which figures. His phone number is 720 7529. He speaks a little German. (This is surprising, given his attitude to the country if his conversation with Kreiber is anything to go by, but then, he always was a sucker for beauty. He was probably stationed there during his time in the army.) Marikka is an old flame – now married to a German film-maker with diplomatic links – with a mad, anarchist brother. Bodie trusted her before, and it all went horribly wrong then, too.

Doyle buys the flowers from the old lady with a pound note. Ah, the nostalgia of it. Doyle may be a philatelist. He seems to be just moving into the new flat we see him in during this episode.

Third Season

Eight 60-minute episodes
An Avengers Mark 1 Production/London Weekend Television
Created by Brian Clemens

Associate Producer: Chris Burt
Producer: Raymond Menmuir
Executive Producers: Albert Fennell, Brian Clemens

Title music by Laurie Johnson

Regular Cast: Gordon Jackson (George Cowley),
Martin Shaw (Ray Doyle), Lewis Collins (William Bodie),
Sally Harrison (Susan, 24, 27[1])

24: 'The Purging of CI5'
27 October 1979

Writer: Stephen Lister
Director: Dennis Abey

Cast: Simon Rouse (Phillips), Norman Gregory (Lake),
Chris Fairbank (Billy), Ian Gelder (King),
Paul Antony-Barber (Matheson), Ben Thomas (Williams),
James Smith (Pennington), Leo Dolan (Murray),
Peter Jolley (Parks), Bill Treacher (Dave),
Martha Nairn (Wakeman), Terry York (Catrell),
David Gretton (1st Doctor), Nalini Moonasar (2nd Doctor)

Somebody is going around blowing up CI5 operatives.
Cowley, not unreasonably, is a bit concerned by this, and
wants to get the bomber and give him a good talking to.

---

[1] Credited as 'Chauffeuse' in this episode.

Keep Your Mincers Peeled For . . .: Simon Rouse went on to star in *The Bill* as DCI Jack Meadows. *EastEnders* fans will have fun trying to spot Bill Treacher in his tiny role as a telephone engineer (see also *The Sweeney* – 'Selected Target'). Chris Fairbank later starred as Moxey in *Auf Wiedersehen, Pet*.

There are a bunch of football rosettes in the caretaker's flat where Cowley takes his second call from the bomber. Among those you can just make out are Everton and Wolverhampton Wanderers. Watch out, too, for the scene where King and Matheson get blown up in their car. In the background you can see a large lump of cardboard with some graffiti on it. It states DENNIS ABEY RULES OK! So, that's the director managing to get himself name-checked on screen. What next, LEWIS COLLINS IS A TOP ACTOR!?

This is the second episode to feature a London *A–Z*. (This one is prominently positioned on Doyle's dashboard. After another tyre-shredding corner, it falls off, and is later used by Bodie.) Bodie's got a new flat (do he and Doyle have to move around regularly?): items on display include a dartboard, a tallboy, an Andy Warhol Marilyn Monroe print, a flash stereo, an M.C. Escher wall print, a poster with some guns on it, and a full-size firing-range target (a soldier figure) on the back of his door.

Best of all, look out for a bottle of Pagan Man (by Jovan) – one of *the* crap aftershaves of the 1970s – on Billy's dresser!

**Birds: ** ** There's a new secretary in a red sweater and (very) tight jeans who gets admiring glances from Doyle and Bodie as she walks past. Susan is the extremely capable new CI5 token woman, whom Bodie and Doyle both respect but neither seems to fancy. Must be something to do with her ability to arrest thugs like Parks on her own that emasculates them. Either that, or they've tried and she's bombed them both out!

Lisa Wakeman is the well-dressed American-based bomber and partner of Catrell (Bodie and Doyle glance at her as she walks down the corridor, too). Bodie mentions a current girlfriend called Joanna a couple of times, but we don't see her (could it possibly be 'sleepy Jo' from 'Hunter/Hunted'?).

Booze: None.

Shooters: * Catrell's high-velocity rifle. And lots of bombs!

Motors: Williams drives a yellow Marina; Matheson and King a golden Vauxhall Victor (which explodes). Susan drives Billy away in a yellow Cortina (with *red* upholstery!). Were these people colour blind?

Threads: It's worth making the point that from around 1979, when this episode was filmed, flares and big collars suddenly became very unfashionable indeed, and so, for the first time, we see things like straight-legged jeans in *The Professionals*. Confusingly, some of the episodes shown in the third season were actually leftovers from the second filming block, recorded a year before, and therefore much funnier in terms of fashion victims. Bodie's haircut (very short in season three, slightly longer in the 1978 episodes) is normally a useful way of telling them apart. But, if you know your fashion, you'll be able to tell them at a glance!

Nevertheless, it was early days and Doyle's brown cords, straight-legged though they are, are still horrible! His green T-shirt is pretty nasty, too. And Billy's rich-blue open-necked shirt is a relic from a different age.

***Shaft* Guitar?:** There's some dramatic chase music, with horns and piano and a bit of hot rock guitar on Billy's radio as he dries his hair.

Slash Fiction Moment: The pair indulge in a bit of *Boy's Own* horseplay as they go into the lift after Bodie makes a crack about Doyle having a yellow streak. Then there's a lovely moment when Bodie elects to stay in the car, despite the possibility of its being booby-trapped, as Doyle turns the key.

Jargon: Catrell: 'Keep your cannon covered up.'

Laughable Dialogue: Doyle: 'If you'd released that dial earlier, it would've been the last cheap-rate call you ever made.'

Bodie: 'There's a little bloke inside my head whistling a tune, and I think he's forgotten it.'

Notes: 'What a way to make a living.' A top-quality start to the season. Really excellent cast (Simon Rouse is in particularly good form). The explosion of the caravan is breathtaking. Only the end lets it down a bit.

Doyle carries a Swiss Army penknife, as did Bodie in 'Hunter/Hunted'. Bodie can do a fairly poor German accent (see 'Fall Girl'). Phillips is nicknamed 'Brains' (after the *Thunderbirds* character, presumably).

25: 'Backtrack'

3 November 1978

Writer: Don Houghton
Director: Christopher King

Cast: Liz Fraser (Margery), Michael Elphick (Garbett),
John Bennett (Truitt), Brian Gwaspari (Pulman),
Brian McDermott (Miller), Stacy Davies (Sammy),
Michael Halphie (Gunman 1), Charlie Price (Gunman 2),
Kevork Malikyan (Sniper), Luke Hanson (Alf),
Rudi Patterson (Herbie), Antony Scott (Kabil Kammahmi)

CI5 discover a cache of illegally imported arms, a number of dead Arabs – and a cat burglar who has seen too much . . .

Keep Your Mincers Peeled For . . .: For Michael Elphick, see *The Sweeney* – 'One of Your Own'. For Brian Gwaspari, see *Sweeney 2*. Liz Fraser was one of the *Carry On* film series regulars.

The magazine Doyle is reading is called *Boat Owner*. There's a Singapore calendar on the wall of the observation room.

Birds: * Garbett's snout Margery Harper takes a shine to Doyle (but not Bodie, who she reckons has 'shifty eyes'!). 'I bet the birds are just putty in your hands, aren't they?' she says. 'Well, that's more his department,' replies Doyle, indicating Bodie. Bodie finds the time to look at a porn mag during the break-in at the Arab residency.

Booze: * Margery's Lightning is a cocktail of her own creation: gin, rum and green chartreuse ('Very sexy').

Shooters: *** Bodie and Doyle's entrance into the house at the beginning is the stuff of a thousand parodies (with music to match). They discover (literally) crateloads of arms. There are off-screen sub-machine-gun attacks on some Arabs. Doyle wears an ankle gun in addition to the usual when he and Bodie break into the opulent houses. 'Shooters – I hate them,' exclaims Margery.

Motors: Garbett and Truitt arrive for the clandestine meeting in a Triumph 2000. The Arabs drive a light-blue Merc. Marge prefers a big Chevvy.

Threads: Doyle looks cool in his matching black leather jacket and gloves; Bodie goes for more of a dark, velvety look.

***Shaft* Guitar?:** There's a nice hi-hat-driven theme during the first pursuit of 'a pair of Arabs'.

Slash Fiction Moment: The very tender 'Thanks' from Doyle after Bodie shoots his attacker, Doyle's weapon having jammed.

Jargon: Garbett: 'He went up before the beak this morning.'
   Bodie: 'Every professional thief's got a pet fence.' (How would Bodie know this, anyway? Doyle's the ex-copper!)

Laughable Dialogue: Garbett: '[Sammy] regarded being nicked as an occupational hazard.' (Laughable, because this is an obvious homage to *Porridge*. Doyle belabours the point by calling Sammy 'a habitual criminal!')
   Margery: 'The third [husband] . . . wanted to send me out on to the streets to tart for him.' Doyle: 'You'd have made a fortune, Marg.' Margery: 'Oh, that's one of the nicest compliments that anyone's ever paid me.'

Notes: 'They can't go on this caper with a pair of bomb-happy uglies on their tail.' Simple plot, but the script is vibrant enough. The break-in scenes are excellent, although the escape from a well-placed bomb is extremely contrived.

Reference is made to Clint Eastwood (whose movies Bodie seems to watch rather a lot of), and to the 'argument' across the Irish Sea (see 'Old Dog with New Tricks'). During the break-in operation, Bodie and Doyle are 'Chaucer', the support car containing Hanson is 'Able 1'.

Major cock-up: Cowley speaks, briefly, to Truitt about Sammy (we see the entire conversation) yet, at the end of the call, he is able not only to ask for details about 'Samuel Augustus Blaydon' when Truitt has mentioned only the name 'Sammy', but also to initiate a check on Frank David Truitt despite never having been told the policeman's first name. Later, Doyle says Sammy's full name is 'Samuel Thomas Blaydon' – to add to the confusion!

Doyle can play a bit of football (at least, when the opposition is made up of ten-year-olds). There are references to the Israeli–Arab Yom Kippur War (October to November 1973), the late 60s supergroup Blind Faith (Eric Clapton, Stevie Winwood, et al), and E.W. Hornung's gentleman thief Raffles.

26: 'Stopover'
17 November 1980

Writer: John Goldsmith
Director: William Brayne

Cast: James Laurenson (Meredith),
Michael Gothard (Kodai), Morris Perry (Radouk),
Peter Cartwright (Sir Peter Pelham),
Morgan Sheppard (Malenski), Paul Dawkins (Tramp),
Frank Jarvis (Dale), Alec Linstead (Doctor),
Jacob Witkin (Captain), Robert Booth (Stevens),
Godfrey Jackman (Customs Official)

A stowaway, found on a ferry, demands to see George Cowley of CI5 . . .

Keep Your Mincers Peeled For . . .: Michael Gothard was

Keith, the groovy vampire in Amicus's classic 1960s film *Scream and Scream Again*. Morris Perry will be familiar from *The Sweeney*.

Cowley's collapsible phone is terribly 'of the era'.

Birds: * Watch out for the blonde barmaids. The first wears a purple gypsy skirt and white blouse; her mate in the tight brown top, complete with heaving bosoms, looks like a right little raver.

Booze: ** 'The only spirit we've got is surgical.' Meredith drinks lots of whisky. There's a great scene in a bar with adverts for Burton's Ale and Martini, and a Schweppes bar towel. They've got Skol and Double Diamond on draught. It's Doyle's round. He and Bodie have been drinking pints (presumably of lager – Bodie later gets himself a bottle of Skol). Bodie asks for a Harvey Wallbanger to cheer himself up (it's full of vitamins, he tells Doyle). When it's Bodie's round he gets Doyle an orange juice (with a large vodka in it), which, together with his bottle of lager, comes to £1.35. Doyle downs the orange virtually in one. By the time they leave the pub they're surely over the drink-drive limit – and as for their aim . . .

Shooters: *** This episode features a *massive* gun battle every ten minutes or so (there's a sniper with rifle at the docks, a sub-machine-gun attack on the safe house, and the shooting of Cowley at an RAF base). We get our first proper look at Bodie's stainless-steel, high-calibre revolver (probably a Smith & Wesson 629).

Motors: The sniper at the docks is rescued by a black Alfa Romeo 2000 Saloon. Kodai and Radouk drive off in a russet-coloured Princess. Kodai and his goons arrive at the safe house in a red Vauxhall VX.

Threads: Meredith's tie. Is it any wonder they locked him up for two years?

***Shaft* Guitar?:** Check out the terribly OTT wild stabs of brass at the beginning, and during the lengthy warehouse scenes. There are some funky disco riffs in the bar.

Jargon: Doyle: 'From the moment we left Malenski we were on RT, no tail, and yet Kodai knew.' Bodie: 'Well, it's like Meredith says, isn't it? Do the job and blow.'

Laughable Dialogue: Cowley: 'Bodie, I am sure you have many hidden talents, but, *if* acting is one of them, I didn't want to put it to the test.'

Notes: 'In all, a stopover of less than ten minutes . . .' The sort of episode in the middle of which it's quite possible to lose the will to live. Sleep-inducing. What's the deal with the scene with the tramp other than pure padding?

Colin Meredith was one of the best men Cowley ever had working for him in the Hong Kong station. He was 'missing, presumed dead' two years ago in Cambodia, but has spent most of the time in a Khmer Rouge concentration camp, before being 'turned' by Radouk. Cowley once shot Kodai (he was quicker, he says). The CI5 HQ call sign in this episode is 'John Brown'. Cowley is (amusingly) 'Queen Vic'.

Kim Philby is mentioned (which rather screws up the *Professionals*-universe continuity of 'A Stirring of Dust'). There's a misquote from Tennyson's 'The Charge of the Light Brigade' ('Ours not to reason why'), and references to Concorde and to the contemporary telephone advertising campaign featuring Busby.

This episode was the highest-rated of the season, achieving 15 million viewers, and number twelve in the weekly viewing charts.

27: 'Dead Reckoning'
17 November 1979

Writer: Philip Loraine
Director: Denis Lewiston

Cast: Derek Godfrey (Stefan Batak 1),
Carol Royle (Anna Batak), Alan Tilvern (Stefan Batak 2),
Milos Kirek (Paul), Michael Hadley (Michael),

Gabor Veron (Vashunin), Jeffrey Chiswick (Bulgarian Officer),
Walter McMonagle (Reporter), Jane Sumner (Bride)

Can CI5 trust a high-ranking Bulgarian double agent, recently
returned to Britain? Moreover, can they trust his daughter?

Keep Your Mincers Peeled For . . .: Poor Carol Royle. Fine
actress, second appearance in *The Professionals*, second stint
as the daughter of a double agent (see 'A Stirring of Dust').
   Look out for the hand-held 8 mm camera Doyle uses.

Birds: * Anna Batak, a music student and the illegitimate
daughter of a Bulgarian spy. Doyle takes a shine to her, but
Bodie ends up with her.

Booze: None.

Shooters: * There's a shotgun ambush on Bodie and Doyle's
car when they are transferring Batak.

Motors: The foreign agents have turned up to the handover in
a Volvo. Susan drives the usual red Granada (and there's the
usual silver Capri/white Escort for the boys). The man who
shoots Batak escapes in a red-brown Maxi. Michael drives a
Renault. At the end, Batak attempts to escape in a blue
Peugeot 604.

Threads: Bodie's horrible jacket. Doyle, in those glasses,
does (vaguely) look like a reporter. One of the Bulgarian
agents at the handover looks like a Burton's advert from
1976, in his light-blue suit.

***Shaft* Guitar?:** Chopin's Mazurkas piano concerto, as played
by Anna Batak, amid the overblown disco cast-offs and the
dreadful syrupy strings at the end.

Jargon: Bodie, inevitably, tells Doyle to 'Cover me!'

Laughable Dialogue: Michael: 'Hare like head, or like rabbit?' Doyle: '. . . Like Burke and . . .'

Notes: 'You know your trouble, don't you? Underneath that
hard shell you're just a great big softie.' The plot runs out

long before the final credits ... A very bland episode which fails to deliver any sort of punch.

Doyle's chest isn't all that hairy. His alias, though, is John Hare! Bodie seems to be in yet another new flat (perhaps all CI5 operatives moved after the events of 'The Purging of CI5' – look at the state of Cowley's 'office', for instance). Bodie calls Anna 'Mata Hari' after the infamous World War I German spy. Cowley refers to Batak as 'Great Uncle Bulgaria', of *The Wombles*. Doyle is aware of the film style *cinéma-vérité* (very popular in the 1960s). Bodie makes an oblique reference to the Georgi Markos case (see 'Close Quarters') when telling Cowley that his 'Bulgarian mojo' is 'a cross between a force beam and a poisoned umbrella'. According to Batak, the Soviets encourage the trade in heroin in the West.

28: 'The Madness of Mickey Hamilton'
24 November 1979

Writer: Christopher Wicking
Director: William Brayne

Cast: Ian McDiarmid (Mickey Hamilton),
Marjorie Yates (Kay Costa), Barry Stanton (Frank),
Shaun Curry (Sergeant Bellager), Clifton Jones (St Jacques),
David Henry (Captain Tepper), David Calder (Inspector Shannon),
John Saunders (Mr Pagett-Munro), Dick Sullivan (Priest),
Maurice Thorogood (Doctor 1), Olu Jacobs (Sylvester),
Kevin O'Shea (Dr Dyson), Anni Domingo (Sister Noel),
Myrtle Moss (Nun), Benjamin Feitelson (1st Doctor),
Rufus Collins (Mr Lemon), Shelagh McLeod (Toni),
Lynne Ross (Pat), Susie Jenkinson (Nurse),
Lydia Lisle (Computer Operator),
Andrew Hawkins (Dr Norris)

CI5 are called in when an African diplomat is shot outside a hospital. But who would want to kill him?

Keep Your Mincers Peeled For ...: Another of our favourite actors, the RSC regular David Calder's credits include *Chimera*, *A Question of Attribution*, *The Trial of Klaus Barbie*, *Tumbledown* and, most memorably, Commander Nathan Spring in *Star Cops*. For Barry Stanton, see *Sweeney 2*.

The secondary headline of the *Evening Standard* is 'CLASH OVER RECORD RATES'.

Birds: ** Bodie's current girlfriend is Pat, a redhead. He says he's 'not a nine-to-five guy,' and is horrified when she pecks him on the cheek ('Everyone's looking!'). He tells Doyle 'she's my plumber ... Come to fix me S-bend.' Doyle's young lady, a brunette, is much more cynical. 'Don't get too excited,' she tells Pat when the boys return. 'Look at them. I can tell. "Goodbye, girls, give you a ring soon. Duty calls." If we're lucky we'll get a lift home in the squad car.' And she's right.

Bodie reckons if he was a copper he would arrest the busty girl in a very short skirt crossing the road for a '217' (presumably soliciting). The CI5 computer girl wears a pair of hip-hugging jeans.

Booze: * Mickey has a bottle of whisky in his wardrobe along with his arsenal.

Shooters: *** Micky uses a rifle to shoot at the hospital, accidentally hitting the foreign ambassador. He has stolen a variety of sub-machine-guns, grenades and Broadsword antipersonnel mines from the army base. He shoots three doctors in the hospital before planting remote-controlled mines at the Wembley Conference Centre.

Motors: The usual Escort/Capri/Granada combo for Doyle, Bodie and Cowley. The African gangsters drive a big silver-grey Yank car.

Threads: The clothes are pretty standard for the era, but, check out the Afro haircut on the black man getting off the bus behind Hamilton.

Bill the Driver: One of the ambulance men looks familiar ...

Jargon: Sylvester: 'Who's the aadvark?'

Laughable Dialogue: Cowley: 'OK, OK, a wee bit less Freud, and a lot more action.'

Doyle: 'Maybe he's got a death wish.' Cowley: 'I noticed. He wishes some doctors were dead . . .'

Bodie (exhausted, having finally climbed the stairs to the top floor of the tower block): 'If I'm not back in ten minutes, send up a St Bernard.'

Notes: 'It's all you can do. Soldier on.' Wonderful! This week on *The Professionals* we have a villain who isn't, a gripping storyline and oodles of good characterisation. Real motivations and a proper back story – how refreshing! An almost Shakespearean meditation on the nature of insanity and blind revenge, the opening is reminiscent of Dennis Potter (all it needs is a 'Which one?' narration). There are some brilliant locations used, too, especially the views from Hamilton's high-rise. Only the convenient discovery of the newspaper covering the medical conference disappoints.

Bodie says he can't stand the smell of hospitals. Bambwezi is an African state, apparently. The army bomb range that Bodie visits seems to be the same disused factory the CI5 boys used to test their experimental gun in 'Hunter/Hunted', but minus the Chelsea graffiti. There's a reference to the Hundred Years War.

Admirably, this episode achieved 14.3 million viewers, and topped the weekly ratings chart during a repeat broadcast on 10 January 1981. See, the British public *have* got taste after all.

29: 'A Hiding to Nothing'
1 December 1979

Writer: Ted Childs
Director: Gerry O'Hara

Cast: Sylvia Kay (Frances Cottingham),
Lise Hilboldt (Shelley), Nadim Sawalha (Doad),
Christopher Reich (Luis), Gerald Sim (Colonel Masterson),

Phillada Sewell (Mrs Cottingham),
Adam Hussein (Hassam Alousha),
Yvonne D'Alpra (Mrs Waller), Nicholas Amer (Khadi),
Leticia Garrido (Pilar Hernandez), Frederick Warner (Smith)

A female terrorist is shot while covertly recording a 'dummy run' to deliver a Palestinian leader to a top-secret meeting. CI5 must find the security leak before the real meeting takes place.

Keep Your Mincers Peeled For . . .: Another year, another Arab diplomat, another page in the Nadim Sawalha CV (see *The Sweeney* – 'Visiting Firemen', et al.). Sylvia Kay was James Shelley's pot-smoking mum in *Shelley*. And there's Nosher Powell again, as one of the burglars.

There's a Chopper bike on the landing outside Doyle's flat. Look out, too, for a bottle of Head & Shoulders in Shelley's bathroom. (Dandruff? Her? *Never* . . .) Then there's the extremely cheap and nasty Interbrand C60 cassette CI5 use for recording their interviews. We used to get three for a pound down the market . . .

Birds: **** Shelley Hunter (phwoar!) is the American air hostess room-mate of the dead terrorist Pilar Hernandez. Bodie stares at her bum when she bends over to pick up a newspaper, but it's Doyle (pretending to be a literature student who has moved into the rooms below) who beds her. (We get to see about a quarter of a bare buttock as she follows Doyle from her bed at one point.)

Booze: * Bodie says he doesn't drink on duty (you lying git!). Doyle has a whisky after chasing the two terrorists from Shelley's flat.

Shooters: *** Hernandez carries a loaded pistol, and isn't afraid to use it. The men who break into Shelley's room carry pistols with silencers. At the end, CI5 and their Israeli attackers have sub-machine-guns; the latter also use a grenade launcher.

Motors: The dummy run uses a brown Merc. The Israeli

diplomat drives a red Lancia Beta saloon. A yellow VW van interrupts Bodie's pursuit of him in the Capri. Frances Cottingham walks out in front of a yellow Triumph 2000. The false Khadi changes from a red Wolsey Princess to a black Daimler limousine.

Threads: Shelley Hunter's tight-fitting jeans and brown silky blouse (and pink dressing gown). Doyle looks *so* macho in his brown leather jacket sans shirt. Also, check out Hassam's nasty kipper tie.

Shaft **Guitar?:** There's a nice trumpet theme as they trail the Israeli agent to the false meeting place.

Doyle Cooks a Bit of Pasta: He knows a bit about Mary Shelley. He says he'll cook Shelley Hunter a meal after her bath, but they end up eating a biryani takeaway.

Bodie Cooks a Bit of Pasta: In a rather worrying development, we see Bodie twanging away on a guitar. He's not bad, either, though his G chord could do with a bit of work. We always thought that, if you had an acoustic guitar, it meant that you were a protest singer . . .

Non-PC Moment: Doyle's flat is rented from a (male) ballet dancer (Bodie thinks he's 'very nice!').

Laughable Dialogue: Bodie: 'He's forensics, CID. I'm CI5.' Shelley: 'What's the difference?' Bodie: 'He's a technician, I'm an intellectual.'

Bodie: 'How come the bionic golly gets all the best bits?'

Shelley: 'I'm flying at six.' Doyle: 'Doesn't it make your arms ache?'

Cowley: 'You're a hard man, Bodie.' Bodie: 'Do you think you recruited a cream puff?'

Notes: 'The unacceptable face of espionage.' Two good stories on the trot. We're impressed. This one rattles along nicely, with everything in its place. Shame Shelley doesn't turn out to be just a normal air hostess, as she strikes us as the kind of girl Ray's been looking for.

The episode features a number of scenes outside the Royal

Albert Hall. Shelley quotes from her famous namesake Percy Bysshe Shelley's 'To a Skylark'.

30: 'Runner'
8 December 1979

Writer: Michael Feeney Callan
Director: Martin Campbell

Cast: Michael Kitchen (Duffy), Barbara Kellerman (Sylvie),
Ed Devereaux (Albie), James Cosmo (Glover),
Sean Caffrey (Ted), Billy Murray (Morgan),
Valerie Hollman (Alice), Keith Marsh (Old Man),
Forbes Collins (Harry), Denis Boyd (Davis),
Robyn Gurney (Girl in Betting Shop),
Debbie Linden (Bodie's Girl),
Samantha Bransden (Young Housewife),
Jeh Welcome (Ted's Girl), Barbara Allen (Albie's Girl)

The theft of a huge consignment of arms leads CI5 to the suspicion that the Organisation has become active again. But, when the weapons turn up dumped in a river, they just haven't got a clue what's going on . . .

Keep Your Mincers Peeled For . . .: Michael Kitchen was superb as the Prince Charles-like regent in *To Play the King*, and as the despised landowner's agent in *The Hanging Gale*. Barbara Kellerman will be well known to telefantasy fans for her performances in *1990* and *Quatermass*, and as the White Witch in *The Chronicles of Narnia*. For Billy Murray, see *The Sweeney* – 'Stoppo Driver'. James Cosmo was in *The Sweeney* – 'Hard Men'.

Doyle's high-speed arrival at the gun shop is pretty poor, clipping the kerb quite badly. Graffiti in the episode includes LONG LIVE OUR RHODESIA. The back page of the *Evening News* has the headline 'ENGLAND SQUARES THE SERIES', suggesting it's referring to a test series in cricket. But, since the episode was filmed in 1979, the only two test series England took part in that year (Mike Brearley's boys' 5–1 massacre of the Australians during the winter, and a 1–0 victory over India during the summer) didn't have an occasion when England were behind in order to draw level.

Birds: ** Sylvie – 'That little bitch from the Pineapple Club' – is first seen in a white dressing gown. Bodie chats up a blonde at the club and she ends up in his bed.

Booze: *** 'A pub crawl in broad daylight?' Much of the episode takes place in a club. Sylvie reaches for the gin when Doyle comes to interrogate Morgan. Bodie and Doyle go to several pubs, including one called the Favourite. Doyle seems to be drinking ginger beer, and Bodie asks for a lemonade (which will cost 30p); he suggests Sylvie put some vodka in it! (He's pulled that trick before – see 'Stopover'.)

Shooters: **** The opening scene features an armed raid on . . . a gun shop! We see Bodie's natty little stainless-steel pistol again. Bodie and Doyle come under rifle and sub-machine-gun fire at the deserted buildings, and again following their tip-off about the armed raid on the casino. A sniper takes out Morgan. Then he attempts to bump off Doyle and (successfully) Duffy. Doyle proves to be a bit of a crap shot with an Armalite.

Motors: Poor Doyle's Escort gets its windscreen blown out. Occupational hazard, we suppose. The villains variously drive a dark-blue Vauxhall Viva, a gold Vauxhall Ventora, a blue Datsun Laurel and a red BMW 323i. After the robbery at the gun shop, some CI5 men scream on to the scene . . . in a Hillman Hunter. Morgan goes to meet Doyle in a dark-green Morris Marina.

Threads: Doyle's nasty jacket and green T-shirt put in yet another appearance. Bodie sports a pair of really rather cool shades as he bursts into the turf accountant's.

***Shaft* Guitar?:** There's a tuneless little melody at the start with off-key piano and horns. Later, what sounds like a glockenspiel joins in.

Doyle Cooks a Bit of Pasta: He starts the episode eating crisps in his car, which doesn't seem very healthy at all.

Slash Fiction Moment: The bit just after they defuse the bomb. If they'd started hugging we wouldn't have been surprised.

Jargon: Morgan: 'And you keep away from that nark, all right?'

Laughable Dialogue: Morgan: 'All this free time is just one of the perks of being unemployed.'
 Alice: 'Got you out looking for truants, have they?'
 Bodie: 'Hey, what you got that's potent and legal?'
 Bodie: 'Who's the heavy boys round here?' Sylvie: 'Ask me about the heavy girls, and I might be able to tell you!'

Notes: 'Could have a runner.' What a load of codswallop! 'The Organisation'? Brilliant name for an, erm, organisation, that . . . Who exactly are they? What are their aims? Where do they come from (two of them are Scottish, one Australian)? Utter bollocks from start to finish. There's a good scene on the roof, with Doyle and Duffy, but the episode also features the crappiest bomb-disposal sequence ever, and thus no real ending at all.

 Five years ago, Doyle shot and killed Duffy's brother during a bank raid.

31: 'Servant of Two Masters'
15 December 1979

Writer: Douglas Watkinson
Director: Ferdinand Fairfax

Cast: David De Keyser (Otta Hahn),
Glynn Edwards (Alfred Cole), Christina World (Jutta),
John Savident (Robert Plumb), Dennis Burgess (Dr Forbes),
Tony Scannell (Man 1), James Lister (Karl),
Kenneth Owens (Groves), Will Stampe (Ted),
Frank Ellis (Man 2), Ryan Michael (Wilf)

Can Cowley really be a traitor, selling an experimental PS2 nerve gas to a bunch of naughty foreigners for a huge wad of cash? Is the civil service pension really *that* bad? Go on, guess ...

Keep Your Mincers Peeled For ...: Glynn Edwards was Dave the barman in *Minder*. Tony Scannell (appearing in a tiny role) went on to play Ted Roach in *The Bill*.

Birds: * Doyle sees Bodie's rocking car: 'He's never found himself a milkmaid?'

Booze: ** Doyle, Bodie and Alf drink treble Scotches – since it's Doyle's round. Cowley drinks red wine at Hahn's house.

Shooters: ** Plenty of tasty steel is stored at Alf Cole's CI5 armoury, but the big stand-off at the end resolves itself after only two shots are fired.

Motors: We first see Cowley's red Granada being filled up. Bodie tracks his boss in a Morris Marina van. Cowley switches to what seems to be a rust-coloured Marina estate. Doyle is probably grateful to be able to drive around in his Escort. Hahn and the others arrive at the airport in an Audi 100 Coupé S; two Transits carry PS2 to the light aircraft. CI5 agents turn up in, among other things, a yellow Granada.

Threads: Doyle's purple shirt and, later, his grey sweatshirt.

Shaft **Guitar?:** 'Auld Lang Syne' is sung at Alf's leaving do in the bar. There's some good harpsichord-like effects as Cowley is under surveillance. And discordant music at the end.

Doyle Cooks a Bit of Pasta: During their early-morning jog through the cemetery to get rid of their hangovers, Doyle says that he thinks that Bodie eats too much. Bodie says he has heard jogging is bad for you since people drop dead while doing it. 'You're in the right place then,' notes Doyle.

Slash Fiction Moment: Bodie telling Doyle that he'll miss him when the latter gets out of the car to talk to Alf, and then warning him 'not to speak to any strange men'.

Jargon: Bodie: 'He's done the old switcheroo. Looks like our bug is US.' Doyle: 'Any chance he clocked you?' Bodie: 'No.' Doyle: 'Any sign of RT on the new chariot?'

Laughable Dialogue: Bodie: 'You haven't got a cure for a hangover, have you?' Plumb: 'Yes. Know when you've had enough.'

Notes: 'We're just hired hands, it's our masters who are bent.' A very slow and ordinary episode with a risibly obvious denouement.

Doyle says he has 20/20 vision (normally). He wasn't a Boy Scout: he took dancing lessons instead (see 'Involvement' for proof!). Doyle reckons Johan Cruyff (then coming to the end of his career at Barcelona) is the best all-round footballer in Europe. Bodie goes for Kevin Keegan (at that time the European Footballer of the Year during his two brilliant years at SV Hamburg). Given the state of Doyle's perm, one might have thought he'd agree with his partner. Charlie is mentioned – nice to see he survived getting shot in the lung in 'Blind Run'.

The title is a biblical allusion (Luke 16:13). In some countries, this episode is mistakenly titled 'Master of Two Servants'! Jutta is said to have devised some brutal punishments for political prisoners in her country, including one 'somewhat similar to what Salome thought up' for an ex-lover (presumably, it involved beheading). Doyle makes reference to *Alice in Wonderland*. The swinging light in the opening sequence may be a subtle nod to *Callan*. There's a reference to the West German special forces rescue of hostages on a hijacked Lufthansa airliner in Mogadishu, Somalia, in November 1977.

Fourth Season

Fifteen 60-minute episodes
An Avengers Mark 1 Production/London Weekend Television
Created by Brian Clemens

Associate Producers: Chris Burt (32, 34–37, 40, 43–44),
Roy Stevens (33, 38–39, 41, 46)
Producer: Raymond Menmuir
Executive Producers: Albert Fennell, Brian Clemens

Title music by Laurie Johnson

Regular Cast: Gordon Jackson (George Cowley),
Martin Shaw (Ray Doyle), Lewis Collins (William Bodie),
Steve Alder (Murphy, 38, 42, 45)

32: 'The Acorn Syndrome'
7 September 1980

Writer: John Kruse
Director: Martin Campbell

Cast: Michael Craig (Guthrie), Ronald Hines (Copeland),
Lynda Marchal (Viv Copeland), Ian Redford (Lucas),
Alun Lewis (McCabe), Oona Kirsch (Sandy Copeland),
Kate Dorning (Nancy),
John Michael McCarthy (Inspector Grainger),
Nigel Humphreys (Joe), Stewart Harwood (Sam),
Gennie Nevinson (Eva), Sean Chapman (Coleman),
Alan Igbon (Angadi), Christopher Saul (Male Hostage),
Jennifer Granville (Female Hostage), Becci Hunt (Child),
John Joyce (Langton), Hilary Crane (Miss Kendall),
Sue Nicholls (Mrs Forbes), Charles Pemberton (Styles),
Patricia Marks (Landlady)

On a rare day off, Bodie and Doyle go to collect an antique

desk for Cowley, and end up involved in a car chase, gun battle and siege.

Keep Your Mincers Peeled For . . .: Michael Craig has had a long and distinguished career in film and TV, though he's probably best known as the captain in *Triangle*. Ronald Hines starred in two legendary 1960s sitcoms, *Marriage Lines*, and *Not In Front of the Children*. Gennie Nevinson was the doomed girlfriend of Nathan Spring in *Star Cops*, while Alan Igbon was terrific as Loggo in *Boys From the Blackstuff*. Probably the best-known face in the episode is Sue Nicholls, a pop star in the 1960s, and a veteran of *Crossroads*, *The Fall and Rise of Reginald Perrin* (as Joan) and *Coronation Street* (as Audrey Roberts). Amazingly, she gets only about four lines.

There's a Che Guevara poster on the wall of the students' flat (did somebody sell the production team a job lot of these, or is it the same one they keep on using over and over again?). Also, watch out, in the flat, for a bottle of Brut aftershave (*the* cosmetic accessory of the 1970s), a book of the Turin Shroud, and a Status Quo poster. When Doyle cases the deserted farm, we wonder if Martin Shaw was *supposed* to get snagged on that rose.

Birds: * Schoolgirls in peril; Doyle seems vaguely interested. 'Down boy,' notes Bodie. Later Mrs Forbes tries to chat him up while he's pretending to be a horse-delivery man.

Booze: No time for that sort of thing.

Shooters: ** It's a half-revealed pistol that gets Bodie and Doyle involved in the case. There are a couple of shortish exchanges of gunfire towards the end, the latter of which has Doyle shooting a man dead despite the hostage he has in front of him. What a guy!

Motors: The student villains drive a gold-coloured Vauxhall Victor. Bodie and Doyle collect Cowley's desk in (or, rather, on) a black Cortina estate (check out the fantastically functional roof rack). Towards the end of the car chase, Lewis Collins accidentally smashes into the kerb. During the course of the episode we also see police Rovers and Triumphs, a whole load of tanks, a black Beamer, a silver Volvo 164, a grey Mercedes 280SE (which Bodie shuts himself into the boot of), a blue Hillman Avenger, a red, and a blue Peugeot 504. Doyle gets to drive a blue horse box, and spots what looks like a greyish Jag at the farm where Copeland's daughter is being held.

Threads: Nancy the precocious schoolgirl describes Bodie and Doyle as 'scruffy'. Out of the mouths of babes . . . Check out Doyle's wellies!

***Shaft* Guitar?:** The standard, somewhat ponderous, bass and strings.

Jargon: Bodie: 'How much was it?' Man: 'Eight hundred and twenty-five nicker.'

Doyle: 'They didn't look that heavy.' Bodie: 'Had the tools, though, didn't they?' Doyle: 'Oh yeah, very brave with women and kids.' Bodie: 'Yeah, marvellous. This green and pleasant land, riddled with bandits.'

Laughable Dialogue: Cowley: 'I suppose you heard what these two did to my desk, McCabe?' McCabe: 'It's the talk of the department, sir.' Cowley: 'Battered beyond recognition, minus its drawers.' McCabe: 'Nasty. On that evidence, I'm surprised you don't charge them with rape!'

Notes: 'First day off in months, he gives us a desk job!' As obvious a plot as they come, with some elements drawn from the (real-life) Balcombe Street siege in December 1975 (four IRA gunmen barricaded themselves in a Marylebone flat, holding a couple hostage for four days).

Bodie's reference to Cowley turning into 'a pillar of salt' indicates a knowledge of the Old Testament (Lot's wife, Genesis 19:26). The Angie Dickinson TV series *Police Woman* is mentioned.

'Photostats' are referred to: this *was* the early days of photocopying in Britain, after all.

33: 'Wild Justice'
14 September 1980

Writer: Ranald Graham
Director: Dennis Abey

Cast: Larry Lamb (Jack Craine),
Sarah Douglas (Dr Kate Ross), Jenny Twigge (Sally),
Ziggy Byfield (King Billy), Marsha Fitzalan (Jennifer Black),
Frances Low (Cheryl), Paul Humpoletz (DCI Botham),
Robert Lee (Shusai), Llewellyn Rees (Dr Philip Hedley),
Jack McKenzie (Rose), Robert Ashby (Mediator),
Richard Huw (Bike Kid), Brian Attree (Terrorist),
Kenneth Hadley (Desk Sergeant),
Tommy Wright (Race Official)

Is Bodie cracking up?

Keep Your Mincers Peeled For . . .: Marsha Fitzalan played
the lesbian wife of Alan B'Stard in *The New Statesman*. Larry
Lamb's credits include *Fox* and *Triangle* (as Matt Taylor).
Robert Lee was in LWT's appallingly racist sitcom *Mind
Your Language*, and played Johnny Ho's wrongly imprisoned
father in *The Chinese Detective*. (Isn't it a pity that Ziggy
Byfield and Jenny Twigge weren't brother and sister? Then
he'd be Ziggy Twigge . . .)

The aftershave that Doyle splashes on all over looks like
it's coming from an Old Spice bottle. Also briefly glimpsed in
Doyle's flat are a very 70s-design bedside reading lamp and
what might be a bean bag (in the corner of one shot).

Birds: * Dr Ross is very sexy in a cold, scientific sort of way.
At least Doyle thinks so. 'What are you doing tonight?' '. . .
As for taking refuge in sexual chauvinism, you've already
branded yourself loud and clear.' (Doyle later calls Ross the
Queen of Cybernetics.) Bodie claims to have always been a
good finisher. Can't imagine what he's alluding to. Doyle
takes a short-haired brunette with him to the motocross
event.

Booze: * Bodie has a half-pint in the Chequered Flag pub. Later, he runs into the bikers there when with Jennifer Black. Cowley and Jennifer share a red wine.

Shooters: *** A vast amount of guns, explosives, etc., are used during the various training exercises. At the end, Cowley places a revolver at Bodie's head.

Motors: We see Doyle riding a Suzuki motorbike and, later, Bodie is on a BMW. There is a green Cortina (complete with a big dent in the back of it). Talking of dents, Bodie puts one into the side of his yellow MGB. Doyle drives to the scrambling event in a bright-yellow Suzuki Jeep-type thing, complete with trailer. Because the episodes were transmitted out of production order, 'Wild Justice' gives us our first look at Bodie's new silver Capri S (OWC 827W). Actually, it seems just the same as the previous one . . .

Threads: Doyle looks a complete knob with his balaclava half on, and resembles a cut-price Rambo a few minutes later. The fur collar on his brown jacket seems to get bigger with every passing episode. Watch out for Bodie's burgundy leatherish jacket, Doyle's sunshine-yellow T-shirt, Bodie in full biker's leathers, plus, of course, a whole load of Hell's Angels . . .

Shaft **Guitar?:** One of the bikers wears a Black Sabbath T-shirt.

Slash Fiction Moment: Doyle: 'You wreck my bike, I'll burn your rubber duck.'

Jargon: Bodie: 'Oh, don't be so snotty, son. Some of these cowboys are no mangoes, you know.'

Laughable Dialogue: Dr Ross: 'Do you call a glass of water half empty or half full?' Cowley: 'If it was a small glass, and it had malt whisky in it, I'd say it was half empty.'

Bodie: 'Well, the first bandit I ever tackled, doctor, was one-armed.'

Dr Hedley (on Bodie): 'We could enter him for the Derby and wager our pensions.'

Dr Ross: 'Oh, as long as their mental capacities are un-impaired, they can have as much simple, hairy, masculine fun as they like.'

Notes: 'Game, set and match, Bodie.' A cracking story, one of Lewis Collins's finest moments. From the opening re-creation of the ending of the Iranian Embassy siege (May 1980 – which must have been the event of the *decade* as far as *The Professionals* was concerned) to the tense denouement, via some really impressive kendo sequences and Eastern philosophy, this barely puts a foot wrong. Really good direction, too. Would Cowley have pulled the trigger at the end? Do bears sh–

The other members of Bodie's special-service platoon have all died subsequent to demob – only Bodie survives. Doyle's moved again. He now lives in a first-floor flat, in rooms that seem reasonably old, and are white-walled and covered with various prints. Jack Craine is agent 7-7.

Reference is made to the *Star Wars* arcade game and Splodgenessabounds's hit single 'Two Pints of Lager and a Packet of Crisps Please' (though here the head biker asks for six pints of lager). (This must have been a fairly late ad-lib or addition to the script: this episode was second in the filming block that commenced in June 1980, and the single first charted on the fourteenth of that month.) Dr Ross quotes from Shakespeare's sonnet 'Shall I compare thee to a summer's day?' when the computer wishes to check her voice pattern. There is some location filming near Tower Bridge, the Tower of London and Windsor.

There are references to the boxer Randolph Turpin and (possibly) the Four Tops song 'Still Water' (by Cowley).

34: 'Fugitive'
21 September 1980

Writer: Gerry O'Hara,
from a story by Anthony Read
Director: Denis Lewiston

Cast: Michael Byrne (Werner), Vickery Turner (Karen),

Brigitte Kahn (Christina), Andrew Seear (Heinrich),
Conrad Asquith (Klaus), Paul Antrim (Slater),
Eleanor Davis (Julie), Tony Sibbald (Silverstein),
Jillian Mack (Receptionist), Christopher Asante (Quentin),
Maureen Darbyshire (CI5 Girl),
Ronald Alexander (1st CI5 Sniper),
Malcolm Hughes (2nd CI5 Sniper),
Pat Connell (3rd CI5 Sniper), Chris Hallam (Man at Door),
Tania Rogers (Black Girl)

When a CIA man falls to his death from his hotel room, Cowley suspects the involvement of the German terrorist Christina Herzog, who is working in the UK as an assistant librarian.

Keep Your Mincers Peeled For ...: Vickery Turner appeared in three of the most important television productions of the 1960s, *Up the Junction*, *Cathy Come Home* and *The Year of the Sex Olympics*. Brigitte Khan would subsequently play Denis's German girlfriend, Dagmar, in *Auf Wiedersehen, Pet*.

In a gorgeous panning shot just after the credits, you get brief glimpses of billboard adverts for Benson and Hedges and Levi's.

Birds: ** Bodie takes a fancy to 'Anne Lawson'. 'She can stamp my book any day,' he says. CI5 agent 6-7 – Julie, an attractive redhead – is an 'old friend' of Bodie's. The black girl we see near Herzog's second flat has a pleasantly mobile chest.

Booze: * When Doyle and Bodie visit Slater, the arms dealer, Doyle has a large Scotch, and Bodie a small Cuba libre. (Slater himself has a pink gin, giving away his naval heritage.) Karen drinks gin and tonic with both Slater and, subsequently, Bodie.

Shooters: *** Christina Herzog has a cache of weapons under the floorboards of her second flat, which she throws into the canal. She and Doyle exchange fire. A few interesting-looking weapons can be glimpsed in Slater's back room. Bodie and Doyle have a mock gun battle so that the former will be accepted by the terrorists; trouble is, the cell leader, Werner, is watching, and he sees Doyle (seemingly shot in the chest) get up unharmed. There's a big shoot-out at the end, and a rucksack of explosives.

Motors: Christine drives a dark-brown Mini. Bodie and Karen make their escape in a green Volvo. (Bodie is back with the T-reg silver Capri.)

Threads: Doyle's silky maroon shirt (with holster over the top, of course!). We also get a lingering shot of his cowboy boots.

***Shaft* Guitar?:** Some very cheesy (and not very reggae) 'West Indian' music from the flat above as Christina removes the guns from under the floorboards. There's also a loud rock theme at the start as Silverstein is bundled out of the window.

Slash Fiction Moment: Doyle leaping on top of Bodie to rip off the explosives.

Laughable Dialogue: Cowley: 'Bodie, I never thought that you would believe that popular misconception of the Scots. You couldn't find a more generous race.'
  Cowley: 'Interrogation of Christina Herzog, resumed at nineteen a.m.' (Eh? Since when has there been a 19 a.m.?)
  Bodie (on the man he has just shot): 'Dead?' Doyle: 'Considerably.'
  Young woman: 'Bobby's free.' (Bodie and Doyle look over at the camp-looking hairdresser.) Doyle: 'Hell, I'm sure he is.'
  Werner: 'What happened to Klaus?' Bodie: 'Ah, Santa Klaus. Yeah, well, he doesn't exist, don't you know?'

Notes: 'We've got your man.' This finally gets going when Bodie is captured, and then bottles its conclusion in a mist of smoke and gunfire. Still, intermittently diverting stuff, and a nice freeze-frame ending. (Shame that's then ruined by the brash title music. How wise it was to have a second, slower, end theme for *The Sweeney*!)

There is a mention of the (real-life) Italian terrorist group, the Red Brigade. The library books Cowley gives his lads are *Medieval England* and *Chaucer the Poet* (for Bodie – who's got a 'twelve pee' fine to pay on them!) and *End of Term* and *Emma in Love* for Doyle (closet romantic!). Inside the library, Doyle reads a book by Gaston Diehl, and we see posters for the Sadler's Wells Royal Ballet company, and a book called *William Blake and his Followers*. There are references to Sleeping Beauty, and another nod towards the Angolan civil war (see 'Where the Jungle Ends').

Locations seen include Wembley Park tube station.

35: 'Involvement'

28 September 1980

Writer: Brian Clemens
Director: Chris Burt

Cast: Patricia Hodge (Ann), William Russell (Charles Holly),
Ray Ashcroft (Turner), Christopher Guard (Tony),
Valentine Pringle (Buzz), Peter Holt (Marli),
Peter Godfrey (Vicar), Kirstie Pooley (Secretary),
Peter Burton (Conroy), Philip Anthony (Butler)

Bodie shoots a suspect dead in a block of flats in front of a horrified witness. And, inevitably, she and Doyle fall in love. Well, you would, wouldn't you?

Keep Your Mincers Peeled For ...: Patricia Hodge first shot to fame in *Rumpole of the Bailey* and *The Naked Civil Servant*. Her subsequent career included *Holding the Fort*, the starring role in *Jemima Shore Investigates* and *The Life and Loves of a She Devil*. William Russell was the star of *The Adventures of Sir Lancelot* in the late 1950s before playing Ian Chesterton in *Doctor Who*.

Keep your eyes on the dreadful running action of the guy Doyle and Bodie are chasing in the opening sequence. Oh, and there's a brown Adidas sports bag used to carry the drugs.

We used to take our sports kit to school in ours. Doyle has a new flat that includes a pinball machine and a wrought-iron staircase.

Birds: **** 'Oh, Ray, I do love you.' A 'Doyle falls in love' episode (first one of those in a while), and as such, full of little gems like 'I'm never off duty' and 'That must be a treat for your girlfriends'. Ann says she is not 'the crying type' and, interestingly, when Doyle is visibly upset after Benny's death and Bodie suggests he needs 'a drink and some female company', it's her he goes running to. Bodie says he's never tried flowers on a girl before. Fancy.

There are two girlie posters in Tony's flat, and Bodie reads a copy of *Mayfair*, which he quickly hides in his desk when Cowley walks in. Shortly afterwards, he's back to flirting with the secretaries (in this case, Kirstie).

Booze: ** In Ann's flat Doyle shares a whisky with her (she's also got a bottle of Smirnoff on display). There's Trophy Bitter on draught in the pub where Doyle and Ann drink white wine.

Shooters: ** 'He had a .38 on Doyle. What was I supposed to do?' In addition to the opening, there's a bit of a shoot-out at the end.

Motors: Bodie photographs Charles Holly's Jag. The red CI5 Cortina (HPU 724T) from 'The Acorn Syndrome' reappears, briefly pursuing a green Cavalier (Bodie later falls asleep in it). We see a couple of Suzuki Jeep-y type things. Ann drives a white Suzuki SC100 Coupé.

Threads: Tony's American high school jacket. Doyle's skinny tie actually *was* pretty fashionable in 1979, but it just doesn't go with the rest of the gear. His pale, enormous cardigan thing (very *Starsky and Hutch*) is foul. The white Harrington jacket worn by one of the villains. Buzz's red poloneck and navy-blue velvet jacket.

Check out the threads on the man Cowley is talking to as he, Doyle and Bodie wait for the light aircraft to land. He's on screen for only about five seconds, but in that time you can spot a grey leather jacket, black poloneck shirt, flared strides and a medallion. Disco shit, man, or what?

Non-PC Moment: Much of Bodie's dialogue concerning Ann is petty and overtly sexist. Big surprise. Then there's the moment where Buzz, the big black man, gets into his flash American car and Bodie notes, 'Didn't get *that* from honest toil.' Bodie also calls him a 'Spade'.

Shaft Guitar?: There's a good cello theme at the start, and two scenes in a disco. The accompanying soundtrack mixes pounding funk (seemingly called 'Give it All You've Got') and some tinkly, smoochy music.

Doyle Cooks a Bit of Pasta: Actually he cooks a *lot* of pasta in this episode, beginning with 'Spaghetti à la Benny' – named for one of his snouts – which he serves to Ann with a red wine. (He very sensibly has concluded that spaghetti always tastes best with lashings of fresh Parmesan.) 'You doing all the cooking now?' asks Bodie. Doyle says he is, and that Ann can't cook.

Slash Fiction Moment: Bodie displays a huge amount of jealousy regarding Ann, despite what he might want Doyle (and maybe himself) to believe. 'She's a toughie ... Mind of her own,' notes Doyle, to which Bodie huffily replies, 'Thought it wasn't her mind you were interested in.' He tells Cowley that Doyle is a 'crafty, randy old toad'. Significantly, Bodie wants all the details the morning after and, when Doyle procrastinates, Bodie believes, 'That means you *didn't*.' Cowley tells Bodie that no operative can get married without his permission (it's in the small print). Bodie says he didn't know this, to which Cowley notes that it's hardly likely to affect *him*. Of course, it all ends up in a big boys' fight, in which Bodie goads Doyle into punching him ('I think she's too good for you, mate'), and the episode concludes with the pair with their arms around each other. If ever one episode could be used as an example of this element of *The Professionals*, so brilliantly parodied in *The Bullshitters: Roll Out the Gun Barrel*, then this is it.

Jargon: 'Are you carrying?'

Laughable Dialogue: Bodie, on being told there are no clues on Conroy's body: 'What, no book of matches with a nightclub name on them?'

Bodie (sniffing the air suspiciously): 'You bought a cat?' Doyle: 'I just figured out who you are. You're the guy who murdered Vaudeville, aren't you?' Bodie: 'Oh, it's your *aftershave*! Oh . . . Never mind . . .'

Notes: 'You're a paradox. You're much more complex than I imagined.' One of the best episodes of *The Professionals*, not so much for what actually happens, but for the ideas behind it. Lovely sequence filmed in Highgate Park. There is one utterly stupid bit, though: how does Ann manage to get into CI5 HQ (presumably a high-security building) without being challenged?

Doyle's a lovely little mover, as the disco scenes prove. He has Italian contacts. Benny was one of his snouts – they first met when Doyle was a copper and he caught Benny nicking apples. Bruce Lee and the photographer David Bailey are mentioned.

36: 'Need to Know'
5 October 1980

Writer: Brian Clemens,
from a story by Chris Menual
Director: William Brayne

Cast: Patrick O'Connell (Manton), Norman Jones (Drake),
Karin McCarthy (Ryan), Niall Buggy (Gorky),
Simon Oates (Tully), Richard Parmentier (Ivan),
David King (Ambassador), Tom Georgeson (Pymar),
Bernard Gallagher (Minister), Chua Kahjoo (Chou),
Yuri Borienko (Maroff), Anthony Chinn (Sikor),
Kristopher Kum (Minder), Nigel Miles Thomas (1st Cop),
Mike Kemp (2nd Cop)

A Special Branch officer arrests Drake, a leading man in the Department, for espionage. It was Cowley who recruited Drake to the section many years ago, so it is not surprising when the finger of suspicion begins pointing in his direction too.

Keep Your Mincers Peeled For . . .: Patrick O'Connell took over from Glyn Owen playing Ted Hammond in *The Brothers*. Simon Oates was John Ridge, one of the dashing young scientists in *Doomwatch*. Norman Jones was one of the stars of Granada's excellent historical drama *The Stars Look Down*. For Bernard Gallagher, see *The Sweeney* – 'Jackpot'. For Tom Georgeson, see 'In the Public Interest'.

See if you can spot the famous (and very stylised) 1930 portrait of Lenin in the Soviet Embassy.

Birds: * Bodie says he's never had a 'Chinese bird'. Doyle seems to have had (see also 'Take Away').

Booze: * Bodie, Cowley and Doyle drink whisky at Cowley's house.

Shooters: ** There are loads of pistols and guns (some antique) visible on Bodie's wall. Cowley takes an enormous rifle out of the boot of his car; Bodie, Doyle and Cowley all have pistols as they break into the farmhouse.

Motors: Drake is taken away by the 'KGB boys' in a yellow Range Rover. Pymar has a bluish Triumph 2000.

Threads: Doyle's ginger T-shirt and green spectacles. Bodie's 'pod' shoes. Doyle's white plimsolls. Plus, Bodie and Doyle in police uniforms (surely Doyle's hair is too long and too curly for this to be convincing?).

***Shaft* Guitar?:** There's a rather tuneful bass-and-glockenspiel effort.

Non-PC Moment: 'Our yellow friends.' The completely unsubtle racism shown by Bodie and Doyle in the Oriental club ('I suppose no one's seen a Chinaman come in, have they?').

Laughable Dialogue: Bodie, on their police uniforms: 'How'd you ever do anything in these outfits?' Doyle: 'You'd be surprised, mate.'

Minister: 'I just hope you're taking the right precautions.' Cowley: 'Och, you sound like a wee lassie behind the pub on a Saturday night!'

Doyle: 'Just to confirm that your order's been filled. One Chinese takeaway.' Cowley: 'With lots of rice . . .?'

Notes: 'Accessories to murder, mate, that's what we are. Either that, or magnificent bloody patriots.' Similar themes to 'Servant of Two Masters'. Slow and ordinary, despite the excellent cast (O'Connell, Oates, Georgeson, etc.). Is the Chinese drug-pusher left at the scene of Drake's snatch? We don't see him in the car with Doyle and Bodie afterwards so it's probably safe to assume so. In which case, isn't he going to blow the plan as soon as he opens his mouth? There are a couple of good kung-fu sequences, and the attack on the prison van is good. The ending is rather nasty (Cowley shooting a fleeing man in the back).

Doyle used to walk a beat in Chinatown. Bodie was beaten in a judo competition in Amsterdam by a Sergeant Mackay (he says he was ill). Mention is made of Cowley's antique desk ('worth a fortune'), which we see at his home, but this presumably isn't a replacement for the desk that gets trashed in 'The Acorn Syndrome', as that was intended for his office. Cowley can speak a little Chinese.

If an agent's passport is taken, it is a serious matter and handcuffs should be used in the following arrest. Bodie and Doyle didn't follow this when bringing Cowley in. Cowley seems to have moved house since 'In the Public Interest'. He first met Drake at a recital of Bach, Beethoven and Chopin at the Edinburgh Festival. They were introduced by Sir Geoffrey (now Lord) Aimsworth. Cowley says Prokofiev is not his style (not enough melody!).

There are references to the recent introduction of the radio broadcasting of Parliament. Kim Philby is mentioned for the second time (see 'Stopover'). The taxi Drake takes costs £4, a *huge* figure in 1980, so he must have come a fair distance.

37: 'Take Away'
12 October 1980

Writer: Roger Marshall
Director: Douglas Camfield

Cast: Chai Lee (Esther), John Forgeham (DS Colin),
James Marcus (DC Jack), Gary Shail (Jimmy),
Phil Brown (Callahan), Sharon Duce (Annie),
Pik Sen Lim (Chai Ling), Arnold Lee (Chi Sang),
Fiesta Mei Ling (Siu Sang), George Little (Meyer),
Andy Ho (Ngan Hung), Richard Rees (Johnny Chong),
Ken Watson (Boss), Ann Coombs (Girl in Bed),
Vincent Wong (Kidnapper), Rex Wei (Kidnapper),
Peta Bernard (Girl Companion), John Rumney (Diter Kroll),
Gertan Klauber (Helmut Brenick), Dennis Matsuki (Cheng),
Jason Forgeham (Child), Jonesta Forgeham (Child)

Bodie and Doyle go undercover to crush a complicated East German/Chinese triad plot to destroy the special relationship between Britain and America.

Keep Your Mincers Peeled For . . . : Sharon Duce played Robby Box's wife in *Big Deal*. James Marcus had a long-running role as Tate on *London's Burning*. For John Forgeham, see *The Sweeney* – 'The Placer'. Presumably Jason and Jonesta Forgeham are John's children.

There are posters of the Boomtown Rats and Bob Marley in Johnny Chong's flat. Graffiti in the squat includes the memorable BOWIE WOZ HERE and, on the stairs, SPG RULE OK (a reference to the infamous Special Patrol Group).

Birds: **** As close as *The Professionals* ever got to full 'boobies alert'. Chong's girlfriend manages to cover her dignity as Colin and Jack burst into the flat. Doyle is sharing a flat with Esther, the pretty sergeant on secondment from the Hong Kong police. (She looks especially hot in the last scene in a silky grey blouse.) Bodie can't help but look closer at the notices for a strip club he passes (advertising 'Swedish Playgirls' and 'Sexy Virgins'!). Watch out, also, for the guy in the hotel room with his volume of porno pictures ('Don't forget the family album') and his (ahem) 'friend' in the shower.

Booze: ** Doyle and Esther drink white wine (Pouilly-Fumé), and have a lengthy discussion on Australian wine (Doyle thinks it pretty poor, which it might well have been back then). She buys him a bottle in an attempt to combat his prejudices.

Shooters: ** When attacked, Esther has a pistol (Doyle uses his hands, kung-fu-style!). Bodie has a sub-machine-gun. Doyle asks Colin, whose men are disguised as dustmen, 'Are you tooled up, apart from your brushes?'

Motors: Chi Sang's 'wife' is abducted in her own orange-ish Vauxhall Cavalier. Chi Sang leaves his restaurant in a blue Datsun (looks like a Skyline to us). Kroll arrives in a silver Merc. Oh, and that red CI5 Cortina – check out the vile scarlet upholstery – appears again.

Threads: We've got to mention Jimmy's classic early-80s haircut *somewhere* . . . Also, watch out for Bodie's stomach-churning grey leather jacket, Doyle's pyjama bottoms and Meyer's horrible stripy tie.

***Shaft* Guitar?:** There's a neoclassical opening, until the French horns come blaring in.

Slash Fiction Moment: Bodie: 'These peaches are bruised.' Doyle: 'Trouble with you, sailor: don't know your own strength.'

   After they find Kroll has 'diplo-bloody-matic immunity', there is a tangible anger about Doyle and Bodie. They're going to the nearest pub: anybody in their way is advised to get out quickly.

Non-PC Moment: Colin, on the diary with Chinese writing in it: 'It's full of chinky-chonky 'ere.' In fact, Colin and Jack are just about the last two coppers you'd want to investigate a sensitive case in Chinatown.

Jargon: 'Bitten by the elephant' is a euphemism for heroin addiction. In fact, there's loads of drugs-speak during the episode.

Jimmy: 'If he hadn't been such a chunk-head he'd still have a daughter instead of a couple of sticks of charcoal.'

Jimmy: 'So I come up with a face, right? Take it out of the frame. Next day there's another one there. It's just like fungus.'

Laughable Dialogue: Roger Marshall at his finest. Jimmy: 'Don't patronise me. Just because I don't conform doesn't mean I'm a cretin.'

Cowley, on entering the squat: 'What's the smell, washing or cooking?'

Notes: 'All that, and we end up with a fistful of smoke.' Take one of the best writers of series TV and one of the best directors of series TV and put them in charge of a *Professionals* episode, and what do you get? Probably the best episode of the series. This is an excellent multilayered script, crammed full of good dialogue and characterisation. Forget the normal macho nonsense and posing around with guns and explosions: this is *real* drama that looks as good as it sounds, and is full of great little moments, like Doyle's revenge against the patronising coppers.

Bodie has a mate who works on the *Daily Express* (maybe *that* explains why everybody on the Squad, not to mention the production team, seem to read it) who told him that the recently deceased PPS of a government minister died a victim of a 'heart-attack hump'. Bodie seems not to have been very good at chemistry at school. His cover name is 'Kilroy'.

Doyle can do a reasonable Australian accent. His Chinese connections were mentioned in 'Need to Know'. Cowley knows his art history (correctly identifying who the Pre-Raphaelites were): see 'It's Only a Beautiful Picture.'

The £1-per-hour wage Esther is offered for a job as a drinks waitress in the Chinese restaurant seems outrageously low now, and it was *still* pretty bad in 1980 (especially as two peaches cost 20p). There are references to Bruce Lee, *Le Morte d'Arthur*, *Nineteen Eighty-Four* (Big Brother) and *The World of Suzie Wong*.

Location filming took place around Soho and Chinatown, plus Heathrow and on the Piccadilly Line.

38: 'Blackout'
19 October 1980

Writer: Brian Clemens
Director: William Brayne

Cast: Ben Cross (Stuart), Linda Hayden (Gerda),
Jill Martin (Mrs Parker), Slyvester Morand (Mr Parker),
Timothy Stark (Henry), John Arnatt (Humber),
Gareth Armstrong (Dr Marsand),
Kevin Quarmby (PC Fenton), Amanda Leigh (Betty Fenton),
Derek Ensor (Bank Manager), John Cording (Minter),
Louis Mahoney (Doctor), Fionn O'Farrell (Nurse),
Cyril Conway (Rector), Paul Gale (Corrigan),
Julia Blalock (Barmaid)

A dishevelled girl wearing only her underwear staggers into a church. So, who do you think the surprised clerics call for . . .?

Keep Your Mincers Peeled For . . .: Ben Cross shot to fame playing Harold Abrahams in *Chariots of Fire*. Linda Hayden was one of the Hammer starlets of the early 1970s, appearing in *Taste the Blood of Dracula*. For Louis Mahoney (that geezer was *seriously* typecast!), see 'Klansmen'.

Birds: ** Doyle: 'The dispatcher could have got it wrong, you know. She might have been *pink in the face*, and *panting*!' Bodie: 'Nah, you heard it loud and clear . . . "Pretty girl, just bra and pink panties."' As they accompany the traumatised girl to hospital, Bodie says that he reckons doctors 'get all the perks'. Still, we suppose we should be grateful he doesn't try chatting her up!

Booze: *** Gerda drinks red wine in the first Kentish pub (she says she likes bier kellers). Cowley sends Bodie to find whisky at some obscure hour of the morning as a test of his initiative. He passes with flying colours! At the end, in the pub with Stuart, Doyle's on the white wine, while the others drink pints.

Shooters: ** The sub-machine-gun attack on the ambulance. In order to make his point at the bank, Bodie has to wave his gun around.

Motors: To go with Bodie's new Capri (see 'Wild Justice'), this episode affords us our first look at Doyle's gold Capri S (OAR 576W). At long last, the issue of tyre wear is addressed (with Bodie saying that they're not his, but the government's!). Red and blue Cortinas attack the ambulance.

Threads: Check out Doyle's white jacket: *disco-king smoothy*, or what? Corrigan's checky jacket. Stuart's flares are enormous.

Shaft **Guitar?:** To tie in with Doyle's jacket, lots of disco brass.

Doyle Cooks a Bit of Pasta: Doyle refuses Stuart's offer of a bacon roll (see 'Cry Wolf').

Non-PC Moment: Bodie to Gerda: 'What about that, Fritz?'

Laughable Dialogue: Cowley on the girl: 'Just wandered in here in her underwear.' Bodie: 'Yes, we made haste with all speed.' Cowley: 'Yes, you would!'
   Cowley: 'You're incorrigible, Bodie.' Bodie: 'Thank you, sir!'

Notes: 'Trouble is our business.' A bit of a run-around, though Ben Cross puts in a very impressive performance as Doyle's temporary partner. Cool car explosions, and lots of good scenes with the police helicopter. Beautiful filming in the Kent countryside, and on the South Bank of the Thames. One utterly stupid moment, though: Cowley says that no one answering the girl's description has come through immigration in the past two weeks, which is silly because (a) it implies that customs officials remember or record such details, and (b) hundreds of pretty but otherwise unremarkable blondes must have entered the country during that period.

Bodie can play skittles passably. He's just bought a new watch – it's a TAG Heuer Manhattan. Doyle's watch is also Swiss (an Orfina), while Cowley's is German, an ICW. Cowley can speak German. Bodie knows the range of an antitank missile. Doyle tells Stuart he's been active for three years (which seems way too short – it's probably closer to six going on the time scale established in 'Close Quarters'). The Trust & Mutual Bank is the one featured in the story's conclusion.

Three strawberry cones cost 60p, which seems a bit steep by 1980 standards (Bodie is surprised, too!). One of the CI5 men is called O'Hara after the script editor, Gerry O'Hara.

39: 'Blood Sports'
26 October 1980

Writer: Gerry O'Hara
Director: Phil Meheux

Cast: Yves Beneyton (Rene Lacoste),
Michelle Newell (Anita Cabreros),
Michael Griffiths (Captain Hidalgo),
Harry Towb (Harry Spence), Oliver Smith (Killer),
Elizabeth Spender (Helen Tippett), Ruby Wax (Lonnie),
Sue Robinson (Killer's Girl), Stephen Bent (Norman),
Pierce Brosnan (Radio Man),
Leonard Trolly (Sir Basil Benton),
Mike Savage (Spray Operator), Prim Cotton (Mrs Davis),
Jonathon[1] Morris (Jaime Cabreros),
Rory McCallum (CI5 Man 9.3[2]), Ben Roberts (CI5 Man 9.4),
Terry Yorke (Team Manager), Jim Barclay (Police Driver),
Jon Cartwright (CI5 Chauffeur),
Jonathan Milton (Golf Partner), Gerald Martin (CI5 Butler),
Peter Francis (West Indian)

[1] Incorrectly spelt 'Johnathon' on screen.
[2] See footnote on p. 30. The use of points in agents' call signs is unique to this episode's on-screen credits.

The murder of the son of a South American president at a polo match gives Doyle a chance to try out his chat-up techniques on some prime Patagonian totty.

Keep Your Mincers Peeled For . . .: Jonathon Morris would go on to star in *Bread*. Hidden away three-quarters of the way down the cast, *yes*, that *is* the future James Bond Pierce Brosnan with a two-scene role as the radio man, and *yes*, that *is* the chat-show host Ruby Wax playing a loudmouthed American in one scene.

Birds: * Doyle has taken a pretty blonde in a yellow blouse along to see Bodie play cricket, but he has to leave her at the match when they get the call from Cowley. There are two girlie pictures in the garage (as there seem to be in every garage in this series).

Booze: ** In the nightclub, Doyle drinks something green, with a slice of lime stuck on the glass. He has more luck than Bodie, whose drink is pink. Doyle later drinks white wine at the club with Anita. He also drinks Pepsi at one point (what with the junk food mentioned in **Doyle Cooks a Bit of Pasta** he must be *ill* or something . . .). Cowley and Bodie head off to a local pub at the end.

Shooters: ** The silencer-fitted weapon used by the killers (and which dispatches Norman so discreetly: a bullet to the head, and barely a drop of blood). Bodie takes on the killer, who ditches his rifle for a pistol. Lacoste, armed with a sub-machine-gun, tries to shoot Anita.

Motors: The 'light-blue coupé' with the tinted windows used by the assassins is a Lancia Beta Coupé. Anita arrives in a Daimler DS420 limousine. Norman drives a white MGB; his killers travel in a blue-green VW Caravette. CI5 agent 1-1-8 drives a gold TR7. An 'orange' BMW drops the killer off at the Gold Club; Lacoste drives a blue Beetle to Anita's house. The CI5 green Granada, seen in 'Wild Justice', reappears, forcing the BMW off the road.

Threads: Mrs Davis's pink trousers are shocking and rather daring for a polo match. Cowley's plus-fours are hilarious.

***Shaft* Guitar?:** Some jingle-jangle harpsichord music, with a hint of oboe thrown in. There's lots of percussion, and a Latin tinge to some of the guitar work. When Bodie switches on Anita's radio, there is Spanish flamenco guitar music on whatever station it's tuned to!

Doyle Cooks a Bit of Pasta: Bodie and Doyle decide not to eat at the restaurant, despite the fact that they could have done so on expenses, but rather intend to get a takeaway burger and go back to Doyle's place to watch 'a good game on the box'. Good lads, that's what we want to hear!

Laughable Dialogue: Bodie: 'What's it like, this San Ebress?' Cowley: 'The haves have it all. The peasants have what they stand up in.'

Notes: 'Bit like a polo pony. Quick on the turn.' A slow, ponderous episode, in which Doyle falls for a girl who should be way out of his league but he is still in her flat as the episode ends.

Bodie is a good cricketer, representing his 'old mob' (the Paras, possibly, since the SAS are unlikely to play team sports in public) against the Met (so why isn't Doyle playing for them, then?). Despite what Doyle says, most of the bowling is crap (and down the leg side), and Bodie's on 97 when Doyle's whistle interrupts him, and he's bowled. Bodie and Doyle plan a game of squash together, but it will have to be quick because Doyle wants to take Anita to see a Luis Buñuel film (we reckon it's probably *That Obscure Object of Desire*). Bodie reads *Private Eye* at one point (that's a bit radical and anti-establishment for him, though later we see him reading the *Daily Express*, which would seem to be more his style). Doyle speaks a bit of French. There are certain aspects of his job that Doyle is 'not entirely happy with' (bugging his girlfriends' bedrooms for one!).

The polo match is between England and 'South America' (that's impressive, taking on a whole continent). Evel Knievel is mentioned, as is the long-running Rice Krispies slogan ('Snap, crackle, pop'). Anita went to Rodean (she says her headmistress often had to write 'could do better' on her reports).

Some location work took place at Chalk Farm underground station.

40: 'Slush Fund'
2 November 1980

Writer: Roger Marshall
Director: William Brayne

Cast: Stuart Wilson (Van Neikerk), Matthew Long (Hope), David Swift (Sir Kenneth), Lynda Bellingham (Betty Hope), Jeremy Young (Geiser), Timothy Carlton (Seymour), Victoria Burgoyne (Kookie Girl), Raymond Brody (Hotel Receptionist), John Eastham (Barman), Len Howe (Hotel Porter), Mario Renzullo (First Youth), Ricky Wales (Second Youth), Chris Sullivan (Reporter), Simon Tasker (Boy on Bike)

A South African assassin is arrested on entry to the UK. Doyle and Bodie must discover who his intended target was.

Keep Your Mincers Peeled For . . .: David Swift's most memorable creation was the alcoholic newsreader Henry Davenport in *Drop the Dead Donkey*. For Lynda Bellingham, see *The Sweeney*'s 'Trojan Bus'.

Watch out for the kid on the Chopper who thinks Doyle's talking to himself.

Birds: ** This episode begins with a whole load of bikini-clad lovelies frolicking in the pool. Apparently they're celebrating somebody's fifteenth birthday, but they seem . . . er, rather well developed for their age. Doyle takes a shine to the 'Kookie Girl'. Later, Doyle and Bodie ogle the busty blonde delivering something to the Hopes' address. ('Whatever she's selling, we need it.' 'She'd stiffen up your chewing gum . . .')

Booze: ** Doyle drinks in the hotel bar and in his room. He takes a small bottle of something alcoholic to Bodie while the latter is watching the Hope house. Cowley manages a quick drink with Geiser.

Shooters: ** Geiser sends a parcel containing a small revolver to Doyle at the hotel. Bodie has a spare gun hidden in his Capri. Suitably armed, Bodie and Doyle chase Van Neikerk through the newspaper plant at the episode's conclusion.

Motors: The Hopes have a brown Renault 5. Doyle finds himself in the boot of a red Jaguar XJS – obligingly, the boot flies open, *Sweeney* style, to allow him to escape. Check out, also, the glee on Bodie's face when he is told to drive 'as fast as possible' to Hope's office.

Threads: Doyle's check jacket. Then again, he is trying to play a vulgar South African. The 'Kookie Girl' has a Bjorn Borg-ish white headband, and, later, she wears a pair of tight black leather trousers and a white T-shirt (she gets it wet in the shower, but, unfortunately, she is being strangled to death at the time). With his usual insensitivity, Bodie wears the headband at the episode's end, much to Doyle's understandable irritation.

Shaft **Guitar?:** Doyle whistles what sounds like the Laurel and Hardy theme. The two youths who kidnap Doyle spend their time blowing a blues/folk harmonica (*very* Bob Dylan).

Doyle Cooks a Bit of Pasta: He is close to completing a large jigsaw puzzle in the hotel room. Bodie offers Doyle a cheese-and-onion sandwich. 'On white?' asks Doyle. Sensibly, he refuses it when told that it is 'Well, sort of off-grey!'

Slash Fiction Moment: When Bodie arrives to collect Doyle in the Capri, Doyle gets to his feet, rubbing his arse. 'Aw, you've banged your head,' says Bodie with mock concern. 'I'll bang yours in a minute,' is the predictable response. Bodie then reaches out of the car to pat Doyle's hip.

Non-PC Moment: Bodie adopts a thick Scouse accent when pretending to be a thief. So, it's easier to convince people that you're dishonest if you come from Merseyside . . . (Although, as Bodie is supposed to come from Liverpool, maybe he knows what he's talking about.) Van Neikerk, the nasty South African, talks of black women in terms of 'dark meat' and 'little ravers'.

Laughable Dialogue: Van Neikerk: 'Save it, dad. I've had it from experts, man.'

Cowley: 'Remember, the world is full of Monday-morning footballers. On your bike, boy!'

Notes: 'Honest truth is, it's not air-worthy . . .' 'It's been developed over dead bodies. Pilots' dead bodies.' A pleasant enough story, with the usual trademarks of Roger Marshall – plenty of witty dialogue, and characterisation. It's the little things that impress, like Martin Shaw's Afrikaans accent, and the early sequence on the plane and at the airport. The dummies in the Jag that crashes (the director even gives us a slow-motion sequence, just so that we can be absolutely sure) are horribly obvious: one of the heads falls off!

Bodie learnt Afrikaans in Angola (though we see no evidence of this until after Van Neikerk comments on the fact), and certainly reacts strongly to be called a Kaffir-lover (see 'Klansmen'). Bodie shares his love of the novels of Harold Robbins with Jack Regan (see *The Sweeney* – 'On the Run'). His 'sob story' to Mrs Hope mentions a 'duplicating shop' and 'Photostatting', and the fact that VAT is at fifteen per cent. Bodie also claims to have worked on a pleasure boat that went from London to Southend, but he may be joking.

The Fohn Fighter plane is made by an international consortium, with fuselage and tail made in Germany, nose and final assembly in France, and wings and flaps in the UK. 'Basically, it was a rush job. Politically expedient not to buy American, Europe flexing its new-found muscle. Short cuts, insufficient testing, flaws in design.' This sounds eerily like (certain people's criticisms of) the modern Eurofighter, although the contemporary British–German–Italian Tornado is the more likely allusion. The Fohn Fighter's poor service record, on the other hand, reflects that of the notorious Starfighter. The nickname 'Widow Maker' had previously been used in the episode 'Wild Justice' as the hill the bikers race up.

Hope mentions the Air Bus. There are references to the Tower of London, Carnaby Street and Savile Row, the tennis players Bjorn Borg and John McEnroe, the gentleman thief Raffles, and Leonardo da Vinci. Sir Kenneth quotes from *Julius Caesar*. Judging from the scenes in the printing plant, Hope works for the *Evening Standard*.

41: 'The Gun'

9 November 1980

Writer: Christopher Wicking
Director: Denis Lewiston

Cast: Celia Greogry (Inger), Robert Gwilym (Gary), Barry Angel (Tony), Peter Kelly (Franco), Zoot Money (G.G. Lesley), David John (Jerry Lee), Nigel Pegram (Wendell), Sylvestra Le Touzel (Patricia Buchanan), Martin Milman (Dr Schulman), Burt Caesar (Paul), Joss Buckley (Devlin), Ray Marioni (Café Manager), Francesca Whitburn (Claudine), Prudence Rennick (Mrs Bergen), Michael F. Kenny (Vicar), Tom Wredden (Plainclothesman), David Vann (CI5 Man)

A youth is shot after passing on information about a major shipment of heroin that is due to arrive soon. The murder weapon is thrown away in a panic by the killer, and found by two young boys . . .

Keep Your Mincers Peeled For . . .: Celia Gregory played the likable Ruth in *Survivors*. Sylvestra Le Touzel was Sarah Teale, Tony Clark's girlfriend, in *Between the Lines*. Zoot Money, who plays a rocker, was a genuine pop star himself in the 1960s in his own band, Zoot Money's Big Roll Band, and in Eric Burdon's New Animals.

There's another Adidas sports bag in this episode, a black one. Also, two punks with leather-studded jackets and dyed hair. Doyle is seen using a Kienzie 6100 computer, with a massive Memorex removable disk drive, a green VDU and a dot-matrix printer. Might as well be chiselling out calculus on a stone table. Jerry Lee has a weird electronic chess computer game, and his dad mentions getting him more games in France, Bullfighting and Assassinating Hitler.

Birds: ** Bodie's teacher girlfriend, Inger, looks lovely in an orange towel and, later, in white football shorts ('That's the best-lookin' ref I've ever seen!'). She tells Bodie that carrot juice is good for the libido (he doesn't think he needs it). Actually this is something of a bottom-lover's dream, particularly that shot of the club girl Claudine's buttocks jiggling away into the distance.

Booze: * Although not much is featured in the episode, two of the locations are the City of York pub, and the Ace's High club.

Shooters: ** The whole episode is about a Parabellum P08 (Luger). Given that, there are surprisingly few shots fired. Funny how Doyle can't help but play with the toy guns at school.

Motors: There's a running gag about Doyle having mislaid his car (losing a gold Capri – yeah, *that* takes some accomplishing). This episode sees the introduction of Cowley's *black* Granada (OWC 822W). Gary drives around in a powder-blue Jag XJ6; Tony drives a flash American motor.

Threads: The school football team wear Bukta sports kit – whose particularly horrid design graced several First Division teams of the era (one of us can still remember the year his beloved Newcastle United wore Bukta, and got relegated . . .). Tony's red T-shirt. And, check out G.G. Lesley's white jacket and tie. Rock and roll!

***Shaft* Guitar?:** There's some loud rock guitar on the radio in Bodie's car. And some horrible, sugary violin as Lesley sees his son in hospital.

Jargon: Doyle, on G.G. Lesley: 'He's got a very heavy record, and I don't mean number three in Japan either!'

Laughable Dialogue: Patricia: 'CI5?' Doyle: 'Like MI5.' Patricia: 'What's the difference?' Doyle: 'They invent the problems, we have to solve them!'

Notes: 'Us outlaws have to stick together.' This one works quite well. A good basic plot, though it runs on coincidence and contrived escalation for a lot of the time. Inger's a great character and should have been used more. (We love her advice to her football team: 'Make it simple, make it quick, make the football do what *you* want it to do.' Ah, the Graham-Taylor-inspired infatuation with the long-ball game was still some way off . . .)

Doyle says he and Bodie almost trapped Nick Lucas during a previous case, Operation Hamper.

A gram of heroin is said to cost between £30 and £50. Grosvenor Square is mentioned. Inger is putting on an adaptation of the Orson Welles musical version of *Julius Caesar* set in Nazi Germany as the school play (one of the swastikas is backwards, incidentally). Tony's grandfather was a patriot in the Spanish Civil War.

G.G. Lesley is a rock star ('I thought you older fellers were fans of his,' Bodie tells Doyle). His current record, 'Arrow to the Heart', is number three in Japan. His son is named Jerry Lee (presumably after the veteran rocker Jerry Lee Lewis). Among the 'junk' Lesley brings back from his foreign trip are home and away strips for the French football team St Etienne (during the late 70s one of the most exciting European club sides, thanks to the influence of players like Michel Platini and Dominique Rocheteau).

There are references to the Mexican revolutionary Emiliano Zapata.

42: 'Hijack'
30 November 1980
(originally scheduled for 16 November 1980)

Writer: Roger Marshall
Director: Martin Campbell

Cast: Dave King (Harry Walter), Jill Baker (Amanda),
Dennis Lill (Merhart), Rachel Davies (Deborah),
Stephen Yardley (Swetman),
Richard Murdoch (Sir Alan Sternfield),
Robert Rietty (Ambassador), Mark Eden (Ross),
Anthony Douse (Dusty), Patrick Durkin (Wally),
Jill Dixon (Amanda's Mother), Lloyd McGuire (Sergeant),
Nicholas Donnelly (Chief Inspector), James Snell (Hitman),
Charles Baillie (Receptionist), Maurice Lane (Taxi Driver),
Vic Tablian (Room Service Waiter), Gora Dasgupta (Boy),
Verne Morgan (Waiter), Michael Worsley (CI5 Man)

A consignment of Soviet silver bullion, valued at £4 million, is stolen by armed men. What connection does Doyle's girlfriend and her flatmate have to all of this?

Keep Your Mincers Peeled For ...: Most readers will recognise Dennis Lill as Rodney's father-in-law in *Only Fools and Horses*. Richard *Stinker* Murdoch was a national radio star even before television was out of its infancy. Arthur Askey's straight man on *Band Waggon*, he later collaborated with Kenneth Horne on *Much-Binding-in-the-Marsh*. Mark Eden was the man every *Coronation Street* fan hated most, Rita's murderous husband Alan Bradley. For Rachel Davies, see *The Sweeney* – 'One of Your Own'. For Stephen Yardley, see *The Sweeney* – 'Regan'.

Bodie and Doyle play the board game Mastermind. The back page of the *Evening Standard* has a picture of the 800-metre world-record holder, and now ex-Tory MP, Sebastian Coe on it.

Birds: ** Doyle's girlfriend, Deborah, shares a flat with Mandy, who works in the Ministry of Defence. 'Come in, at least to the top of the shaft.' 'Sound's exciting!' Debbie's father used to be in oil, apparently. When Doyle hears that Mandy has two men with her, he comments, 'That's ambitious.' Bodie and Doyle look on in great admiration at the girl doing exercises in her garden ('Bet she's got a lovely full lotus!'). They find a naked 'Arab girl' in a bath. Trouble is, she's got an electric heater with her, and so is quite dead.

Booze: *** 'How was dinner?' 'Boozy!' Mandy is preparing a Buck's Fizz. Bodie has a meal with Ross of MI6 at an Indian restaurant. For some reason, Ross is surprised that curry houses serve wine (a Portugese rosé). The lager on sale is Carlsberg. Mandy and Doyle share a sherry. At the hotel, Mandy drinks Pepsi while Bodie and Doyle go for two cans of beer.

Shooters: ** Harry Walter asks Merhart about the shipment: 'Are they tooled up? Er . . . shooters? Guns?' The hit man carries a rifle in his attaché case for the intended hit on Mandy. Swetman carries a natty little sawn-off for *his* attempt on her life.

Motors: Doyle seems to have found his gold Capri since the previous episode. The red Skoda Estelle seen by Doyle in the car park carries diplomatic plates. Walter and Swetman watch the truck containing the silver from the front of their Rolls-Royce. Dusty arrives for his first meeting with Swetman in a white Citroën GS. We see Mandy washing her black Mini. A red Opel Rekord accompanies the silver shipment.

Threads: Mandy's light-blue T-shirt, and her big-collared blouse. Her mum's lilac blouse is pretty nasty, too. Runs in the family, obviously.

***Shaft* Guitar?:** Lots of cellos and violins.

Jargon: 'Your man with the shooter. He didn't deliver.'

Laughable Dialogue: Doyle: 'Somewhere to the north of Katmandu, there's a little green-eyed, grey-haired, sober little Scotsman who wouldn't approve.'

Bodie: 'Seven little dwarves sitting in the bath, all feeling Happy. Happy got out, they all felt Grumpy!'

Bodie (on the silver consignment): 'Regular?' Driver: 'As in All-Bran.'

Notes: 'Your friends get ripped off, that's fine. When it's not your friends, send for CI5.' A bit formulaic, especially for Roger Marshall. Nicely characterised, though, and it's not without its charm. Why doesn't Mandy get sent down for a long time, though? After all, she seems to have been involved up to her eyeballs! We love the bit where the actors playing the security guards have to pretend that the props really *are* heavy bars of silver.

The production team's Che Guevara poster puts in another appearance! There are references to Karl Marx, *Morning Cloud* (Ted Heath's yacht), 'The Colonel' (Gaddafi), Lyublyanka Street (the notorious Cheka interrogation headquarters in Leningrad), J. Milton Hayes (see **Laughable Dialogue**), and the Sadler's Wells, and there's another allusion to Tennyson ('Theirs not to reason why'). There's an *Evening Standard* visible in Mandy's flat: the headline, 'BULLION ROBBERY: GANG USE FAKE CENSUS POINT IN LORRY HIJACK', is so implausibly long it takes up half of the front page!

The locations include Wembley Stadium. Dave King calls his character 'Harry Walters' at one point. This episode was the highest-rated *Professionals* story, achieving 17.6 million viewers, and number three in the weekly ratings chart.

43: 'Mixed Doubles'
7 December 1980

Writer: Brian Clemens
Director: Roger Tucker

Cast: Michael Coles (Rio), Ian McCulloch (Macklin),
David Beames (Coney), Nickolas Grace (Joe),
Paul Herzberg (Serpoy), Bill McGuirk (Callard),
Lesley Daine (Barmaid), Mark Wingett (Big Punk),
Lindsay Campbell (Diplomat),
Walter Randall (President Parsali),
Ena Cabayo (Chambermaid), John Berrard (Scruffy Man),
Clifford Earl (Plain Clothes Sergeant),
Charles Cork (Security Guy)

A pair of hit men are hired to assassinate an Arab President whom Bodie and Doyle are guarding. But are the two pairs of men so very different?

Keep Your Mincers Peeled For . . .: Ian McCulloch became
a telefantasy icon playing Greg Preston in *Survivors* (a series
for which he also wrote several episodes). Nickolas Grace
had a huge following as the Sheriff of Nottingham in *Robin of
Sherwood*. Mark Wingett's film appearances include *Quad-
rophenia* and *Breaking Glass*. Readers will be most familiar
with him in his decade-long role as Jim Carver in *The Bill*.
For Michael Coles, see *The Sweeney* – 'I Want the Man'.

The book in Rio's hotel room is *Eenmaal Niet Genoeg* by
Jacqueline Susann.

Birds: ** 'Listen, sunshine, thinking about it, that's worse
than doing it!' Doyle warns Bodie in the first pub scene as
they watch the (very) big-chested barmaid ('She's got a bit of
form on her'). Later, Bodie and Frank get to stare down her
cleavage. There are three or four girlie pictures in the garage
(including one charming shot of a girl bending over and
revealing her, ahem, assets . . .). Frank is looking forward to
finding out if it's true what they say about girls in the
Bahamas. Doyle's current girlfriend is called Claire and
works at a hospital.

Booze: ** Frank and Rio drink whisky in a car at the former's
garage. Bodie and Doyle drink (pints, then halves, of) bitter in
the White Lion. Joe and Frank, meanwhile, have more whisky.

Shooters: ** Notably .44 Magnums – 'stoppers'. There's a
tasty fist fight involving Bodie, Doyle, Frank and four leather-
clad kids who seem to be bikers but are described as 'punks'
on the end credits. Doyle has moral objections to the use of
dumdum bullets (but has to use them on this mission). There
is a great scene of Bodie and Doyle practising their moves
under the watchful eye of Cowley, their fingers held out like
children playing a game.

Motors: Serpoy arrives with instructions for the hit in a white
Mercedes with red upholstery (where do they get these colour
schemes?). Cowley's back in a red Granada, temporarily. Rio
uses a red Vauxhall Victor. Bodie is a bit miffed when his
silver Capri gets its windscreen smashed – as always, it's
mended soon enough.

Threads: Rio's red socks and cream slacks. Towzer's red tracksuit top seems to be the same kind Bodie and Doyle wore in 'Long Shot' (departmental issue?). Bodie's and Doyle's sweat-covered T-shirts! The barmaid's various costumes include tight purple blouse and leather miniskirt, and leopardskin-print top. Doyle's Doc Martens.

***Shaft* Guitar?:** The sharp violin stabs at the opening are quite impressive. There is a lot of snare drum in evidence, and scratchy strings as Frank and Joe break into the second venue.

Slash Fiction Moment: The very protective way Bodie helps Doyle from the floor after he's received a kicking from Macklin. The scenes where Bodie and Doyle lie in their sleeping bags, discussing the afterlife, and later when they admit to each other how scared they are.

Jargon: Frank Coney: 'It's a kill job?' Rio: 'Naturally.' Frank: 'And a Ferrari at the end of it, which I may not get to drive . . .'
  Cowley: 'He's our pigeon. We're providing cover . . .'

Laughable Dialogue: Bodie: 'Bad medicine. Next minute you'll be asking me if I've made a will.'

Notes: 'I always knew you boys would turn out to be useful one of these days.' A genuinely great episode, Clemens creating a mirror image for Bodie and Doyle in Frank and Joe. The former were a pair of tearaways who were converted to 'right' only by spells in the army and police, while Frank and Joe were born in the wrong place at the wrong time and took another path. There are so many great little moments, but the highlights are the scenes cutting back and forth between the two pairs, as they philosophically discuss their respective jobs. Frank and Joe realise it's a suicide mission, but carry on because it's all they know. Other great moments: the children playing on Bodie's car, and Bodie and Doyle tucking into their scrambled eggs. As so often with even the best *Professionals* episodes, though, it lacks a truly satisfying come-down after the climax.
  Doyle was a 'right tearaway'. He 'cut up' one kid when he

was still a kid himself, but he never got caught. He joined the police to get some discipline. He was glad to join CI5, however, seeing a narrowing of the lines between what the police and what the criminals did during his time with the Met. He seems to believe in heaven (Bodie mocks him because Cowley 'punches the Bible, reads the lesson' and therefore 'he'll be up there with you').

Bodie, on the other hand, is 'going the other way'. He doesn't believe in an afterlife. ('I believe in *me*. I was born tall, dark and beautiful – and engagingly modest, of course!') He says he joined CI5 for the money, though Doyle doesn't believe this is the whole truth. Bodie has, however, made a will.

Macklin was a top operative in CI5 until he got a gut shot in Hong Kong some years ago and lost his nerve in combat. Now he runs the training branch. He believes Bodie and Doyle are good, but have got out of shape.

There are references to the Swedish tennis star Bjorn Borg, Muhammad Ali, the assassination of Mahatma Gandhi and the Trojan Horse. The pub, the White Lion, in Chiswick, had previously been used as a location in 'Everest was Also Conquered'.

44: 'Weekend in the Country'
14 December 1980

Writer: Gerry O'Hara
Director: James Allen

Cast: Bryan Pringle (Case), Sarah Lawson (Mrs Shaw),
Brian Croucher (Georgie), Louisa Rix (Judy),
Ray Burdis (Vince), Jacqueline Reddin (Liz),
Marcus D'Amico (Daniel), Brian Hawksley (Ben),
Brian Coleman (Golf Partner),
Gordon Honeycombe (Announcer), Susan Wooldridge (Sally),
Barry Woolgar (Police Driver), Colin Rix (Duty Sergeant),
Tim Meats (Inspector Cross), Peter Hill (Onlooker),
Catherine Riding (Receptionist), Pat Gorman (Security Man)

Enjoying a weekend in the country with two girlfriends, Bodie and Doyle get taken hostage by three armed and desperate men. Don't you just *hate* it when that happens?

Keep Your Mincers Peeled For . . .: Bryan Pringle's performance as Arthur in *Auf Wiedersehen, Pet* will be long remembered by that series' fans. He was also one of the stars of Jack Rosenthal's legendary sitcom *The Dustbinmen*. Brian Croucher donned a leather one-piece suit, and an eye patch, and won a legion of female fans as Servelan's villainous henchman Travis in *Blake's 7*, before going on to terrorise Albert Square in *EastEnders*. Louisa Rix was Mel Smith's wife in the excellent *Colin's Sandwich*. Gordon Honeycombe, long-running ITN newscaster, is seen on the TV describing the robbery. Susan Wooldridge was Daphne Manners in *Jewel in the Crown*.

Cowley passes a Jobcentre in his car.

Birds: ** Bodie and Doyle are sharing their weekend of fishing and riding with Judy Shaw (who works in the Ministry of Defence) and her friend Liz. CI5's Sally is, as always, attractive and briskly efficient.

Booze: *** Bodie's drinking a can of light ale at the start. Liz goes for a white wine. In the golf clubhouse, they have Heineken and Young's Special Bitter on draught (and a bar towel for Trophy Bitter). George has a half of lager rather than his usual whisky, while his partner drinks a Bloody Mary. Lots of whisky *is* drunk during the siege.

Shooters: ** Judy is menaced by Case, who carries a small pistol. Georgie and Vince are tooled up as well.

Motors: 'It's the law! The law!' cries Vince as a Vauxhall Chevette panda car turns up at the farm. Bodie tries to fix the Land Rover in the Shaws' garage: Vince says he doesn't drive a 'clapped-out heap' like the Land Rover but has a 'decent motor'. The head gasket has, apparently, gone on the Land Rover. Cowley is still in his red Granada. Sally turns up at the farm in a red Renault 20.

Threads: Doyle's sheepskin bomber jacket. Liz's very tight corduroy pants and silky, sexy top. Cowley's bathrobe.

***Shaft* Guitar?:** A dramatic and rather tuneless melody at the beginning gives way to plenty of snare rolls later on as the tension builds.

Bill the Driver: The lorry driver who asks Judy, 'What's up darlin'? Not good enough for ya?' is Bill the driver from *The Sweeney*! (Maybe he left the Squad soon after Regan and became a trucker.)

Jargon: Georgie: 'You bitch! You grassed!'
   Georgie: 'Yeah, if you're going to spew your ring up, you might as well do it out there.'
   Case: 'Still in the cape-carny?'

Laughable Dialogue: Case: 'One move, and she gets it!'

Notes: 'We don't lock our doors in the country.' A very obvious plot line, but one reasonably well handled. Little tension because the only thing the viewer is waiting for is when Bodie and Doyle get to kick the crap out of the robbers (the loathsome Vince in particular) – and, typically, it's all over in the blink of an eye.
   Bodie is a keen fisherman, and can play chess. He was in the Scouts, and has always had an interest in cars. He tells the robbers he is a civil servant. Neither Bodie nor Doyle smokes. Doyle can ride a horse pretty well. He has a degree of medical competence (standard police training?), being able to perform basic surgery. Cowley plays golf.
   There are references to *Jaws 3*, Louis Pasteur, *Jim'll Fix It*, and the US TV doctor Ben Casey. There seems to be an extremely violent cop show on TV at one point judging by the screeching tyres and gunfire (maybe it's *The Professionals*!).

45: 'Kickback'
20 December 1980

Writer: Stephen Lister
Director: Ian Sharp

Cast: Norman Eshley (Jimmy Keller),
Meg Davies (Sheila Kaufman), Peter Whitman (Benedek),
James Faulkner (Major Nairn), Hal Galili (Travaioli),
Ben Howard (Spelman), Job Stewart (Russell),
Christopher Mitchell (Simms), Roy Purcell (Richardson),
Marc Boyle (Donatti), Val Musetti (Valerii),
Ian Fairbairn (Price)

Investigating an Italian terrorist cell active in London, Bodie discovers that an old SAS colleague, Keller, has infiltrated the group.

Keep Your Mincers Peeled For . . .: For Norman Eshley, see *The Sweeney* – 'Taste of Fear'. For Meg Davies, see *The Sweeney* – 'Latin Lady'.
There's a flash 70s entertainment centre in Sutherland's office. Billboard posters briefly seen include adverts for Fosters lager and Marlboro cigarettes.

Birds: * Sheila Kaufman is Keller's German bird. Bodie notes, 'I leave you alone for a couple of years, what happens? You get shacked up with some half-baked terrorist groupie.' He gets to dump her in a trough of water at the end.

Booze: * A wagon carrying Woodpecker cider passes Sutherland's car. Bodie drinks gin straight from the bottle.

Shooters: *** Bodie practises his shooting on wine bottles (and a bottle of Teachers whisky) – presumably full of water – and on some eggs. He uses an M16 rifle, and later proves how good a shot he is by taking out the front tyre of the Bentley. Benedek carries a sub-machine-gun, but doesn't get to fire it. Towards the end, shots are exchanged between the Cortina and the helicopter. But that still leaves time for one last shoot-out.

Motors: Benedek drives a yellow Fiat X1/9 (well, he's Italian, right?); he meets Keller on a motorway bridge, driving a yellow Mk II Cortina. Spelman is sprung from a black Granada, and jumps into a grey TR7. (Cowley's black Granada also appears.) Sutherland is ferried around in a Merc (with telephone in the back, complete with scrambler). Bodie and Keller, in the yellow Cortina, are followed by a blue Mark III. Richardson's journey in the Bentley limo is 'interrupted'. Travaioli arrives for his meeting with Sutherland in a dark Triumph Toledo.

Threads: Check out the girl jogger's thick woolly socks, Benedek's cheap trainers and Bodie's wellies and green parka. Doyle's yellow sweatshirt clashes awfully with his white disco jacket.

***Shaft* Guitar?:** Percussion and violins (the music at the beginning, for the boat scene, is reminiscent of the *Jaws* theme), and a soulful trumpet tune.

Slash Fiction Moment: Bodie and Doyle in rubber diving suits. Need we say more?

Laughable Dialogue: Bodie: 'I don't trust you as far as I could throw you.' Sheila: 'And how far is that?'

Notes: 'Bodie? Is he toeing the line nowadays?' Bodie betrayed by an ex-friend is something of a regular theme in *The Professionals*, this one falling just the right side of ridiculous. It looks great, however, with an excellent helicopter chase (the production team certainly got their money's worth from the hiring of the chopper – it's on screen for *ages*).

Sergeant William Bodie was on active service with the SAS from 1971 to 1976 (the implication is that immediately after this he joined CI5, which would fit in with the time scale established in 'Close Quarters'). Jimmy Keller was in Bodie's unit, and once took a bullet for Bodie (possibly in Northern Ireland). He was last heard of in 1978 doing deep-cover special ops in Italy.

There are reference to the (real) Italian PLA (People's Liberation Army). Does anybody else agree with us that Bodie's entry on to the boat under the cover of darkness is just crying out to be made into a Milk Tray advert?

46: 'It's Only a Beautiful Picture . . .'

27 December 1980

Writer: Edmund Ward
Director: Denis Lewiston

Cast: Moray Watson (Jeremy Sangster),
Jonathan Newth (James Tibbs), Prunella Gee (Sarah Gresham),
Neil McCarthy (Sam Armitage),
Anthony May (Snapper Ullmann), Anthony Carrick (Ralston),
Dennis Burgess (Galbraith), Jo Rowbottom (Betty Marlow),
William Moore (Gillespie), Andrew Hilton (Ebert),
Peter Rutherford (Perce Wilmot),
James House (Works Manager),
Roger Martin (George Gorton), Charmain May (Miss Piper),
Stephen Churchett (Supervisor), Hugh Morton (Smithson),
Noreen Leighton (Receptionist)

A bunch of right tasty geezers are ripping off the art and industrial worlds in equal measure. Doyle rejoins the police, and Bodie goes undercover to catch the thieves.

Keep Your Mincers Peeled For . . . : Moray Watson was one of the stars of the BBC's first soap opera, *Compact*. Fans of *Rumpole of the Bailey* will remember him as the blustering George Frobisher. For Prunella Gee, see *The Sweeney* – 'Cover Story'.

The sports page of the newspaper Tibbs is reading (it looks like the *Sunday Express*) features the headline 'COE HANDS OVETT THE GOLDEN PRIZE' – this presumably means the episode was filmed around the time of the 1980 Moscow Olympics, and refers to Steve Ovett winning a gold medal, and Seb Coe a silver in the 800 metres.

**Birds: ** Sarah Gresham, Sangster's posh bird. Bodie and Doyle wander around various Soho strip joints and porn shops. After leaving one peepshow featuring 'exotic dancers', Bodie comments, 'What a turn-off!' He finds a photo of a nude woman among the snapper's pictures.

Booze: ** Bodie and Doyle drink champagne at the art gallery. In the village pub Bodie gets his first drink (a half of lager) on the house from Betty the barmaid. Later Bodie and Doyle drink pints (sometimes out of a pewter tankard). Sangster drinks Scotch in his garden with Sarah and Tibbs. Galbraith's drinks cabinet contains, among others, lots of cans of Skol, a couple of cans of McEwan's Export, two bottles of Martini, a bottle of vodka (Smirnoff), a gin bottle, and some Teachers Scotch.

Shooters: The thieves who do the Acme truck are tooled up. Tibbs's sub-machine-gun. Bodie carries a Magnum.

Motors: Doyle's bike is a Suzuki. Bodie drives a red Opel Rekord estate. Cowley whisks Henry away in a Daimler limousine. Sangster, of course, has a Roller (looks like a Phantom). He uses it when robbing the Acme lorry. Sarah tries to escape from the airport in a Mini. The police turn up in a Rover 2000 and an SD1.

Threads: There's another appearance of the vile combination of Doyle's yellow sweatshirt and white disco jacket. Later, his biker jacket is equally garish.

***Shaft* Guitar?:** Listen out for the terribly funky version of the theme in Soho. There's some chunky rock guitar on Doyle's radio. Plus strident piano music.

Jargon: Snapper: 'Who are you? You the buttons?'
   Doyle: 'Don't give us some ancient moody about some Samaritan you met in a pub.'

Laughable Dialogue: Doyle: 'When did Cowley become an art lover? Bodie: 'When he saw his first pound note!'
   Doyle: 'Why send us here?' Bodie: 'To improve our minds, he said.' Doyle: 'Well, with yours he's got plenty of room to manoeuvre.'
   Cowley: 'Who was it said inspiration is nine-tenths perspiration?' Bodie: 'Last year's Derby winner?'
   Sangster: 'The whole country's riddled with petty dishonesty and drunkards on the dole.'

Tibbs: 'Haven't you ever gloated in private, darling?'
Sarah: 'Not in a bank vault!'

Doyle: 'Detective Sergeant Doyle, reporting for duty among the hayseeds!'

And: 'I used to be in the Mounties, but my horse was retired.'

Notes: 'Gentlemen, we're up against a fellow professional.' At the end of a generally very impressive bunch of episodes during this season, the closer is a bit of a let down, being both slow and lacking in any great tension or plot. Bodie and Doyle know who the villains are from quite early on but spend most of the episode faffing about before getting the gang at the climax. Nice locations in Trafalgar Square, Soho and Leicester Square, though. In Trafalgar Square, several passers-by stare at Collins and Shaw in fascination.

Doyle says he should have been artistic. Given previous references to painting being a hobby in 'The Rack', 'In the Public Interest' and 'Rogue', this may suggest he's given it up due to Bodie's constant ribbing. Cowley is a member of a gentlemen's club.

Cowley misquotes the popular song 'Tiptoe Through the Tulips'. There's a reference to another song, 'Ragtime Cowboy Joe'. The line 'Eliminated with extreme prejudice' is (almost) a direct quote from *Apocalypse Now*. Calling the company 'Acme Drilling' may be a nod to the Roadrunner cartoons ('Acme' was the company that many of Wile E. Coyote's fantastic devices were bought from).

One silly aspect. Isn't a Roller with personalised number plates a rather ostentatious hijack vehicle? The van driver and his mate are killed by Tibbs, but what if somebody else had been watching?

Fifth Season

Eleven 60-minute episodes
An Avengers Mark 1 Production/London Weekend Television
Created by Brian Clemens

Associate Producer: Chris Burt (50, 52–53, 56–57)
Producer: Raymond Menmuir
Executive Producers: Albert Fennell, Brian Clemens

Title music by Laurie Johnson

Regular Cast: Gordon Jackson (George Cowley),
Martin Shaw (Ray Doyle), Lewis Collins (William Bodie),
Steve Alder (Murphy, 47, 49, 51, 55)

47: 'Foxhole on the Roof'
7 November 1982

Writer: Brian Clemens
Director: William Brayne

Cast: Stanley Meadows (Roddy Barker),
Karl Howman (Stacey), Ron Pember (Jack Cobber),
Robert Putt (Inspector Newton), C.J. Allen (Sergeant Wood),
Roderic Leigh (Dunston), Barbara Keogh (Maisie),
Richard Simpson (Doctor), Lorrain Grey (Nurse),
Kim Goody (Tessa), Alan Polonsky (Bob),
Peter John (Merton), Sarah Kenyon (Bob's Girl),
Peter Joyce (Bud), Peggy Bullock (Patient),
Jean Campbell-Dallas (Patient)

A man has holed up on a roof with a vast amount of ammo,
a hostage and the intensive-care unit of a hospital in his
sights . . .

Keep Your Mincers Peeled For . . .: For Karl Howman and

Ron Pember, see *The Sweeney*'s 'May' and 'Regan' respectively. Barbara Keogh was one of the stars of *Making Out*.

The factory used in this episode appears to be the one used in *The Sweeney* episode 'Victims'. Bob's girl is wearing a Crystal Palace scarf.

Birds: * Bob's girl is seen in a green sleeping bag with what appears to be very little on. Bob, on the other hand, is fully clothed. That's convenient.

Booze: * Jack's got a pint in his hand in the first scene. Roddy and Jack drink whisky while looking over London.

Shooters: *** Barker steals a box of grenades, plus launcher, two SLRs, four pistols, one Stirling, and a sub-machine-gun from the army base. He uses the grenades against the police and CI5, and sprays the hospital with sub-machine-gun fire. We see loads of CI5 marksmen, and a tense stand-off develops between the two sides.

Motors: Doyle continues with his gold Capri, Cowley the black Granada. Roddy Barker uses an army truck and a yellow Ford Transit ('Simpson & Wells Roofing Contractors') to advance his plans. The police have Rover SD1s (one of which – WVP 150T – also appeared in 'The Gun') and Land Rovers. The getaway car is a green Talbot Alpine – no wonder they prefer the helicopter option . . .

Threads: Doyle's tartan scarf. He looks a complete prat in the scenes where he wears his black flak jacket *on top* of his chunky leather flying jacket. Stacey in drag ('Give us a kiss!').

***Shaft* Guitar?:** There's some funky, psychedelic jazz on Doyle's radio (he appears to be really enjoying it, too). His trip to Camberley is accompanied by an OTT, full-on brass version of the main theme.

Jargon: Doyle: 'Unless they were tooling up for one specific job.'

Doyle: 'You're busted, love.' Tessa: 'Busted, for one lousy joint?'

Barker: 'Let's ginger 'em up a bit.'

Laughable Dialogue: Cowley: 'He's got us . . . Got us by the short and curlies.'

Notes: 'They owe us, Jack.' Super premise, and the execution is well realised, despite an occasional lack of tension. Some fine directorial touches, particularly the exploding blood bag. And excellent shots of the choppers whizzing over Parliament, St Paul's and Tower Bridge. The ending is rather enigmatic – and, frankly, Bodie should be reprimanded, seeing as he embarked upon his plan to climb the chimney without liaising with Cowley. (Odd, too, that Doyle didn't radio in before the end. It only really makes sense because of – understandable – dramatic licence.)

There is another reference to the 'small print' ('Leave it to CI5') in the governing articles of the police force. Doyle seems to believe that prisons are drug-free. Poor, naive soul. 'Murph' Murphy is the best mountaineer in the Squad, having climbed the Eiger. He's also an A-class marksman, but reckons Bodie is better. He's shot in the shoulder in this episode, but is back in action again by the time of 'You'll Be All Right'.

This episode achieved 13.7 million viewers (in the new slot of 9:15 on Sunday nights), and fourth place in the weekly ratings chart.

48: 'Operation Susie'
14 November 1982

Writer: Ranald Graham
Director: Ian Sharp

Cast: Alice Krige (Diana Molner),
Ewan Stewart (Rudiger Molner),
Harold Innocent (Northcott), Maggie Henderson (Jane),
John Line (Somerfield), Donald McKillop (MacLean),
Alexander Davion (Torres), George Raistrick (Smith),
Robert McBain (Deville), Andrew Maclachlan (Powell),
Robert Morgan (Philip Latimer), P.H. Moriarty (Harris),
Geoffrey Freshwater (Dodds), Bernard Finch (DI Harrington),
Colm Daly (Student), Jim Wiggins (Dr Roberts),

Jackie Downey (Receptionist), Roger Owen (Driver),
Barry Copping (1st Ambulance Man)

When three student revolutionaries are caught up in a deal
concerning artificial cocaine, the murder of two of them leads
Bodie and Doyle into a deadly game to protect the third.

Keep Your Mincers Peeled For . . .: P.H. Moriarty recently
gained critical acclaim for his performance as Hatchet Harry
in *lock, stock & two smoking barrels*. Alice Krige played the
Borg Queen in *Star Trek: First Contact*.
   There's a STOP BRITAIN BURNING poster at the university. In
the students' flat watch out for a box of Shredded Wheat, and
some Anchor butter.

Birds: * Jane, the CI5 girl with the Princess Di hairdo and
dress sense. Diana Molner, radicalised student daughter of a
left-wing member of a right-wing dictatorship. Doyle fancies
her. Inevitably, she dies!

Booze: None.

Shooters: **** The episode begins with a shooting. Harris
and Rudi are both armed, the latter with a small, silver
revolver. An attempt is also made on Diana's life, which
Doyle foils with a smoke canister. There is a massive armed
stand-off at the end, with numerous rifles and sub-machine-
guns.

Motors: Rudi drives a grey left-hand-drive VW camper van
(or 'microbus', according to CI5). Harris is seen behind the
wheel of a green Cortina. When Rudi is injured, he stops a
yellowish Range Rover at the hospital. The red Cortina that
follows Doyle and Bodie in the gold Capri is the same one as
seen in 'Blackout'. Northcott and Torres travel in a black
Rover SD1. Bodie and Doyle decide to drive 'something
foreign' while on Operation Susie, so they ditch the Capri for
a 5 series BMW.

Threads: Rudi's brown tank top. Bodie's light-brown
poloneck. Doyle's enormous tartan scarf.

***Shaft* Guitar?:** There's some slow, whistly flute and trumpet music.

Slash Fiction Moment: Bodie comforting Doyle after Diana is shot.

Notes: 'Whatever happens, I want those kids alive.' Talky and rather uninvolving, despite the subject matter, and another rubbish, hurried conclusion. It's frightening, but not altogether unsurprising or unrealistic, that an organisation like CI5 has 'Photographed on anti-National Front march' and 'Signatory of petition against Econdora military dictatorship' listed alongside (and equivalent to) criminal offences. (Incidentally, there is a spelling mistake on the computer screen we see 'Arrested during proptest'.)

The safe house Bodie and Doyle use is the 'Old Southbank terminal' (a specially designed railway carriage, unique to them). Doyle describes their standard walkie-talkies as being 'SIS issue'. Cowley is an old friend of Alex Maclean, a Scottish militant union leader with connections in government.

MI17 ('one of the funny ones') is described by Cowley as 'DDT – the Department of Dirty Tricks'. The CI5 telephone number is 373 0029 (a direct line to Cowley's red phone). An 'Operation Susie' is an operation in which deniable plausibility is maintained (the agents must act without official sanction). 'This order will be erased,' says Cowley, which may be an oblique reference to *Mission: Impossible*. He also says, 'Anticipate interference with maximum prejudice. You are not alone!', which is a possible nod to both *Apocalypse Now* (see 'It's Only a Beautiful Picture . . .') and *Close Encounters of the Third Kind.*

49: 'You'll Be All Right'
21 November 1982

Writer: Gerry O'Hara
Director: John Crome

Cast: Derrick O'Connor (Jack Stone),
Geraldine Sherman (Chrissie Stone),
Melissa Wilks (Linda Stone), Jason Savage (Nick Stone),
Derek Francis (Len Hatch), Janet Davies (Roz Hatch),
Hazel McBride (Liz Spalding),
Malcolm Storry (Ned Turner), Don Hawkins (Barney Moss),
Sally Faulkner (Anne), Shirley Dixon (Mrs Johnson),
Freddie Boardley (Billiard Player),
Arthur Whybrow (Gardener), Stephen Mackenna (Rod),
Richard Albrecht (Pearson), Grant-Ashley Warnock (Lou),
Graeme Eton (CI5 Mechanic), James Butchart (Labourer),
Tex Fuller (Pat Weaver), Kellie Byrne (Schoolgirl),
Joanne Bell (Schoolgirl)

Jack Stone, an armed blagger, rings Doyle and offers to give himself up in return for protection for his family.

Keep Your Mincers Peeled For . . .: Derrick O'Connor was in the excellent Euston drama *Fox* (see also *Sweeney 2*). Derek Francis was Frankie Howerd's Wazir in *Whoops Baghdad!*. Janet Davies spent a decade hiding her relationship with 'Uncle' Arthur Wilson from her son, as Mavis Pike in *Dad's Army*.

Watch out for a billboard advertising Rothman's King Size. The children play bar football.

Birds: * Doyle gets rather flirty with one of the girls in the computer section. Liz Spalding (9-1) is one of CI5's top women. She likes Bodie but is less keen on Doyle.

Booze: * Cowley shares a small Scotch with Hatch (Cowley's is without water). Doyle and Bodie drink cans of Coke in the Hustler Snooker Club (ah, the not-that-long-ago nostalgia for cans with removable ring pulls!).

Shooters: * Weaver arrives with a gun to kill the Stones, but is himself shot.

Motors: The children are taken to and from school in a white Triumph 1300 *(another* car with bright-red upholstery). The two schoolboys are nearly killed by a white Mercedes SL saloon (if Bodie is right, it's got false number plates). Cowley's black Granada has been serviced by the CI5 mechanic, Fred. 'Sounds a bit rough, doesn't she?' says a less than convinced Bodie. Chrissie drives a pale-blue Morris Minor Traveller; when the family try to escape in this they are pursued by a black 3½-litre Rover. Bodie gets to drive a taxi cab.

Threads: Bodie's crimson jacket. Stone's suede boots.

***Shaft* Guitar?:** At the beginning, there's that *Jaws*-ish theme again, followed by some fairly standard horn music. Plus woodwind and slushy strings as Jack and Chrissie are in bed, and the really funky, modulated guitar and driving strings so often used by *The Professionals* in moments of tension.

Jargon: Ned: 'You some sort of God-botherer?' Doyle: 'You could say I'm a concerned person, yes!'

Laughable Dialogue: Liz: 'Linda's detained for a while. Bad marks in home economics.' Bodie: 'What, screwed up on the rice pudding?'

Doyle (on CI5): 'It's a living.' Barney: 'So's feeding pigs.'

Doyle: 'Rat poison. In a high-rise flat?' Bodie: 'Maybe they use the lifts?'

Notes: 'Some heavy money fronted the job.' A very unusual storyline for *The Professionals*: it's rather ordinary, but, in some ways (because the drama is more realistic), more satisfying than the usual terrorists-and-drug-dealers fare. Nice ensemble performances from a very good cast.

Doyle's beat for a while included Limehouse in London's East End. He takes his tea without milk or sugar. He claims to be a *Guardian* reader (as we suspected), and carries a set of skeleton keys with him. There seem to be two separate but connected telephone lines into Doyle's house (how else could he pick up the other phone and ask for a trace without being heard by Stone?). Notice how Doyle doesn't exactly deny being a 'God-botherer' (see 'Mixed Doubles').

There are references to James Fenimore Cooper's *The Last of the Mohicans*, the Stevie Smith poem 'Not Waving

But Drowning' and Houdini. Stock footage of the Isle of Wight (the Needles at Alum Bay and Parkhurst Prison) is used.

50: 'Lawson's Last Stand'
28 November 1982

Writer: Ranald Graham
Director: Ian Sharp

Cast: Michael Culver (Lieutenant Colonel Peter Lawson), John Hallam (Tug Willis), Michael Angelis (Len Clarke), Donald Pickering (Brigadier Tennant), Helen Cherry (Lavinia Lawson), Stephen Greif (Dr Lowe), Eve Bland (Doreen), Allan Mitchell (Professor), Prentis Hancock (Army Major), Doyne Bird (Lieutenant Colonel Tony Manning), Roger Nott (Police Chief), Tim Swinton (Army Guard), Robert Cavendish (Senior Guard), Brian Binns (Guard), Max Harvey (Pedestrian)

Lieutenant Colonel Lawson has disappeared from a military hospital, suffering from psychiatric problems. He recruits some ex-soldiers, and sets out to raid a chemical-research establishment.

Keep Your Mincers Peeled For . . .: The Liverpudlian actor Michael Angelis played the rabbit-loving Lucien Boswell in *The Liver Birds* and Chrissey Todd in *Boys from the Blackstuff*. Stephen Greif was the villainous Commander Travis in *Blake's 7*. Prentis Hancock (who gets a tiny, one-line part here) played Paul Morrow in *Space: 1999*. John Hallam was the star of Catherine Cookson's *The Mallens*, and was also in the film *Flash Gordon*, and *EastEnders*. Eve Bland was Ellie Hughes in *Between the Lines*. For Michael Culver, see *The Sweeney* – 'Money, Money, Money'.

There's a large cardboard box in Len's forge which once contained Horlicks!

Birds: * Doreen Clarke notes that Len is off 'playing games', but not the sort that she likes to play. Fnaar, fnaar.

Booze: * There's a pub scene in which Guinness, Double Diamond and Woodpecker cider are all on draught. But, significantly, we don't see what Lawson, Clarke and Willis are drinking. Later, as Manning prepares for a 'snifter' with Lawson, his friend clobbers him on the bonce.

Shooters: *** At first Lawson and the others seem a pretty pathetic bunch, practising in a field without weapons, but later they use sub-machine-guns during a bank job. One teller may lose an arm. They then steal various explosives, grenades and mortar bombs from the military (British army security must have been abysmal in 1982 – see 'Foxhole on the Roof'), although ultimately Lawson plans to use an altogether different weapon to get his way.

Motors: Lawson uses a battered white Cortina and an army Jeep. Bodie gets a new silver Capri in this episode (it looks the same as all the others, but the registration is VHK 12W).

Threads: Doreen Clarke wears some shocking-pink overalls. And a disgusting pink-and-black-striped jumper. Watch out for Bodie's rather frightening tracksuit.

Laughable Dialogue: Doyle on Lawson's promotions: 'He's gone through these ranks like food through a goose.' Bodie: 'That's *downwards* . . .'

Cowley: 'He's given us one hour in which to blow up the entire chemical-warfare research establishments at three separate locations . . . He wants two million pounds transferred to a Swiss account . . . And he wants the national anthem played on Radio Two. On the hour, every hour. For ever.'

Notes: 'What we're going to fight for is this country's soul.' Really rather silly, though the stunt work during the mortar attack on the chemical-research place (which takes up about ten minutes of the episode) is fantastic. The scene with Lawson singing 'God Save the Queen' is startling, but the ending is a mess, with Lawson, equipped with rear-view mirrors, looking a less than credible threat. And how many people practise javelin-throwing with their families in public parks in the shadow of Battersea power station . . .?

Liquefied C29 is said to be 'the most toxic substance on the planet' and that 'one part in a million' can be lethal – it's a bit moronic, therefore, to keep it in a room with only a (locked) wooden door for security. Lawson was commissioned to the 16th Rifle Brigade and saw action in Aden and the Far East (in the late 60s/early 70s? Must have been a war we missed . . .). He volunteered for the SAS and did three tours of Northern Ireland (presumably not during the period Bodie was there), receiving two commendations. Captain at staff college, he was promoted to major and transferred to BOAR. He's currently battalion commander of 31st Tank Regiment. He's 37. Willis was a (highly decorated) corporal in the Paras, and served in Borneo, Aden, Cyprus, Sudan and Northern Ireland. He also did some undercover work (possibly also in Ulster).

51: 'Discovered in a Graveyard'
28 November 1982

Writer: Christopher Wicking
Director: Anthony Simmons

Cast: Derek Waring (Dr Seigel), Philip Latham (Hogan),
Megumi Shimanuki (Mayli Kuolo),
Vincent Wong (Colonel Lin Foh), Richard Moore (Malone),
Owen Holder (Coronor), David Yip (Editor),
Rayner Bourton (Caretaker), Julie Sullivan (Rita),
Toni Kanal (Nurse Hale), Linda Lou Allen (Blonde),
Michael Maynard (Desk Clerk), Betty Lawrence (Old Lady),
Elisabeth Choice (German Lady), Brian Abbott (CI5 Man),
Rex Wei (Embassy Man), Peter Polycarpou (Waiter),
Heather Emmanuelle (Nurse), Gary Taylor (Ambulance Man)

Doyle is shot, and hovers between life and death . . .

Keep Your Mincers Peeled For . . .: Three really big TV names appear in this episode, though all are featured in only a couple of scenes each. Derek Waring was Roland in Thames's hit sitcom *Moody and Peg*. Philip Latham shot to fame as Willy Izzard in *The Troubleshooters*, and later starred in *The Pallisers* (he also had a great role in Hammer's *Dracula – Prince of Darkness*). David Yip took the part of the eponymous Johnny Ho in *The Chinese Detective*.

Birds: * The second of the 'three single women' whom Bodie and Cowley check up on wears a sexy pink nightgown and manages a very unsurprised and sultry 'Hi'.

Booze: None.

Shooters: *** A veritable blood bath. People get shot left, right and centre here, chiefly by Mayli with her silencer-fitted pistol. Bodie's silver-coloured revolver makes another appearance.

Motors: A couple of less salubrious motors than usual, the episode beginning with a Bedford van exploding. It's probably the only episode in the history of crime-drama TV in which the murderer drives around in a yellow Citroën 2CV van! (Odd bit when Bodie phones in with the licence number: he says, 'George William Lionel 656 Jane' rather than 'Golf Whiskey Lima . . . Juliet'.)

***Shaft* Guitar?:** Mozart. Plus a very discordant piano-and-trumpet segment, and an almost *Carry On*-style tinkly version of the main theme used towards the end.

Doyle Cooks a Bit of Pasta: There's a beautiful sequence of Doyle shopping (buying milk and fruit) accompanied by Mozart's Piano Concerto No. 21 (the 'Elvira Madigan'). Tragically, this wonderful scene is normally the first casualty in cuts when the episode is repeated in syndication, or on satellite TV.

Slash Fiction Moment: The whole episode! Bodie wanting to stay at the hospital with Doyle, despite the fact there's nothing he can do, rather than search his flat. Bodie's reaction when he discovers the identity of Doyle's would-be assassin ('*Bitch!*'). The horseplay of the scenes as Bodie pushes Doyle out of hospital in a wheelchair. Let's face it, they *love* each other . . .

Jargon: Bodie: 'She's got wheels now. I'm in pursuit.'

Laughable Dialogue: Bodie: 'Can't afford to give a damn, might make you hesitate. Forget the book. You shoot to kill. He will!'

Doyle: 'A row of graves, that's the bottom line of all your noble sentiments. Lives wasted.'

Bodie: 'Give Ray half a chance, he'll blame himself for the invention of gunpowder.'

Doyle, on death: 'Now I've done it once, it'll be easier next time.'

Notes: 'We don't want your war here, Colonel.' Stunning. One of the best episode of the series, both for its daring use of quasi-telefantasy elements, and its quite brilliant direction – from the slow-motion explosion in the pre-titles, through to the 'first-person' camera work in the attack on Doyle and the ensuing dream sequences. Great use of hand-held camerawork all round, in fact. An episode that not only throws light on Doyle's character, but Bodie's too. A wonderful and *Callan*-ish reflection on the nature of killing, and what happens to people who do this for a living.

Doyle is in yet another new flat. He seems to be collecting militaria. Bodie (in a flashback to their first meeting) says he's heard Doyle has a hot temper, and it seems that he also had quite a few run-ins with his police superiors. Cowley says Doyle is 'an idealist'. Doyle uses a launderette for his washing (he normally does it on a Friday).

Doyle has a framed epitaph/poem on his bedroom wall, 'Discovered in a Graveyard – Baltimore 1692', which reads 'Go placidly amid the noise and haste . . . and remember what peace there may be in silence. Do not distress yourself with imaginings; many fears are born of fatigue and loneliness. You are a child of the universe, no less than the trees and the stars. Be at peace with God, whatever you conceive Him to be; in the noisy confusion of life, keep peace with your soul. With all its sham, and drudgery, and broken dreams, it is still a beautiful world.'

Bodie has never thought of 'getting out' (where else would he go?). He says 'to the pure, all things are pure', a New Testament quotation (Titus 1:15) (cf. 'The Acorn Syndrome'). He has basic medical knowledge (checking airways, staunching blood, etc.) – cf. Doyle in 'Weekend in the Country'. Cowley speaks French (even describing the 2CV as a 'Deux Chevaux'). An 'A3' is a medical emergency.

Film locations include Camden Town (a shot of the famous rock club Dingwalls can be seen from Bodie's car) and Lock and, judging from the equipment at Doyle's bedside, Northwick Park hospital near Harrow.

A repeat of this episode on 8 April 1984 achieved (a staggering) 11.7 million viewers, and fourth place in the weekly ratings chart.

52: 'Spy Probe'
12 December 1982

Writer: Tony Barwick
Director: Dennis Abey

Cast: Paul Daneman (Dawson), Graham Crowden (Minister), Joyce Grant (Miss Walsh), Patrick Ryecart (Williams), Barry Stanton (Ferris), Nick Stringer (Twig), Raymond Brody (The Voice of Kovac), John Hart Dyke (Flynn), Christopher Banks (Mitchell), Patrick Brock (Lewis), Jim Dowdall (Man), John Ashbury (CI5 Man), Susan Worth (CI5 Girl)

Bodie and Doyle infiltrate a group who are being paid to exterminate a series of retired, middle-ranking spies and civil servants. Few of the intended victims had any access to any top-secret material, so why are their lives at risk?

Keep Your Mincers Peeled For . . .: Graham Crowden will

be familiar to viewers of *A Very Peculiar Practice* and *Waiting for God*. For Barry Stanton, see *Sweeney 2*.

Birds: None, though Miss Walsh is clearly just the sort of person to warm the cockles of Cowley's heart.

Booze: ** Dawson and the minister are surprised that Cowley is too busy to have a drink with them. Cowley and Miss Walsh have drinks as Bodie arrives to 'kill' the latter.

Shooters: *** Bodie carries a Walther PPK (as used by James Bond, of course); Doyle uses a stainless-steel revolver that 'pulls to the right' in the scene with the dummies. In fact, lots of pistols are in evidence during this story, though few of the intended targets are killed. Williams has a rather explosive way of proving his MI5 membership.

Motors: Doyle is watched from a white Cortina Mk III estate. Dawson and the minister drive through Whitehall in a Daimler. Bodie drives a powder-blue Cortina Mk III. Kovak escapes from the hotel in a black Mercedes saloon, pursued by Doyle in the bronze-coloured Capri. (This is our first proper look at the new car, VHK 11W; Bodie also drives the silver VHK 12W from 'Lawson's Last Stand'.) Dawson drives a Jag XJ12.

Threads: Doyle's nasty biker jacket puts in another appearance.

***Shaft* Guitar?:** There's some pounding music to accompany the shoot-out with Twig.

Jargon: Kovac: 'I am not your "guv".'

Laughable Dialogue: Doyle: 'You wouldn't want to be shot from this angle, would you? Could alter your whole outlook on life.'

Notes: 'End of the line, fat man.' A little bit ordinary, although Patrick Ryecart is very good in it, and the direction is terrific (Doyle shooting the heads off showroom dummies is suitably surreal). The hotel scenes are reminiscent of similar moments in *The Thomas Crown Affair*. The dramatic slow-motion somersault that the stuntman playing Mitchell pulls when he gets shot is hilariously funny. There are some good 'interrogation' scenes, and a nice speedboat chase at the end.

Elizabeth Walsh has the highest level of security clearance. She was Under-Secretary to the Cabinet Office in the 1950s, and is another old friend of Cowley's (he considers her the cleverest woman he knows). According to Dawson, the PM 'looks on Cowley with favour' (it is implied that he has lasted as head of CI5 for as long as he has because of this: yeah, we can see Thatcher being suitably impressed by the boot boys of CI5!). Dawson is the acting head of MI5. There are references to one of the great governmental buzz theories of the 1980s, 'cost-cutting'.

A repeat of this episode on Friday, 28 August 1987 (yes, *five years* after the series ended!), achieved 10.1 million viewers and seventh place in the weekly ratings chart.

53: 'Cry Wolf'
9 January 1983

Writer: Paul Wheeler
Director: Phil Meheux

Cast: Sheila Ruskin (Susan Grant),
Alan MacNaughton (Laughlin), Rona Anderson (Mrs Grant),
David Neal (Bauer), Ian Bartholomew (Miller),
Simon Templeman (Neville Grant), Timothy Block (Smith),
Zoe Gonord (Joan), Barrie Cookson (Mason),
Iain Blair (Sergeant Watson),
Rex Robinson (Superintendent), Vass Anderson (Doctor),
Aimee Delamain (Old Lady), Duncan Miller (Sergeant),
Rob Heyland (PC), Arthur Nightingale (Night Porter)

Who would possibly want to hurt Susan Grant, a charity worker? Is she just a spoilt little rich girl crying wolf? CI5 try to find out.

Keep Your Mincers Peeled For . . .: For Alan MacNaughton, see 'A Stirring of Dust'.

In Susan's flat you can just make out a black-and-white print of Marilyn Monroe. A carton of fresh orange juice seems to cost 25p. Also visible in Laughlin's flat is a clipping from William Hickey's column in, yes, you guessed it, the *Daily Express*.

Birds: ** Susan Grant, who, her mother says, usually 'gets involved with Chelseaites', instead spends the episode dating Bodie (of course, she calls him 'Bodie' throughout!).

Booze: ** Susan and Bodie share a red wine in the Chinese Garden restaurant. Bodie tells her he likes 'good company, good food, hot sun, cold beer'. Don't we all? Cowley drinks malt whisky with Margaret Grant. Bodie gets a drink for Susan after one of her encounters.

Shooters: ** The gunman carries a pistol with a huge silencer. Bodie blows him away, of course! The usual bullet-ridden climax (Doyle's shot on the pilot, while driving full-tilt at the plane, is well hard).

Motors: Neville's gold TR7. Susan has a brown Porsche 924. A Vauxhall Cavalier gets in the way of Bodie's tailing of Susan. The man with the ski mask drives about in a yellow-green Hillman Hunter. Bodie's silver Capri has a tracking unit built into it.

Threads: The police sergeant's brown and light-blue tie. Henry's sheepskin. Bodie wears not one but two horrible suede jackets in this episode. Doyle's white, black and red tartan scarf is on display again, but all the awards in this episode go to his nasty leather jacket with the huge fur collar. Oh, and his disguise as a parks gardener.

***Shaft* Guitar?:** The plucking cello music often used for sinister moments in *The Professionals* puts in another appearance.

Doyle Cooks a Bit of Pasta: There is a definite hint that, like the actor playing him, Doyle is a vegetarian. Mind you, Bodie

doesn't like liver-sausage sandwiches either, and there's no
suggestion that Bodie is a carrot-cruncher. Doyle seems to
know an alarming amount about roses!

Laughable Dialogue: Cowley: 'You were after the silver?
. . .What were you going to do, chloroform it?'

A special mention for Doyle's appalling joke with the
punchline 'Nein, W.'

Notes: 'What do you want her for?' Slow and obvious,
despite some nice directorial touches (the rose on the car
windscreen for instance) and a gripping opening. Sheila
Ruskin is very good, and Lewis Collins has one of his finest
moments in the series, but it's all a trifle obvious. Still, at
least Cowley has the utmost respect for the free-thinking
Laughlin.

Susan's foster father, Anthony, was another old friend of
Cowley's (the man must have a hell of a Christmas card list!).
Laughlin's books include *The Realm of Evil* (1959), *The
Covert Society* (1963) and *The Enemy Within* (1968), all
left-leaning volumes about covert state secrecy. A sort of
1960s version of Duncan Campbell, no doubt.

This episode achieved 13.6 million viewers and eighth
place in the weekly ratings chart.

54: 'The Untouchables'
16 January 1983

Writer: Brian Clemens
Director: William Brayne

Cast: Keith Washington (Rahad), Marilyn Galsworthy (Anna),
Robert Flemyng (Sir John), John Junkin (Hollis),
Joe Marcell (Nero), Nick Brimble (Hart),
Lucy Hornack (Clare Terringham), John Francis (Taylor),
Andrew Sargent (Fisk), Andy Pantelidou (George),
Ramsay Williams (Al), Brogden Miller (Gregory),
Vicki Michelle (Tina), Clive Panto (TV Commentator),
Linda Spurrier (Anna Jones),

Imogen Bickford-Smith (Blonde), Terry Paris (Lucho),
Neville Rofaila (Kaffir)

Rahad keeps murdering the enemies of his Arabic state and getting away with it because of his diplomatic immunity. CI5 decide it's time to put a stop to his exploits.

Keep Your Mincers Peeled For ...: Joe Marcell found fame on the other side of the Atlantic, playing the butler in *The Fresh Prince of Bel Air*. For Vicki Michelle, see 'Hunter/Hunted'; for Nick Brimble, see 'Look After Annie'; for John Junkin, see *The Sweeney* – 'Feet of Clay'.

Check out the enormous, wood-veneered entertainment centre that Bodie puts into the boot of his car. Must be a Bang & Olufsen if he's hoping to get any money for it. And you can't miss the enormous, stuffed sailfin marlins on the walls of the gambling house. Later, there's a lovely bit of CND graffiti.

Birds: *** Bodie claims to be dating Sir John's pretty daughter, Clare (who says she isn't an actress, so we must presume at least the second kiss is for real!). Judging by his instructions to the chauffeur to 'take the long way home', our Bodie's been taking method acting to its absolute limits. Rahad enjoys a clearly postcoital cigarette as his high-class hooker dresses at the embassy. Rahad's taste is for tall, long-legged, blonde, European women ('Must be all that rice and sheep's eyeballs!').

Then there is the blonde tart in the back of the pimp's car who lacks 'class', and 'Anna' (or whatever her real name is), who doesn't. Anna is a horse-riding ex-debutante, and the product of some of England's finest finishing schools (she obviously got expelled more than once), who speaks French, and a smattering of Arabic and Japanese ('You pick these things up in my profession!'). Cowley knew her father well. Why doesn't that surprise us?

Booze: **** Doyle drinks a can of Heineken with Jackson. Following this, Doyle and Cowley drink whisky, and Bodie drinks a whisky (which he takes without ice) with Nero at the club. Anna drinks a (very) Bloody Mary with Doyle. More

drinking follows with Rahad, and at the gambling house, and
there's champagne at the end.

Shooters: * Amazingly, none, bar the one Rahad uses in the
opening scenes.

Motors: In the pre-titles, Rahad drives a dark-blue Mercedes.
Bodie gets intimate with Sir John's . . . silver Rolls-Royce. The
prostitute drives a silver and black Porsche 924 Turbo. Hart
tails Bodie in a light-blue Cortina 2.0 GL. George the pimp
has a big yellow Cadillac, complete with flash white-leather
upholstery. There's also a big white limo in evidence.

Threads: Bodie's white jacket and wide-collared black shirt
(we've not seen *that* for quite a while . . . thankfully); just the
thing for a night down the disco with Clare Terringham. (Dig
that black hanky in his pocket, too.) Doyle's purple dressing
gown is terribly girly. The barmaid wears a foul, stripy,
one-sleeved top.

Shaft **Guitar?:** Standard stock trumpet-and-piano music.

Doyle Cooks a Bit of Pasta: He's seen in his kitchen a
couple of times, but it's only to make the coffee (while
whistling tunelessly).

Slash Fiction Moment: 'You must know all the hard boys in
London!' The staged fight between Bodie and Doyle (over
a woman) speaks volumes! And, of course, the astonishing
moment when Bodie is apparently run over by Rahad and Doyle
starts checking for a heartbeat ('Never knew you cared!').

Jargon: George: 'This is the best john ever.'

Laughable Dialogue: Remarkably for such a naff episode,
this includes some great dialogue, including Rahad's
memorable 'Mr Cowley, I had heard of you. You are much
smaller than I imagined!'

  PC Fish: 'You want him nicked, eh? . . . Obstruction?
Loitering? Breathing too hard in a public place?'

  Doyle: 'Do you ride?' Anna: '. . . Do you mean horses?'

  Anna: 'I used to do it for a dinner and a disco. I nearly did
it for an Earldom. Now I just do it for money. Cheers!'

Notes: 'Smash male dominance!' A laughably bad episode that is actually hilariously funny after a while (not, we assume, the production team's intention). A genuine case of an episode achieving high camp without really trying. The take on Arab terrorism is so silly it resembles what *The Comic Strip* would have done if *The Bullshitters* had really existed! And yet something keeps on cropping up every few moments – a good line of dialogue, a nice bit of action (death by exploding newspaper has got to be one of the most brilliant set pieces the series ever devised) – just to remind the viewers that the people making this ludicrous engine of destruction weren't complete idiots.

Doyle now lives in a (very tastefully decorated) house, complete with a piano (does he play, we wonder, or is it just for decoration?). Bodie, who considers himself married to the job, seems violently antiracist in this episode, which proves he's had his consciousness raised since 'Klansmen' (nice one, Brian).

55: 'The Ojuka Situation'
23 January 1983

Writer: David Humphries
Director: Christopher King

Cast: Clarke Peters (President Ojuka),
Shope Shodeinde (Katunda), Geoffrey Palmer (Avery),
John Horsley (Headmaster), Charles Dance (Parker),
Al Matthews (Faroud), Harry Fowler (Salesman),
Robert Swan[1] (Major Danby), Colin McCormack (Inspector),
Michael Bertenshaw (Doctor), Jane West (Receptionist),
Derek Smith (2nd Doctor), Emma Relph (CI5 Girl),
Bruce Alexander (Detective), Paul Medford (Felix Ojuka)

[1] Note: Spelt incorrectly on screen as 'Swann' (see 'Not a Very Civil Civil Servant' and *The Sweeney* – 'Country Boy').

Someone wants to assassinate the deposed African dictator Ojuka. As usual, it's down to CI5 to get in the way of the bullets.

Keep Your Mincers Peeled For . . .: Charles Dance made his name playing Guy Perron in *Jewel in the Crown*, and Edward Forrester in *First Born*. Fans of the James Bond movies will remember his highly regarded one-line appearance in *For Your Eyes Only*. The cockney comedy actor Harry Fowler was the chirpy Flogger Hoskins in *The Army Game*. Emma Relph starred opposite John Duttine in the BBC's 1981 adaptation of *The Day of the Triffids*. Paul Medford played Kelvin Carpenter for many years in *EastEnders*, and has recently been seen in *Invasion: Earth*. For Geoffrey Palmer, see *The Sweeney* – 'Feet of Clay'. For John Horsley, see 'Long Shot'.

There's a cracking shot of a bidet in the hotel room when Doyle is washing.

Birds: * Bodie had a woman called Louise 'lined up' for an evening date. He and Doyle swap sexist remarks as a pretty (and possibly bra-less) secretary passes them in the CI5 building.

Booze: * Cowley offers Ojuka a whisky which, as a Muslim, he of course refuses. (He does, however, gamble with Doyle.)

Shooters: ***** Pistol fire is exchanged right at the outset between two gunmen and Ojuka and his bodyguard (check out Ojuka's silver-plated Remmington .45). More shooters are seen, and used, in the attack on the 'safe house', and again when pursued by a car.

Motors: The gunmen arrive in a pea-soup-coloured Maxi (death is too good for them). Bodie and Doyle make Ojuka sit in the back of their silver Capri (OWC 827W), which hardly befits so prominent a person. (One of us used to own a Capri, and there ain't much room back there!) They are pursued by a black Merc, and when the Capri crashes Bodie looks at the damage and says that it's 'hardly worth calling the RAC'. The Transit (OHJ 280V) seen prominently in this episode is the same as in 'Foxhole on the Roof', only this time it's white. Cowley has his usual black Granada.

Threads: Bodie's green, parka-ish coat and matching polo-neck (Murphy also wears a horrible fawn one). Highlight of the episode: the quick flash of Doyle's garish, headache-inducing, sky-blue belt!

Shaft **Guitar?:** Another 'big-band' version of the theme.

Doyle Cooks a Bit of Pasta: Well, he uses 'priapismic' as an insult (against Bodie), and suggests he look it up in a dictionary. So we did, and it's definitely worth doing! (Bodie later impresses with his quotation from John Keats's 'La Belle Dame sans Merci', which Cowley recognises.) We presume that Doyle's reference to postponing his next violin practice is facetious . . .

Slash Fiction Moment: The hotel receptionist asks if Bodie and Doyle wouldn't mind sharing a bath: they seem rather pleased at the idea.

Laughable Dialogue: Doyle: 'What's the Fourteenth Heavy Metal brigade doing here? It's not war, is it?' Cowley: 'It's never anything else.'

Avery: 'The notion of calling in CI5 for a school visit seemed akin to asking the SAS to rescue a cat from a tree.'

Cowley: 'John Avery at the Home Office has more interests in African finance than you've got in air hostesses, Bodie.'

Notes: 'You understand the mechanics of the game.' Well scripted and not too bad a stab at a non-Western culture, though the intended plot twists are about as obvious as an Agatha Christie novel with only one suspect. There's an astronomical body count in this episode (we got to twelve shootings within half an hour before giving up). It also runs on coincidental remarks (like Murphy's 'closer to home' leading Cowley to working out who the leak is coming from) and locations.

Doyle's family used to keep tropical fish (including guppies and angel fish), thus his ad-libbed cover that he and Bodie are tropical-fish salesmen (with Ojuka as 'Mr Guppy'!). The young Doyle was very upset when the family cat went fishing one morning. Probably made him the man he is today, in fact. Doyle carries a lighter in his back pocket. Bodie disobeys a direct order (cf. 'Foxhole on the Roof', etc.).

Ojuka is the former leader of the Islamic state of Battan, where a left-wing junta now rules. The episode mentions in passing the Muslim origin of the word 'assassin'. There are references to the Great Train Robbery, and *All Quiet on the Western Front*. Ojuka reads *The Times*, and the book we see him leafing through at one point is called *The Eagles Die*.

56: 'A Man Called Quinn'
30 January 1983

Writer: Tony Barwick
Director: Horace Ové

Cast: Del Henney (Quinn), Steven Berkoff (Krasnov),
Bernard Archard (Granger), Peter Howell (Howard),
Linal Haft (Jack Canon), Johnny Shannon (Harris),
Christopher Ettridge (2nd Interrogator),
Margo Cunningham (Landlady),
Christopher Scoular (Doctor), Malcolm Mudie (Male Nurse),
Peter Woodward (Policeman), John Owens (Johnson)

Quinn, an ex-spy, escapes from a secure hospital and starts bumping off his former colleagues. Well, guess who's top of this list. Go on, it'll surprise you . . . (OK, it's Cowley).

Keep Your Mincers Peeled For . . .: Steven Berkoff is best known (as here) for his villainous roles, his films including *A Clockwork Orange*, *Octopussy*, *Beverly Hills Cop*, *Rambo: First Blood II* and *The Krays*. Bernard Archard was the star of *Spycatcher* in the late 1950s.

Birds: None.

Booze: Nothing even remotely alcoholic.

Shooters: **** Quinn's sub-machine-gun, wrapped in plastic and buried in the woods. He uses grenades and smoke bombs against Bodie and Doyle. There's a rifle-launched grenade attack on Cowley, and a massive gunfight at the end.

Motors: Doyle's silver Capri gets pulled over for speeding. Jack Canon has a grey Mercedes. Quinn steals a blue Vauxhall Victor from Johnson. Another Victor, a white one, gets blown up by Major Howard, an explosives expert.

Threads: Quinn's light-brown cord pants. Doyle's white shoes.

Shaft **Guitar?:** Blaring trumpets at various points.

Jargon: Policeman: 'Good morning, Flash Gordon.'

Notes: 'This is where it all started. This is where we can finish it.' Sometimes you just can't find anything new to say about an episode. This one is just . . . ordinary. Some good direction, chiefly in the pre-titles (the surrealism becomes a little wearing after that) and during the lads' raid on Quinn's digs. The plot's not too bad, either (the episode actually feels very like a *New Avengers* caper).

Cowley's nickname was 'Morris', after the prewar car Morris Cowley. Cowley doesn't take sugar in his tea. He always called Quinn (with whom he was a field agent in Special Forces) 'laddie'; Quinn, Cowley notes, 'practically wrote the book'.

Location filming took place on the A4 Great West Road and around Notting Hill.

57: 'No Stone'
6 February 1983

Writer: Roger Marshall
Director: Chris Burt

Cast: Sarah Neville (Ulrike), John Wheatley (Jimmy Kilpin), Philip York (Hockley), Godfrey James (Ross Kilpin), Briony McRoberts (Tessa Kilpin), Philip Martin Brown (Cook), Chrissie Cotterill (June Cook),

Brian Miller (Prison Officer), Simon Dutton (Tree),
Seymour Green (Wilfred Robard), Milton Johns (Clerk),
Brian Southwood (Allison), Mark Drewery (Joe),
Nicholas Owen (Jones), James Simmons (Terrorist/Foreman),
Michael Praed (Terrorist), William McBain (Terrorist),
Jonty Miller (Policeman), Earl Robinson (Plainclothesman),
Maria Harper (Jackie)

A grass has revealed the location of an arms dump. He then
finds himself in still further trouble – facing a kangaroo court
for his 'crimes'.

Keep Your Mincers Peeled For . . .: A very young-looking
Michael Praed (later of *Robin of Sherwood* and *Dynasty*) has
a tiny role. Sarah Neville was Mary in *The Fainthearted
Feminist*. Simon Dutton would later play Simon Templar in a
short-lived 1990s version of *The Saint*. Milton Johns will be
familiar to readers from a number of comedy series, including
Butterflies, *Foxy Lady* and *Murphy's Mob*, in which he had a
long-running role.

Check out the Ferguson cassette player, and Memorex C90
tape. There's a massive poster warning of the dangers of
rabies on display at Luton Airport. The terrorists read the
Daily Mirror (well, it *was* vaguely left-wing in those days!).

Birds: * Brian Cook's wife June, according to Doyle, isn't
Bodie's sort: she's witty, attractive, intelligent . . . Jackie,
Hockley's bird, emerges from a side room in a very fetching
white gown.

Ulrike Herzl was originally known as Judy Wynettc; she
was convent-educated and went to a Swiss finishing school
before becoming active with German terrorists. She was
responsible for a political murder in the Hague. Her pet
rabbit, when she was nine or ten, was called Lenin (the
headmistress made her change it to Winston). She killed it.

Booze: None.

Shooters: * Sub-machine-gun fire as Jimmy Kilpin is captured.

Motors: There's a 'very nice' Porsche 911 at the beginning (the registration is OPR 911!). Cowley's in another dark Granada (UNO 375W). The last episode, and thus the last outing for the silver and bronze Capris. The capture of Kilpin involves a blue Hillman Avenger estate, a yellow Cortina (GUL 748L: the policeman considers it odd that it has a 1972–3 registration as it looks like a Mk IV – i.e. 1977 vintage – car), and a grey Jag that blows up. A white police Rover arrives to pick up the photographs.

Threads: Doyle's white, black and red tartan scarf, again.

Shaft **Guitar?:** There's a rather sprightly, new-wave-style rock song coming from Ulrike's caravan in the opening scene.

Slash Fiction Moment: Bodie and Doyle share a coffee.

Non-PC Moment: Bodie tells Doyle a story about a cage full of gay rats. (Respect, though, for the sequence where the sexist legal chaps get their just deserts!)

Jargon: Ulrike: 'We've removed your supersnout, your jumped-up Judas.'
 Hockley: 'In other words, a routine, made-in-Britain, good old-fashioned fit-up.'
 Doyle: 'Ulrike Herzl. Judy Wynette. You're nicked!'

Laughable Dialogue: Hockley, on the recording of his telephone conversation: 'That supposed to be me? ... Could have been anyone from Donald Duck to Mao Tse-tung.'

Notes: 'It's all right for you. You haven't got anyone ... You can go and play cowboys for the rest of your miserable, selfish life.' Which sums up the better episodes of the series in a nutshell. It's a shame, then, that much of the episode disappoints, and that the ending is rather underplayed – they doubtless did not imagine that this episode would be the last. And it includes positively the worst pre-title sequence ever in the history of television! Still, the themes are very appropriate for a finale (even if it wasn't intended to be).
 Bodie doesn't like raspberry jam, though he seems to think

strawberry is OK. Doyle recruited Brian Cook to CI5 from
the Fraud Squad. Hockley's books include volumes by Hegel
and Timothy Leary. Doyle also seems familiar with the
works of Leary. Hockley's apartment overlooks Lord's cricket
ground. The terrorist group is financed by the KGB and the
PLO.

Some of the filming took place at Temple tube station.

The Power of Guv

Throughout the 1970s and into the 1980s, *The Sweeney* and *The Professionals* were two of television's most popular series with the viewers. (That the former had a critical standing that the latter never managed to acquire is somewhat incidental, the critic Phillip Drummond noting that in *The Sweeney* 'Regan, Carter and Haskins ... form an almost perpetual ensemble versus opponents inevitably characterised by fictional ephemerality.') The playground discussions about whether *Starsky and Hutch* or *Kojak* was the best cop show on TV were constant among the children of the revolution, but, as one Newcastle schoolteacher was memorably quoted as saying, 'I prefer the rough and tumble of *The Sweeney* myself!' As late as 1987, a repeat of the *Professionals* episode 'Spy Probe' achieved over 10 million viewers, and reached number seven in the weekly ratings charts, right up with *Coronation Street*, *EastEnders* and *Surprise, Surprise*.

But times change, and by the late 1980s – with television examining closely its relationship with action and violence – such series as these seemed like relics from a bygone age, as relevant to the present as *Z Cars* or *Dixon of Dock Green*. *The Sweeney* was relegated to late night, twenty-to-midnight repeat slots around the ITV regions (where nostalgic twenty-something insomniacs would spend most of the next day at work bemoaning the inability to get two double whiskies for 'seventy-eight pee' any more). *The Professionals* would, but for the power of Martin Shaw's veto on repeats, have joined it there. The fact that both John Thaw and Martin Shaw ended up taking highly publicised roles as 'modern', 'thinking' policemen, in *Inspector Morse* and *The Chief* respectively, seemed to have laid the ghosts of their past. Jack Regan and Ray Doyle were surely safe in a little box marked 'gone for ever'. But ever is a long time, especially in TV.

Television's fascination with its own past is only really equalled by its ability to turn excess into parody, and subsequently, into new forms. When *Lost in Space* began a hugely successful rerun on Channel 4 in the late 1980s, it took those in the television industry some time to realise that what had once been science-fiction melodrama had magically been transformed via two decades of postmodernism into a sitcom. Older viewers may have watched it for a touch of nostalgic kitsch, but 'the kids' tuned in because they wanted to laugh at the costumes, and the haircuts, and the 'groovy' dialogue. In this climate, and with the emergence of satellite and cable channels with many hours of scheduling to fill, the possibilities for digging something out of the archives and reinventing it were too good to miss.

It wasn't as if this style of programming had ever entirely gone away. The first of two *Comic Strip Presents . . .* parodies – *The Bullshitters: Roll Out the Gun Barrel* – aired in 1985. Written by Peter Richardson and Keith Allen, and starring them as 'Foyle' and 'Bonehead' respectively ('Cover me!'), this concerned Commander Jackson (Robbie Coltrane) of DI5 and his attempts to bring his two closet-homosexual agents back into the fold. (Allegedly, Martin Shaw approved of the parody!) It was followed by *Detectives on the Verge of a Nervous Breakdown* (1993), which widened the targets still further ('I'm a ten-guv-a-day man, guv'). In addition there were little gems like Mark Cullen's legendary *Alas Smith and Jones* sketch ('This man is a well-known tablecloth!'), which ruthlessly lampooned *The Sweeney*'s propensity for impenetrable cockneyesque dialogue. 'And you don't need a daffodil . . .'

Then there were those Nissan ads . . . The first aired in 1996, and had two Bodie and Doyle lookalikes testing out the new Almera GTi 2.0. Its 60 seconds of screen time were filled with outrageous rolls over the bonnet and slides into cardboard boxes. The dialogue was achingly accurate, too: 'This car's well sprung!' 'Yeah – just like your perm!' And: 'Go faster!' 'I'm doing nearly thirty!' The second promoted the Primera 2.0 GT in similar fashion, this time with *The Sweeney* ('Oi! Squealer!') as its target. 'Stop shout-ing,' says 'Carter'. '*I can't!*' bellows 'Regan'. (In these ads, Phil Cornwell – the *Spender* equivalent in *Detectives on the*

Verge of a Nervous Breakdown – played both 'Bodie' and
'Regan' with chilling accuracy, especially the latter's 'Oh,
blimey!'.) All these postmodern, very arch takes on *The
Sweeney* and *The Professionals* were like Rosetta stones for
translating these old texts into the modern era. Suddenly, UK
Gold and Bravo (and eventually Channel 5) had a pair of
bona fide cult items on their hands.

Another element, too, was present in this landscape: the
growth of 'New Lad'. The basic concept behind this 'trend' –
tied in with the post-Italia '90 revival of football culture, the
emergence of Britpop (and its variants), television series like
Fantasy Football League and *Men Behaving Badly*, and
magazines like *Loaded* and *FHM* – is that 'The Lad' never
really went away. 'The Lad', as represented by Bob Ferris and
Terry Collier in comedy, Len Fairclough in soap opera and
Jack Regan, George Carter and Bodie and Doyle in crime
drama, was the man that many TV viewers desired to be. He
normally had working-class roots, with an angry disrespect
for authority, particularly if that authority came from a class
above his own. He didn't give a monkey's about *their* rules,
and *their* attitudes. He liked his alcohol and his football and
his bacon sandwiches, and he loved a bit of danger as much
as he loved women. In another life, 'The Lad' (especially
Jack 'The Lad' Regan) could have been a poet, a clipped
philosopher casting a jaundiced eye upon the delicious ironies
of life.

'New Man' was all about discovering the feminine side,
about being considerate rather than brutish, about accepting
that feminism has been around for an awfully long time, and
that it isn't going to go away. All right, we've done that.
What's next? Next, was the 'New Lad', something of a
balance between the extremes.

So, we can watch *The Sweeney* and *The Professionals*, but
because we're so modern and self-aware, we can see the
sexism, the macho stupidity, for what it is. Many men tend to
like, if they're quite honest, the fantasy of loose women and
fast cars (or is it the other way round?). We *recognise* that it's
a fantasy, but what is television about if it's not about giving
the viewer a little slice of something different?

Of course, the problem with all of this is that, inevitably, there is the need to recreate (via television's perpetual ability to feast upon itself). There are, at present, revivals of both *The Sweeney* and *The Professionals* in development. Is this a Good Thing, or should the spirits of Regan and Carter, Bodie and Doyle, remain where they are, trapped in the amber of televisual nostalgia for ever?

Time, and the ratings, will tell. They usually do.

Glossary

Adam and Eve	Believe
Apples	Stairs (apples and pears)
Aris	Bum (Aristotle – bottle and glass – arse)
Badger game (or job)	To incriminate with pornographic or salacious photographs
Barnet	Hair (Barnet fair)
Beak	Judge
Bell	Telephone
Benghazi	Toilet (karsey)
Bent	Corrupt
Bent	Homosexual
Bird	Imprisonment, prison sentence (bird lime – time)
Bird	Woman
Bird bandit	Man on the pull (q.v.)
Blag	Robbery (often with violence)
Blagger	Robber
Blower	Telephone
Boat	Face (boat-race)
Bob Hope	Drugs
Boob	Prison
Boozer	Public house
Boracic	Penniless (boracic lint – skint)
Bottle and glass	Bottom (arse)
Bottle out	To lose one's nerve, to lack courage
Bracelets	Handcuffs
Brahms	Drunk (Brahms and Liszt – pissed)
Brass	Prostitute (from alternative meaning, 'money')
Bread	Money
Brief	Lawyer
Bubble	Greek (person) (bubble and squeak)
Bull and cow	Row
Bum steer	(Deliberately) misleading information
Bunny	Talk (rabbit and pork)
Bust	Arrest (or prevent a crime)
Butcher's	Look (butcher's hook)
Cape-Carny	Army
Cat man	House breaker
Champers	Champagne
Chelsea potter	Squatter
Chocolate	Judge (chocolate fudge)
Chunk-head	Uncool, square or stupid person
Chump	Idiot, loser
Clean	Not incriminated, not guilty, no criminal record
Clock	Watch, observe, notice
Cockle	Ten (cock and hen)
Con	Convict
Connaught	Stranger (Connaught Rangers)
Currant bun	Sun
Cushty	see *Kosher*
Dabs	Fingerprints
Dan Dares	Flares
Desmond	Jacket (Desmond Hackett)
Diddlo	Stupid
Dickie	Shirt (Dickie Dirt)
Doing a royal	Turning Queen's evidence
Dog	Telephone (dog and bone)
Dogs	Feet (dog's meat)

Drum	House
Drummer	A thief, especially of unoccupied houses
Duke of Kent	Rent
Ear	Phone tap
Elephant	Heroin
Face	Criminal or person
Factory	Police station
Farmers	Piles (Farmer Giles)
Fence	Handler of stolen goods
Filth	Police
Firm	Gang
Fit up	To incriminate someone with falsified evidence
Form	Criminal record
Funnel	Courage, bravery
Frame	To name or to incriminate someone (with falsified evidence)
Gaff	House
Geezer	Man
Germans	Hands
Ginger	Dubious, untrustworthy (cf. *Stone Ginger*)
Ginger up	Enliven
God-botherer	Christian
Gold watch	Scotch
Grand	Thousand (pounds)
Grass	Informer, or to inform
Gregory	Cheque (Gregory Peck)
Gregory	Neck (Gregory Peck)
Grief	Trouble, unpleasantness, hardship
Guv(nor)	Superior (officer)
H	Heroin
Hampsteads	Teeth (Hampstead Heath)
Hans Christian	Fiction, a fairy tale (Hans Christian Andersen)
Harry Rag	Cigarette (fag)
Harry Ramp	Tramp
Hoist, to go on the	To become a prostitute
Hooter	Nose
Hump	Sexual intercourse
Hump, the	Fit of anger, irritation or depression
Ice cream	Man (ice cream freezer – geezer)
Iron	Roof (iron hoof)
Jacks	Five (pounds) (Jack's alive)
Jack the Ripper	Stripper
Jam jar	Car
Jam tart	Heart
Jar	Glass of beer
Joanna	Piano
John	Prostitute's client
Jug	Bank
Junk	Heroin
Karsey	Toilet
King Creole	Dole
Kosher	Truthful, legitimate, genuine
Lallies	Legs
Lemon	Flash (lemon dash)
Lemon	Stupid or gullible person, or defective objective (esp. car)
Long one	One thousand pounds
Loop-the-loop	Soup
Luke	Black person (Lucozade – spade)
Manor	Area (often police district)
Meet	A meeting or appointment, especially with criminals
Mincers	Eyes (mince pies)
Monkey	Five hundred pounds

Motor	Car
Mug	Face (as in mug shot – photograph)
Mug	Stupid person, or blackmailed or incriminated person
Mutton	Deaf (Mutt and Jeff)
Nark	Informer
Naughties	Illegal goods
Naughty	Illegal
Nevis	Ten (stretch) (Ben Nevis)
Nick	Arrest, imprison, prison
Nick	Steal
Nicker	Pound sterling
Nonce	Sex offender, child molester, deviant
North	Mouth (north and south)
Nosh	Food
Not many	(sarcastic agreement, to a considerable degree, similar to 'not half')
Obo	Observation
Old Bill	Police
Old King Cole	Dole
Oner (or oncer)	One hundred pounds
On your Jack	On your own (Jack Jones)
Oppo	Partner, companion (opposite number)
Palmer's	Draw(ers) (Palmer's Doors)
Pear-shaped, to go	To go wrong, to fail catastrophically
Peckham	Tie (Peckham Rye)
Pen and ink	Stink
Penny stamp	Tramp
Peter	Cell
Pig	Police officer
Pigeon	Informer
Pin	Leg
Pinch	Arrest
Plates	Feet (plates of meat)
Ponce	Gay man, or general term of abuse
Ponce	Pimp
Pony	Twenty-five pounds
Poppy	Money (poppy-red – bread)
Porkies	Lies (pork pies)
Porridge	Imprisonment, prison sentence
Pull	Search, look for or find (sexual) partner
Quaker	Coat (Quaker oats)
Queen's Park Ranger	Stranger
Quid	Pound sterling
Rabbit	Talk (rabbit and pork)
Richard	Girl (Richard III – bird)
Rickit	Mistake, blunder (also *ricky*)
Rock 'n' roll	Dole
Roller	Rolls-Royce
Rub (out)	Kill
Rubber	Public house (rub-a-dub – pub)
Ruby	Curry (Ruby Murray)
Sauce	Alcohol
Saucepan	Child (saucepan lid – kid)
Saucepan	Pound sterling (saucepan lid – quid)
Scarper	Run away, escape (Scapa Flow – go)
Schmock	Stupid or contemptible person
Schtuk	Trouble
Schtum	Quiet
Score	Twenty (pounds)
Scotches	Legs (Scotch eggs)
Scrape clinic	Abortion clinic
Screw	Prison officer

Screw	Robbery
Screwsman	House breaker, robber
Sexton	Fake (Sexton Blake)
Shake	Threaten, intimidate
Shell-like	Ear
Shooter	Gun
Shop	Inform on someone
Short one	Fifty pounds
Shovel, the	Prison
Six-and-eight	Straight
Skin and blister	Sister
Skip(per)	(Senior) sergeant
Skirt	Woman
Sky	Pocket (sky rocket)
Smoke	Cigarette
Smudge	To photograph (secretly)
Snout	Informer
Snow	Cocaine
Snow	Lie, mislead
Sob	Pound sterling (from earlier slang *sov* – sovereign)
SP	Information (starting prices)
Spade	Black person
Spiel	Talk
Squeal	Confess
Steel	Car
Steel	Gun, weaponry
Stir	Imprisonment, prison sentence
Stone ginger	Absolutely true or genuine (information)
Stoppo driver	Driver of getaway car
Straight	Honest, not corrupt
Strawberry	Heart
Stretch	Prison Sentence
Strides	Trousers
Swede	Head
Syrup	Wig (syrup of figs)
Tail	To follow, to keep under surveillance
Taters	Cold
Tea leaf	Thief
Team	Police squad
Tickle	(Successful) robbery
Tiddlywink	Chinaman (chink)
Tie	Back (tie rack)
Tin tack	Sack
Titfer	Hat (tit for tat)
Tod	On one's own (Tod Sloane)
Tom	Jewellery (tomfoolery)
Tom	Prostitute
Tooled up	Armed
Trombone	Telephone
Trumpet	Telephone
Tumble	Discover, establish, work out
Two-and-eight	(Agitated or distressed) state
W	Search warrant
West Ham	Scam
Wheels	Car
Wheels man	Driver
Whisper	Rumour
Whistle	Suit (of clothes) (whistle and flute)
Wind-up	Joke, hoax
Woodentop	Uniformed police officer
Zero	Kill

Additional forms appear throughout when these cannot be derived from the forms given or when it is considered helpful to list them. Only those irregular verbs judged to be the most useful are shown in the tables.

abattre *as* BATTRE.

accueillir *as* CUEILLIR.

acquérir ● *Pres.* acquiers, acquérons, acquièrent. ● *Impf.* acquérais. ● *Past hist.* acquis. ● *Fut.* acquerrai. ● *Pres. sub.* acquière. ● *Past part.* acquis.

admettre *as* METTRE.

aller ● *Pres.* vais, vas, va, allons, allez, vont. ● *Fut.* irai. ● *Pres. sub.* aille, allions.

apercevoir *as* RECEVOIR.

apparaître *as* CONNAÎTRE.

appartenir *as* TENIR.

apprendre *as* PRENDRE.

asseoir ● *Pres.* assieds, asseyons, asseyent. ● *Impf.* asseyais. ● *Past hist.* assis. ● *Fut.* assiérai. ● *Pres. sub.* asseye. ● *Past part.* assis.

atteindre ● *Pres.* atteins, atteignons, atteignent. ● *Impf.* atteignais. ● *Past hist.* atteignis. ● *Fut.* atteindrai. ● *Pres. sub.* atteigne. ● *Past part.* atteint.

avoir ● *Pres.* ai, as, a, avons, avez, ont. ● *Impf.* avais. ● *Past hist.* eus, eut, eûmes, eûtes, eurent. ● *Fut.* aurai. ● *Pres. sub.* aie, aies, ait, ayons, ayez, aient. ● *Pres. part.* ayant. ● *Past part.* eu. ● *Imp.* aie, ayons, ayez.

battre ● *Pres.* bats, bat, battons, battez, battent.

boire ● *Pres.* bois, buvons, boivent. ● *Impf.* buvais. ● *Past hist.* bus. ● *Pres. sub.* boive, buvions. ● *Past part.* bu.

bouillir ● *Pres.* bous, bouillons, bouillent. ● *Impf.* bouillais. ● *Pres. sub.* bouille.

combattre *as* BATTRE.

commettre *as* METTRE.

comprendre *as* PRENDRE.

concevoir *as* RECEVOIR.

conclure ● *Pres.* conclus, concluons, concluent. ● *Past hist.* conclus. ● *Past part.* conclu.

conduire ● *Pres.* conduis, conduisons, conduisent. ● *Impf.* conduisais. ● *Past hist.* conduisis. ● *Pres. sub.* conduise. ● *Past part.* conduit.

connaître ● *Pres.* connais, connaît, connaissons. ● *Impf.* connaissais. ● *Past hist.* connus. ● *Pres. sub.* connaisse. ● *Past part.* connu.

construire *as* CONDUIRE.

contenir *as* TENIR.

contraindre *as* ATTEINDRE (except *ai* replaces *ei*).

contredire *as* DIRE, except ● *Pres.* vous contredisez.

convaincre *as* VAINCRE.

convenir *as* TENIR.

corrompre *as* ROMPRE.

coudre ● *Pres.* couds, cousons, cousent. ● *Impf.* cousais. ● *Past hist.* cousis. ● *Pres. sub.* couse. ● *Past part.* cousu.

courir ● *Pres.* cours, courons, courent. ● *Impf.* courais. ● *Past hist.* courus. ● *Fut.* courrai. ● *Pres. sub.* coure. ● *Past part.* couru.

couvrir ● *Pres.* couvre, couvrons. ● *Impf.* couvrais. ● *Pres. sub.* couvre. ● *Past part.* couvert.

craindre *as* ATTEINDRE (except *ai* replaces *ei*).

croire ● *Pres.* crois, croit, croyons, croyez, croient. ● *Impf.* croyais. ● *Past hist.* crus. ● *Pres. sub.* croie, croyions. ● *Past part.* cru.

croître ● *Pres.* crois, croit, croissons. ● *Impf.* croissais. ● *Past hist.* crûs. ● *Pres. sub.* croisse. ● *Past part.* crû, crue.

cueillir ● *Pres.* cueille, cueillons. ● *Impf.* cueillais. ● *Fut.* cueillerai. ● *Pres. sub.* cueille.

débattre *as* BATTRE.

décevoir *AS* RECEVOIR.
découvrir *AS* COUVRIR.
décrire *AS* ÉCRIRE.
déduire *AS* CONDUIRE.
défaire *AS* FAIRE.
détenir *AS* TENIR.
détruire *AS* CONDUIRE.
devenir *AS* TENIR.
devoir ● *Pres.* dois, devons, doivent. ● *Impf.* devais. ● *Past hist.* dus. ● *Fut.* devrai. ● *Pres. sub.* doive. ● *Past part.* dû, due.
dire ● *Pres.* dis, dit, disons, dites, disent. ● *Impf.* disais. ● *Past hist.* dis. ● *Past part.* dit.
disparaître *AS* CONNAÎTRE.
dissoudre ● *Pres.* dissous, dissolvons. ● *Impf.* dissolvais. ● *Pres. sub.* dissolve. ● *Past part.* dissous, dissoute.
distraire *AS* EXTRAIRE.
dormir ● *Pres.* dors, dormons. ● *Impf.* dormais. ● *Pres. sub.* dorme.
écrire ● *Pres.* écris, écrivons. ● *Impf.* écrivais. ● *Past hist.* écrivis. ● *Pres. sub.* écrive. ● *Past part.* écrit.
élire *AS* LIRE.
émettre *AS* METTRE.
s'enfuir *AS* FUIR.
entreprendre *AS* PRENDRE.
entretenir *AS* TENIR.
envoyer ● *Fut.* enverrai.
éteindre *AS* ATTEINDRE.
être ● *Pres.* suis, es, est, sommes, êtes, sont. ● *Impf.* étais. ● *Past hist.* fus, fut, fûmes, fûtes, furent. ● *Fut.* serai. ● *Pres. sub.* sois, soit, soyons, soyez, soient. ● *Pres. part.* étant. ● *Past part.* été. ● *Imp.* sois, soyons, soyez.
exclure *AS* CONCLURE.
extraire ● *Pres.* extrais, extrayons. ● *Impf.* extrayais. ● *Pres. sub.* extraie. ● *Past part.* extrait.
faire ● *Pres.* fais, fait, faisons, faites, font. ● *Impf.* faisais. ● *Past hist.* fis. ● *Fut.* ferai. ● *Pres. sub.* fasse. ● *Past part.* fait.

falloir (impersonal) ● *Pres.* faut. ● *Impf.* fallait. ● *Past hist.* fallut. ● *Fut.* faudra. ● *Pres. sub.* faille. ● *Past part.* fallu.
feindre *AS* ATTEINDRE.
fuir ● *Pres.* fuis, fuyons, fuient. ● *Impf.* fuyais. ● *Past hist.* fuis. ● *Pres sub.* fuie. ● *Past part.* fui.
inscrire *AS* ÉCRIRE.
instruire *AS* CONDUIRE.
interdire *AS* DIRE, except ● *Pres.* vous interdisez.
interrompre *AS* ROMPRE.
intervenir *AS* TENIR.
introduire *AS* CONDUIRE.
joindre *AS* ATTEINDRE (except *oi* replaces *ei*).
lire ● *Pres.* lis, lit, lisons, lisez, lisent. ● *Impf.* lisais. ● *Past hist.* lus. ● *Pres. sub.* lise. ● *Past part.* lu.
luire ● *Pres.* luis, luisons. ● *Impf.* luisais. ● *Past hist.* luisis. ● *Pres. sub.* luise. ● *Past part.* lui.
maintenir *AS* TENIR.
maudire ● *Pres.* maudis, maudissons. ● *Impf.* maudissais. ● *Past hist.* maudis. ● *Pres. sub.* maudisse. ● *Past part.* maudit.
mentir *AS* SORTIR (except *en* replaces *or*).
mettre ● *Pres.* mets, met, mettons, mettez, mettent. ● *Past hist.* mis. ● *Past part.* mis.
mourir ● *Pres.* meurs, mourons, meurent. ● *Impf.* mourais. ● *Past hist.* mourus. ● *Fut.* mourrai. ● *Pres. sub.* meure, mourions. ● *Past part.* mort.
mouvoir ● *Pres.* meus, mouvons, meuvent. ● *Impf.* mouvais. ● *Fut.* mouvrai. ● *Pres. sub.* meuve, mouvions. ● *Past part.* mû, mue.
naître ● *Pres.* nais, naît, naissons. ● *Impf.* naissais. ● *Past hist.* naquis. ● *Pres. sub.* naisse. ● *Past part.* né.
nuire *AS* LUIRE.

obtenir *as* TENIR.
offrir, ouvrir *as* COUVRIR.
omettre *as* METTRE.
paraître *as* CONNAÎTRE.
parcourir *as* COURIR.
partir *as* SORTIR (except *ar* replaces *or*).
parvenir *as* TENIR.
peindre *as* ATTEINDRE.
percevoir *as* RECEVOIR.
permettre *as* METTRE.
plaindre *as* ATTEINDRE (except *ai* replaces *ei*).
plaire ● *Pres.* plais, plaît, plaisons. ● *Impf.* plaisais. ● *Past hist.* plus. ● *Pres. sub.* plaise. ● *Past part.* plu.
pleuvoir (impersonal) ● *Pres.* pleut. ● *Impf.* pleuvait. ● *Past hist.* plut. ● *Fut.* pleuvra. ● *Pres. sub.* pleuve. ● *Past part.* plu.
poursuivre *as* SUIVRE.
pourvoir *as* VOIR, except ● *Fut.* pourvoirai
pouvoir ● *Pres.* peux, peut, pouvons, pouvez, peuvent. ● *Impf.* pouvais. ● *Past hist.* pus. ● *Fut.* pourrai. ● *Pres. sub.* puisse. ● *Past part.* pu.
prédire *as* DIRE, except ● *Pres.* vous prédisez.
prendre ● *Pres.* prends, prenons, prennent. ● *Impf.* prenais. ● *Past hist.* pris. ● *Pres. sub.* prenne, prenions. ● *Past part.* pris.
prescrire *as* ÉCRIRE.
prévenir *as* TENIR.
prévoir *as* VOIR, except ● *Fut.* prévoirai.
produire *as* CONDUIRE.
promettre *as* METTRE.
provenir *as* TENIR.
recevoir ● *Pres.* reçois, recevons, reçoivent. ● *Impf.* recevais. ● *Past hist.* reçus. ● *Fut.* recevrai. ● *Pres. sub.* reçoive, recevions. ● *Past part.* reçu.
reconduire *as* CONDUIRE.
reconnaître *as* CONNAÎTRE.
reconstruire *as* CONDUIRE.
recouvrir *as* COUVRIR.
recueillir *as* CUEILLIR.

redire *as* DIRE.
réduire *as* CONDUIRE.
refaire *as* FAIRE.
rejoindre *as* ATTEINDRE (except *oi* replaces *ei*).
remettre *as* METTRE.
renvoyer *as* ENVOYER.
repartir *as* SORTIR (except *ar* replaces *or*).
reprendre *as* PRENDRE.
reproduire *as* CONDUIRE.
résoudre ● *Pres.* résous, résolvons. ● *Impf.* résolvais. ● *Past hist.* résolus. ● *Pres. sub.* résolve. ● *Past part.* résolu.
ressortir *as* SORTIR.
restreindre *as* ATTEINDRE.
retenir, revenir *as* TENIR.
revivre *as* VIVRE.
revoir *as* VOIR.
rire ● *Pres.* ris, rit, rions, riez, rient. ● *Impf.* riais. ● *Past hist.* ris. ● *Pres. sub.* rie, riions. ● *Past part.* ri.
rompre *as* VENDRE (regular), except ● *Pres.* il rompt.
satisfaire *as* FAIRE.
savoir ● *Pres.* sais, sait, savons, savez, savent. ● *Impf.* savais. ● *Past hist.* sus. ● *Fut.* saurai. ● *Pres. sub.* sache, sachions. ● *Pres. part.* sachant. ● *Past part.* su. ● *Imp.* sache, sachons, sachez.
séduire *as* CONDUIRE.
sentir *as* SORTIR (except *en* replaces *or*).
servir ● *Pres.* sers, servons. ● *Impf.* servais. ● *Pres. sub.* serve.
sortir ● *Pres.* sors, sortons. ● *Impf.* sortais. ● *Pres. sub.* sorte.
souffrir *as* COUVRIR.
soumettre *as* METTRE.
soustraire *as* EXTRAIRE.
soutenir *as* TENIR.
suffire ● *Pres.* suffis, suffisons. ● *Impf.* suffisais. ● *Past hist.* suffis. ● *Pres. sub.* suffise. ● *Past part.* suffi.
suivre ● *Pres.* suis, suivons. ● *Impf.* suivais. ● *Past hist.* suivis. ● *Pres. sub.* suive. ● *Past part.* suivi.

surprendre *as* PRENDRE.
survivre *as* VIVRE.
taire
- *Pres.* tais, taisons.
- *Impf.* taisais. ● *Past hist.* tus. ● *Pres. sub.* taise.
- *Past part.* tu.

teindre *as* ATTEINDRE.
tenir
- *Pres.* tiens, tenons, tiennent. ● *Impf.* tenais.
- *Past hist.* tins, tint, tînmes, tîntes, tinrent.
- *Fut.* tiendrai. ● *Pres. sub.* tienne. ● *Past part.* tenu.

traduire *as* CONDUIRE.
traire *as* EXTRAIRE.
transmettre *as* METTRE.
vaincre
- *Pres.* vaincs, vainc, vainquons. ● *Impf.* vainquais. ● *Past hist.* vainquis. ● *Pres. sub.* vainque. ● *Past part.* vaincu.

valoir
- *Pres.* vaux, vaut, valons, valez, valent. ● *Impf.* valais. ● *Past hist.* valus.
- *Fut.* vaudrai. ● *Pres. sub.* vaille. ● *Past part.* valu.

venir *as* TENIR.
vivre
- *Pres.* vis, vit, vivons, vivez, vivent. ● *Impf.* vivais. ● *Past hist.* vécus.
- *Pres. sub.* vive. ● *Past part.* vécu.

voir
- *Pres.* vois, voyons, voient. ● *Impf.* voyais.
- *Past hist.* vis. ● *Fut.* verrai. ● *Pres. sub.* voie, voyions. ● *Past part.* vu.

vouloir
- *Pres.* veux, veut, voulons, voulez, veulent.
- *Impf.* voulais. ● *Past hist.* voulus. ● *Fut.* voudrai. ● *Pres. sub.* veuille, voulions. ● *Past part.* voulu. ● *Imp.* veuille, veuillons, veuillez.